This book is sponsored by the Theological
Commission of the World Evangelical Fellowship

WORSHIP:

Adoration and Action

*Also produced by the Faith and Church Study
Unit of the Theological Commission of the
World Evangelical Fellowship:*

BIBLICAL INTERPRETATION AND THE CHURCH:
Text and Context

THE CHURCH IN THE BIBLE AND THE WORLD:
An International Study

TEACH US TO PRAY:
Prayer in the Bible and the World

RIGHT WITH GOD:
Justification in the Bible and the World

WORSHIP:
Adoration and Action

edited by

D. A. CARSON

Published on behalf of the
World Evangelical Fellowship by

BAKER BOOK HOUSE
Grand Rapids, Michigan

THE PATERNOSTER PRESS
Carlisle UK

Unless otherwise stated, Scripture quotations in this
publication are from the Holy Bible, New International Version.
Copyright © 1973, 1978, 1984 International Bible Society.
Published by Zondervan and Hodder & Stoughton.

British Library Cataloguing in Publication Data

Worship: Adoration and Action
I. Carson, D. A.
264

ISBN 0–85364–523–X

Library of Congress Cataloging-in-Publication Data

Worship : adoration and action/edited by D. A. Carson.
    p.   cm.
    "Produced by the Faith and Church Study Unit of the Theological
Commission of the World Evangelical Fellowship."
    Includes bibliographical references and indexes.
    ISBN 0–8010–2584–2. — ISBN 0–85364–523–X (Paternoster)
    1. Public worship.   2. Liturgies.   I. Carson. D. A.
II. World Evangelical Fellowship. Faith and Church Study Unit.
8V15.W65   1993
264–dc20   93-25994
                                                      CIP

Typeset by Photoprint, Torquay, Devon
and printed in the UK by
The Guernsey Press Co. Ltd., Guernsey, Channel Islands
for the publishers.

Contents

Acknowledgement

Unless otherwise stated, Scripture quotations in this publication are from the Holy Bible, New International Version. Copyright 1973, 1978, 1984 International Bible Society. Published by Zondervan and Hodder & Stoughton.

Abbreviations

(Names of certain journals are given in full in the text and notes, and are therefore not listed below.)

AB	Anchor Bible
ANRW	*Anstieg und Niedergang der römischen Welt*
ASV	American Standard Version
AV	Authorised Version
BDT	*Baker's Dictionary of Theology*
Bib	*Biblica*
BJRL	*Bulletin of the John Rylands Library*
BNTC	*Black's New Testament Commentaries*
BR	*Biblical Research*
CBQ	*Catholic Biblical Quarterly*
CT	*Christianity Today*
CU	Christian Union (local chapter of IVCF)
EBC	*The Expositor's Bible Commentary*
EDT	*Evangelical Dictionary of Theology*
EQ	*Evangelical Quarterly*
ET	*English Translation*
EVV	English versions
ExpT	*The Expository Times*
Fs.	*Festschrift*
GBU	Federación de Grupos Bíblicos Universitarios de España
GTT	*Gereformeerd Theologisch Tijdschrift*
HTR	*Harvard Theological Review*
ICC	International Critical Commentaries
IDB	*Interpreter's Dictionary of the Bible*
IFES	International Federation of Evangelical Students
Int	*Interpretation*
Inst.	John Calvin, *Institutes of the Christian Religion*
ISBE	*International Standard Bible Encyclopedia*
JBL	*Journal of Biblical Literature*
JES	*Journal of Evangelical Studies*

JR	*Journal of Religion*
JRS	*Journal of Religious Studies*
JSNT	*Journal for the Study of the New Testament*
JSNTSS	Journal for the Study of the New Testament Supplement Series
JSS	*Journal of Semitic Studies*
JTS	*Journal of Theological Studies*
KJV	King James Version
LW	*Luther's Works*, ed. J. Pelikan and H. T. Lehrmann and published by Concordia & Fortress in 55 volumes
LXX	Septuagint
NASB	New American Standard Bible
NCB	New Century Bible
NDT	*New Dictionary of Theology*
NEB	New English Bible
Neot	*Neotestamentica*
NICNT	New International Commentary on the New Testament
NICOT	New International Commentary on the Old Testament
NIDNTT	*New International Dictionary of New Testament Theology*
NIV	New International Version
NovT	*Novum Testamentum*
NTS	*New Testament Studies*
NTT	*Nederlands Theologisch Tijdschrift*
OTL	Old Testament Library
RB	*Revue Biblique*
RRR	*The Review of Religious Research*
RSPT	*Revue des Sciences Philosophiques et Théologiques*
RSV	Revised Standard Version
RTR	*Reformed Theological Review*
SNTSMS	Society of New Testament Studies Monograph Series
SOTSMS	Society of Old Testament Studies Monograph Series
TDNT	*Theological Dictionary of the New Testament*
TDOT	*Theological Dictionary of the Old Testament*
ThBeit	Theologische Beiträge
TNTC	Tyndale New Testament Commentaries
TOTC	Tyndale Old Testament Commentaries
TSCF	*Tertiary Students Christian Fellowship*
TWOT	*Theological Wordbook of the Old Testament*
WA	*Weimar Ausgabe* [see chapter 7, note 8 of this book]
WCF	*Westminster Confession of Faith*
WUNT	Wissenschaftliche Untersuchungen zum Neuen Testament
VT	*Vetus Testamentum*
ZAW	*Zeitschrift für die alttestamentliche Wissenschaft*

Preface

This is the fifth and final volume of a series of studies produced by the Faith and Church Study Unit of the Theological Commission of the World Evangelical Fellowship. The first two (also published by The Paternoster Press and Baker Book House) dealt respectively with hermeneutical issues relating to the doctrine of the church (*Biblical Interpretation and the Church: Text and Context*), and with the doctrine itself (*The Church in the Bible and the World: An International Study*). Recognizing the worldwide interest in 'spirituality', the third dealt with prayer: *Teach Us to Pray: Prayer in the Bible and the World*. The fourth, *Right with God: Justification in the Bible and the World*, sought not only to untangle some of the contorted lines of debate over justification since the majesterial Reformation (not least those of recent years), but to show the relevance and applicability of justification to the promulgation of the gospel in various cultures around the world.

This final volume of the series (it is 'final' only in the sense that my responsibilities as Convenor of this Study Unit have now come to an end, and the direction and leadership of the Unit now fall to new hands) tries to respond to current interest in worship. Much of this, we fear, focuses on the mere mechanics of worship; relatively little has sought to establish a biblical and systematic theology of worship, and in that light attempted to critique and revise current practices.

That, at least, was the aim of this volume when it was first envisaged. I am only too aware how far short of the ideal we have fallen. The disagreements of the members of the Study Unit have not been papered over. I can only say that they are less severe and nuanced now than when we began our studies, and I would like to think that if we had more time we would have achieved still greater unanimity. I am sorry, too, that we did not have better worldwide representation. Two scholars, one from India and one from West Africa, proved unable to devote the time to this project that would have assured better coverage. Nevertheless, in its attempt, and partly in its execution, this book represents a fresh effort to think through Scripture on the subject of worship, and then to apply our findings to the way we actually think about worship and gather for congregational worship in various parts of the world. I cannot imagine that anyone will agree with all the opinions here expressed;

equally, I cannot imagine how anyone could come away from this book without having horizons enlarged and thought clarified.

As with the first four volumes in the series, so here: members of the Study Unit agreed to write chapters in advance of a meeting where all the papers were subjected, paragraph by paragraph, to discussion and critique. That was where a certain degree of uniformity was hammered out; on so sensitive an issue, where the ecclesiastical traditions that have nurtured us have often (and sometimes unwittingly) achieved near-canonical status, it is not surprising that we did not always convince one another. It was gratifying to me to observe how much common vision we came to share, and especially to acknowledge the degree of courtesy and honest listening that were present, even in the midst of strongly felt opinions. These discussions were summarized in written form, and members revised their papers in that light. The task of editing the revisions fell to me – yet another place where the indulgence of the members was greatly appreciated.

On a rather mechanical note, I should perhaps explain that where a contributor thought it wise to provide bibliographical information on his or her topic, beyond what was actually cited in the essay, a bibliography has been appended. Where the only bibliography relating to an essay was already cited in notes, no separate listing at the end of the essay was permitted.

The meeting itself took place in the autumn of 1990 in Cambridge, England. Once again Tyndale House provided the excellent facilities, while members and friends of Eden Baptist Church provided most of the hospitality. One of the elders of that church, Mr Stan Blake, saw to all the local logistics, an unenviable task he expertly discharged.

I should mention that, as with other volumes in this series, moneys are put aside to assist in the translation and publication of any part of these books in areas of the world where the church has little money. Applications from recognized Christian institutions may be made in the first instance to the Publications Working Group of the World Evangelical Fellowship.

Working on this book has convinced all of us not only that we need to understand worship better, but that we ought to worship better. As one of the contributors notes, God is not seeking true worship, but true worshippers (John 4:23). If in God's mercy this book contributes to the growth and multiplication of true worshippers, we shall be satisfied with our labours.

Soli Deo gloria.   D. A. CARSON

1

'Worship the Lord Your God': The Perennial Challenge

D. A. CARSON

According to Matthew and Luke, the devil took Jesus to a high mountain and showed him 'all the kingdoms of the world and their splendour.' The gauntlet he threw down before Jesus invited apostasy as it promised glory: 'All this I will give you if you will bow down and *worship* me.' Jesus' answer was unequivocal: 'Away from me, Satan! For it is written: "*Worship* the Lord your God, and serve him only" ' (Matt. 4:8–10; cf. Luke 4:5–8).

This was not an invitation to change styles of 'worship' – to move, say, from pipe organ to guitars. In fact, it was not properly an ecclesiastical or corporate matter at all. It was private and personal; more importantly, it dealt with the fundamental question, the question of ultimate allegiance: Whom do you serve?

This, surely, is where all questions about worship must properly begin. The critical issue is not the techniques of worship, or the traditions of worship, still less the experience of worship, but who is being worshipped, and who is worshipping. The Puritans understood the point, connecting worship with true godliness:

Worship comprehends all that respect which man oweth and giveth to his Maker. . . . It is the tribute which we pay to the King of Kings, whereby we acknowledge his sovereignty over us, and our dependence on him. . . . All that inward reverence and respect, and all that outward obedience and service to God, which the word [viz. 'godliness'] enjoineth, is included in this one word worship.[1]

If the heart of sinfulness is self-centredness, the heart of all biblical religion is God-centredness: in short, it is worship. In our fallenness we constrict all there is to our petty horizons. I think of all relationships in terms of their impact on me; my daydreams circle around my own life and circumstances; my goals and hopes invariably turn on my place in the universe. Such profound self-centredness may result in wild cruelty that the world thinks of as social pathology, or it may result in religious cant; it may issue in war and racism as masses of little people who want to be first exploit and harm others who want the same thing but may lack the means, and it may issue in piety and discipline full of self-satisfaction and fervour. Still the demon SELF marches on. The sign that self is broken is true worship: God becomes the centre, the focus of delight, the joyfully acknowledged King, the Creator, the Redeemer. In this sense, none but the transformed can truly worship – and they too discover how much more transformation is still needed. Thus all worship becomes an eschatological sign, a marker of what will be in the new heaven and the new earth, the home of righteousness, when the children of God have been 'glorified' (Rom. 8:30), and God is all in all. In anticipation of that day, and 'in view of God's mercy', we offer our bodies 'as living sacrifices, holy and pleasing to God', for this is our 'spiritual worship' (Rom. 12:1).

Unfortunately, however, in much of the world the term 'worship' has been restricted in a number of ways. This would be of minor importance – after all, words regularly change their meaning with time – were it not for the fact that 'worship' has become attached to a fair bit of ecclesiastical practices. When we want to reform 'worship', we really mean we want to reform certain ecclesiastical practice. But if the modern word 'worship' is now associated with a lot of ideas with little biblical warrant, then those who wish to reform theology and practice by the Bible must pause and ask some basic biblical questions before following any of the siren voices that beckon.

At the risk of oversimplification, we may discern three approaches to 'worship' that are, finally, reductionistic, and that would greatly benefit from larger, biblical-theological categories:

1. The most common tendency restricts 'worship' to what happens in a corporate setting when a number of Christians gather together for a 'service'. The word may then be further restricted to what happens in only *part* of that 'service': we have 'worship', and then we have the sermon; we assign part of the service to a 'worship leader' or a 'worship team', and then another part to the 'preacher' or 'pastor' or 'minister'. The implications are unambiguous. Worship has nothing to do with Christian life all through the week, but only with corporate activity during a designated hour or so. Or worse, it refers to only a part of that designated hour, when *we* are actively voicing something *corporately* (in songs, prayers, liturgical responses, corporate Bible reading, and so forth). At this point 'worship' is something *we do*, where the *we* ensures its corporate nature, and the *do* ensures corporate *activity*. One thinks of the engaging title of a book by Robert E. Webber, *Worship is a Verb*.[2]

2. Another approach to worship during the past few decades, especially in North Atlantic countries, has been to ransack the New Testament for any hint of liturgy, and thereby to establish afresh the importance of more formal liturgy today. Thus passages such as Phil. 2:6–11 and Col. 1:15–20 are thought by many to be quotations from early Christian hymns; some of the responses in Revelation are judged to be drawn from liturgies actively used in the churches; 1 Peter is thought by some to be something akin to a baptismal liturgy. Moreover, we are told, the church established many of its practices by modelling itself on the ancient synagogue, and since the synagogue system had developed its own liturgies, *a priori* we must assume that the church followed suit.

But the evidence turns out to be very slender. It has been repeatedly shown that all the evidence for liturgy in the Jewish synagogue system is considerably later than the New Testament documents: we simply do not know what a synagogue service looked like in the first century. Most scholars today rightly reject the notion that 1 Peter is a baptismal liturgy. And if, say, Col. 1:15–20 is a hymn well-known to the church, and something Paul is quoting (certainly quite possible, though hard to prove), it says nothing about the kind of 'service' from which it was drawn.

More importantly, these studies – both the more practical approaches of the first reductionism, and the more theoretical approaches of the second – are so heavily focused on *congregational* worship, i.e. what happens when the church meets together, that it ignores the overwhelming tendency in the New Testament to associate 'worship' terminology with the full range of Christian life and thought and experience. At its worst, it so narrows down to what *we* experience, or what *we* do, or how *we* participate, or what *we* should sing, that we return to self-centredness by another route. A little over a century ago, it was not uncommon to find Christians in some traditions asking after a sermon, 'How did you get on under the Word?' Now we ask, 'How did you enjoy the sermon?' Now the latter question is extended: 'How did you enjoy the worship?' (i.e. the rest of the service apart from the sermon). Worship can be rated according to our degree of enjoyment. It is part of the *genus* 'entertainment industry'.

Should we not remind ourselves that worship is a *transitive* verb? We do not meet to worship (i.e. to experience worship); we aim to worship *God*. 'Worship the Lord your God, and serve him only': there is the heart of the matter. In this area, as in so many others, one must not confuse what is central with byproducts. If you seek peace, you will not find it; if you seek Christ, you will find peace. If you seek joy, you will not find it; if you seek Christ, you will find joy. If you seek holiness, you will not find it; if you seek Christ, you will find holiness. If you seek experiences of worship, you will not find them; if you worship the living God, you will experience something of what is reflected in the Psalms. Worship is a transitive verb, and the most important thing about it is the direct object.

All this was better understood in an earlier age:

It is a principle deeply fixed in the minds of men that the worship of God ought to be orderly, comely, beautiful and glorious. . . . And indeed that worship may be well suspected not to be according to the mind of God which comes short in these properties. . . . I shall add unto this, only this reasonable assertion . . . viz, That what is so in his worship and service, God himself is the most proper judge. If then we evince not that spiritual gospel worship, in its own naked simplicity, without any other external, adventitious helper or countenance, is most orderly, comely, beautiful, and glorious, the Holy Ghost in the Scripture being judge, we shall be content to seek for these things where else, as it is pretended, they may be found. . . . In the spiritual worship of the gospel, the whole blessed trinity, and each person therein distinctly, do in that economy and dispensation, wherein they act severally and peculiarly in the work of our redemption, afford distinct communion with themselves unto the souls of the worshippers. This is the general order of gospel worship, the great rubric of our service. . . . If either we come not unto it by Jesus Christ, or perform it not in the strength of the Holy Ghost, or if it go not unto God as a Father, we transgress all the rules of this worship. This is the great canon, which if it be neglected, there is no decency in whatever else is done in this way. And this in general is the glory of it. . . . Acting faith on Christ for admission, and on the Holy Ghost for his assistance, so going on in his strength; and on God, even the Father, for acceptance, is the work of the soul in this worship. That it hath anything more glorious to be conversant about, I am yet to learn. . . .[3]

3. Almost in reaction against these tendencies, a number of scholars have argued that whatever it is that the church in the New Testament gathers for, it is *not* for worship. The worship language of the New Testament, they argue, is tied restrictively to *all* of life; it is simply not tied to what goes on in the Christian assembly. There we read of instruction and of mutual edification, but not of worship. To think otherwise is to be bound to the cultic focus of pre-Christian times.

But one must ask if this is a new reductionism. If the New Testament expands the horizons of worship to embrace all of life, does it intend to exclude those times when Christians assemble together? Is there nothing to be learned from the apocalyptic vision of what occupies the saints when they gather around the Throne? Do the 'psalms, hymns and spiritual songs' (Eph. 5:19; Col. 3:16) serve *exclusively* to edify the saints mutually?

It appears, then, that recent discussions about worship have tended to be either minimally biblical and primarily pragmatic, or narrowly biblical and without adequate integration with inner-canonical development of major themes. The temple of Solomon had choirs: what does that say to us today? The old covenant specified the nature of the priesthood that could offer sacrifice: how do such specifications fare, or in what ways are they transmuted, under the new covenant? Is it appropriate to think of church buildings as 'tabernacles' or 'temples'? If so, why? If not, why not?

The fact of the matter is that none of these and a host of related questions can be responsibly answered apart from the careful articulation of biblical theology – theology that sorts out how the parts of the Bible hang together. Suddenly the subject of worship becomes complex, the more so because by and large the contemporary church has not disciplined itself to think in biblical-theological terms. When one starts asking questions about, say, the relationship between the covenants, one is immediately embroiled in historic questions about law and grace, circumcision and baptism, Sabbath and Lord's Day, and a host of more recent debates that turn, often in unrecognized ways, on the way one reads the Bible as a whole book – in short, on biblical theology.

In modest measure, that is what the second and third chapters of this book attempt. The authors themselves would be the first to acknowledge the preliminary nature of their work, but the results are fascinating and important. They become the backdrop for the rest of the chapters in the book.

Chapters 4 through 12 describe and usually offer some critique of the traditions of worship in various Christian bodies around the world. We might have cast our net still more widely; some will be daunted by the breadth already displayed. It may help to draw attention to several features of these chapters.

First, in every case what 'worship' means in some particular tradition is taken up by those associated with that tradition. We did not ask a Presbyterian cessationist to describe and criticize the worship traditions of the charismatic movement – or vice versa. We did not ask a Latin American Baptist to describe and criticize the Anglican *Book of Common Prayer* – or an Anglican to describe and criticize Free Church traditions. In each case, we have provided an 'in-house' look. The advantage, of course, is that each view of what 'worship' means is set forth in its most attractive form. That is valuable if we are to understand one another and avoid alien stereotypes. It does not mean we will always agree; it does mean we will be better able to grasp how some of those within these traditions perceive what is going on.

Second, each writer was asked not only to describe but also in some measure to offer thoughtful critique of his or her own tradition, *on the basis of the biblical theology attempted in chapters 2 and 3* of this book. The degree to which this was successful you must judge. Speaking editorially, I can assure you that the revised drafts were far more sensitive to the weaknesses of the traditions they represented than the first drafts – owing, no doubt, to the strenuous debate and exposure to the biblical papers. In two or three of the revisions, writers have taken exception to some of the emphases or details in the biblical papers, and justified their views: again, the measure of success achieved must be carefully weighed by the reader.

Thirdly, although there was a fair bit of mutual criticism, in good spirit, at the meeting, we did not invite contributors to offer written criticisms of the stances adopted by others. That would have been a logical next step; it would also have made this book too long. Perhaps, too, such an exercise would have been more than some of us could have borne. But the thoughtful reader cannot help but be fascinated by the way, say, that Clowney deploys Scripture in seeking to establish (and delimit!) the regulative principle ('Presbyterian Worship'), and the way that Alistair Brown deploys Scripture in defence of 'Charismatically-Orientated Worship'. One cannot help thinking about how each would reply to the other in print. And this, of course, is not the only pair of polarities in the book.

Fourthly, even where there was widespread biblical and theological agreement (and eventually more agreement was achieved than might be suggested by these introductory remarks), one cannot escape the conclusion that not a few practices in *congregational* worship have been moulded rather more by cultural and historical factors than some have thought. As the articles by Houghton and Méndez make clear, it is no accident that the charismatic flourishes in Latin America but not in Japan or Madagascar. The paper by Yri makes clear the extent to which classic Lutheranism has defined itself by its historic emergence from Roman Catholicism. What, then, does reformation of our worship by the Word of God look like in various cultures of the world? How *should* cultural factors be shaped by Scripture? These questions, it must be said, have been addressed only peripherally in this book.

Fifthly, in the final revisions most of the essays in this section attempt some comment on the relation between, on the one hand, biblical evidence that under the new covenant, worship first and foremost means God-centred living in every area of life and thought and action and relationships, and, on the other, the demands and constraints of *congregational* worship. But clearly much more work needs to be done on this relationship.

The final essay attempts some theological synthesis, and provides the title for the book. Worship as adoration of God is a distinctive activity; it embraces both understanding and emotions, the whole person in the presence of the God of creation and redemption.

Worship is an act of the understanding, applying itself to the knowledge of the excellency of God, and actual thoughts of his majesty. . . . It is also an act of the will, whereby the soul adores and reverenceth his majesty, is ravished with his amiableness, embraceth his goodness, enters itself into an intimate communion with this most lovely object, and pitcheth all his affections upon him.[4]

Even so, this does not mean turning away from the world. It involves, rather, the right perception of how God relates to the world, and the world to God. In such a framework, worship, embracing both adoration and action, is nothing but the outworking of God-centredness in the individual and corporate experience of the people of God.

Part One

Toward a Biblical Theology
of Worship

2

Theology of Worship in the Old Testament

YOSHIAKI HATTORI

In the beginning, there was worship.

Although critical voices might be raised in response to such a statement, it is not out of step with biblical theology. According to the Bible, the relationship between God the sovereign Creator and the human beings created in his image is the foundation upon which all theological concepts rest (Gen. 1). As beings created by God, men and women are responsible for keeping in right relationship with God their Maker: they are to respond to him, to pay him due service. In fact, such a concept of 'service'[1] expresses the fundamental idea of worship, and is entirely in line with the definition of worship offered by Allen and Borror:

> Worship is an active response to God whereby we declare His worth. Worship is not passive, but is participative. Worship is not simply a mood; it is a response. Worship is not just a feeling; it is a declaration.[2]

Accordingly, worship is the entire attitude of one's life or being in relationship to God the Creator.[3] Of course, the externally visible expressions of worship may take many forms, in the history of redemption, in the course of the history of the Christian church[4] and in the experiences of geographically and culturally distinct traditions within the worldwide Christian church.

Our purpose in this chapter is to look into some basic elements of worship in the revealed history of the Old Testament. Beyond that, we shall probe their organic and canonical relationships with the New Testament understanding of worship. Ultimately something must be said about the relation of our findings to worship today.[5]

In this essay the term 'worship', tied to its Old Testament roots, focuses rather more on corporate than on private or individual forms.

I. WORSHIP ELEMENTS IN THE EARLY HISTORY

In the first two chapters of Genesis, the divine initiative is the fundamental factor that determines the divine/human relationship. God creates the world and everything in it, including human beings. Accordingly, the relationship

21

between God and his human creation was initiated by God himself (Gen. 2:15, 19). The first man and woman simply responded to the divine provision, maintaining the right and normal relationship with God the Creator. If worship embraces the basic attitude of human response to the Creator-God, the original beauty of the responding relationship in the act of worship can be seen even before the fall.

A. Pre-patriarchal Period

However, that basic relationship between God and humanity was broken by human rebellion, this profoundly evil response to God (Gen. 3:6–10). Though so greatly provoked, God graciously revealed the first steps in the wonderful covenant of redemption (Gen. 3:15, 21). To the man and the woman, he graciously restored something of their original ability to respond to and worship God – but now in connection with sacrifice. Thus, the very first formal element of worship is an offering (Gen. 4:3–4).[6] Although there is no mention of any form of altar for the offering in this case, nevertheless since it is the *minḥāh* ('gift') offering, it must be considered as including some element of worship.[7]

It is worth pausing to ask whether this early worship is to be construed as an individual or a corporate act. Although corporate and cultic worship predominates in much of the Old Testament, the crucial expression in Gen. 4:26 is simply 'calling the divine name' – and it is difficult to decide, from the expression used in the Hebrew text,[8] whether corporate or individual worship is in view. Some translations (including KJV, RSV, ASV, NEB, NASB, NIV) rather freely render the text in plural form.[9] Similar expressions are found in Gen. 12:8, 13:4, 21:33 and 26:25, however, and they are all expressed in the singular. Some argue that although the expression of the text is in the singular, the actual activity of 'calling the divine name' might have been done with others present, such as the members of the household. Certainly there are other singular forms that envisage more than one person, as in the case of Solomon's building of his houses (by himself alone? or with the help of other people?) (1 K 7:1–2). In any case, as Rowley observes, at least in the early days of the patriarchal age the act of 'calling the divine name' might well have been done individually rather than in a corporate manner or even as a family affair.[10]

What does the expression 'calling the name of YHWH' (Gen. 4:26) mean? It should be taken as almost synonymous with 'praying to YHWH': 'We have here an account of the commencement of that worship of God which consists in prayer, praise, and thanksgiving, or in the acknowledgement and celebration of the mercy and help of Jehovah.'[11] In fact, all of the similar occurrences in the Old Testament may be divided into two categories: those that are virtually synonymous with prayer to God (Ps. 116:4, 13; Lam. 3:55; [2 Kings 5:11]), and those that are joined with some cultic act of worship such as 'building an altar' or 'planting a tree', etc. (Gen. 12:8; 13:4, 16:13; 21:33; 26:55, 1 Kings 18:24; Ps. 16:17). Gen. 4:26 is to be classified with the former.

Although one may well imagine that there was some kind of altar for the offerings of Cain and Abel (Gen. 4:4–5), no such details surface in the biblical text. In fact, in the Old Testament the first explicit reference to the building of an altar is found in Gen. 8:20. Here building an altar is closely related to offering sacrifice, and these two notions make their contribution to the idea of worship.[12]

B. Patriarchal Period

Sacrifice is more prominent in the patriarchal period. The first occurrence in the Bible is at Gen. 8:20. Thereafter the worship of the patriarchs is intimately connected either with 'building an altar'[13] or with the act of sacrificing upon the altar.

Sacrifice is an indication of devotion to God on the part of the one who is performing the act.[14] Thus the offering of a sacrifice, together with the act of building an altar, must be considered basic elements of worship among the people of Israel in the patriarchal period.[15] Of course, the significance of sacrifice changes with time: in the cult the role of sacrifice was progressively revealed and enriched across the history of the Old Testament period. For example, the significance of sacrifice in the Passover Feast, and its ultimate connection with the promised Messiah, can be satisfactorily appreciated only from the standpoint of salvation-history.[16]

During the life of Abram/Abraham, the act of worship, whether bound up with building an altar or calling on Yahweh's name, seems to be related to some location, frequently a place where God has revealed himself (see Gen. 12:7–8; 13:4, 18; 21:33; [22:9]). Meeting with God or encountering God is an essential component of worship. Thus the experience of encountering the living God at a specific location was easily tied to the idea of a particular sanctuary. However, it is necessary to distinguish these sites from other holy places or sanctuaries established by the non-Yahwistic religions. Although there were doubtless similarities between the two,[17] the significance of any site for the patriarchs was necessarily bound up with the peculiar nature of the theophany they had experienced there. Several patriarchal sites clearly served as sanctuaries at least until the temple was built in Jerusalem: e.g. Gilgal (Josh. 5:7–12), Shiloh (Josh. 18:1–10), Mizpah (Judg. 20:1–3; 21:1–8), Gibeon (1 Chron. 16:39; 21:29), Ophra (Judg. 6:11–24), Dan (Judg. 17–18).

Another element that might be considered to be related to worship in the life of Abram/Abraham is the act of circumcision as a sign of Yahweh's covenant with him (and with all of his descendants). Of course, the practice of circumcision was not found exclusively amongst the people of Israel; it was practised by other ancient peoples as a sort of magical or religious initiation rite. However, it was utilized as a sign of the divine covenant by the people of Israel (Gen. 17:10–14).[18] The covenant established a binding relationship between the two parties, and detailed their responsibilities and principles. Any worship directed toward the God of the covenant is naturally to be understood as part of the worshipper's proper response.[19]

One of the most general expressions for the act of worship in the Old Testament is the verb 'to bow down' or 'to prostrate' (Hebrew *šāhah* – so the older works. More recent philologists think the root is *ḥ-w-y*).[20] This verb is commonly used to mark respect to certain great men in the narratives of the patriarchs in the Book of Genesis (Gen. 18:2; 19:1, 23:7, 12; 27:29; 33:3, 6, 7; 37:10; 43:26, 28; 47:31; 48:12; 49:8), but in a few places God is understood to be the object (Gen. 22:5; 24:26; 48, 52).[21] As to the outward expression or posture, the idea of 'bowing down' or 'prostrating' oneself then takes on an overtone of worshipful reverence, as suggested by the linkage of verbs in Gen. 24:48.[22]

Further, we find in the Book of Genesis some emphasis on seeking after God's goodness or help for such blessings as healing (Gen. 20:7, 17)[23] and child-birth (Gen. 25:21).[24] Finally, there is an element of praising in the worship of the patriarchs. They praised their God, and the words used in the narratives are mainly two: *bārak* ('to bless', Gen. 9:26; 14:20; 24:27)[25] and *yādāh* ('to put forth', Gen. 29:35).[26]

In summary, in the patriarchal narratives the following elements are constitutive of worship: (1) setting up a place of worship, in particular 'building an altar' and offering a sacrifice upon it[27a] and calling upon the divine name (with or without an altar present); (2) adopting the practice of circumcision as an important covenantal rite tied to worshipful response to God; (3) 'bowing' or 'prostrating oneself' as a reverential posture in worshipping God, (4) acknowledging the need of seeking God's intervening help for practical living; and (5) praising God as an expression of thanksgiving to God and his goodness. E. W. Nicholson's observation seems sound: 'It is probable that Yahweh was worshipped in the pre-Exodus period and few today would deny that a community bearing the name Israel may have existed in the pre-Mosaic period and, further, that it may already have been a Yahweh-worshipping community.'[27b] Of course, these elements of worship become somewhat more definite patterns or forms in the next period of history.

II. WORSHIP AROUND THE TIME OF THE EXODUS

The first part of the Book of Exodus summarizes the transition from the period of the patriarchs to the period of the Exodus (Exod. 1:1–7).[28] The rest of the first chapter sets forth the background of the event of the exodus, viz. the increase of the Israelite populace in Egypt and eventually the oppression they suffered at the hands of the Egyptians, who feared the potential dangers inherent in such an increase.

Then, in the second chapter and in the first part of the third chapter the narrative indicates that the God who revealed himself to Moses with the command to bring the Israelites out of the land of Egypt according to his faithful fulfilment of the covenant (2:24–25), was the very same God whom the patriarchs had been worshipping during the preceding period of history. The so-called Kenite hypothesis is to be excluded.[29] God's self-revelation (seen in Exod. 3:6, 15–16 as well as in Exod. 6:3) is to be understood in terms of the theological framework the text establishes: the God of the patriarchs is the same God who has revealed himself to Moses.

Building on this line of continuity, we may inquire in what ways the people of Israel worshipped God in their day.

A. Moses and the Israelites in Egypt (Exod. 3–15)

(1) Moses' attitude toward God

God reveals himself to Moses and identifies himself as the God of the patriarchs, saying, 'I am the God of your father, the God of Abraham, the

God of Isaac and the God of Jacob' (Exod. 3:6). Moses' response to God was 'fear',[30] as expressed in the text: 'At this, Moses hid his face, because he *was afraid* to look at God' (3:6). God responds with instruction and a commission to lead the Israelites out of the land of Egypt (Exod. 3:7–12). Included in that commission is God's declaration that the people he redeems are to be a people of worship:[31] 'And God said, "I will be with you. And this will be the sign to you that it is I who have sent you: when you have brought the people out of Egypt, you will *worship* God on this mountain" ' (Exod. 3:12). Moses is instructed to say to the king of Egypt, 'Let us take a three-day journey into the desert *to offer sacrifices*[32] to the Lord our God' (Exod. 3:18).

Although various terms expressing worship are found in the text,[33] the central feature of their worship was 'offering of sacrifices (*zebāḥîm*) and burnt offerings (*'olot*)' (Exod. 10:25),[34] and the most common verb referring to their worship seems to be *'ābad* ('to serve') which is often rendered 'to worship' (e.g. NIV, NEB).[35] In these chapters, which deal with the history of the Israelites immediately preceding their redemption from slavery in the land of Egypt, the emphasis seems to be on the fact that the Israelites were to be a people of worship, acknowledging their responsibility as the recipients of the grace of the covenant of redemption.[36] Their repeated requests to leave the land of Egypt for the purpose of 'worshipping'/'serving' their God' (Exod. 3:18; 5:1, 3; 7:16; 8:1 [Heb 7:26]; 8:8 [Heb 8:4]; 8:20 [Heb 8:16]; 8:27 [Heb 8:23]; 9:1, 13; 10:3, 7, 9, 25, 26) establish the point. Apparently the sacrifices they wished to offer might not be welcomed by the Egyptians in the land of Egypt (cf. Exod. 8:26–27) – whether because of the animals being offered or the procedures involved.[37] In any case, the covenant community was clearly conscious of being a people called to worship their ancestral God.

(2) Passover and the Israelites

The event of the Exodus has been commemorated by the Hebrews throughout their history in the observing of the Passover. Exodus 12 establishes that the Passover was covenantal in nature, and was given prior to the event of the Exodus itself (at least according to the structure of the text), and then the event took place just as it had been promised.[38] Ensuing generations have observed the rite of the Passover with thanksgiving for the saving act of God in the past, understanding it to be the archetypal act of redemption that anticipates all later acts of redemption (hence Israel's use of exodus motifs).

Christians cannot forget that the feast of Passover was observed by Jesus Christ himself, most notably at the time of the last supper (Matt 26:17–29; Mark 14:12–25, Luke 22:7–23). The central themes of deliverance and redemption surface again.[39] Small wonder Christ is referred to as the Passover lamb in 1 Cor. 5:7 (cf. also John 19:36).

Although there were times when the observance of Passover was neglected,[40] from the beginning the event of the exodus was to be kept in mind as God's great work of deliverance (Exod. 13:3–16). Explaining the relationship between the *event* of the exodus and the book that takes that name, C. F. Pfeiffer says: 'It refers more specifically to the crucial event of that book – God's redemption of his people Israel from Egypt. This divine act in human history, recounted from generation to generation, was never lost sight of, even in the N. T. (Acts 7:36).'[41]

In fact, the feast of the Passover brought forth two theological channels by which the organic and progressive nature of the divine revelation toward the New Testament practice of worship was developed. The first opened the way to the Lord's Supper. R. S. Wallace draws attention to this biblical-theological motif in the Passover when he says,

> In this, the people of God not only remembered, but again lived through the events of their deliverance from Egypt under the sign of the sacrificed Paschal lamb as if they themselves participated in them (see Exod. 12). In this context, giving the bread and wine as his body and blood, with the words, 'This do in remembrance of me,' Jesus points to himself as the true substitute for the Paschal lamb, and to his death as to the saving event which will deliver the new Israel, represented in his disciples, from all bondage. His blood is to be henceforth the sign under which God will remember his people in himself.[42]

A second channel tied to the Passover feast is the notion of the Sabbath and its connection, on the one hand, with creation (Gen. 2), and on the other, with the sabbath-rest of God (Heb. 4). The biblical-theological line runs through the Sinai covenant. When God's 'rest' from his labours is first introduced in Gen. 2:2–3, two concepts[43] are especially significant. They are the concept of 'sabbath'/'rest' and the concept of 'setting-apart'/'sanctifying'. Of this, W. C. Kaiser, Jr. says,

> Thus God made the seventh 'day' holy as a perpetual memorial to the completion of the entire universe and all that was in it. His 'rest' was to be symbolic for man both in his own rhythm of work and cessation from labor as well as for his eternal hopes.[44]

Exodus 16:23–30 introduces a practical example of God's marvellous provision in regard to the Sabbath.[45] This is the first occurrence of the word *šabāt* ('Sabbath') in the Old Testament (though there is the basis of the idea of the Sabbath in Gen. 2:2–3). Perhaps, as A. Cole supposes, if the Israelites did not observe the Sabbath during their stay in Egypt (as the silence of the text might suggest), it was because of their constrained circumstances as slaves.[46] But what is clear is that the formal institutionalization of the Sabbath, as presented in the process of the progressive revelation in the course of salvation-history, occurred in the context of the theophany at Mt. Sinai (Exod. 20:8–11).

As is well-known, the reasons given for sabbath-observance are not the same in Exod. 20:11 and in Deut. 5:15. The former grounds sabbath-observance on the fact that God the Creator rested on the seventh day and thus set it apart from the other six days (Gen. 2:2–3), while the latter grounds sabbath-observance on the fact that God delivered the people of Israel out of bondage in the land of Egypt. Yet we need to acknowledge the organic and progressive relation between the two. Entering into the rest of God by enjoying the Sabbath is tied on the one hand to the rest that God himself exemplifies at the end of his creative work and before human rebellion, and it is tied on the other to the rest that God graciously provides for his fallen and enslaved people. As Cole observes in his comments on Exod. 20:11,

Exodus gives the reason for sabbath observance as being the memory of God's 'rest' from His great work of creation. Deuteronomy 5:15 regards sabbath as commemorating the 'rest' that came to the Israelite slaves in Egypt, when freed by YHWH, and (typical of Deuteronomy) as offering an opportunity of similar 'rest' to Israel's slaves now (Dt. 5:14). These explanations are not mutually exclusive, since both deal with 'rest'; but they do tend to reinforce the view that the shorter form of the commandment was original, perhaps 'Remember the sabbath' alone. In either case, in the sabbath observance, as in all Hebrew festivals, an act of God is commemorated.[47]

Before we consider the next phase of the history of the Israelites reflected in the structure of the Book of Exodus, a little space must be devoted to another issue that is especially relevant to the concept of 'worship' in the Old Testament. I refer to the praising or singing that celebrates God himself or his great work, the deliverance of the Israelites from the land of Egypt. This is especially noteworthy in Exod.15, vs.1–21 in particular.[48] In summary:

(1) Even the title, the 'song of Moses', demonstrates that this praise of God is musical.

(2) There are elements both of retrospection, commemorating God's great work of deliverance of the Israelites from Egypt and his greatness (vv. 2–12),[49] and of anticipation, projecting their trust in God for the future (vv. 13–18).[50]

(3) In a summarised form, there is articulated a theology of salvation and judgment in the context of the Exodus and especially of the crossing of the Red Sea (in vv. 19).

(4) There is mention of the use of musical instruments and dancing along with singing (vv. 20–21).

B. Moses and the Israelites at Sinai
(Exod. 16–40; Lev. 1–27; Num.1–36; Deut.1–34)

Although Moses built an altar, most probably by way of commemorating the victory over the Amalekites and expressing his gratitude for it (Exod. 17:15), the next major event that reveals to us some important elements related to worship is the divine theophany and the law-giving to the Israelites through Moses at Mt. Sinai.[51]

(1) Theophany at Sinai (Exod. 16–19)

Because Moses had stayed with Jethro (Reuel in 2:18) in the land of the Midianites (Exod. 2:15–22)[52] we are probably justified in suggesting that Jethro was beginning to believe in the God of Moses as the true God, not least because of the powerful witness of the event of the exodus – a point suggested by confessional words in 18:10–11. In this light, Exod. 18:12 appears to be an act of worship in anticipation – in anticipation of the divine theophany depicted in the following chapters. Cole writes:

Jethro's own words here seem to favour the view that YHWH was a new god, as far as he was concerned. Those who hold to the 'Midianite hypothesis' (or 'Kenite hypothesis') think otherwise: they think that Moses learned not only the name of

God, but also much of His ways of worship, from this Midianite kinsmen. They thus easily explain the puzzling fact that Jethro leads the worship on this occasion – not as a 'new convert' but as a recognized priest and teacher. However, this explanation is not necessary. Jethro's status as priest, and his senior relationship to Moses, would seem to be adequate grounds. Priesthood as such did not yet exist in Israel: it was a function of the 'elder' of the clan. BURNT OFFERING is usually expressive of thanksgiving, or of the fulfilment of a vow: both would be appropriate here. This is probably the 'whole burnt offering', in which everything is devoted to God and nothing eaten. The general term SACRIFICES would cover the 'communion meal', fasting in the presence of God, as here and in Exodus 24:11, where the 'elders' again appear, possibly in a primitive priestly capacity.[53]

It is almost as if it was necessary to have some sort of worship-like preparation for the great theophany at Mt. Sinai. To meet God and to receive the divine message it was – and is – important to have some such time of preparation.

Furthermore, in the light of this, the word of God to Moses, reported in 19:10–15, seems very significant. In order to meet God they were to be cleansed and to be holy. Gispen states:

> Moses now received further instructions concerning the impending theophany. Verses 10–13 describe how the people were to prepare themselves for the Lord's coming down on Mount Sinai. Moses was to go to the people and consecrate them, that is, separate them from anything unclean, so that they were in the appropriate condition for approaching the Lord (cf. Amos 4:120. Even their clothes had to be clean (cf. Gen. 35:2).[54]

With this preparation completed[55] there was theophany: God revealed himself to Moses and to the Israelites at Mt. Sinai.[56]

In the narrative that follows (Exod. 19:16–25), there are two elements to the theophany. One is the visible phenomena, themselves unusual or supernatural; the other is the audible speaking, the word of God. Both elements are to be understood as components of the divine revelation. Of course, it is necessary to see that the entire experience of this revelation, this encounter between God and his people, was firmly based upon the covenant (Exod. 19:4–6), which was tied to the past (God's redemptive act, v. 4), the present (Israel's responsibility, v. 5a), and the future (God's promise, vv. 5b–6).[57]

(2)   The Law at Sinai (Exod. 20–40; Lev. 1–27)

Though there was a manifestation of supernatural phenomena at the theophany at Sinai, the truly lasting significance of the event lay in the fact that at that time God gave his law to his people. The law included many kinds of commandments, statutes, ordinances, and precepts, among which the ten commandments (the decalogue) occupied the central place. At the beginning of chapter 20, where the decalogue is recorded, absolute obedience to God the Creator and Redeemer is required as the basic necessary attitude of the people who truly worship God. Then, in chapters 21–23, the laws that deal with their concrete social life are set out as the divine revelation: they are the requirements for the people of the worshipping community. To live holy lives in accordance with these regulations is nothing other than to serve God. It is truly the spirit of '*ābad* ('to serve') and the basis of all forms of worship for the old covenant people of God.[58]

In Exodus 24 the following elements are relevant to our study of worship:

(1) The priestly responsibilities of Moses and his line become evident as the statutes and ordinances governing ritual are articulated, not least those related to the tabernacle (Exod. 25–31). Starting with the responsibilities and duties of Moses, Aaron, Nadab and Abihu,[59] the ritual elements of priesthood are introduced as a body of regulations. The expression of the text, v. 1 is, 'You are to worship.'[60] As for the people involved in this corporate worship, Gispen observes a sort of ecclesiastical order: 'Then Moses himself, but not the others, was to approach the Lord. There were thus three degrees of approach: i) Moses, ii) the elders with Aaron, Nadab, and Abihu, and iii) the people.'[61]

(2) It was a 'word-oriented' worship, and 'all the Lord's words and the laws'[62] were told to the people by Moses. Then there was the response of the people to the Lord's words and laws (v. 3). Thus it was covenantal in nature, a covenant confirmed by various offerings (vv. 7–8). In this corporate worship, then, God's people are to be instructed by the word of God, and to confirm their covenantal relationship to God by their response in word and offering.

Following the introductory summary (Exod. 24), the detailed regulations are set forth, not least the instructions relating to the building of the tabernacle (chaps. 25–40).[63] Of course, this section, Exod. 25–40 (especially chaps. 25–31, 35–40), is often (and rightly) considered to contain the essential regulations for worship.[64] Every minute detail in these regulations was in one way or another significant for the worship of the people of God, not least the physical structure and layout of the tabernacle. We cannot ponder here all their bearing on the concept of worship. For our immediate concern it will suffice to mention the following:

First, in the outer court or 'courtyard' (NIV) of the tabernacle there were two objects. One was the altar for burnt offering (Exod. 27:1–8). It functioned as a reminder for the worshippers that sacrifice was necessary in order to approach God. The other was the bronze laver (Exod. 30:17–21), which was mainly for the priests. Those who come to the place of worship to minister must be clean.

Secondly, as to the tabernacle within the courtyard, curtains divided the space within the tabernacle into two parts, the holy place and the holy of holies (Exod. 26:31ff). Access into the holy of holies was restricted to the high priest, who entered but once a year (on the day of atonement), and even then only with the blood of the prescribed sacrifice – details to which the NT writers are quick to draw attention (e.g. Mark 14:38 par.; Heb.9).

Thirdly, in the holy place there were three objects. The first was the table for the 'showbread' (NIV 'bread of the Presence'; Exod. 25:23–30; 37:10–16). It constituted an act of thanksgiving for life here on earth and an indication of one's dedication in worship to the God who sustains life. The second was the golden lampstand (Exod. 25:31–40; 37:17–24), providing seven golden lamps. Perhaps it symbolizes the light of God's glory, the light of God's revelation, the light of God's word as it shines upon the covenant community, while they in turn reflect that light in their lives. The third was the altar of incense (Exod.

30:1–7; 37:25–28) situated in front of the dividing veil. It was used for both morning and evening incense offering (Exod. 30:7ff.), and symbolized the worshipper's dedicated prayer life (cf. Lk. 1:10; Rev. 5:8; 8:3).

Lastly, in the holy of holies at the innermost part of the tabernacle, there were two objects. One was the ark of the covenant. It stood as a solemn reminder of the mutually binding covenant relationship; it marked the place where God met with the priestly representative of his own people on the basis of the merciful atonement. Of course, it contained the tablets of the ten commandments (Exod. 25:16). The other was the 'mercyseat' or 'atonement cover' (NIV) with the cherubim (Exod. 25:17ff.) upon the ark of the covenant. Here the high priest sprinkled the blood of atonement on the day of atonement (Lev. 16:14ff.).

Thus, the tabernacle was the centre of worship, prior to the building of the temple.[65] By way of anticipation, it is worth reminding ourselves what new covenant believers saw in these details. As J. G. S. S. Thomson summarizes:

> The tabernacle symbolism found its fulfilment in Christ. He was tabernacle, priest, altar and sacrifice. He is our High Priest who has passed into the heavens now to appear for us, and to give us access to the holiest by his blood, the blood of the everlasting covenant. God who tabernacled with Israel, and with men in the Word incarnate (John 1:14), does so still in the body of Christ (Eph. 2:21f.) and in the believer (I Cor. 6:19).[66]

While we reflect on the law at Sinai, we must briefly consider the bearing of the contents of the book of Leviticus on our topic. Adopting a traditional understanding of Leviticus, we observe that the regulations in the book were given to the people of Israel through Moses at Sinai, and were considered a further expansion of the laws and regulations in the book of Exodus.

Leviticus sets forth three components in the pursuit of holiness. In other words, there are three ways for the people of Israel, God's worshipping community, to be holy. One way is to keep away from impurity and uncleanness. The regulations for that purpose are in the first part of the book (chaps. 1–16), and the tone is largely negative. The second way is to act with justice in all of life, and to observe the regulations and feasts God stipulates: there are positive things to be performed. The regulations for that purpose are in the second half of the book (chaps. 17–26). And thirdly, when there are breaches in the first two, cleanness and holiness can be regained only through certain God-sanctioned restrictions and sacrifices. Various offerings and sacrifices were required to take away uncleanness (chaps. 1–7). Such regulations were a necessary element in one's approach to the holy God. To officiate at these required rituals, various regulations for the priests were needed (chaps. 8–10).

After the lists of regulations relating to daily, practical life (chaps.11–15), the regulations concerning the day of atonement are presented (Lev. 16) – the precursor to the so-called 'holiness code' (chaps. 17–26), which contains the regulations the people must observe in order to be God's holy people. The grace that springs from the great and decisive work of atonement does not end there; the appropriate response is to observe the regulations and rites set forth in these chapters (Lev. 17–26). These regulations and rites are to be considered as the reasonable service that must be performed or observed by

God's people, whose sins have been atoned for. It is in this sense that the holiness code (Lev. 17–26) offers a very significant perspective on the concept of worship. Nevertheless, we must not minimize the sheer mechanical detail in the regulations governing priesthood and priestly offerings (chaps. 21–22), and those governing religious festivals such as Sabbath, Passover, Seven-weeks, New Year, Atonement, Feast of Booths, daily worship, Sabbath-year, and Jubilee (Lev. 23–25). To these are added the regulations related to blessing-and-curse ordinances (chap. 2).[67]

(3)   Journey from Sinai (Num. 1–36; Deut.1–40)

Some mention is necessary here of the contents of the books of Numbers and Deuteronomy, so far as they bear on our study of worship. Doubtless there were religious activities, which would be related to worship, during the journey from Sinai to the east side of the Jordan river, but no noteworthy description of such activities is preserved in the book of Numbers, except for some suggestive and fragmentary expressions. These are related to the work of the Levites in the Tent of Meeting (1:53; 4:3–4), the work of the priests (Moses and Aaron) such as offerings and the benediction (3:6–8; 5:25–26; 6:24–26), the prophetic ministry of Moses and the elders with some ecstatic phenomena (11:25–30), the prayer of Moses and Aaron (14:5; 16:4; 45; 20:6; 21:7), the memorial service (?)(31:54), and a few similar matters. The laws and regulations in the book of Numbers are mostly supplementary to those mentioned in Exodus and Leviticus, and the main dramatic feature of Numbers is the history of the journey of the Israelites through the wilderness for forty years.[68]

As for the Book of Deuteronomy, a similar brevity is maintained. The first part of the book, in the main, is a review of the journey following the exodus from Egypt (chaps. 1–3). The second part, though it could be divided several ways, is composed of instructional laws and regulations applicable more specifically to the life of the covenant community in the land of Canaan, although they are based upon the laws set forth in the books of Exodus, Leviticus, and Numbers. Of course, the contents of Deuteronomy have been influential upon many concepts in both Jewish faith and Christian faith.[69] Nevertheless, there is not much new material pertinent to our study of worship, except for the well-known 'Shema',[70] which could be adopted as a creed in our corporate worship.

We may usefully pause here to summarize:

(1) There seems to be some need of preparation for theophany – or at least there is anticipation of it – in worship (Exod. 16–19).
(2) The Israelites were to be clean and holy when they encountered God in worship (Exod. 19:10–5).
(3) There were two elements in the people's experience of the theophany, i.e. in their encounter with the living God: (a) visible visionary pheno-mena, and (b) audible revelation in the divine word (Exod. 19: 16–25).
(4) The audible word, giving law and instruction, and culminating in written form, played the central role in the divine revelation at Sinai, providing a lasting influence on both Jewish and Christian faith (Exod. 20–40; Lev. 1–27).

(5) The office and responsibilities of the priest were becoming more manifest through this period. Two distinctive features are worth mentioning. The priests served the society, the entire covenantal people; and the regulations/rites that governed them were based upon the covenant (Exod. 24).
(6) The structure of the tabernacle indicates its significance. It is the meeting place between God and human beings. Such a meeting can take place *only* on the conditions that God himself stipulates, including specified times, intermediaries, and sacrifices (Exod. 25–40).
(7) The laws and injunctions of Leviticus are designed to specify conditions under which God's people will be holy and acceptable to him (Lev. 1–27).
(8) Much of Numbers and Deuteronomy can be viewed as the setting forth of the conditions and times in which God's people did, or more commonly did not, worship God aright. ˙

III. WORSHIP DURING THE TIME OF THE CONQUEST/SETTLEMENT

At the time of the conquest of the land of Canaan by the Israelites under the leadership of Joshua, priests were doubtless at work, and occasionally some extraordinary function is described, such as the carrying of the ark of the covenant (Josh. 3:1–17; 6:1–21). Yet it is difficult to see clearly how the Israelites maintained the stipulated pattern of worship during such a period of transition.[71] Certainly they were enjoined, as the community of people who were worshipping the sovereign God, to preserve their identity as the people of God even in the midst of the culture and religions of the land, which they were commissioned both to conquer and to settle in. During the period of the conquest the Israelites had to face the temptations of syncretism to a much larger degree than in their previous experience.

A. Worship in Challenge – Book of Joshua

The fourth chapter of Joshua depicts an early phase of this challenging struggle of the Israelites in the land of Canaan. 'When the whole nation had finished crossing the Jordan, the Lord said to Joshua, . . .' So reads the opening verse and it indicates that the event described in chapter 4 happened soon after the Israelites had completed their crossing of the Jordan river. They were now in the land of Canaan. More importantly, because it shows that all of the twelve tribes of Israel had crossed into the land of Canaan, it signals that the covenantal promise made to their forefathers was fulfilled at that time. This becomes more definite in v. 3: 'And tell them to take up twelve stones from the middle of the Jordan from right where the priests stood and to carry them over with you and put them down at the place where you stay tonight.' Commenting on v. 3, M. Woudstra says, 'The emphasis of the command lies in the participation of all Israel in the ritual of the ceremonial stones (See 1:2; 3:1, 12).'[72] In a similar way, in v. 4 the twelve tribes are repeatedly mentioned, corresponding to the twelves stones in v. 3. Still further, in v. 5 both the twelve stones and the twelve tribes are brought together in a close relationship with the ark of the Lord: 'And [Joshua] said to them, "Go over before the ark of the Lord your God into the middle of the

Jordan. Each of you is to take up a stone on his shoulder, according to the number of the tribes of the Israelites . . ." ' (v. 5). The purpose of setting these stones was, as the first part of the text of v. 6 clearly shows, *that it might become a sign among the Israelites* ('to serve as a sign among you' (=the Israelites, NIV)), and the time reference is futuristic. This is especially evident in the expression 'when your children ask (you) *in time to come*' (American Jewish translation = Soncino Bible). Contextually and exegetically speaking, the answer to the question 'What do these stones mean?' (v. 6) is in the first half of v. 7, and both its content and its structure connect the crossing of the Jordan with the covenantal truth of the 'Exodus-motif'.[73] The second half of the verse (v. 7) discloses still further the covenantal concerns of the crossing narrative, as the writer establishes that the purpose of the stones is to foster faithfulness to the covenant in the following generations: 'Thus these stones shall become a MEMORIAL [emphasis mine] for the children of Israel forever.'

The following verses (vv. 8–18) recapture the actual event, and in the narratives we observe some few cultic elements, such as the work of the priests and the role of the ark of Yahweh. The people camp at Gilgal, and there at Gilgal in the land of Canaan the Israelites, the community of the people who were worshipping the sovereign God, participated in an act of corporate worship, most probably the first such activity after entering into the land of Canaan.[74] As in the case of the Passover in Exod. 12:25–27 and Exod. 13:14, both the retrospective significance and the prospective significance of the event are stressed in this chapter, especially in the repeated expressions, 'When your children ask you, "What do these stones mean?" ' (4:6, 21), and in the answers to the question. In the land of Canaan, therefore, the Israelites during this early stage were concerned to foster covenantal fidelity, and thus also faithful worship. In other words, they were concerned to transmit to the next generation the covenantal structure of their worship inherited from the exodus and Sinai.

Throughout the book of Joshua we find occasional pieces of evidence of their effort to maintain their identity as the community of Yahweh – worshippers of the sovereign God in the land of Canaan during this challenging period of conquest. The following might be addressed:[75] keeping the Passover (5:10), the priestly duty of carrying the ark of the covenant (chap. 6), building altars and sacrificing as well as reading the Torah at Mt. Ebal and Mt. Gerizim (8:30–35), the building of a memorial altar (22:10–11, 34), and renewal of the covenant at Shechem (24:25–28).

B. Worship in Transition – Book of Judges

The contents of Joshua and Judges are often contrasted. While the former is positive and victorious the latter is negative and failing.[76] During the days of the judges, many Israelites were tempted to compromise their identity, especially their religious identity as Yahweh-worshippers. It was a time of struggle for those concerned to keep the covenant, under the unceasing pressure of syncretism.

Although there are some depictions of religious activities in the book of

Judges – such as sacrificing to the Lord in repentance at Bokim (2:5), crying to the Lord for help (3:9, 15; 4:3; 6:6),[77] building an altar to the Lord (6:24, 28), worshipping the Lord (7:15), seeking after the Lord's help (16:28), fasting and sacrificing in repentance (20:26), building an altar and sacrificing (21:4) – most of them are set in a rather negative context. By and large these passages portray repentance and cries to God for help after there has been a prolonged period of rebellion and consequent punishment. Indeed, the entire course of life of the Israelites described in Judges is a saga of the cycle of rebellion and repentance.

With this as the dominant theme of the book, it is not easy to see exactly what kind of religious activities the Israelites were engaging in during these years in the land of Canaan. Doubtless they established some local places of worship – sanctuary, shrine, etc. – but they had to adjust their activities to the new society of the land of Canaan one way or another. Although Rowley's view may be too pessimistic, the picture he draws is probably not far off from the reality the Israelites experienced at that time. Rowley says,

> In the post-settlement period, as reflected in the Book of Judges, we find abundant signs of a new syncretism, which fused Yahwism with the religion of Canaan and brought it down to the level of Canaanite religion. This was fertility religion, marked by practices quite alien to the religion of the Decalogue. The Israelites were surrounded by Canaanites and offered worship at existing local shrines according to Canaanite customs, learning the arts of agriculture and viticulture and taking over with them the local rites associated with them.[78]

It has been commonly understood that the Israelites had formed a religio-social pattern of living, called an 'amphictyony' by modern scholars, in the land of Canaan after entering into the land. However, in recent years various questions have been raised about this consensus. Was there a central shrine or were there several local ones? Was this social arrangement rather more political and military than religious and cultic? Indeed, even the suitability of 'amphictyony' itself, as a category, has been questioned.[79]

At one level, the Israelites were facing what we would call 'cross-cultural adjustment'. Some of this was bound up with arrival in the promised land. Although they understood this to be the fulfilment of the promise given to their forefathers that their place of settlement would be the land of Canaan (Gen. 12:1–8; 15:18–21), arriving in the land entailed a massive social change: they would no longer be semi-nomadic, but adopt a more sedentary and settled life-style. They were to change their ways of living as part of what it meant to be Yahweh-worshippers in that land of Canaan which was given to them by their God. However, they were not to change their religion, their God. They were to be continually faithful to the Lord, God the Creator and Redeemer, even in this land surrounded by other cultures and religions. While they were engaging in agriculture, they were not to follow the practices of those who believed in the fertility gods of Canaan.

Thus, it was a period of transition. Largely for this reason, it seems inappropriate to seek any definite principle or idea of worship in this particular time of history, the time of the Israelites' settlement in the land of Canaan, save the ongoing warnings in Scripture against religious syncretism.

IV. WORSHIP DURING THE TIME OF MONARCHY

We have already observed the dark and failing picture of the age of the judges through the Book of Judges. And the same book ends with the sad event on the day of the annual festival of the Lord[80] in Shiloh, where had been the Tent of Meeting as a centre of worship (Josh. 18:1). In addition, the book closes with a verse which reflects the unstable conditions of that time in history: 'In those days Israel had no king; everyone did as he saw fit'(21:25).

A. Worship in Pre-Monarchical Society

In the first part of 1 Samuel, large parts of the picture described in the last part of Judges continue, not least the importance of the sanctuary in Shiloh. Shiloh was playing an important role as a centre of worship,[81] with Eli and his two sons as resident priests (1 Sam. 1:3). Worship included some system of offerings, and rituals such as sacrificing, ceremonial eating,[82] wearing of an ephod, and so forth (1:7, 9, 21, 24; 2:13, 18, 28). J. Gutmann says of Shiloh's importance, even beyond these religious aspects,

> What does seem fairly certain is that the Shiloh sanctuary containing the ark, which appears to have been the visible symbol of God's presence, was a major supra-tribal institution of the pre-monarchial period. It served, apparently, as the guarantor of the political autonomy of those tribes who were willing to subscribe to the religious traditions of Yahwism, as upheld at the Shiloh shrine, and to allow those traditions to serve as a unifying force in times of war.[83]

Of course, it was the presence of the ark of the Lord which gave Shiloh its importance (1 Sam. 3:3).[84]

However, in spite of the mention of Shiloh and its importance as the place of worship for the Israelites, the biblical narrative in the first part of 1 Samuel is largely dark and negative. This is especially clear as the plot follows the life of the priestly family of Eli and his two sons. We even read that this was a time of scarcity of the divine revelation: 'In those days the word of the Lord was rare; there were not many visions' (1 Sam. 3:1). Theologically speaking, this moral and spiritual failure in the priesthood connected with the tabernacle/sanctuary might be considered to be an embryonic starting point of the critical attitude of later prophets towards the priestly hierarchy. It eventually developed into the profound prophetic criticism preserved in the Old Testament.[85]

B. Worship under the Leadership of Saul

The dissatisfaction with the depraved priestly line centred on Shiloh prompted the people of Israel to seek a king. The Israelites were losing their trust in their priestly leaders, and ultimately in the divine and kingly authority of their invisible God. So they sought a visible king, following the example of neighbouring countries that pursued other religions. In spite of Samuel's personal dislike of this demand, the course of history went against him. While this course of action won God's permission, it was attended with dire warnings, and in effect it constituted the people's rejection of God as their king, the formal rejection of the theocracy (1 Sam. 8:7).[86]

Samuel performed his prophetic ministry (1 Sam. 3:20–21), and the people often responded (1 Sam. 7:3–4, 17). In this period of history, the ministry of the prophet apparently extended beyond the solemn declaration of the word of God to include priestly functions such as offering sacrifices and pronouncing blessings on the people and the sacrifice at the 'high place' (1 Sam. 9:5–14). At this juncture in history, therefore, the place of meeting with God was not necessarily the sanctuary at Shiloh but might be a 'high place' (1 Sam. 9:12–14). With the rise of the prophetic ministry the place of meeting with God for corporate worship was not restricted to the central sanctuary in Shiloh. The Hebrew expression *bāmāh* ('high place') has been extensively debated, and the problem of finding a suitable translation has not been resolved.[87] However, it has been generally agreed that the word was linked to the varied expressions of religious cults in the geographical area of Canaan; it was certainly used in other religions in the area.[88] Of course, it was also used by the Israelites to refer to a meeting place with God or to a place of theophany, before the building of the temple in Jerusalem (cf. 1 Kings 3:2–5). Later in the history of the Israelites 'high place' became almost synonymous with idolatry, a place of pagan worship (1 Kings 11:7; 2 Kings 18:4; 23:8, etc.).

Since it was a place of meeting with God, there might be some use of musical instruments (1 Sam. 10:5). Although this occasion might have been a festival procession rather than an act of corporate worship more properly conceived, some of these musical instruments were used later in Israelite worship.[89]

At this point, it is important to observe another nascent sign of the rising prophetic criticism of the formalism or ritualistic legalism of priestly functions. Samuel, a prophet, speaks to Saul, a king, in terms that clearly insist that obedience to the divine Word is of greater importance than the formal offering of prescribed sacrifices: 'Does the Lord delight in burnt offerings and sacrifices as much as in obeying the voice of the Lord? To obey is better than sacrifice, and to heed is better than the fat of rams. For rebellion is like the sin of divination, and arrogance like the evil of idolatry. Because you have rejected the word of the Lord, he has rejected you as king' (1 Sam. 15:22–23).[90] This sounds much like the voice of later prophets such as Jeremiah (7:22–23), Hosea (6:6), and Micah (6:6–8).

C. Worship under the Leadership of David

David was a man chosen by God to be a king over Israel (1 Sam. 16:12–13). Perhaps his greatest bequest to the worshipping people of God is the body of psalms that reflect the astonishing diversity of his experiences – all tied to the knowledge of God. One thinks, for instance, of this beautiful song of praise for divine deliverance from danger:

> The Lord is my rock, my fortress and my deliverer;
> My God is my rock, in whom I take my refuge,
> My shield and the horn of my salvation.
> He is my stronghold, my refuge and my saviour,
> from violent men you save me (2 Sam. 22:2–3).[91]

David was a man who praised his God with his whole being: 'David . . .

danced before the Lord with all his might' (2 Sam. 6:14; cf. also vv. 5 and 21). He utilized various musical instruments for praising God with his people (2 Sam. 6:4–5; 1 Chron. 16:4–36, 41–42). In addition, David organized the Lord's service (1 Chron. 23–25). Various responsibilities in the corporate worship of the Lord were delegated to different groups of people. Eventually, what was needed was the actual temple – and that was to come under the leadership of Solomon (cf. 1 Kings 8:17–19; 1 Chron. 22:5–11).

D. Worship under the Leadership of Solomon

The construction of the Temple marks a decisive step in the development of Israelite worship. On the one hand, this marks the culmination of the sacrificial system set out at Sinai, the concretization of the laws and regulations often carried out rather more in the breach than in faithfulness. It pulls all faithful corporate worship into the centre – Jerusalem, Mount Zion, the city where God meets with his people. On the other hand, it sets up the dynamics that lead to the division of the kingdom, and ultimately to the exile and the razing of the Temple.

Perhaps the most convenient way to focus discussion will be to survey 1 Kings 8, which might almost be called 'Solomon's theology of the Temple' – or even 'Solomon's theology of worship'. We may usefully adopt the following four divisions: (1) preparatory activities for the dedication of the Temple, vv. 1–13; (2) Solomon's speech at the dedication, vv. 14–21; (3) Solomon's prayer of dedication, vv. 22–53; (4) Solomon's benediction and the people's thanksgiving at the dedication, vv. 54–66.

(1) Preparatory activities for the dedication of the Temple (vv. 1–13)

All the leaders of Israel were gathered together, including the elders, the heads of the tribes, and the princes. They were there for the purpose of carrying the ark of Yahweh and the Tent of Meeting along with the sacred utensils into the newly built Temple. The priests and the Levites were particularly involved in the work of carrying them. Here again we observe the retrospective elements of worship in their cultic activities on this occasion. The ark of the Lord (=the ark of covenant), the two tablets of stone representing the Torah/Law (1 Kings 8:9), the Tent of Meeting[92] – all three theologically and historically related to the great work of God's deliverance, the exodus from Egypt.[93] Moreover, the ark of the Lord was in cultic use in the crossing of the Jordan.

Another cultic activity found in this place is the sacrificing of sheep and cattle (v. 5), although there is no *specific* indication as to the purpose of these sacrifices.[94] However, two observations on vv. 10–13 need to be articulated in order to see both Solomon's view of the Temple and the view of the writer of 1 Kings.

First, the time when the cloud,[95] the glory of the Lord, filled the temple was the very moment of the priests' coming out of the holy place of the Temple after depositing the ark of the Lord there. The physical structure of the Temple had already been completed at the site, but until the ark of the Lord, in which were deposited 'the two tablets of stone' which represented the Law,[96] was placed in the holy place of the Temple, the glory of God did not descend. Thus the author carefully underscores the fact that God's word, his verbal self-disclosure, his law, was the basic and essential element of the Temple. We may call this the 'Torahism' of the theology of the Temple, and we can be sure that the Word of God must play the central role in our worship today.

Secondly, the attitude of Solomon toward the Temple, which he had built using great wealth and the best of his effort, needs to be noticed. When the glory of the Lord had filled the Temple, *then*[97] Solomon articulated his desire to the Lord in a form of prayer, going so far as to say, 'I have indeed built a magnificent temple for you, a place for you to dwell forever' (v. 13); however, these words of Solomon need to be understood in the context of his later words in v. 27: 'But will God really dwell on earth? The heavens, even the highest heaven, cannot contain you. How much less this temple I have built!' After having done his very best for God in building that incomparably magnificent Temple Solomon confessed that God was so great that he could not be reduced to any building, even this Temple. Solomon's theological apprehension was right and profound.[98]

(2)   Solomon's speech at the dedication of the Temple (vv. 14–21)

As the text says, 'While the whole assembly of Israel was standing there, the king turned around and blessed them' (8:14), and Solomon made a speech to the congregation. The following details should be noticed: (a) Solomon understood the completion of the Temple to be the fulfilment of God's promise made to his father David (v. 15); (b) Solomon was strongly aware of the fact that God had given to him the special and personal task of building the Temple (vv. 18–20); and above all, (c) Solomon knew that he had built the Temple to house the ark of the covenant of the Lord, which was related to the great events of the exodus (v. 21).[99]

(3)   Solomon's prayer of dedication (vv. 22–53)

The longest section in this chapter is Solomon's prayer of dedication. This prayer is so tightly arranged that it might very possibly have been written for the occasion. After the description of Solomon's posture for the prayer in v. 22, his prayer starts with v. 23. Solomon addresses God, acknowledging that God is Yahweh, the God of Israel, the God of the whole world and the faithful Keeper of the covenant (vv. 23–26).

The main part of the prayer (vv. 27–53) displays Solomon's concept of the Temple, the people's place of worship, as the place of the divine presence. The basic structure of the prayer is clear:

Basic introductory words, soliciting God to hear his people and forgive them and answer their supplications (vv. 27–30),
a) in the case of troubles in human relationship (vv. 31–32)
b) in the case of defeat in war (vv. 33–34)
c) in the case of disaster/famine (vv. 35–36)
d) in the case of plague and other disasters (vv. 37–40)
e) in the case of foreigners who seek God's face (vv. 41–43)
f) in the case of battle/war (vv. 44–45)
g) in the case of being taken away as captives (vv. 46–51).
Concluding words (vv. 52–53).

Of course, these seven areas do not cover all aspects of the life of the Israelites, yet they represent the main spheres, certainly the most troubling spheres of their life.

Moreover, the structure of these seven petitions (the basic introductory words at the beginning as well) unaminously reveals the fundamental 'triangle' of themes: God, Temple, and people. We may schematize as follows:

Basic introductory words (vv. 27–30):

(A) God in heaven (v. 27)
     God in heaven hears the prayer of his people (v. 30b)

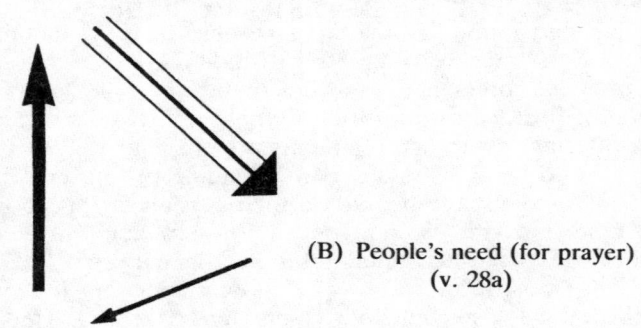

(B) People's need (for prayer)
       (v. 28a)

(C) People coming to the Temple for prayer
     or praying toward the Temple from a distance (vv. 28b–30a)

The same triangle is seen in the first specific petition (vv. 31–32):

(B) People's need (for prayer), in this case
     when a man wrongs his neighbour (v. 31a)

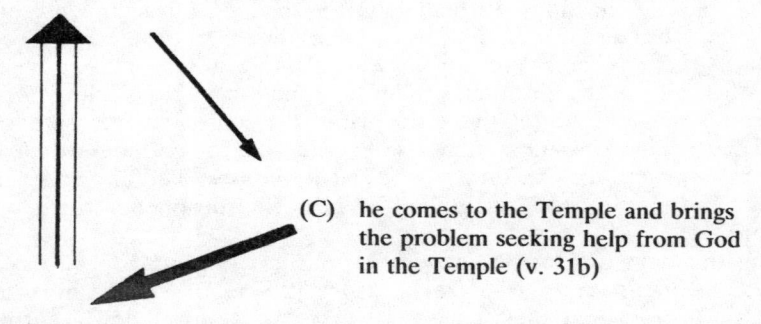

(C)   he comes to the Temple and brings
      the problem seeking help from God
      in the Temple (v. 31b)

(A) God in heaven hears the prayer of people (v. 32)

In other words, when a person has problems in life he or she *needs to come to THE TEMPLE IN JERUSALEM to pray*, but *God himself listens to his or her prayer IN HEAVEN* (not in the Temple).

This pattern is repeated in all the petitions, with the additional factor that in the third (vv. 35–36), fourth (vv. 37–40), sixth (vv. 44–45), and seventh

(vv. 46–51) petitions, Solomon says that the petitioner may pray where he or she is, but facing toward the Temple in Jerusalem.

(4)   Solomon's benediction and the people's thanks-offering at the dedication (vv. 54–66)

As verses 54–55 record, when Solomon finished his prayer he turned toward the people who were gathered for the occasion and blessed them. 2 Chron. 7:3 tells us there was a great manifestation of God's glory in the Temple when Solomon finished his prayer.

Solomon's benediction consists of three parts: (a) praising God for his faithfulness in fulfilling all the promised blessings (v. 56), (b) seeking God's blessing and guidance for the congregation (vv. 57–60), and (c) Solomon's exhortation to the congregation ('But your hearts must be fully committed to the LORD your God [It "must be completely with the LORD"],[100] to live by his decrees and obey his commands, as at this time.').

At the occasion of this dedication of the Temple, the closing cultic ritual was the thank-offerings with great numbers of slaughtered animals (vv. 62–64),[101] followed by a joyous festival extending to fourteen days.[102] There was great joy amongst the people on the occasion of this dedication service of the Temple, and a great and joyous response to their king Solomon. It is as if whole-hearted corporate worship, this meeting between God and his covenant community, must result in transparent and exuberant joy.[103]

In summary, the following elements of worship during the united monarchy may be highlighted.

In the pre-monarchical period, the centre of corporate worship became increasingly the sanctuary at Shiloh, administered by the priest Eli and his family. Yet at the same time the corruption of the priests called forth prophetic oracles that are the start of the later prophetic criticism of the massive formalism and hypocrisy surrounding the Temple worship at its most corrupt stages.

During the days of Samuel's leadership, with the failure not only of the priestly classes but also of Samuel's sons, Israelites began to seek change. The 'high place' (*bāmāh*) had come to be utilized more and more as a meeting place with God, as the prophets' religious function in the society became more prominent, and the relative influence of the central shrine waned. The demand for a king was motivated less by a desire for godliness than by a desire for order and for conformity with pagan nations. The first experiment issued in multiple disasters, including the blistering prophetic criticism of 1 Sam. 15:22–23.

During the days of David's leadership, music, song and dance were all deployed in worship on some special occasions (2 Sam. 6:1–23; 1 Chron. 13:8; 15:16, 28). Professional musicians were taken on as the central shrine in Jerusalem gained lustre (1 Chron. 24–25).

During the days of Solomon's reign, the Temple in Jerusalem became the centre of the Israelites' worship, its physical structures a visible fulfilment of the former tabernacle. Theologically, Solomon's theology of temple and worship highlighted (1) historical recapitulation, the event of exodus in particular; (2) the Torah, the word of the Lord, as the centre or core of the Temple's significance; (3) humble acknowledgement of God's sovereign greatness; (4) the centrality of the Temple as the place where God meets his people, and to which they therefore address themselves; and (5) the exuberant joy that is the byproduct of whole-hearted corporate worship of the living God.

V. WORSHIP DURING THE TIME OF THE DIVIDED MONARCHY

In the history of the people of Israel, the period of the divided monarchy was in general a dark time of declension, even though there were some peaceful times under good leadership. Far too many kings are described with the formula, 'he did evil in the eyes of the Lord'. After all, the Israelite kingdom was at one level the result of the people's rejection of Yahweh's kingship (1 Sam. 8:7), and the division of the kingdom into two after the reign of Solomon was the result of the divine judgment upon the faithlessness of King Solomon (1 Kings 11:9–13). Nevertheless, God graciously preserved a remnant, and many of the people of Israel continued as faithful worshippers of Yahweh.

Among features of Israelite experience during this period that bear most directly on the theme of worship, the following might be enumerated:

A. The 'high place' (*bāmāh*), which I have already discussed to some extent,[104] was more and more becoming the site of idolatry for the Israelites, beginning with the latter part of Solomon's reign (1 Kings 11:7–8). Eventually the expression 'high place' became almost a synonym for idolatry (1 Kings 13:32–33; 14:22–24; etc.).

B. Tied to this degeneration of the 'high place', one of the most characteristic signs of the failure of the Israelites to keep their identity as Yahweh-worshipers throughout this period was the rapidly developing religious syncretism – the careless adoption of heathen religious rites or cultic practices into the worship patterns of the Israelites themselves. One thinks of such egregious instances as the making of two golden calves and saying to the people, 'Here are your gods, O Israel, who brought you up out of Egypt'. (1 Kings 12:28–33; cf. also 14:22–24; cf. the earlier failure in Exod. 32:1–10). (Perhaps we should note that the challenge of religious syncretism is ever with us: it seems to be a recurring issue in the history of the Christian church, especially when missionaries attempt to communicate the gospel in another culture, but also when culture invades the church without the church exercising critical judgment.[105]) The Israelites went so far as to institute their own system of selecting their priests for serving the idols on the high places (1 Kings 12:31–33; 14:24; etc.).

C. As God had raised up the judges during the days of the Israelites' settlement in Canaan, so he raised up his servants the prophets in the days of the divided monarchy. This was the rise of the Old Testament prophetic movement proper. These prophets were primarily the speakers of God's Word rather than God's agents in performing the miracles that were more common among the earlier seers/prophets. Accordingly, these prophets criticized the priestly ritualism and lifeless legalism that was becoming, if not always dominant, at least generally accepted in society. They soundly condemned the 'religiosity' of the leaders both in religion and politics. For too many leaders, keeping the regulations and rituals themselves became their

major interest – even while they were indifferent toward the demands of
morality and justice in the land. To such people, Hosea preached God's
words, saying, 'Therefore I cut you in pieces with my prophets. I killed you
with the words of my mouth; my judgments flashed like lightning upon you.
For I desire mercy, not sacrifice, and acknowledgment of God rather than
burnt offering' (Hosea 6:5–6).[106] The word here translated 'mercy' is *hesed* in
Hebrew and could be rendered 'love'.[107] In the Hebrew text, it is emphatically expressed. This word *hesed*[108] is also used in Hosea 4:1: 'Hear the word
of the Lord, you Israelites, because the Lord has a charge to bring against you
who live in the land; there is no faithfulness, no love, no acknowledgment of
God in the land' (cf. also 10:12). Similar prophetic criticism is found in Micah
6:6–8.[109] Since the fundamental attitude of worship is 'to serve God' (*'ābad*
discussed earlier) with our whole being, these blistering prophetic criticisms
went to the heart of the people's (and especially the leaders') failure as those
called to worship Yahweh.[110]

D. Despite the general decline that characterized the divided monarchy,
God did raise up from time to time leaders who would guide his people to
periods of widespread covenantal fidelity. Among them was King Josiah,
under whose reign a great religious reformation took place in 621–620 B.C.
This was a reformation based upon the Book of the Law[111] (1 Kings 22:8; 2
Chron. 34:14–15). It was characterized by a dramatic purging away of all the
idolatries and the evil practices related to them (2 Kings 23:4–25). Moreover,
it was accompanied by the physical reconstruction and repair of the Temple (2
Kings 22:4–7). The place of worship, God's Temple, needs to be holy and
clean as the place of God's presence.

E. As the place of corporate worship, at least for the southern kingdom and
doubtless for many from the north, the Temple in Jerusalem was filled with
various forms of music and praise, especially during the festivals. Solomon
himself was a man of literature, composing over 1,000 songs (1 Kings 4:32).[112]
In our Book of Psalms, Ps. 72 and Ps. 127 are considered to be by Solomon,
and many more by David. Regardless of the dates of composition of each
psalm, the book clearly preserves some considerable number of the Psalms
used for rituals or services in connection with the Temple.[113] Doubtless an
appreciable number were used in post-exilic days in connection with the
second temple and its cultus. Even so, the tradition of music and psalm was
co-extensive with the Temple(s). Martin writes:

> At Solomon's Temple services there were choirs and musical contributions,
> according to the Chronicler's account (2 Chron. 5:11–14). Several antiphonal or
> responsively sung psalms in the Davidic psalter may belong to this period (Ps. 24,
> 118, 136), even if that accumulation of psalms is better called 'the hymn-book of the
> second Jewish Temple,' erected after the exile (cf. Ezra 3:11; Neh. 12:24, 36). The
> so-called 'Royal Psalms' in praise of the Hebrew monarchy may well have been
> linked with enthronement ceremonies, royal anniversaries, preparations for battle,
> and so on (Pss. 45, 72, 110).[114]

Although there is some ambiguity in the text, one may suppose that various
musical instruments and various forms of singing were used for the festival at
the time of the dedication of the Temple. The text says (1 Kings 8:65):

So Solomon observed the festival at that time, and all Israel with him – a vast assembly, people from Lebo Hamath to the Wadi of Egypt. They celebrated it before the Lord out God for seven days and seven days more, fourteen days in all.

And the expression of 1 Kings 10:12 may also suggest the presence of musical instruments in the Temple:

> The king used the almugwood to make supports for the temple of the Lord and for the royal palace, and to make harps and lyres for the musicians. So much almugwood has never been imported or seen since that day.

2 Chron. 23:18 also suggests the use of song by special groups of singers.

In summary, we observe the following features during the divided monarchy:

First, the period as a whole was marked by spiritual decline, rising injustice, growing syncretism, and formalism in worship. What began as cultural assimilation, worship of Yahweh at 'high places', sank into compromising idolatry.

Second, to counter this drift there was rising prophetic criticism against the lifeless ritualism, legalism and corruption of the organized priestly system.

Third, just as the centre of Solomon's Temple was the Holy of Holies where the Torah/the Law/the Word of God was deposited in the ark of the covenant, so also the centre of the great religious reformation under King Josiah in 621–620 B.C. was bound up with the Word of God, in this case the rediscovery of the 'Book of the Law'.

And, lastly, in the Temple, music and praise constituted an essential part of worship. This music embraced both songs and the playing of musical instruments. Praising God is to be an essential part of our worship.

VI.   WORSHIP AROUND THE TIME OF THE EXILE

The kingdom of Judah fell, and the glorious centre of worship, the Temple of Solomon, was destroyed by the Babylonians under the leadership of king Nebuchadnezzar. The Jews were carried away as exiles. Although this was a great tragedy, increasingly the Jews themselves came to see it as God's judgment.[115]

For over seventy years they had to keep their identity as worshippers of Yahweh, in the midst of quite different religions and culture. Nor could any stability or sustenance be derived from the Holy City of Jerusalem and their meeting place with God, the great temple now destroyed. Small wonder the people were in despair, saying, 'Our bones are dried up and our hope is gone; we are cut off' (Ezek. 37:11). Under such circumstances, how did they preserve their identity? The following four elements related to the subject of worship seem to be relevant.

A.   The Torah/Word of God and the Synagogue

With the destruction of Jerusalem in 586–587 B.C., sacrificial worship in the Temple came to an end. Many Jews were soon conscious that if they were to continue in the worship of Yahweh, they needed to do what they could: they read and learned the Scriptures together with or under their leaders, such as priests or prophets. Although there are several theories concerning the origin of the Jewish synagogue system,[116] most commonly it has been related to the Babylonian exilic background. Worship in the context of Temple sacrifice and ritual was no longer possible; what was possible, and therefore what became important, was the diligent study of the Scriptures. The text, 'Although I sent them far away among the nations and scattered them among the countries, *yet for a little while I have been a sanctuary for them* in the countries where they have gone' (NIV, Ezek. 11:16) was soon tied in the public mind to the origin of the synagogue. In fact, the American Jewish translation (Soncino Bible) renders this verse: 'Yet I have been to them as *a little sanctuary . . .*',[117] and the gathering of the exiled people to Ezekiel's place mentioned in Ezek.8:1; 14:1; 20:1 is likewise considered to be a synagogue in embryo. Surely the Word of God/the Torah might be a great channel through which the exiled Israelites could receive the divine revelation and respond in worship. In fact, such a view may be in accord with Solomon's view of the Temple, as we have already noted. Similar emphasis on the importance of the Scriptures, especially the Torah, in the life of Yahweh-worshipers, is found in Psalm 119, which expressed the renewed decision (of those returned from the exile) to search the Scriptures diligently in order to avoid repetition of the divine judgment of captivity.[118] One of the exilic psalms, Psalm 137, vv. 1–6 in particular, typically demonstrates this strong desire to pursue God's Word.

B.   Cooperation in Corporate Worship

Returning from the lands of exile after a little over seventy years to their homeland was not easy, and the desolate destruction doubtless made their resettlement there all the more difficult. There were those who had been in Babylon and returned to Canaan, and those amongst the poorest people who somehow had remained in Canaan throughout those seventy years of captivity; there were those who had lived in the northern kingdom of Israel and had been exiled to Assyria and then had returned and wanted to join with those returned from Babylon, and there were those who themselves had returned from Babylon; there were the elderly returnees who had seen Solomon's Temple before the exile, and the younger ones who were born in Babylon during the exile and had never seen the glorious Solomonic edifice – between these there were differences and disagreements (cf. Ezra 3:8– 4:24).[119]

Because of such disagreements, the work of reconstructing the temple, to which all the exiles had so passionately looked forward, was interrupted (Ezra 4:24). To overcome this situation, which was directly related to the worship of God's people, God raised up a reforming prophet who forged fresh co-operation among the different leaders (Haggai 2:1–4).

The initiative in dealing with the wretched divisions and inertia came from God, as the text (v. 1) indicates: 'On the twenty-first day of the seventh month, *the word of the Lord came* through the prophet Haggai.'[120] The call of God to rebuild the place of worship came through the prophet, not through priest or governor.[121] However, the call to the leaders – Zerubbabel the governor of Judah and the high priest Joshua – was fashioned in a slightly different way from that directed to the remnant of the people (cf. v. 2).[122] Doubtless the people themselves heard the appeal in different ways, depending on whether they were elderly and had seen the glorious Temple of

Solomon and returned from Babylon to Jerusalem, or were amongst those who were born in Babylon during the period of the exile and accordingly had never seen the Temple of Solomon. Their different perspectives, as we have noted, generated different assessments of the significance of the new foundation as it was laid.[123]

Under such circumstances, the message from God was a message of encouragement urging cooperation. The civil ruler Zerubbabel, Joshua the high priest, and the prophet Haggai were charged with leadership. Their task was to ensure cooperation in the work of restoring the centre of their community life (Ezra 5:1–2).

Of course, other communal endeavours by those who returned from the exile were carried out, and some of these reflect the corporate worship of the community: priestly works connected with various offerings and sacrifices (Ezra 3:2–6; 6:16–22; 7:72; 8:9–18; etc.), and the praise offered by musicians and singers (Ezra 3:10–11; 7:7, etc.). For many contemporary scholars, the use of the psalms in cultic contexts has been assigned to the post-exilic period.[124] Although in some cases this judgment seems reasonable, in many others the exilic community doubtless tried to restore the traditions of praise – and psalms used in praise – in force at the fall of Jerusalem. If we may draw an analogical argument from the creation of modern hymns, we may also suggest that some psalms used in the post-exilic cultus had their genesis as privately composed expressions of personal piety, and were then taken up for public worship.

C. Messianic Perspectives in Worship

We cannot here embark on a comprehensive articulation of the messianic hope in the Old Testament. However, since there are numerous Old Testament passages that link exilic and post-exilic practices and expectations of worship with messianic hope, it seems wise to sample two or three of them.

When the returned exiles undertook the rebuilding of the Temple as the central place for corporate worship, they needed to have both retrospective convenantal assurance and prospective Messianic hope. They were not to be afraid of any circumstance that might arise, because they were to trust the promises of their covenant-keeping God, the God who had revealed himself so decisively and triumphantly in and through the event of the exodus. But the exodus itself pointed beyond itself to still great deliverance to come – a theme articulated in the Pentateuch, and mightily enlarged upon in Isaiah. Thus if Haggai looks back to the covenant established at the time of the exodus (2:5), he looks forward to a time of transcendent judgment and blessing for the whole world (2:6–9). The glory of those last days is tied to the Temple even now being reconstructed: 'and I will fill this house with glory' (v. 7), 'the glory of this present house' (v. 9). Indeed, declares the Almighty, 'the glory of this present house will be greater than the glory of the former house' (v. 9).

It is well known that the second Temple built by Zerubbabel after the exiles was not by any means in physical size or in its degree of beauty and splendour greater than that of the first Temple built by Solomon. Did the prophet Haggai give a false prophecy? Has the divine prophecy failed? Small wonder

Christians have rightly detected here an adumbration of messianic splendour, a veiled messianic prophecy. In such perspective, the last half of v. 9 [after Athnah in the Hebrew text] 'And in this place I will grant peace (*šālōm*)') is a key to the best contextual understanding of this text.[125] The 'peace' granted in 'this place' will spring from the 'promise of peace' (Isa. 9:6).

A similar connection between worship and messianic hope is found in the message of Ezekiel, an exilic prophet with a priestly background, especially in the last part of his book, chaps.40–48.[126] Doubtless the strong longing among the exiles to return to their homeland (Ps. 137) was accompanied by a desire to see *Jerusalem* restored (Ps. 137:5) – and especially the Temple as the place at which the covenant community met the living God.

The prophet Ezekiel well knew the best way to minister to them. His picture (in the last nine chapters of his book) of an ideal Temple held out hope for the future. He never intended these descriptions to be followed as an actual plan upon their return from Babylon to their homeland.[127] The fact that Ezekiel himself was a prophet *with a priestly background* doubtless contributed to the extremely detailed descriptions of the Temple structure and its services.[128] Such a description was best for both the exiles and for the prophet himself. The centre of the message of hope is the re-establishment or restoration of the covenant relationship between God and his people. Above all, the restored people will be characterized by holiness. To the priestly mind of the prophet Ezekiel, material or ritual holiness (expressed in these nine chapters) cannot properly be separated from spiritual or moral (ethical) holiness: to him there is no conflict between the two. Ezekiel at that point is faithful to the spirit embodied in the Mosaic laws (of the Pentateuch).

The details of ritual related to the Temple that are seen in these nine chapters are to be understood as the prophet's expression of that holiness which is essential to a genuine covenant relationship with the holy God. All the details he sees in his visions are to be passed on to his people as God's message. So he is told:

> Son of man, look with your eyes and hear with your ears and pay attention to everything I am going to show you, for that is why you have been brought here. Tell the house of Israel everything you see (Ezek. 40:4).

A similar idea is found in Ezek. 43:10. This relationship – a relationship characterized by holiness as expressed in all the detailed descriptions of ritual – is nothing but the final and ideal relationship to be established between God and his covenant people.

To the exiles, such a message through the prophet Ezekiel surely nurtured hope. But the message expressed in these detailed descriptions transcends the details. It anticipates a perfection of holiness, of glory, of dwelling with God, that could not be realized in the post-exilic cultus. Its only adequate fulfilment is described by John in the closing chapters of the Apocalypse. Ezekiel 40–48 is the most adequate prelude or introduction to John's Revelation (chaps. 21–22 in particular) found in the Old Testament.

> I saw the Holy City, the new Jerusalem, . . . Now the dwelling of God is with men, and he will live with them. They will be his people, and God himself will be with them and be their God (Rev. 21:2–3).

The last word of the Book of Ezekiel (48:35) is our last word on this point as well: 'And the name of the city from that time on will be "the Lord is there".'

D. Holiness in Worship

Turning our attention again to Haggai, we discover that, a bare two months after his previous prophecy, Haggai conveys a charge from God addressed to the priests (v. 2:10–23). Although the priests are addressed ('Ask the priests . . .', v. 11), the burden of the message is that the covenant community, the people who worship Yahweh, are to be 'holy' *both in cult and life*. Of course, the holiness of the Temple and of the priests serving in the Temple was to be the holiness of the Torah: the law's detailed prescriptions were to be observed. However, what was needed beyond ritual observance was such holiness of life that it governed attitudes and priorities in all of their living before God. In vv. 12–13, using a Levitical law (Lev. 6:20; Num. 19:22), Haggai shows that the 'infectious' power of a holy thing (v. 12) is less than the 'infectious' power of a defiled thing (=unclean thing) (v. 13).[129] As Hildebrand argues:

> Thus the prophet used the priestly ruling that uncleanness is more contagious than holiness to bring into focus the effect of the remnant's sinfulness: prescripts that applied to meat and clothes and corpses were given a personal and moral application. The prophet here used the cult as a paradigm of holiness.[130]

The prophet Haggai's message becomes clear in v. 14 with the repeated 'so' (in the Hebrew text). The prophet insists that the people are unclean, the nation is unclean and all their works are unclean (the Hebrew text is well rendered in the NASB: '*So* is this people, and *so* is this nation before Me, declares the Lord, and *so* is every work of their hands; and what they offer there is unclean.')

In 2:15–19, Haggai declares that when we are holy as God's people we are able to receive God's blessing according to our work; but on the other hand, when we are unclean and are under God's judgment we are not able to receive God's blessing in spite of our hard work. The seriousness of this truth is underscored by the repeated expressions, 'Give careful thought!' (vv. 15,18). If the people were unclean and under God's judgment, as evidenced by their indifference to the Temple (which was to be the centre of life for the Israelites as God's people), they could not reasonably expect blessings from God, in spite of their hard labour (v. 16). Indeed, they did not return to God even when his hand of judgment fell on them (v. 17). But if they would respond to God's urging through the prophet Haggai, and get on with the rebuilding of the Temple and the pursuit of holiness, they would enjoy God's blessing henceforth (v. 19).

We may usefully summarize the highlights of the Israelite patterns of worship during and after the time of the exile.

First, in pagan Babylon, the land of their captivity, many Israelites tried to maintain their identity as Yahweh-worshippers by reading and learning the Scriptures. This led in practice to an understanding of corporate worship that was tied to what became the primitive synagogue, rather than to the Temple.

Second, prompted by leaders such as Haggai, Ezra, and Nehemiah, whom

God raised up in the post-exilic period, the Israelite leadership in Jerusalem eventually attained sufficient cooperation and determination to rebuild the Temple, the centre of their corporate worship.

Third, exilic and post-exilic prophets not only pointed to God's faithfulness in arranging a return of his people to the Promised Land, but to the eschatological and messianic hope at the End.

And finally, Haggai makes it clear that the Israelites were to be holy in all of their living before God, if they were to be true worshippers of Yahweh.

VII. THEOLOGICAL ANALYSIS OF THE CONCEPT OF WORSHIP IN THE CANONICAL OLD TESTAMENT

Thus far we have made our observations *ad seriatim* as we have worked our way through the Old Testament. None of this has been exhaustive; nor will this closing section approach such an ideal. Nevertheless a few closing reflections may offer some analysis and synthesis.

A. Theological Structure and Worship in the Old Testament

(1) Organic Unity in Two Basic Covenants

W. J. Dumbrell begins his book *Covenant and Creation: A Theology of Old Testament Covenant*, with a first chapter entitled 'The Covenant with Noah – A Recall to a Basic Pattern of Creation'.[131] Another book, though a little older, which has often been cited in evangelical circles for its unique treatment of Old Testament theology (and some New Testament as well) is G. Vos, *Biblical Theology, Old and New Testaments*.[132] Vos begins his treatment with the 'Adamic covenant'. Whether one thinks of 'recall' or primary reference, there can be little doubt that the canonical Scriptures open with creation and a sin-free relation between God and human beings. This sin-free relationship is shattered by the fall (Gen. 3). The rest of the Bible is tied, one way or the other, to God's redemption purposes in the wake of that fall. In Reformed circles, one commonly speaks of 'the covenant of creation' and the 'covenant of redemption', but whatever the terminology the focus is the same: human beings who once served God, 'worshipped' him, in sin-free obedience and dependence, are now, this side of their catastrophic rebellion, pursued by him as he displays his gracious redemptive purposes in calling out a new humanity where worship of him will ultimately be unalloyed and unchallenged. God's redemptive purposes take his people to the perfect worship of the new heaven and the new earth (Rev. 21:22).

Thus the theology of worship in the Old Testament must be placed in the largest canonical context. The bliss of creation is superseded by the rebellion and curse of the fall (Gen. 3). Immediately we begin to perceive adumbrations of God's redemptive purposes, starting with the so-called 'proto-evangelium' (Gen. 3:15, 21). The first reported offerings to Yahweh, by Abel and Cain (Gen. 4:1–7), must likewise be understood in the context of 'the covenant of redemption'.[133] From there to the end of the period of the Old Testament, the developing and growing self-disclosure of God must be understood in the light of its ultimate focus, which is the decisive work of redemption by Jesus Christ as revealed in the New Testament. Christian worship, we maintain, is necessarily shaped by this framework.

(2)   The Changing Face of Worship in the Progress of Redemptive History

Almost inevitably, as 'the covenant of redemption' unfolds, the people of God responded in patterns of worship that changed over time. At any given point there are at least two axes to observe: the redemptive-historical axis (and therefore what God *required* of his people at this point), and the historical-cultural context (and therefore what forms of corporate worship were judged admissible, appropriate, not improperly syncretistic and so forth).

We have observed a diversity of elements that were relevant to the worship of the people of God at various points in their history. We recall such expressions as 'calling the divine name', 'building an altar', 'offering sacrifice', 'serving', 'prayer'/'supplication', 'praising', etc. These and others are to be understood as the means by and through which the people of God worshipped and served their God in their period of history.[134] Of course, there were more explicitly cultic activities related to worship, such as 'burning incense',[135] and corporate (and even professional) activities such as Temple 'singing'[136] etc. But what is most decisive and enduring is 'the covenant of redemption' revealed in the Old Testament – i.e. God's purpose to redeem and reform and even transform his people for his own praise and for their good, and in many cases his stipulation as to which is their appropriate response.

(3)   The Relative Nature of Cultic Activities

Granted the changing nature of the formal elements of (corporate) worship in the Old Testament, one is left with the need to distinguish what is enduring – or, to put it otherwise, what distinguishes an appropriate cultural form from an inappropriate and spiritually dangerous syncretism.

From a Christian perspective, part of the answer to such a question must await study of the New Testament – the burden of the next chapter. But one observation may help to clarify the issue. Whatever the inner-canonical connections, among the *forms* of corporate worship, the experience and fidelity (or infidelity!) of the people of God in any generation is more tightly tied to the *significance* they assign those forms, than to the forms themselves.

Rowley emphasizes the importance of the 'meaning' or 'spirit' (what I have called the 'significance') of the form in the worship of the Israelites.[137] Similarly, R. de Vaux maintains:

> By 'rites' we mean the outward forms which this service takes. Israelite ritual may be similar to the rituals of other religions, or even borrowed from them; but its important feature lies in the new meaning which these rites received, a meaning which was determined by the religious ideas of Israel's faith. Without trespassing into the domain of biblical theology, we must underline the characteristics of the Israelite cult, and see what distinguishes it from other Oriental cults, even when the rites are the same.[138]

In fact, de Vaux lists three characteristics of Israelite worship different from other cultic religions. They are: (a) The Israelites worshipped a God who was the only God.' (b) 'The Israelites worshipped a personal God who intervened in history; Yahweh was the God of the covenant.' (c) 'The Israelites had no image in their cult. Both versions of the Decalogue contain the prohibition of images (Exo. 20:4 and Deut. 5:8), and the prohibition certainly dates back to the age of Moses.'[139]

3

Worship in the New Testament

DAVID PETERSON

If you want to start a lively conversation amongst Christians, introduce the subject of worship! For most of us that means debating styles of music, ways of conducting church services or methods of preaching. Disagreements can be heated, reflecting denominational traditions or individual preferences. Yet dissension can also reveal profound theological differences about the nature and significance of Christian gatherings. For example, to what extent do we meet together to encounter God and to what extent to minister to each other? Is God especially present in the gathering of his people and, if so, how? Is worship fundamentally a response to God's word in prayer and praise or is it something more? What is the relationship between congregational worship and the worship or service due to God in everyday life? Is there any warrant in the New Testament for sacred times and sacred places?

A recent publication, jointly written by a theologian and a church musician, has urged Evangelicals to rediscover 'the missing jewel' of worship.[1] It is one of an increasing number of books attempting to investigate what people did when they went to church in New Testament times, with a view to revitalising congregational worship today. Although there is clearly a need for this sort of stimulation and for creative experimentation on the basis of biblical teaching, there is little attention in contemporary literature to the more fundamental question of a *biblical theology of worship*. Perhaps it is assumed that this is being developed when biblical teaching about praying, singing and ministering the Scriptures to one another is expounded. However, there is a fundamental flaw in this approach, when such specific issues are not considered in the light of what the New Testament teaches about the theme of worship more generally or when the profound differences between the Old and New Testaments on this subject are not discussed. These are not merely academic questions or prolegomena to the real issues. Biblical theology is the broad context in which detailed exegesis regarding any topic must take place.

Worship has been aptly described as 'the supreme and only indisputable activity of the Christian Church',[2] but what does it really involve? Ralph Martin, for example, defines it as 'the dramatic celebration of God in his supreme worth in such a manner that his "worthiness" becomes the norm and inspiration of human living'.[3] John Burkhart similarly describes Christian worship as 'the celebrative response to what God has done, is doing, and promises to do.'[4] However, with such a starting point, the focus of their books is too narrow, obscuring other important biblical perspectives.[5]

Worship is a comprehensive category in the New Testament, describing *our engagement with God through faith in Jesus Christ and what he has done for us*. Such faith will express itself in daily obedience or service to God in every sphere of life. What we do 'in church' must be considered as a vital part of that engagement with God but it is misleading to confine the notion of worship to that activity: 'our traditional understanding of worship as restricted to the cultic gathering of the congregation at a designated time and place for rite and proclamation will no longer do. This is not what the New Testament means by worship.'[6]

This chapter begins by noting the meaning of certain key words for worship in the Greek Bible. It then develops the argument from several contexts that only Jesus could offer the worship that is truly pleasing to God, fulfilling and replacing the way of approach to God established in Old Testament times. By this means he made it possible for Jews and Gentiles to draw near to God together, to honour, serve and praise him, and to enjoy all the benefits of the new covenant. Acceptable worship is something that *God makes possible for us*, through Christ: it does not depend on our own initiative, creativity, skill or worthiness. Apart from a faith-relationship with God through Jesus Christ there is now no worship that pleases him.

The worship that Jesus makes possible has many dimensions. So this chapter goes on to discover from a number of key passages how we may glorify and serve God in everyday life. Within this framework of thought, the evangelization of unbelievers, the support of gospel work, and the edification of fellow believers have a priority. Thus, the chapter concludes with some attention to what the New Testament says about such ministries, with special reference to the function and significance of the congregational gathering in God's purposes.

SOME KEY WORSHIP TERMS

There are many worship terms in the Old Testament, relating to the priesthood, the sacrificial system and the temple service ordained by God for Israel. When these are used in a transformed way by the writers of the New Testament, they point to a new way of thinking about worship. To highlight this radically different perspective on worship, it will be helpful to know something about the use and meaning of three particular sets of terms in the Greek version of the Old Testament (LXX). Reference will then be made to the use of these terms in various New Testament passages as this chapter progresses.

Grateful Submission to God

By far the most common word translated 'to worship' in the New Testament is the verb *proskynein*. From earliest times, this term expressed the widespread oriental custom of bowing down or casting oneself on the ground, kissing the feet, the hem of a garment or the ground, as a total bodily gesture of respect before a great one. As applied to the honouring of the gods, it meant bending over or falling down before an image or making some literal gesture of homage to the god. At an early stage *proskynein* also came to be used for the inward attitude of homage or respect which the outward gesture represented.[7] In the LXX, *proskynein* is virtually the only word used to render some form of the Hebrew *hištaḥᵃwâh* (i.e. Hithpael of the root *ḥ-w-y*). Recent scholarship has suggested that the literal meaning of this verb, which occurs one hundred and seventy times in the Hebrew Bible, is 'bend oneself over at the waist'.[8]

'Bending over to the Lord' in the Old Testament expressed *surrender or submission to God*. In many contexts this was an immediate and spontaneous reaction to a divine action or revelation, specifically motivated by *awe and gratitude* (e.g., Gen. 24:26–7, 52; Exod. 4:31; 34:8; Judg. 7:15). The only command in the Mosaic law for Israelites to bend over before the Lord was in connection with the presentation of the first-fruits at the Lord's sanctuary (cf. Deut. 26:1–11). Elsewhere, there is mention of this gesture as a spontaneous expression of grateful submission to the Lord, associated with sacrifice and public praise (e.g., 1 Chr. 29:20–1; 2 Chr. 7:3–4; 29:28–30; Neh. 8:6).[9]

Gestures of homage were a regular part of ancient near-eastern religion (e.g., Exod. 32:8; Num. 25:2; Ezek. 8:16) and so the act of bending over to honour a god came to represent the religion itself. In many Old Testament contexts *the customary worship of idols* is intended by the use of *hištaḥᵃwâh* and *proskynein* (e.g. Exod. 20:5; 23:24; Deut. 4:19; 5:9). Even though bending over before the Lord appeared to be like the ritual bowing of pagans before idols, it was simply a *recognition of his kingly presence in their midst*, without confusing that presence with any image or physical representation of God.[10] Occasionally this terminology is used in the New Testament with reference to those going up to Jerusalem in the traditional way to pay homage to God at the temple (e.g., Jn. 12:20; Acts 8:27). However, mostly it is used to describe the response that people make to Jesus in his earthly ministry (e.g., Matt. 14:33; 28:9, 17; Jn. 9:38) or to God and the Lamb in the heavenly realm (e.g., Rev. 4:10; 5:14). The use of this terminology in Jn. 4:20–4 and 1 Cor. 14:25 is especially interesting.

Since the same Hebrew and Greek words could be used to express surrender or homage to kings and others worthy of special respect (e.g., Gen. 18:2; 23:7, 12; 33:3, 6,7; Exod. 18:7; 1 Sam. 25:23; 2 Ki. 4:36), it is not legitimate to suggest that in religious contexts the terminology expressed intimacy with God or affection towards him.[11] *Submission* is the fundamental disposition indicated by these words, with the note of adoration or praise being suggested by certain particular contexts.

The Service of all God's People

The other verb most often translated 'to worship' in the New Testament is *latreuein*. Considering its use in non-biblical as well as biblical literature, this word is more adequately rendered 'to serve'.[12] It was one of a number of terms for service in the Greek language but was rarely employed until the translators of the LXX gave it special prominence, using it to refer exclusively to *the service rendered to God or to heathen gods*, especially service by means of sacrifice or some other ritual. However, it should be remembered that the underlying Hebrew verb *'ābad* with a direct object means 'to serve' in religious and non-religious contexts alike.[13] At least in the Hebrew text, the close link between the service of the gods and the service of human masters is clear.

According to the Book of Exodus, the purpose of Israel's redemption from slavery was to release them for service to the Lord (e.g., Exod. 3:12; 4:23; 8:1). When the parallel expressions 'to sacrifice to the Lord' (Exod. 3:18; 5:3, 8, 17; 8:8, 25–9) and 'to hold a festival' (Exod. 5:1) are used, it is clear that *cultic service* is in view. In general terms, the word cult means 'the expression of religious experience in concrete external actions performed within the congregation or community, preferably by officially appointed exponents and in set forms.'[14] The Israelite cult was the complex system of sacrifices and rituals carried out for the people by the priesthood at the Lord's sanctuary. Yet it is important to note that some contexts set cultic service within the broader framework of *fearing him, walking in all his ways, and observing all his commands and decrees*. In Deut. 10:12–13 in particular, 'to serve the Lord your God with all your heart and with all your soul' implies a total lifestyle indicating allegiance to God (cf. Josh. 22:5; 24:14–24).[15]

In the New Testament, *latreuein* and related terms are still used to refer to Israel's cultic worship (e.g., Acts 7:7; Rom. 9:4; Heb. 8:5; 9:1, 9). However, much more significantly, this terminology is used to describe the new way of relating to God made possible by the Lord Jesus Christ (e.g., Rom. 1:9; 12:1; Phil. 3:3; Heb. 9:14; 12:28).

Priestly Service

When the translators of the LXX specifically wanted to describe *the priestly service* of the God of Israel, they used the verb *leitourgein* and related words (e.g., 2 Chr. 11:14, Joel 2:17, Ezek. 45:4).[16] This terminology was not used to designate the worship or service of the Israelite nation as a whole but only the ministries of priests to God, as accredited representatives of the nation, and of Levites to priests. There are occasions when the people represented by the priests are explicitly designated as the beneficiaries of the priestly ministry (e.g., 2 Chr. 35:3; Ezek. 44:11). However, the nation is served by the priests only to the extent that it is enabled to offer its sacrifices through their mediation: fundamentally, God is the recipient of all cultic service in Israel.

Although there was a specialised cultic usage of this terminology in pagan Greek literature and inscriptions, it first appears in a technical political sense, with reference to *the discharge of specific services to the body politic*, either levied by law or rendered voluntarily.[17] This usage was then extended to cover any service to the community and then service in general, such as that of slaves to masters, or of friends to one another. Some New Testament examples have a literal or transformed cultic reference (e.g., Lk. 1:23; Acts 13:2; Rom 15:16; Phil. 2:17; Heb. 8:2; 9:21; 10:11). Others may emphasize the idea of service to others, without necessarily viewing this as a ministry to the Lord (e.g., 2 Cor. 9:12; Phil. 2: 25, 30).

THE PERFECT WORSHIP OF JESUS CHRIST

Jesus' Obedient Service to the Father

In his decisive encounter with Satan in the wilderness, Jesus affirmed the teaching of the Old Testament that the essential response demanded by God is *submission and service to him alone* (Matt. 4:8–10=Lk. 4:5–8). Challenged to 'fall down and worship' the devil, Jesus refused to surrender his allegiance to God's rival by some decisive act of loyalty. With a quotation from Deut. 6:13, Jesus asserted, '*Worship* the Lord your God and *serve* him only' (*kyrion ton theon sou proskynēseis kai autǭ monǭ latreuseis*). Satan was dismissed as the Son of God expressed his devotion to the Father and renewed his commitment to do his will exclusively.

This narrative highlights the notion that Jesus' life is to be the expression of perfect worship. He will offer consistent loyalty and devotion to the Father, in the face of every temptation to idolatry. Where Israel failed, the Son of God will be faithful and obedient. Thus, he is portrayed in the Gospels as a pious Jew, participating in activities associated with the temple or synagogue, fervent in prayer, and constantly seeking to discern and do the Father's will (e.g., Lk. 2:41–50; 4:14–30; 6:12).

Jesus is never presented as offering a sacrifice in the temple, though his instruction to the disciples to prepare the Passover would have involved sacrificing a lamb in anticipation of their meal together. In some texts, he clearly takes the sacrificial system and the associated cult as given (e.g., Matt. 5:23–4; Mk. 1:44; 12:41–4). Yet his teaching is generally more concerned with the ethical than the cultic. He often stands with the Old Testament prophets in condemning the cultic practices and traditions of his contemporaries, without criticizing the law itself (e.g., Matt. 12:1–14; Mk. 7:1–23). Those traditions were often designed to protect the pious from infringing the commandments of God. Yet so radical is Jesus' challenge concerning such traditions that he raises questions about the continuing role of the law itself. The impression is given 'of a life neither geared to nor drawn up against the Law, but one that is *moved by quite different considerations*, yet to which observance of the Law can indirectly be made to bear witness.'[18]

In other words, Jesus is not simply a rabbi or a prophet recalling Israel to the service of God. He is the Messiah and the Son of God, with a unique, eschatological mission to fulfil. The New Testament goes on to indicate that by his obedience to the will of his Father, culminating in death, Jesus offers the sacrifice that inaugurates the new covenant, fulfilling and replacing the system of worship associated with the Mosaic covenant (e.g., Lk. 22:19–20; Heb. 10:5–18). The pure worship he offers to God by means of his faith and obedience is the only basis on which we can find acceptance and draw near to God (e.g., Rom. 3:22–6; Heb. 9:1–14; 10:19–22).[19]

In each of the Gospels, Jesus' obedience to the will of the Father clearly culminates in his death. Officially organised opposition to his ministry will not deflect him from completing the task that he believes he has been given (e.g., Matt. 12:14–21; Lk. 13:31–5). The narrative of his last journey to Jerusalem is punctuated in the Synoptics by his predictions of impending rejection and death (e.g., Mk. 8:31; 9:30–2; 10:32–4, 45, and parallels). Yet Jesus continues resolutely on his way. In John's Gospel, laying down his life for his 'sheep' is a command he has received from the Father (Jn. 10:17–18; cf. 4:34), so that the 'hour' of his death is the climax towards which his ministry moves (Jn. 12:23–33). Under the dread of death, Jesus resists the temptation to avoid the approaching anguish and suffering, and rededicates himself to do the Father's will, allowing himself to be delivered into 'the hands of sinners' (Matt. 26:36–46; Mk. 14:32–42; Lk. 22:39–46).

Jesus' Teaching about his Sacrifice

Prior to the Last Supper, Jesus' most pointed saying about the redemptive significance of his death occurs in Matt. 20:28=Mk. 10:45. There he claims that 'the Son of Man did not come to be served, but to serve, and to give his life as a ransom for many.' The reference to his life being given 'as a ransom for many (*lytron anti pollōn*)' suggests that he viewed his death as *a substitutionary atonement for the benefit of others*. Such terminology implies that the 'many' are held in a captivity from which only the self-offering of Christ can release them. The wider context of Jesus' teaching indicates that this captivity is caused by sin. The expression 'to give his life' signifies the voluntary nature of his death and recalls Isa. 53:10–12, which speaks of the Servant of the Lord offering his life as a compensation or payment for the sins of his people.[20] Jesus could also have had in mind Isa. 43:1–4, where different terminology is used to affirm that a ransom will be provided by God to redeem Israel. If both texts are drawn together by Jesus' saying, we may conclude that he viewed himself as the ultimate 'guilt offering' for the sins of his people and the ransom to redeem them from judgment and death.[21]

Jesus' whole life was a ministry to others, designed to serve (*diakonēsai*, Matt. 20:28=Mk. 10:45) their needs. But ultimately his service to them meant offering himself in death, in perfect obedience to the will of his Father, as a payment for their sins. Although the language of worship is not specifically used in this context, *the notion of Jesus' death as an atoning sacrifice is close at hand*.

The so-called eucharistic words of Jesus are crucial for discovering his own view of the significance of his death. There are differences of emphasis in the various Gospel accounts of the Last Supper but each one points to the fact that it was in the context of a traditional Passover meal that Jesus instituted what was later called 'the Lord's Supper'.[22] The Passover was an annual celebration of the way in which God had fulfilled his covenant promises in the time of Moses, rescuing Israel from bondage in Egypt in order to establish them as his own distinctive people in the promised land (cf. Exod. 12:1–30). According to Jewish tradition, the blood of the lambs sacrificed at the time of the exodus had redemptive power and made God's covenant with Abraham operative.[23] When families or groups of friends gathered in Jerusalem to eat the Passover meal, they were reminded in a very personal way of the whole basis of their relationship with God and their existence as a people. Additionally, the Passover had become an occasion for Israelites to express their confidence in a future redemption by God, associated with the coming of the Messiah.[24]

Jesus' longing to celebrate this last Passover with his disciples is especially emphasized in Luke's account, yet his hope of celebrating it anew, when it would be fulfilled 'in the kingdom of God', is expressed in each of the Gospels (Lk. 22:15–16,18; cf. Matt. 26:29; Mk. 14:25). The notion of fulfilment indicates that for Jesus the Passover had a typological significance. He was endorsing the Jewish tradition that this rite pointed forward to an eschatological deliverance of God's people and the subsequent possibility of enjoying the messianic banquet together in the End time (e.g., Isa. 25:6–7; Lk. 14:15). The context makes it clear that his approaching death would be the event to accomplish that deliverance. The Lord's Supper, which has its origin in Jesus' teaching at the Last Supper, is not itself to be regarded as the fulfilment of the Passover but as *an anticipation of its ultimate fulfilment in the fellowship of the new creation* (cf. Lk. 22:29–30; 1 Cor. 11:26). In effect, the Lord's Supper functions as a Christian substitute for the Passover, but with significant differences that will be highlighted below.[25]

Theologically, the Passover came to an end with its final celebration by Jesus. We cannot say with certainty that he identified himself explicitly with the Passover lamb on this occasion, but that link was soon made by early Christian writers (1 Cor. 5:7–8; cf. 1 Pet. 1:18–19).[26] Jesus himself took the unusual step of accompanying the distribution of the bread and at least one of the Passover cups with *his own words of interpretation*. In this way, the food was presented to the disciples as a symbol of his approaching death and of the salvation he would accomplish. Their eating and drinking appears as a symbolic reception of the benefits to be obtained by his death: 'Jesus uses the grace before and after eating to give his disciples one after another the additional personal assurance that they share in the kingdom because they belong to the many for whom he is about to die.'[27]

Some commentators interpret the bread-word and the cup-word differently, since they were separated by the main course of the meal and each saying was meant to be complete in itself. Thus, 'this is my body' is taken to refer to Jesus' *person* – the bread broken and distributed is to be a pledge of his continuing presence with them – and 'this is my blood' is taken to refer to his sacrificial *death*. However, even though the two sayings were originally separate, 'we must surely grant that Jesus intended the two sayings to be in some way complementary to each other. If, then, the second saying speaks of Jesus' sacrificial death, we should expect something similar to be present in the former saying.'[28] With mention of the fact that his blood is to be 'poured out' as a sacrificial offering for many/you, there are allusions again to the role of the suffering Servant, who 'poured out his life unto death . . . and bore the sin of many' (Isa. 53:12; cf. Matt. 20:28=Mk. 10:45; Lk 22:37).

Most significant for our present study is the fact that the cup-word speaks of *the inauguration of a new covenant by Jesus' blood*. The strange expression '*my* blood of the covenant' (Matt. 26:28; Mk. 14:24) recalls Exod. 24:8, where the covenant established by God at Mt. Sinai is said to have been sealed by means of animal sacrifice. Only the version of the saying in Lk. 22:20 and 1 Cor. 11:25 mentions explicitly that Jesus had in view the new covenant promised in Jer. 31:31–4. Jeremiah said nothing about sacrifice but pointed to a definitive and permanent solution to the problem of Israel's sin as a basis for the renewal of God's relationship with his people. Yet it is obvious from the words 'my blood of the covenant' that Jesus envisaged some new demonstration of God's grace, and Matt. 26:28 indicates that Jesus' death was specifically 'for the forgiveness of sins' (cf. Jer. 31:34). Jesus' death functioned to *re-establish the underlying relationship with Israel on a new basis*, making possible the fulfilment of God's ancient promise to bring blessing to all peoples on earth (cf. Gen.12:2–3). The implication of this saying is that the priesthood, the sacrificial system, and all the rites and festivals given to Israel under the old covenant are fulfilled and replaced by the person and work of the Lord Jesus Christ.

Some Pauline Perspectives on the Sacrifice of Christ

The opening chapters of Paul's letter to the Romans illustrate how Jews and Gentiles have failed in their own distinctive ways to reverence and serve God acceptably (note especially Rom. 1:21–3). This refusal to glorify God as God has its consequence in every form of wickedness, abuse, hypocrisy and injustice in human relationships. God's abandonment of men and women to the consequences of their rebellion against him is an expression of his wrath, anticipating the final revelation of his wrath on the day of judgment (1:18, 24, 26, 28; 2:5). Yet Paul's exposition of the work of Christ and its consequences (3:21 – 11:36) shows how God has acted to transform this disastrous situation. Now it is possible for all to engage with God in a new way, *on the basis of Christ's sacrifice*, and to offer the worship that is pleasing to him (Rom. 12:1).

The apostle first explains how believers are justified freely by God's grace 'through *the redemption* that came by Christ Jesus' (3:24). The word *apolytrosis* ('redemption') recalls Israel's deliverance from slavery in Egypt, thus setting the nation free to serve God as a distinct and holy people (cf. Lk. 1:68–75). In view of the fact that such terminology was regularly used in contexts where the payment of a ransom was on view (cf. *lytron* in Matt.20:28=Mk. 10:45), Paul could also be suggesting by the use of this word that Jesus' death is the ransom price paid to release us from sin's captivity (cf. 1 Cor. 6:20; 7:23).[29]

Something more of the nature and significance of this new redemptive act of God is then revealed in the description of Christ as 'a *sacrifice of atonement* by means of his blood, to be received through faith' (*hilastērion dia pisteōs en tō autou haimati*, 3:25).[30] Various commentators have argued that the word *hilastērion* here portrays Christ as the anti-type of the 'mercy seat' or 'place of atonement' which covered the ark in the most holy place of the Old Testament sanctuary (e.g., Exod. 25:17–22; Lev. 16:14,15–16). However, it is more appropriate to view Christ as the 'means of atonement' or 'sacrifice of atonement', rather than as the 'place of atonement'.[31]

The expression 'by means of his blood' points to the atoning significance of his death. The wrath of God is averted by Jesus' death though, paradoxically, as in Old Testament teaching about the sacrificial system, it is *God* who provides the means of atonement. The sprinkling of sacrificial blood was a crucial part of the annual Day of Atonement sin offering (Leviticus 16) and Paul seems to be indicating that *Jesus has fulfilled and replaced that central rite of Old Testament religion* (cf. Heb. 9:11–14), rendering the whole sacrificial system no longer necessary.

The sacrificial and atoning significance of Christ's self offering is also brought out in Eph. 5:2, where Jesus is said to have given himself up 'for us' (*hyper hēmōn*), 'as an offering and sacrifice, whose fragrance is pleasing to God' (*prosphoran kai thysian tō theō eis osmēn euōdias*).[32] This collection of technical terms from the Old Testament suggests again that all the sacrifices of Judaism find their fulfilment in the self-offering of Christ. Yet in this context, Christ's sacrifice is also set forth as *an example* and a motivation for believers, to impel those who benefit from his redemptive work to 'walk in love' as he did (cf. 2 Cor. 5:14–15; Col. 2:6–7).

In Rom. 5:8–9 Jesus' blood/death is again highlighted as the means by which sinners are justified and saved from the wrath of God. It is the eschatological sacrifice, which secures for believers all the blessings of the New Covenant and the kingdom of God. However, in 5:19 it is through his *obedience* that 'the many will be made righteous'. As Adam headed the line of disobedience and sin, Jesus heads the line of humanity which lives under the sign of obedience. The atoning value of his obedience, which culminates in his death, lies in the fact that he surrenders himself completely to the Father as the representative of sinful humanity. Thus, it is implied by Paul's argument that we may related to God only on the basis of Christ's perfect 'worship', which is his self-offering. Jesus' death was a once-for-all sin offering, providing the atonement towards which the propitiatory rites of the Old Testament were ultimately pointing.

The Sacrifice of Christ According to Hebrews

The idea that Jesus' life was the expression of perfect worship, culminating in his sacrificial death for others, is developed more fully in Hebrews than anywhere else in the New Testament. There the writer portrays the ministry of Christ – past, present and future – as a fulfilment and replacement of the priesthood and cult associated with the old covenant. Only Hebrews takes the unusual step of identifying Jesus as the high priest of the new covenant, though there are hints in other New Testament books that his ministry could be understood in such terms (e.g., Rom 8:34; 1 Jn. 2:1–2).

The first indication of this is in Heb. 1:3, where it is briefly mentioned that the Son of God 'made purification for sins'. This expression portrays humanity's fundamental problem as *defilement due to sin*, recalling the teaching of Leviticus in the Old Testament. However, the high-priestly dimension of Christ's work is not made explicit until the writer asserts that the incarnation and suffering of the Son of God was necessary 'in order that he might become a merciful and faithful high priest in service to God, and that he might make atonement for the sins of the people' (2:17–18).

Jesus as Servant of the Lord appears to be one of 'several converging elements that bring the author to see Jesus' death as a priestly act.'[33] Thus, the obedience of the Son, culminating in his death as a sacrifice for the sins of others, is a prominent theme in Hebrews (e.g., 5:7–9; 7:27; 9:14). The victim is *the priest himself* and this unity of the priest and the sacrifice brings the Mosaic cult to an end because its ideal has been fulfilled in Jesus. 'Sacrifices and offerings, burnt offerings and sin offerings' are all set aside by 'the sacrifice of the body of Jesus Christ once for all' (10:5–14).

The role of the high priest on the annual Day of Atonement was to deal with the problem of sin by means of the appropriate rites and thereby to remove from the Israelite community what provoked God's anger (cf. Leviticus 16). Thus, the task of Jesus was 'to expiate' or 'make atonement for the sins of the people' (*eis to hilaskesthai tas hamartias tou laou*, 2:17). In Hebrews it is clear that the blood or death of Jesus is what actually removes sin and makes it possible for sinners to draw near to a holy God (e.g., 9:12–14, 15–22; 10:19, 29; 12:24; 13:12). Yet it is because he offered himself as *a perfectly obedient and unblemished sacrifice* to God that his death has atoning significance (cf. 7:27; 9:14). The proving of his obedience through suffering and temptation was an important aspect of his high-priestly work on our behalf.

Hebrews regularly insists on the *unique and unrepeatable character of Jesus' sacrifice* (cf. 7:27; 9:24–8; 10:10, 12, 14), in contrast with the numerous and repeated offerings prescribed in the Old Testament. It is therefore significant to note that in the portrayal of Jesus as 'priest for ever after the order of Melchizedek' (Ps. 110:4; cf. Heb. 5:6,10; 6:20; 7:1–28) there is a different emphasis. This text is used along with Ps. 110:1 and Ps. 2:7 to indicate that the ascended Christ is both the messianic king and the eschatological priest, who reigns 'at the right hand of the Majesty in heaven' (1:3; cf. 4:14; 8:1; 10:12–14; 12:2). As such, 'he is able to save completely those who come to God though him, because *he always lives to intercede for them*' (7:25). The image of the heavenly intercessor is used to emphasize Christ's willingness and ability to go on applying the benefits of his once-for-all sacrifice to believers, in the midst of all their trials and temptations (cf. 4:14–16; Rom. 8:34; 1 Jn. 2:1–2).[34]

The exposition of Christ's heavenly priesthood in Hebrews 7 leads into the portrayal of his earthly work as a *sacrificial ministry* performed with reference to the heavenly sanctuary in Hebrews 8–10. Jesus is a priestly 'minister' (*leitourgos*) of 'the sanctuary, the true tabernacle, set up by the Lord, not man' (8:2). As such, his 'ministry' (*leitourgia*) is superior to that of the priests of Judaism (8:6), since they serve (*latreuousin*) only at 'a sanctuary that is a copy and shadow of what is in heaven' (8:5; cf. 9:23; 10:1). This is said to have been indicated by the command in Exod. 25:40 for Moses to construct the earthly tabernacle according to the pattern given to him by God.[35] The point of the contrast is that the priests of Judaism served in a God-ordained, but humanly-constructed sanctuary, and in this ministry only foreshadowed the definitive priestly ministry of Jesus Christ, in his death and exaltation to the very presence of God. Now that the ultimate priestly liturgy has been performed, there is no place for the operation of any human priesthood in an earthly sanctuary.

The writer insists in 7:26–7 that the priestly ministry of Jesus is superior because it involves the offering of *himself* as a pure and unblemished sacrifice to God. In 8:6 he indicates that this 'liturgy' is also superior because *it institutes the benefits of the new covenant*. Although Jer. 31:31–4 says nothing about a new priesthood or a transformation of the worship of God's people, it is clear that the final and foundational promise of that prophecy implies some definitive act on God's part to deal with the problem of Israel's sin ('for I will forgive their wickedness, and will remember their sins no more', Jer. 31:34). Between the full quotation of Jeremiah's prophecy in Heb. 8:8–12 and the abbreviated citation in 10:16–17, the writer seeks to establish that the death of Jesus is the means by which that promise is fulfilled and the new covenant is inaugurated. Jesus' death is interpreted in priestly and cultic terms because it is seen to fulfil the method of approach to God instituted in connection with the old covenant. This whole system has been 'set aside' by Jesus Christ in his establishment of the new basis of relationship with God (10:9–14; cf. 8:13).

The writer introduces his detailed exposition of the work of Christ in cultic terms by asserting *the impotence of the old levitical system* (9:1–10). The system as a whole is symbolized by the 'outer tent' or first tabernacle, where the constant daily ritual gave proof that no permanent access to God in 'the Most Holy Place' (*ta hagia*, v. 8) had been achieved. In stark contrast, Jesus Christ as high priest of the new order has fulfilled the ritual of the annual Day of Atonement 'once for all', by means of his death and heavenly exaltation to the Most Holy Place, 'having obtained eternal redemption' (vv. 11–12). His death makes possible a cleansing of consciences from sin, freedom to serve God in a new way in the present, and the certainty of sharing at last in 'the eternal inheritance' promised to God's people (vv. 13–15). Just as the old covenant was inaugurated with a blood ritual, and the law required that nearly everything be cleansed by blood, so *the new covenant order is consecrated by the blood of Christ* and his death suffices to purify his people and to bring them ultimately into the actual presence of God (vv. 16–28).

THE WORSHIP THAT JESUS ALONE MAKES POSSIBLE

If Jesus Christ fulfils and replaces the system of worship ordained by God for Israel under the Old Covenant, how does that benefit us? How can we draw near to God and serve him acceptably under the new covenant?

Jesus and the Temple

The Gospels give various indications that Jesus will somehow replace the Jerusalem temple in the plan and purpose of God. In the debate with the Pharisees about Sabbath-keeping, Matthew alone records his claim that 'one greater than the temple is here' (12:6).[36] Jesus represents *God's royal presence and authority* more fully than the temple. Temple imagery is not explicitly transferred to the Christian community in Matthew's Gospel, though it is easy to see how that application could later be made (cf. 1 Cor. 3:16–17; 2 Cor. 6:16–18; Eph. 2:19–22; 1 Pet. 2:4–5). The well-known saying in 18:20 identifies *Jesus himself* with the divine presence and promises his presence to the most insignificant gathering of two or three in his name.[37]

Jesus' cleansing of the temple is an acted parable of God's imminent judgment against rebellious and unfruitful Israel (cf. particularly Mk. 11:12–21). His contemporaries had obscured the temple's true function as a place where God's holiness was to be revealed and Israel's status as a holy nation was to be renewed and expressed. In particular they had prevented the Gentiles from using the one place set aside for them to pray ('a house of prayer *for all nations*', Mk. 11:17, citing Isa. 56:7). They had done this by turning the temple into a 'den of robbers' (alluding to Jer. 7:11). In Luke's version, Jesus takes possession of the temple as a basis for teaching the people and preaching the gospel, suggesting that the sanctuary is purified in order to become the centre for revelation to Israel once more. Yet the theme of God's inevitable judgment on the city and its temple is highlighted just before Jesus enters the temple (Lk. 19:41–4).

Consequently, the Gospels indicate that *Jesus himself is to become the centre of salvation and blessing for the nations* (e.g., Matt. 28:18–20; Luke 24:46–9; John. 12:20–33). The resurrected Lord promises that, as the disciples preach the gospel to the nations, he will be with them to draw many into relationship with himself through faith and repentance. Thus will be realised the prophetic hope of the nations uniting with the faithful in Israel to acknowledge and serve the Lord.[38] The tearing of the curtain of the temple from top to bottom at the moment of Jesus' death (Matt. 27:51; Mark. 15:38;

Luke 23:45) could be both a sign of the judgment of God on that institution, anticipating the more drastic events to come in A.D. 70, as well as a sign of the opening of a new way to God though the death of Jesus.

The Fourth Gospel has much to say about the way in which Jesus replaces the Old Testament institutions of worship more generally. The divine presence is no longer bound to the temple, but the Word who was with God 'in the beginning' and who in fact 'was God, has become flesh and taken up temporary residence or 'tabernacled among us' (1:14, *eskēnōsen en hēmin*). This terminology recalls the instruction to Israel to make a tent-sanctuary (Exod. 25:8–9, *skēnē*), as the site of God's localized presence on earth, and the later teaching about God's presence in the temple or on Zion, his holy hill. The prophets indicated that in the End time God would 'make his dwelling' (*kataskēnoun*) in the midst of his people forever (Joel 3:17; Zech. 2:10; cf. Ezek. 37:26–8; 43:7) and John proclaims the fulfilment of that promise *in the incarnation of the eternal Word*.[39]

Jesus' cleansing of the temple in John 2:12–22 parallels the Synoptic accounts inasmuch as it is a prophetic-type protest against the profanation of God's house.[40] The immediate context in the Fourth Gospel also suggests that the action was a specifically messianic sign, pointing to the replacement of the temple by Jesus. At the wedding in Cana of Galilee (2:1–12), Jesus changed the water in the six stone jars used by the Jews for ceremonial washing into wine and thus 'revealed his glory' to his disciples. This is the first of a series of signs indicating that Jesus is the one sent by the Father to replace the customs and feasts of Judaism.[41] Jesus does this by bringing in the blessings of the messianic era, here signified by the abundance of choice wine. By cleansing the temple, he further revealed himself as the one sent to replace the institutions of the Mosaic covenant.

On the surface, the pronouncement of Jesus in John 2:19 ('Destroy this temple and I will raise it again in three days') simply refers to the Jerusalem temple and could have been taken as a claim by Jesus to be the builder of another sanctuary for the community of the End time. The insight that this saying referred to his *resurrection body* came only after he had been raised and the disciples 'believed the Scripture and the words that Jesus had spoken' (2:22). The Scripture in question was probably Ps. 69:9 (cited in Jn. 2:17). John indicates the typological and predictive aspect of this psalm of a righteous sufferer by substituting the future tense ('Zeal for your house *will* consume me') for the original past tense ('Zeal for your house has consumed me'). In this context it suggests that Jesus' concern to establish the purpose of God for Israel, Jerusalem, and the temple will destroy him! Because of this zeal, the Jewish leaders will bring about his death, but Jesus will take up his life again.

John indicates that the glory of God is ultimately manifested in the death of Jesus on behalf of God's flock, so that he might raise them up to share the new life of the kingdom with him (cf. 10:14–30). The coming of the 'Greeks' to Jerusalem, in fulfilment of the Scriptures concerning the eschatological pilgrimage of the nations to Zion, is the signal that the hour of his glorification through death has come (12:20–33). His 'lifting up' from the earth will be the means by which he draws the nations *to himself*. The institution of the temple is fulfilled and replaced in John's perspective not simply by the incarnation, bringing God amongst his people in a definitive way, but by the death and resurrection of the incarnate Son of God, securing the ultimate liberation from sin and bringing us to God (cf. 1:29,36; 3:14–18; 8:34–6). The temple of the new age in the Fourth Gospel is not the church but *the crucified and resurrected Son of God*.[42]

A New Way of Worship

In answering the question of the Samaritan woman about the appropriate *place* to worship God, Jesus shifts the focus to the more fundamental question of *how to worship God acceptably* (John 4:20–4). When he says, 'You worship what you do not know; we worship what we know, for salvation is from the Jews', he asserts that Samaritan worship, based as it was on an inadequate knowledge of God, was false. However, despite the implication that Jewish worship was truly based on divine revelation and therefore honouring to God, it is to be superseded:

> Yet a time is coming and has now come when the true worshippers will worship the Father in spirit and truth, for they are the kind of worshippers the Father seeks. God is spirit, and his worshippers must worship (*proskynein*) in spirit and truth. (Jn. 4:23–4)

Jesus does not simply contrast the old external and cultic pattern of worship with a new inward, and universal spirituality.[43] With the expression 'a time is coming and has now come', he continues to develop the notion introduced in v. 21 that his ministry initiates *a totally different way of relating to God*: 'a time is coming when you will worship the Father neither on this mountain nor in Jerusalem'. In the Fourth Gospel the coming 'time' means the hour of Jesus' death, resurrection and return to the Father (e.g., 2:4; 7:30; 12:23; 13:1; 17:1).[44] Through the cross and resurrection of Jesus the new temple of his body is raised up (2:19–22) and then the Spirit is given (7:37–9). Thus, Jesus is to become the means by which the Father obtains true worshippers from every nation (cf. 12:32). The expression '*true* worshippers' suggests that the Old Testament cult was, in effect, only 'a shadow of the good things to come' (Heb. 10:1), pointing forward to the reality which was to come in Jesus.[45]

More specifically, the expression 'in spirit and truth' suggests that Jesus is to be the means by which this new worship is to be inaugurated. The two key words 'spirit' and 'truth' are closely connected in John's portrait of Christ. No one can see the kingdom of God or experience the blessings of the End time without being born again by the Spirit (3:1–8). Thus, in slightly different language, *the Father begets true worshippers through the Spirit*. But it is Jesus who makes the Spirit available to those who come to him, because of his saving work (7:37–9). Again, since Jesus is the truth (14:6), who uniquely reveals the reality of God and his purposes (8:45; 18:37), he alone can bring men and women to a true knowledge of the Father (cf. 17:3), enabling them to honour him by their faith and obedience. Jesus is not the object of worship in this passage but the means to God-honouring worship.

The coming hour is already present as Jesus addresses the Samaritan woman because he draws attention to himself as the giver of living water 4:10, 14), using a metaphor which combines the two key notions: *Jesus gives the ultimate revelation and Jesus provides the life-giving Spirit.*[46] The Father seeks those who would relate to him on this basis because such worship accords with his nature (v. 24).[47] By implication, such worship is possible only for those who recognize the true identity of Christ (vv. 25–6,42) and yield him their allegiance.

At the beginning of this dialogue, *proskynein* clearly refers to the customary worship of God, as practised by Jews or Samaritans (cf. also 12:20). However, as the discussion proceeds, it is used in conjunction with other terms to describe the *relationship with God*, which Jesus alone makes possible, in the present, eschatological hour. This relationship is not tied in any way to any earthly 'place' (v. 20) or cult, for the prophetic hope of the temple as the centre for the universal worship of God in the End time has been fulfilled in the person and work of Jesus. In effect, the exalted Christ is now the 'place' where God is to be acknowledged and honoured. The Father cannot now be honoured unless Jesus is given all the honour due to him as the Son (cf. 5:22–3; 8:49).

Jesus as the Object of Worship

The Gospels indicate in a variety of ways that the God-given cult with its centre in the temple at Jerusalem is fulfilled and replaced by the person and work of Jesus. A related theme, particularly highlighted in the narrative of the Last Supper, is that Jesus is the inaugurator of a new or renewed covenant by means of his death. He establishes a new basis of relationship with God for Israel and the nations and thus a new pattern of worship. The worship of the eschatological era is essentially a relationship with God on the basis of the redemptive work accomplished by Christ. Paradoxically, however, there are also indications in the Gospels that *Jesus himself is worthy of divine honours*. He is not simply the means by which a new allegiance to the Father is initiated and maintained. The Son himself is to be accorded the homage and service due to the Lord God of Israel.

Matthew, for instance, develops a picture of Jesus as the one to whom 'every knee should bow' (cf. Phil. 2:10). The Magi from the East come to prostrate themselves before the new-born king of the Jews (2:2,11), anticipating the submission of the nations to the risen Lord, which is the essence of discipleship according to 28:16–20.[48] Suppliants come to Jesus in the course of his ministry for life and health and even for a place of honour in his kingdom (8:2; 9:18; 15:25; 20:20). In these verses *proskynein* is used to indicate the total dependence of those bowing before him and begging him for help. Despite the fact that these incidents reveal exemplary trust in Jesus and a dawning recognition of his true identity, it is doubtful that the posture should be viewed as 'worship' (so KJV), implying a recognition of his divine sonship.[49] As suppliants in the Old Testament expressed their total dependence on kings and other authority figures (e.g. 1 Sam. 2:36; 2 Sam. 14:4; 16:4), so these people recognized the extraordinary power and authority of Jesus to meet a variety of needs.

However, with the narrative of Jesus walking on the water and stilling the storm we find a spontaneous reaction much like that of people in the Old Testament confronted by divine disclosures (e.g., Gen. 24:26–7; Exod. 34:8; Judg. 7:15). Matthew records that 'those who were in the boat *worshipped* him, saying, "Truly you are the Son of God" ' (*prosekynēsan autō* Matt.

14:33). This confession of Jesus' identity makes the response of the disciples distinctive here and indicates the appropriateness of translating the verb 'worshipped'. The later response of the women to an appearance of the risen Christ (28:9) and the response of the eleven disciples when they met him on the mountain (28:17)[50] is the same expression of grateful and reverent homage found in 14:33. The final encounter with the resurrected Christ involves an unmistakable declaration of divine kingship on his part ('All authority on heaven and earth has been given to me') and the implication of the charge that follows is that the disciples are to call upon people everywhere to express the same homage to Christ as they disciple the nations.

The terminology of worship is not much employed in the other Gospels. John uses *proskynein* at a key point in his narrative to signify the acknowledgement of Jesus' true identity and submission to him by the man healed from blindness (Jn. 9:38). Luke's only use of the term in relation to Jesus is in his account of the ascension.[51] When Jesus was taken up into heaven, the disciples 'worshipped him' (*proskynēsantes auton*) and then returned to Jerusalem with great joy, where they stayed continually at the temple, praising God (Luke 24:52–3). Perhaps Luke reserved the term for this climactic moment to indicate that this was at last *the real recognition of Christ by the disciples*. It would certainly appear that the presentation of Christ in each one of the Gospels is designed to elicit such a response from all who read (cf. Jn. 20:30–1).

All this suggests the centrality of evangelism to an authentic New Testament theology of worship. Indeed, the aim of all Christian preaching should be to bring people to worship Christ in the sense of *yielding their allegiance to him as Saviour and Lord*. 'Bending over to the Lord' in New Testament terms means essentially responding with repentance and faith to the person and work of the Lord Jesus Christ. Those who are concerned about God-honouring worship will be pre-occupied with bringing people to Christ! This perspective will be confirmed as other New Testament documents are examined.

The Apostolic Preaching about Christ

Peter's Pentecost sermon (Acts 2:14–40), with its focus on the prophecy of Joel, is widely recognized as being programmatic for Acts as a whole. Joel 2:28–32 indicates that, 'before the coming of the great and glorious day of the Lord', God will pour out his Spirit *on all flesh*, and all will prophesy. Whereas the Spirit especially designated and empowered the prophets and other leaders of the people under the old covenant, God promised that all his people would be possessed by the Spirit in the last days. Joel's prophecy corresponds to some extent with Jeremiah's prediction of a new covenant (Jer. 31:31–4), with its promise that all God's people would know him and obey him in a new way, and with Ezekiel's vision of the Spirit as 'the life-principle of a nation which truly knows the Lord and is inwardly his people' (Ezek. 36:26–7; 37:14; 39:29).[52] The coming of the Spirit is another way of talking about the coming of God to dwell amongst his people, to fulfil the ideal of the temple and to transform their lives by his presence (cf. Ezekiel 40–8). Acts goes on to show how the Spirit-indwelt community came to include believing Gentiles along with the Jewish disciples of Jesus (10:44–8; 11:15–17).[53]

Peter's sermon proclaims that Jesus has been raised, and the witnesses of his resurrection have received from the exalted Lord *the promised Holy Spirit* (2:32–3). Consequently, these are 'the last days' (2:16–17), and Jesus is the Lord upon whom everyone must call in order to be saved from the coming judgment of God (2:21,33–6; cf. 22:16). Those who do so, being baptised 'in the name of Jesus Christ', are promised that their sins will be forgiven and that they themselves will receive the gift of the Holy Spirit (2:37–9). In this way they will share in the benefits of the new covenant and participate in the community of those who 'call upon the name' of the Lord Jesus.[54]

What were the implications of this preaching for the Jerusalem temple, the priesthood and the sacrificial system? Luke indicates that the earliest disciples met regularly in the temple courts to teach and encourage one another (Acts 2:46; 5:12) and to give public testimony to the gospel about Jesus (3:11–26; 4:2; 5:42). This was not simply for the practical reason that the temple was a place where crowds could be easily addressed but because the disciples, like their master, wanted to take the word of salvation to the centre of Judaism itself. The temple also remained for a while *a place of public prayer* for Christians. As well as meeting 'house to house', where they ate together and praised God as a distinct group or sect within Judaism (2:46–7, cf. 24:5,14; 28:22), the earliest Christians apparently went up to the temple at the set hours of prayer (3:1), continuing their association with the traditional practices of their religion (cf. 21:20–6; 22:17–21). Since 'the ninth hour' (3 p.m.) was the time of the afternoon sacrifice, the most natural way to read Acts 3:1 is to suppose that the disciples participated in the prayers associated with the burnt offering and incense at that time (cf. Exod. 29:38–43).[55]

While it was logical for them to meet together separately, to express their newfound relationship to God through Christ and to strengthen one another in the role given to them by God, if they were to function as the Servant community, to bring Israel back to God (cf. Isa. 49:5–6), that would not be facilitated by immediately disengaging themselves from the temple and isolating themselves from the traditional practices of their religion.[56] By preaching in the temple, the Jerusalem Christians related Jesus most closely to Jewish hopes about the End time. However, since they focussed on Jesus as the only source of eschatological salvation, and warned of divine judgment against those who rejected this gospel, the temple soon became the place where disciples experienced *opposition and arrest* (4:3; 5:25–6, cf. 21:27–30). Acts shows how the gap between Christianity and Judaism progressively widened. Yet, even towards the end of Luke's account, we are reminded that there were still many thousands of Jewish Christians who were 'zealous for the law' (21:20).

The theme of Jesus replacing the temple is not explicit in Acts, yet preaching about the centrality of the resurrected Christ in God's plans for Israel points to Jesus as the fulfilment of the temple ideal (cf. 7:54–8:3). The story of Stephen is used by Luke to summarize the rejection of the gospel by Jerusalem as a whole and Stephen's speech explains why this happened: 'Jerusalem preferred to remain with the Temple and to regard that as the final mark of God's favour, rather than let it lead them to Jesus to whom it pointed.'[57] Stephen asserts that devotion to the temple must not halt the advance of the divine plan for the people of God, which focusses on Jesus the glorified Messiah, who is Lord of all (cf. 10:36). In the perspective of Acts,

Jesus is *the new point of contact between heaven and earth for people of every race without distinction*.

As the earliest disciples proclaimed the exalted Christ and called upon their fellow Israelites to acknowledge him as the giver of the Holy Spirit (Acts 2:33), 'the author of life' (3:15), and their only saviour in the coming judgment (4:12), they were, in effect, summoning their contemporaries to *bend the knee to Jesus*, as they themselves had done. Yet, Luke did not go on to employ *proskynein* in Acts to describe either initial acts of homage and devotion to Christ or the content and purpose of regular Christian gatherings. He restricted the term to a quite technical usage, applying it to those engaged on a pilgrimage to honour God in the traditional temple services (Acts 8:27; 24:11) or to the practice of idolatry (Acts 7:43, adapting Amos 5:26). Such terminology was presumably not applied to Christian meetings in Acts or the Epistles because of its association with the rites of paganism or with the Jewish cult centred at Jerusalem.[58]

Only in Acts 13:2 do we find the technical language of worship specifically applied to a Christian meeting. There, the prophets and teachers of Antioch are said to be 'worshipping' or, more literally, '*serving*' the Lord (*leitourgountōn . . . tǭ kyriǭ*) and fasting, when the Holy Spirit calls for the sending out of Barnabas and Saul. Many commentators take this as a reference to prayer,[59] and it is certainly clear from v. 3 that prayer and fasting were involved in the meeting. If this is correct, Luke will be highlighting prayer as the 'priestly' activity in which all can participate and which replaces the sacrificial approach to God which was at the heart of Judaism.

However, it is possible that Luke means that 'these prophets and teachers were carrying out *their appointed ministry* in the church'[60] In other words, the ministry of prophecy and teaching, which was exercised by those especially gifted for the benefit of other believers in the congregation, was a particular way of serving God under the New Covenant. If the service of God involved a certain lifestyle and ministry in everyday contexts, it also had a definite expression when Christians gathered together. More will be said about the nature and purpose of Christian meetings in Acts later in this chapter.

Paul's Teaching about Worship as the Obedience of Faith

The phrase 'through faith' in Rom. 3:25 indicates how Paul envisaged that the saving benefits of Jesus' unique and unrepeatable 'sacrifice of atonement' might be appropriated. In the following chapters of Romans, the apostle goes on to describe the nature of that faith and its consequences in terms of obedience and sanctification (cf. especially Rom. 6:11–23). Justification by faith opens up the possibility of serving God in a new way in the power of the Holy Spirit. Such a relationship with God is available for Jews and Gentiles alike, since anyone who calls upon Christ as Lord may be saved (cf. 10:9–13).

In Rom. 12:1 Paul begins to draw out the practical implications of the preceding theological exposition, indicating the transition by the use of the word 'therefore' (*oun*):

Therefore, I urge you brothers, in view of God's mercies, to present your bodies as a living sacrifice, holy and pleasing to God, which is your understanding worship (Rom. 12:1)[61]

The basis of this appeal is 'the mercies of God' (*dia tōn oiktirmōn tou theou*), an expression which encapsulates the message of Rom. 3:21–11:36. Jesus' death was a once-for-all sin offering, providing the atonement towards which the propitiatory rites of the old covenant were ultimately pointing. On the basis of this sacrifice, we are to present ourselves to God as 'living sacrifices, holy and pleasing to God'. The verb *paristanai* ('to present') is a standard Hellenistic word for the offering of a sacrifice, even though it never appears to be used in that technical sense in the LXX.[62] The aorist tense is used in this exhortation to indicate the decisiveness required in presenting ourselves to God for his service. However, since disobedience and unfaithfulness are so much a part of ongoing Christian experience, it is clearly necessary to renew on a regular basis that initial presentation of ourselves to God made at conversion or in baptism.

The sacrifice in question is our 'bodies', meaning ourselves as a totality, not just skin and bones (cf. 6:13,16, 'offer yourselves', *paristanein heautoun*)! Christ's obedience makes possible a new obedience for the people of God. Paul is not simply considering some form of inner consecration here but the consecration of ourselves as bodies, able to express our obedience to God in concrete relationships within this world (cf. 1 Cor. 6:20). As those who have been brought from death to life by means of Jesus' death and resurrection (cf. Rom. 6:4–11), we belong to God as a 'living sacrifice' (*thysian zōsan*, cf. 6:12–14). As those called to be saints (cf. 1:7 *klētoi hagioi*), we are to live out that consecrated relationship in terms of practical holiness (*hagian*) and so prove to be acceptable or pleasing to God (*euareston tǭ theǭ*). Thus, Paul has transposed the notion of sacrifice 'across a double line – from cultic ritual to everyday life, from a previous epoch characterized by daily offering of animals to one characterized by a whole-person commitment lived out in daily existence'.[63]

The expression *tēn logikēn latreian hymōn*, which I have translated 'your understanding worship', suggests that *the presentation of ourselves to God in Christ* is the essence of Christian worship. Paul uses the noun *latreia* with reference to the God-given cult of the old covenant in 9:4 but with reference to a different form of service in 12:1. This word is the cognate of *latreuein*, and was employed in the LXX only nine times, five times translating the Hebrew *ʿabōdāh*, and four times appearing in texts for which there is no Hebrew original. It denotes service rendered to other people (3 Macc. 4:14), cultic service to other gods (1 Macc. 1:43), and cultic service to the God of Israel (1 Chr. 28:13). The Passover was a particular 'service' to be observed by Israel, in remembrance of the Lord's redemptive work at the time of the exodus (Exod. 12:25, 26; 13:5). As noted previously, when *latreuein* or *latreia* are applied to the service of God they almost always denote *the worship of the people as a whole*, not the specific work of the priests or Levites.

A great deal of discussion has taken place about the actual meaning of *logikē latreia* in Rom 12:1, in view of the usage of similar terminology and concepts in Hellenistic and late Jewish literature. The adjective *logikos* was a favourite term of the Greek philosophers, especially the Stoics, for whom it meant 'belonging to the sphere of the *logos* or reason' and hence 'spiritual' in the sense of 'suprasensual'.[64] Since rationality is what distinguishes human beings from animals and relates them to the gods, traditional sacrifices were repudiated by some writers and various forms of 'rational sacrifice' (*logikē thysia*) were advocated instead. In some texts this refers to attitudes of mind and purity of life, but in texts influenced by mysticism some form of religious ecstasy or even silence are regarded as the proper worship. The LXX does not employ *logikos*, but the prophets clearly indicated that God was honoured, not merely by ritual observance, but by what might be termed a 'spiritual worship' (e.g. Isa. 1:10–16; 29:13; Mic. 6:6–8). God's essential requirement was repentance, faith and obedience, especially expressed in the concern to establish righteousness and holiness in the community of his people. The sacrificial system was designed to promote a true engagement with God and not to be a cover-up for sin! In late Judaism, while the need for cultic observance continued to be stressed, deeds of love, and activities such as fasting, prayer and the study of the law were often regarded as being as pleasing to God as temple offerings.

If the term 'spiritualization' is to be applied to developments in Judaism, this should not be confused with what such terminology meant in Hellenism. In some Jewish writings, such as the Epistle of Aristeas and the works of Philo, Hellenistic and Jewish ideas about spiritual worship were certainly blended. However, whereas in Hellenism generally there was a movement towards interiorizing worship, culminating in teaching about the importance of *silence* before an impersonal and ineffable divinity, in Judaism the movement was towards a development of the *ethical implications* of ritual worship. The way for New Testament teaching was to some extent forged by Jewish thinkers placing the doing of God's will at the heart of what they said about sacrifice, rather than by Hellenism. Nevertheless, what is distinctive for Paul is not the moralization and spiritualization of the notion of sacrifice but the fact that Christian worship involves the presentation of ourselves to God *on the basis of the atoning sacrifice of the death of Jesus, in the power of the Holy Spirit*.[65]

If Paul's expression is translated 'spiritual worship', there is a danger of accenting the inwardness of Christian worship and not taking sufficient account of the fact that we are to yield our *bodies* to God's service. On the other hand, the translation 'rational worship' may suggest only a contrast between the offering of *rational beings* and the sacrifice of irrational animals. The mind is certainly central to Paul's perspective here, but the focus is not simply on rationality. The service he calls for is the obedience of faith expressed by those whose minds are being transformed and renewed by God, so that they may *no longer be conformed in lifestyle to the values, attitudes and behaviour of* 'this age' (Rom. 12:2; cf. Col. 3:9–10; Eph. 4:22–4). Consequently, it may be best to read 'understanding worship', and to recognize from the context that this means 'the worship which is consonant with the truth of the gospel',[66] or the service rendered by those who truly understand the gospel and its implications.

The first two verses of Romans 12 place the concluding chapters of Paul's letter under the umbrella of *acceptable worship*. The idea of worship emerges again explicitly in 14:18 ('Anyone who serves [*douleuōn*] Christ in this way is acceptable [*euarestos*] to God and approved by men'). The notion of an offering acceptable to God then continues in the section dealing with Paul's particular ministry which begins in 15:14. From Romans 12–15 it is clear that acceptable worship involves effective ministry to one another within the body of Christ, love and forgiveness towards those outside the Christian community, right relationships with ruling authorities, living expectantly in the light of Christ's imminent return and expressing love especially towards those with different opinions within the congregation of Christ's people.

Worship and Christian Ministry

When Paul tells the Christians at Rome how constantly he has remembered them in his prayers, requesting that somehow he might be able to visit them, he affirms that God knows the sincerity of his claim: 'God whom I serve (*latreuein*) in my spirit, in the gospel of his Son is my witness' (Rom. 1:9). The words 'in my spirit' (*en pneumati mou*) primarily refer to Paul's spirit, rather than to the Holy Spirit, yet it is surely right to assume that he means *his spirit renewed and inspired by the Spirit of God* (cf. Phil. 3:3). In this way he differentiates Christian service from other forms of worship as a service flowing from and motivated by a renewed spirit and one in which the whole person is engaged. And the context suggests that this service takes place quite specifically in the sphere of gospel ministry (*en tǭ euangeliǭ tou huiou autou*). Intercessory prayer is certainly a vital aspect of Paul's service to God (1:8–10), but it is clear from what follows that *gospel preaching* is the focus and goal of all his activity (cf. 1:11–15).[67]

At the conclusion of the letter, Paul again describes his gospel work using transformed worship terminology. As 'a minister of Christ Jesus to the Gentiles', he is *God's designated servant* (*leitourgos*), bestowing benefits on (*eis*) the Gentiles with the gospel (Rom. 15:16). The word *leitourgos* need not imply a sacral function.[68] However, what follows shows that he is engaged on Christ's behalf in discharging a 'priestly' ministry in the 'cult' of the gospel (*hierourgounta to euangelion*). This sacral terminology is used metaphorically to portray the ministry of preaching by which *he enables the Gentiles to offer themselves to God* as an acceptable sacrifice, 'sanctified by the Holy Spirit'.[69] The language here recalls Rom. 12:1 and suggests that gospel preaching is necessary to bring about the obedience of faith through Jesus Christ, which is the 'understanding worship' of the eschatological era. His own role as apostle to the Gentiles is foundational to the new 'cult' in the Spirit, with evangelism and teaching about the implications of the Christian message being his God-given 'liturgy'. Since preaching was not regarded as a ritual activity in Paul's world, he clearly gives that ministry a novel significance when he describes it as the means by which he worships or serves God. By implication, other gospel ministries may be similarly described, though there is always a danger that, by so doing, the metaphorical and spiritual dimension to Paul's thought may be obscured.[70]

The related verb *leitourgein* is used in Rom. 15:27 to describe the *financial support* by the Gentile churches 'for the poor among the saints at Jerusalem'. Paul argues that the Gentiles have shared in the Jews' spiritual blessings and owe it to them literally 'to benefit them in material things' (*en tois sarkikois leitourgēsai autois*). Here, and in 2 Cor. 9:12 ('this service that you perform'), the terminology is used with something of its original meaning, namely the bestowal of public benefits on those in need by those with means.[71] Again, in Phil. 2:25 Epaphroditus is described as the one sent by the Philippians to take care of Paul's needs (*leitourgon tēs chreias mou*). The task of Epaphroditus was to bring *the material gifts* of the Philippians, which are described as their 'liturgy' or benefaction to Paul (*hymōn . . . tēs pros me leitourgias*, 2:30), and to provide whatever personal ministrations he could to the imprisoned apostle. In such passages the ordinary secular sense of rendering a service to someone is obvious, although it is clearly a ministry that will glorify God (2 Cor. 9:13) and the gifts are 'a fragrant offering, a sacrifice acceptable and pleasing to God' (Phil. 4:18). The notion of worshipping or serving God *by means of our service to one another* is thus implied.

The service of the Philippians is seen to have a quite specifically Godward dimension in Phil. 2:17, where the apostle writes of *the sacrifice and service of their faith* (*tę thysią kai leitourgią tēs pisteōs hymōn*).[72] This verse suggests that the Philippians offer their faith (or the good works springing from their faith) as a sacrifice of praise and thanksgiving to God. The apostle's life-blood, which may soon be poured out because of his work in establishing such faith all over the Gentile world, is most likely what is meant by the words 'even if I am to be poured out like a drink offering (*spendomai*)'.[73] Their faith was elicited and encouraged by Paul's preaching and now their faith has been expressed in a practical ministry of care and support for the apostle and his ongoing work. If his own life is to be sacrificed, it can only be regarded as a modest 'drink offering', added to the primary offering of their faith! The use of sacrificial language in such a context highlights the importance of such expressions of faith in the life that is pleasing to God (cf. Heb. 11:6).

The Philippians share with Paul in the 'worship' of the messianic age by putting no confidence 'in the flesh' and therefore placing no reliance on rites and ceremonies such as circumcision or animal sacrifice. The worship described in Phil. 3:3 is *the service to God made possible by the Spirit of God* (*hoi pneumati theou latreuontes*). Just as 'the circumcision' was previously a designation of Israel as the covenant people of God, now applicable in a new way to Christians, so 'the service' acceptable to God is now offered by those who are the new covenant community, initiated and led by the Holy Spirit.[74] Through the preaching of the gospel, they have come to put their trust and confidence in Jesus and his redemptive work alone, and to live out that faith with the expectation of sharing in Christ's resurrection life (cf. 3:7–21).

Not every relevant text from Paul's letters has been discussed here. However, the observations that have been made about his use of *latreuein, leitourgein*, and related terminology, are sufficient to show that, according to Paul, *expressions of faith in Jesus Christ* and *ministries that encourage such faith* are the worship acceptable and pleasing to God under the new covenant. Such worship will doubtless find expression in a congregational context. But contemporary Christians need to be reminded that sharing the gospel with unbelievers, supporting gospel work, offering material help to those in need, and serving God in the workplace or wider community is no less important than prayer, praise or participating in the Lord's Supper!

Appropriating the Benefits of Christ's Saving Work

In the argument of Hebrews, sanctuary, sacrifice, altar and priesthood all find their fulfilment in the saving work of Jesus Christ,[75] not in some ongoing activity in the Christian congregation. When Christians throughout the ages have failed to grasp this teaching and its implications, clergy, buildings and objects within those buildings have been invested with a special sanctity. This has obscured the true focus of the New Testament, leading to a pre-occupation with ritual and ceremony, wrong views about Christian ministry and a simplistic application of Old Testament texts to what goes on in church. More fundamentally, people are misled about the way we can relate to God and please him when Christianity is presented as an earthly cult.

However, worship terms are certainly applied to the Christian life in Hebrews. One set of terms is used to urge Christians to draw on all the spiritual resources available to them through Jesus Christ. Another set of terms highlights the service they should offer to God in their everyday lives, expressing their gratitude for the saving work of Christ. Since Jesus fulfilled, and therefore replaced, the Old Testament cult (cf. 8:13; 10:1–10), believers are set free from cultic obligations to serve God in a new way.

In two important passages of exhortation, preceding and concluding the main doctrinal argument, the writer issues the challenge to hold fast the Christian confession and to '*draw near*' to God with confidence (4:14–16; 10:19–23). In both cases, the appeal is based on the fact that Christ is the perfected and enthroned high priest, who has entered the heavenly sanctuary by means of his sacrificial death and heavenly exaltation and opened up 'a new and living way' into that sanctuary for us.

The verb *proserchesthai* occurs at a number of points in the argument (4:16; 7:25; 10:1,22; 11:6; 12:18,22; cf. *engizein*, 7:19) and is clearly a key to understanding the way believers should respond to the person and work of Christ. In non-biblical Greek, *proserchesthai* meant 'to come before', or 'to approach' someone such as a judge or a god. Since this verb was commonly used in the LXX to describe the priestly approach to God in sacrificial ministry (e.g. Lev. 21:17,21;22:3), some commentators understand the usage of Hebrews to imply that the right of priestly approach is 'now extended to Christians'.[76]

There is certainly a hierarchy of drawing near to God in some Old Testament references (e.g., Exod. 19:21–2; 24:2). However, this terminology is also used in the LXX to describe the relationship which *all Israel* could enjoy with God, either in cultic ritual or in prayer.[77] In Heb. 11:6, where there are no specifically cultic associations, drawing near to God means having a relationship with him by faith (cf. Jas. 4:8; 1 Pet. 2:4). Even in cultic contexts, it is most likely that this is the reality behind the writer's use of the imagery of drawing near to God.

Thus, it is simplistic to say that Hebrews uses this terminology to expound the view that the privileges of the Old Testament priesthood find their fulfilment in the priesthood of all Christian believers. The people of God may now draw near without the aid of human priesthood, but only because they rely on *the priestly mediation of Jesus Christ*. This directness of approach to God comes about because the office of priesthood is fulfilled in Christ rather than in us. In 10:1–2, the Israelites generally are described as those who drew near to God by means of the sacrificial system. However, the writer clearly affirms that the system was not able to 'perfect' those who sought to relate to God in this way. On the other hand, the high-priestly ministry of Jesus has 'made perfect for ever those who are being made holy' (10:14). The immediate context suggests that this refers to the fulfilment of the prophecy of Jer. 31:31–34 and the inauguration of the sort of relationship with God envisaged there.[78]

The 'better hope' by which the Christian draws near God (7:19) is due to the 'better covenant' of which Jesus is surety (7:22) and mediator (8:6; 12:24): it is enacted on 'better promises' (8:6) and is eternal in its consequences (13:20). In short, the contrast in these passages is between *the limited effectiveness of the former priesthood and the absolute effectiveness of the priesthood of Christ to bring about a right relationship with God* (cf. 7:25). The work of Christ means that 'the certainty of the actualisation of the drawing near is now stronger and surer and more complete than in the O.T. and later Judaism.'[79]

Consequently, 4:16 and 10:22 must be understood as encouragements to realize the benefit of the new relationship with God made possible by Christ. The tense of the Greek verb in each case (*proserchōmetha*) implies the need for this to be an ongoing activity. Christians have already drawn near to God and the Lord Jesus in the heavenly assembly (12:22, note the perfect tense of *proselēluthate*). Yet they are to 'keep on drawing near with confidence to the throne of grace' (4:16). The direct approach to God 'with confidence' (*meta parrēsias*, 4:16; cf. 3:6; 10:19,35),[80] which is the essence of Christian faith, needs to be expressed continually as *an ongoing relationship of trust and dependence* (10:22, 'with a true heart in full assurance of faith').

The alternative is to 'throw away your confidence' (10:35) and 'shrink back' (10:39), which is another way of describing apostasy. The particular need expressed in 4:16 – to 'receive mercy' and find 'timely help' for running the Christian race – suggests the activity of *prayer* (cf. Jer. 7:16[LXX], Ps. 33:6[LXX]). However, the reference will not be to intercessory prayer in a general sense but more specifically to confession of sin and 'personal appropriation of salvation'.[81] Such prayer will be the means by which the benefits of Christ's high-priestly work will first be grasped, in conversion and baptism. Such prayer will also be the means by which genuine disciples continue to express their dependence upon God through Christ, at any time and in any place, without the mediation of a human priesthood.

Although we must draw near to God in a personal way, it is also true that those who turn to Christ come *together* into the heavenly presence, to join by faith in the celebration of the heavenly assembly (cf. 12:22–4). The notion of collectively drawing near to God is similarly suggested by the context of 10:22. Gathering together is an important means of encouraging one another to persevere in love and obedience (10:24–5). As we expose ourselves to the ministries of others and to the word of God, we are encouraged to *engage with God as the family of God together*.

Serving God in the Perspective of Hebrews

The use of *latreuein* at two key points in the argument of Hebrews (9:14; 12:28) suggests that, as in Paul's teaching, the Christian's response to the work of Christ is *a life of grateful obedience*.[82] The sacrifices of the old covenant were not able to perfect 'the worshipper' (*ton latreuonta*) by dealing with the fundamental problem of a guilty conscience (9:9; cf. 10:1–4). This was so because they were 'external regulations applying until the time of the new order' (9:10). However, the all-sufficient sacrifice of Christ for the forgiveness of sins makes such cleansing possible: the blood of Christ is able to 'cleanse our consciences from acts that lead to death, so that we might serve (*latreuein*) the living God' (9:14).[83] Conscience must be 'cleansed' by the assurance that the blood of Christ provides the necessary forgiveness before one can draw near to God (cf. 10:19–22) and before one can serve him effectively (9:14). But what exactly is the nature of the service that Christ makes possible? The key to interpreting 9:14 is a later passage:

> Therefore, since we are receiving a kingdom that cannot be shaken, let us be thankful, and so worship God acceptably (*latreuōmen euarestōs tǭ theǭ*) with reverence and awe, for our God is a consuming fire (Heb. 12:28–9).

Acceptable worship is clearly related here to the reception of 'an unshakable kingdom.' Thanks to the work of Christ, Christians already participate by faith in the eschatological kingdom of God,[84] having already 'drawn near' to the heavenly Jerusalem, where God is in the midst of his angels and the perfected saints of all generations (12:22–4). At first glance it may appear from 12:28 that acceptable worship is simply defined in terms of expressing gratitude for this great gift: 'let us be grateful . . . and thus (*di' hēs*) let us offer to God acceptable worship.'[85] However, since chap 13 follows immediately, with its many exhortations to faithfulness and obedience, it is more likely that the writer is indicating that *the words and actions that flow from such gratitude* are the worship that is pleasing to God.[86] That is certainly the meaning of 13:15–16.

As in Rom. 12:1, Christian worship is the service rendered by those who have truly grasped the gospel of God's grace and its implications. The motivation and power for such service in Hebrews is quite specifically the *cleansing* that derives from the finished work of Christ (9:14) and the *hope* which that work sets before us (12:28). Gratitude expressed in service is the sign that the grace of God has been apprehended and appreciated. However, the writer introduces a more serious note when he asserts that acceptable worship is characterized by 'reverence and awe' (*meta eulabeias kai deous*), and supports his challenge with an allusion to the coming *judgment* of God ('for our God is a consuming fire').[87]

In the wide range of instructions given in 13:1–7 there is a challenge to persist with the sort of practical expressions of love and patient faith previously commended (cf. 6:10–12; 10:32–36). Here we see what Christian worship means in the context of everyday life: it has to do with entertaining strangers, visiting prisoners, being faithful in marriage, trusting God to provide material needs and imitating the faith of Christian leaders! In 13:8–16 there is a restatement of the theme that the Old Testament cultus finds its fulfilment in the work of Christ, concluding with another reference to the worship that is 'pleasing to God' (vv. 15–16; cf. 12:28).

In 13:15 the 'sacrifice of praise' Christians are to offer to God through Jesus is defined in language borrowed from Hos. 14:2 (LXX) – it is 'the tribute of lips which acknowledge his name' (NEB). Clearly, this could involve the *celebration of Christ as Saviour and Lord in personal or corporate acts of praise*. However, the writer's meaning here cannot simply be restricted to such activities. The verb 'to acknowledge' (*homologountōn*) can be understood in a non-cultic and non-liturgical way to refer to the confession of Christ before unbelievers.[88] Our writer's concern in the immediate context is to exhort believers to acknowledge Christ *in the world*, in the face of opposition and suffering (13:12–14). In its widest sense, this sacrifice of praise will be rendered by those who confess Jesus 'outside the camp', in various forms of public testimony or evangelism.[89] The offering up of praise to God is certainly not just a matter of singing hymns or giving thanks in a congregational context, though these activities can be a stimulus to effective proclamation in other contexts.[90]

'To do good' and 'to share with others' is also acceptable worship, for 'with such sacrifices' (*toiautais thysiais*, v. 16) God is pleased. The writer employs transformed cultic language to show the centrality of these activities to genuine religion (cf. Jas. 1:26–7).[91] Such 'sacrifices' cannot be regarded as cultivating God's favour, since Christian worship is meant to be an expression of gratitude for the care that he first showed us (cf. 12:28).

WORSHIP AND CONGREGATIONAL GATHERINGS IN THE NEW TESTAMENT

It might be concluded from the evidence examined so far that, in the New Testament,

> Sacred times and places are superseded by the eschatological public activity of those who at all times and in all places stand 'before the face of Christ' and from this position before God make the everyday round of so-called secular life into the arena of the unlimited and unceasing glorification of the divine will. At this point the doctrines of worship and Christian 'ethics' converge.[92]

However, while it is true that every sphere of life provides the Christian with the opportunity to glorify and serve God (cf. Col 3:17), it would be a mistake to think that worship in the New Testament is simply synonymous with ethics. For one thing, as we have observed, the terminology of worship is used quite specifically by Paul with reference to gospel preaching and the ministries that support gospel work. There is *a declaratory side* to glorifying God and *a sacrificial service in the cause of the gospel* that needs to be highlighted as a vital part of the Christian's 'understanding worship'. Furthermore, while it may be the logic of New Testament teaching that sacred times and places are superseded, it is still valid to ask whether there is any special significance in the gathering of Christians together. What is the purpose of Christian assembly in the New Testament and how does it relate to the service believers are to offer to God in everyday life?

The Character and Function of Christian Gatherings in Acts

Acts 2:42 provides a brief summary of the activity of the first community of Christians in Jerusalem, where we are told that 'they devoted themselves to the apostles' teaching and to the fellowship, to the breaking of bread and to prayer'. Since 2:44–7 appears to be an expansion of this initial summary, it is not appropriate to regard the four elements specified in 2:42 as a primitive liturgical sequence, implying that their meetings regularly involved instruction, [table] fellowship, then the Lord's Supper and prayers.[93] Luke is giving a brief portrayal of the ministry of these disciples to one another *in a variety of contexts*, not simply telling us what happened when they gathered for 'church'. In 4:32–5:16 many of the same details are presented in a different order and in an expanded form.

Their meeting together in the temple courts (2:46) appears to have been specifically to *hear the apostolic preaching* (cf. 3:11–26; 5:21), though doubtless there were also opportunities for teaching in the home context. We may surmise that these earliest converts desired to be encouraged in their faith but also to identify with the public preaching of the gospel to their fellow Israelites as an act of testimony to its truthfulness. Apostolic instruction continued to be at the centre of church life later in Gentile contexts (e.g., 11:25–6; 20:7–12).

The *fellowship* mentioned in 2:42 (*tē koinōniā*) most likely refers to the sharing of material blessings described in 2:44–5, as a particular expression of the new relationship experienced together through a common faith in Christ (cf. 4:32–7).[94] That relationship brought a certain sense of responsibility to one another. The sharing of goods came to include the distribution of food to the needy in their midst (cf. Acts 6:1–2) and was clearly not restricted to formal gatherings of the believers.

The *breaking of bread* refers to the common meals shared in their homes (2:46), described in terms of the customary Jewish action of initiating the meal by breaking a loaf and distributing bread to all present (cf. Lk. 24:30,35). To 'break bread' was to eat together. Luke goes straight on to say (literally) 'they were partaking of food with glad and sincere hearts'. There is no ground for saying that this table fellowship was a formal 'liturgical' activity, although it must have been 'full of religious content because of the recollection of the table fellowship which Jesus had with his followers during his earthly ministry'.[95] Again, although Acts 20:7 mentions the coming together of the believers at Troas 'on the first day of the week' in order to 'break bread', and to hear Paul teach, it is incorrect to identify this as a celebration of 'the Lord's Supper'.[96] Such gatherings were quite informal expressions of what was later more structured and organized. The reality of Christian fellowship was expressed from the earliest times, as Jesus intended it, in the ordinary activity of eating together. Yet these meals were presumably given a special character by teaching, prayer and praise, focussing on the person and work of their Lord (e.g., they ate together 'with glad and sincere hearts, praising God', 2:46–7). Perhaps the grace at the beginning or end of the meal focussed particularly on the person and work of the Lord Jesus, reminding the believers of the basis of their fellowship in him.

The use of the definite article and the plural in the expression 'the prayers' (*tais proseuchais*, 2:42) suggests that the reference is to *specific prayers* rather than to prayer in general (NIV, 'to prayer'). In the context, this most obviously points to their continuing participation in the set times of prayer at the temple (3:1; cf. 2:46). However, their eating together in households involved 'praising God' (2:47) and must also have involved prayer in the strict sense of petition. Other references to Christian assembly in Acts indicate that they met specifically for thanksgiving and prayer (4:23–31); teaching (11:25–6); prayer (12:5,12); prayer with fasting and prophecy (13:1–3); listening to a report from returning missionaries (14:27); listening to a letter from the Jerusalem council and being exhorted by two prophets (15:30–2); teaching in the context of a meal (20:7–12); and teaching and prayer (20:17–36).

While such passages suggest some parallel with the activities of the synagogue, it must be stressed that Luke presents the community life of the earliest Christians in terms that set it apart from Pharisaical Judaism, with its focus on the study and application of the law. Only a very general correspondence between certain features of the synagogue and Christian gatherings may be discerned from the evidence of Acts.[97] Again, although parallels might be drawn with the Qumran community, there is nothing of the monastic lifestyle, with its focus on ritual and moral regulations, in Luke's presentation of early Christianity. Rather, there is an awareness of being the community of the End time, loosed from the strictures of Judaism, focussing on Jesus and the prophetic Scriptures, with distinctive forms of prayer and praise, relating to one another and serving one another in everyday contexts such as the household.

Serving God when the Church Gathers

Paul's single application of the common worship term *proskynein* is in 1 Cor. 14:24–5, where he mentions the possibility of an unbelieving 'outsider' entering a church gathering when 'all prophesy'. Being convicted of sin, and falling on his face, such a person may 'worship God' (*proskynēsei tǭ theǭ*) and acknowledge his presence among them, thus fulfilling prophecies such as Isa. 45:14. The worship described here is *an act of submission or unconditional surrender to God*, similar to the spontaneous response of people in the Old Testament to divine disclosures (e.g. Gen. 24:26–7; Exod. 4:31; 34:8). Such language implies the conversion of the unbeliever, with the gesture expressing repentance and faith. Although the apostle does not use *proskynein* in connection with the regular gathering of God's people for prayer, praise and mutual encouragement, it is significant that this passage, with its focus on the mutual ministry of all who are prophesying, suggests that God presences himself in a distinctive way in the Christian meeting *through his word and the operation of his Spirit*.[98] The apostle expects that God may be encountered when the church gathers for mutual edification – in the relationships and ministries that the Spirit enables in the body of Christ.

In fact, Paul regularly uses the terminology of *edification*, rather than worship, to describe the purpose and function of Christian gatherings (e.g., 1 Cor.14:3–5,12,17,26,31; 1 Thess. 5:11; Eph.4:11–16), and this concept deserves special attention in connection with our topic. The verb *oikodomein* is used outside the New Testament quite literally for the building of houses, temples and other structures, and figuratively for the establishment of individuals or nations in some situation or way of life. In the LXX it regularly translates the Hebrew *bānāh* in contexts where either a literal or a figurative activity of building may be on view (cf. 2 Sam.7.11–13, where both senses are found). Similarly, in the New Testament both senses of 'building' are found in the usage of this verb. The substantive *oikodomē* is common in Koine Greek but not in earlier stages in the development of the language. It can refer to the act of building (e.g. 2 Cor.10:8) or to the construction which is the result of building (e.g. Matt.24.1).

In contemporary English, to say that something was 'edifying' usually means that it was personally helpful or encouraging. It is easy to misinterpret Paul and to think of edification purely in terms of the spiritual advancement of individuals within the church. As with many other biblical concepts, there is a redemptive-historical framework to be understood before we can apply the apostolic teaching. Paul's notion has its point of departure primarily in the prophetic literature of the Old Testament, where the restoration of Israel after the judgment of exile is promised in terms of God *building a people for himself* (e.g., Jer.24:6; 31:4; 33:7). To 'plant' and to 'build' go together: the opposite is to 'tear down' and 'uproot' (Jer.1:10; 24:6). God does this work by putting his words in the mouths of his prophets (Jer.1:9–10). Furthermore, he promises that if Israel's enemies learn the ways of his people and swear by his name they shall be 'built up' or 'established' among his people (Jer.12:14–17).

From Eph.4:7–11 we learn that Christ builds his church through the people he provides as apostles, prophets, evangelists and pastor-teachers. Priority is given in this context to word ministries (cf. 2:20–2). These people are 'to prepare God's people for works of service, so that the body of Christ may be built up' (4:12).[99] Just as Jeremiah was told that the message given to him by God would be the means of re-establishing Israel (Jer.1.9–10; 24:6), so also the church is built through the preaching of the gospel. From Rom.15:20 it is clear that *oikodomein* primarily refers to Paul's work of evangelism and church planting. However, the use of *oikodomē* in passages like 2 Cor.10:8; 12:19; 13:10 suggests that edification involves also a process of teaching and encouragement beyond the initial task of evangelism. It involves 'founding, maintaining and advancing the congregation',[100] as God's eschatological 'building'.

The concept of edification blends with that of the church as the body of Christ in Eph.4:12–16. Paul's ideal is that the members of the body be 'rightly related to one another, each making its own contribution, according to the measure of its gifts and function, to the upbuilding of the whole in love'.[101] Edification occurs when Christians *minister to one another in word and deed*, seeking to express and encourage a Christ-centred faith, hope and love. Clearly this ought to take place when the congregation meets together but also as individuals have the opportunity to minister to one another in everyday life situations (cf. 1 Cor.8:1,10; 10:23). However, it must be stressed that Paul's primary focus here is not on the need for individual growth to maturity but for individuals to learn to contribute to the life and development of the Christian community. The expression *eis oikodomēn heautou en agapę* (lit. 'for its own upbuilding in love', Eph. 4:16) clearly affirms this corporate focus. The same expression reminds us that although the church has been 'built (by God) upon the foundation of the apostles and prophets' (2:20) it is far from being a completed house of God (cf. 2:22). 'It is both complete and yet it grows. It is a heavenly entity and yet it is an earthly reality. And it is both present and future, with a consummation occurring at the parousia.'[102]

With the metaphor that the congregation is God's 'building' (*oikodomē*, 1 Cor.3:9) goes the notion that Jesus Christ is the 'foundation' and Paul the 'skilled master of works' (*architektōn*, 3:10),[103] who lays the foundation through his evangelistic ministry. In this theological framework Paul warns about the way in which others build on the foundation (vv.10–15). As the divine 'sanctuary' (*naos tou theou*, vv.16–17) where God's Spirit dwells, the Corinthian congregation must be wary of defiling and destroying that dwelling-place of God by party-spirit and quarrelling.[104] The *congregation* is where the sacred presence of God is to be found. Paul's teaching is obscured when notions of holiness are transferred to the building where the congregation meets. The acknowledgement of God's special presence amongst his people and the preservation of the sanctity of the congregation is to take place not by ritual or ceremony but by the pursuit of edification!

The terminology of edification occurs more frequently in 1 Corinthians 14 than in any other chapter of the New Testament and is clearly significant in the development of Paul's argument there about the relative value of prophecy over against tongues. The context indicates that the first issue is *intelligibility*. Being 'inspired' is not enough: when Christians gather together words should convey meaningful truth. The one who speaks in a tongue speaks not to people but to God, 'for no one understands him, but he utters mysteries in the Spirit.' On the other hand, he who prophesies speaks to people 'for their upbuilding and encouragement and consolation' (vv.2–3). Only speech that can be understood by others has the potential for building up or edifying the congregation. Paul may not be saying that prophecy is the *greatest* of the gifts on some absolute scale, but only that it is more important than tongues on the scale of reference adopted.[105]

The tongues-speaker 'edifies himself' (v.4), but the person who prophesies 'edifies the church'. Paul does not rebuke the tongues-speaker for self-edification as such but indicates that *this falls short of the primary goal of Christian assembly* (cf. vv.16–17).[106] Individuals intent on edifying themselves may simply 'seal themselves off from others and concentrate exclusively on their personal experiences'.[107] Paul's teaching challenges the common assumption that church services should be designed primarily to facilitate and encourage a private communion with God, either by spiritual exercises or ritual. The apostle envisages that we come together to draw on the resources of Christ for spiritual growth by the giving and receiving of ministries directed to one another.

To pursue what is beneficial for the church is to fulfil the opening injunction of 1 Corinthians 14 ('Make love your aim') and to apply the teaching of chapter 13. In effect, the argument here, as in Eph. 4:15, is that *speaking the truth in love* is the means by which edification takes place. This emphasis is continued in vv.6–19, where the focus is on bringing to the congregation 'some revelation or knowledge or prophecy or teaching'. Public praying and singing must also be intelligible and truthful so that others may be able to say the 'Amen' and be edified (vv.16–17). It is interesting to note that Paul speaks again of the individual being edified in v.17. Although he is concerned that the Corinthians should abound in spiritual gifts 'for the building up of the church' (v.12), it is clear that such edification cannot take place unless individuals are instructed (v.19) and encouraged (v.31). On the other hand, the chapter emphasizes that edification involves ministry to the congregation *as a body*, and a concern to enhance the life of the church as *a community*.

More precisely, the very act of ministering the truth to one another should be *an exercise of love*: only when a church is functioning in this way can it be said that it is being edified. For this reason, Paul concentrates in vv.26–40 on the manner in which gifts are to be exercised in the congregation. This section begins with the challenge, 'Let all things be done for edification' (v.26) and concludes with the injunction, 'Let all things be done decently and in order' (v.40). Order and not disorder will be a sign of the Spirit's presence and control, since 'God is not a God of disorder but of peace' (v.33). Only one person may speak at a time and only a certain number may speak on each occasion. Encouraging others to exercise their gifts is an aspect of edification. The majority, including those wishing to contribute, should listen in silence and 'weigh what is said' (v.29). Listening with discernment is also part of the task of edifying the congregation, even though it appears to be such a passive role! The aim of these and other controls is 'that all may learn and be encouraged' (v.31).

Intercession, thanksgiving and praise play a very significant role in Paul's letters, as he reports his own personal practice, incorporates wish-prayers or expressions of praise at appropriate points in his argument, and urges his readers to glorify God by following his example. These elements of Jewish worship, transformed in terms of gospel perspectives, were clearly central to the apostle's view of the Christian life and, by implication, the Christian meeting.[108] In Col.3:16 and Eph.5:19, the God-directed ministry of prayer or praise and the notion of edification are intimately linked. Even 'psalms and hymns and spiritual songs', which are *expressions of faith and thankfulness to God*, are to be considered simultaneously as the means of *teaching and admonishing one another*. This does not mean that prayer or praise is a means to an end, namely edification. We worship God because of who he is and because of his grace towards us. However, participating in the edification of the church is an important expression of our devotion and service to God. God is glorified by the growth of the church towards the goals he has set for it.

Mutual ministry is a way by which 'the word of Christ' may dwell richly amongst believers (Col. 3:16), and thus the Lord Jesus himself may be present in their midst, to minister to them and meet their needs through his Spirit. Through the exercise of gifts and ministries, the exalted Christ manifests his presence and encourages and nurtures the faith of his flock. They acknowledge his presence by responding appropriately to those gifts and ministries with expressions of faith. However, those expressions of faith themselves become a means of further encouragement and ministry to the body!

The Corinthian Lord's Supper

Paul's first reference to what he later calls 'the Lord's Supper' is in the context of urging the Corinthians not to attend pagan meals (1 Cor. 10:14–22). The unique relationship shared by Christians with their Lord, and expressed by eating together in his name, makes any association with demon-worshippers at idolatrous feasts an impossibility. Those who participate in pagan sacrifices are 'partners with demons' (*koinōnoi tōn daimoniōn*, 1 Cor. 10:20). By implication, those who 'drink the cup of the Lord' and 'partake of the table of the Lord' are partners with Christ and express their fellowship with him in the common meal.[109]

The final cup at a Jewish meal, for which God was 'blessed' or 'thanked', was called 'the cup of blessing',[110] and this was the cup interpreted by Jesus as 'the new covenant in my blood' at the conclusion of the Last Supper (cf. 1 Cor. 11:25). With the use of this expression Paul implies that some form of thanksgiving for the death of Jesus was associated with drinking together at the Corinthian meals. The 'cup of blessing' was a means by which they demonstrated a 'comon participation' (*koinōnia*) in 'the blood of Christ' –

namely 'in the benefits of Christ's passion'.[111] The idea of sharing in the benefits of the covenant established by Christ in his death meant that they did not consider their table to be an altar where sacrifice was taking place, but 'a fellowship meal where in the presence of the Spirit they were by faith looking back to the singular sacrifice that had been made and were thus realizing again its benefits in their lives'.[112]

'The bread that we break' also recalls the language of the Jewish meal (cf. Acts 2:46; 20:7, 11; 27:35). Eating together, with a focus on Christ's death and its implications for congregational life, is a means of expressing 'a common participation in the body of Christ'. To eat the 'one loaf' is to share with others in 'that company which, through its union with Christ, has by anticipation entered upon the new age which lies beyond the resurrection'.[113] Paul provides a theological rationale for the fellowship meals that were characteristic of Christianity from the beginning. A Christian congregation is not an ordinary association like a club, where people simply meet because of common interests or ideals: it is a gathering that arises out of *sharing together in the benefits of Christ's saving work*. The general flow of the argument in 1 Corinthians 11–14 suggests that the exercise of gifts and ministries was associated with such common meals, further expressing what it meant to be the Messiah's community.

Paul's encouragement to the Corinthians to recognize their unity in the body of Christ as they ate from 'one loaf' (1 Cor. 10:17) prepares for the extended argument of 11:17–34 about divisions in their meetings. These divisions appear to have had a *social dimension* – the 'haves' devouring their own supper at the meal and failing to share with the 'have nots' (v. 21)[114] – as well as a *theological dimension* – not treating one another as fellow members of Christ. By humiliating those who had nothing, those with plenty to eat and drink were 'despising the church of God' (v. 22).

Their behaviour indicated to the apostle that their 'gathering together as the church' was for the worse rather than the better, and that it was not, in fact, 'the Lord's Supper' that they were eating (v. 20)! The noun *deipnon* ('supper') was used in the Hellenistic world for the main meal of the day, usually eaten toward evening or at night. The adjective *kyriakon* ordinarily meant 'belonging to the Lord' but may have been understood in this context to mean 'in honour of the Lord'.[115] As long as individuals were pre-occupied with consuming *their own private meals* (*to idion deipnon*, v. 21), they could not possibly be holding a community meal in honour of the Lord Jesus.

Their purpose in gathering was to share an ordinary meal together (v. 33 '. . . when you come together *to eat*'). However, the technical expressions 'the cup of blessing which we bless' and 'the bread that we break' (10:16), in association with Paul's reminder about the tradition concerning the Last Supper (11:23–5), imply that their common meals were to have a special character. In Jewish fashion, they presumably began their supper with a thanksgiving in connection with the breaking of bread and concluded with a thanksgiving over the shared cup.[116] Jesus' teaching and example at the Last Supper should have transformed these Jewish customs for them into expressions of new covenant theology. In reality, the tradition about the Last Supper was not being observed (v. 23; cf. v. 2), because they were *not reflecting the true meaning of that meal in their life together*.

In v. 26 Paul asserts that eating the bread and drinking the cup is a means of proclaiming the Lord's death until he comes, a means of reminding one another of the significance of his sacrifice. By their disregard for one another they were *negating the very point of that death* – 'to create a new people for his name, in which the old distinctions based on human fallenness no longer obtain.'[117] The paragraph that follows warns them of the dire consequences of continuing to eat and drink 'without discerning the body' (vv. 27–32), that is, without recognizing the significance of their partnership in the body of Christ. The Corinthians were to receive or welcome one another as fellow believers at 'the Lord's table' and to satisfy their personal needs at home if necessary (vv. 33–4).[118]

Although the terminology of edification is not used in 1 Corinthians 11, the issue of *edifying the church* is undoubtedly prominent. The Lord's Supper, which has so often throughout church history been understood as a means of deepening the personal communion of believers with their Lord, is clearly meant to focus the eyes of the participants on *one another* as well as on God. We do not simply meet to have fellowship with God but to minister to one another as we express our common participation in Christ as our Saviour and Lord. It is the 'horizontal' significance of the Lord's Supper that is so often played down in contemporary practice. Yet, according to Paul, those who disregard their responsibility to welcome and care for fellow believers in the local congregation cannot worship or serve God acceptably!

Worship in Church and in the World

Paul's application of transformed worship terminology to the work of Christ, the preaching of the gospel, and the new life-orientation of believers, testifies to the understanding of *a new kind of worship*:

> The New Testament knows no holy persons who substitutionally perform the service of God for the whole people of God, nor holy places and seasons or holy acts, which create a distance between the cultus and the life of every day and every place. All members of the church have access to God (Rom. 5:2) and a share in the Holy Spirit; all of life is service to God; there is no 'profane' area.[119]

This revolutionary use of the terminology of worship with reference to a Christ-centred, gospel-serving, life-orientation is obscured by the common practice in the English-speaking world of restricting any talk of worship to what is done 'in church'. Furthermore, people who emphasize that they are 'going to church to worship God' tend to disregard what the New Testament says about the primary purpose of the Christian assembly. If Christians are meant to worship God in every sphere of life, it cannot be worship as such that brings them to church. 'Corporate worship' may express more accurately what is involved, but Paul's emphasis is on coming together to participate in the edification of the congregation.[120]

To put the focus on edification is not to suggest that the church service is the one area of the Christian life where we do not worship God! The evidence assessed so far suggests that *the exercise of gifts* in any context may be regarded as an expression of worship, if the ministries are genuinely for the benefit of others and for the glory of God.[121] While all ministry must be understood as a response to God's grace, and not in any sense a cultivation of his favour, ministry to others is an aspect of our service or self-giving to God. Moreover, edification is really God's work in our midst.

At the heart of Christian gatherings there should be a concern to proclaim and apply the truths of the gospel, to keep the focus on God's gracious initiative, to stimulate and maintain saving faith and *to elicit appropriate expressions of that faith in the assembly and in everyday life*. Prayer and praise are clearly worship when they are faith responses to the gospel. To highlight the importance of everyday obedience by playing down the significance of corporate prayer and praise is to attack one error with another!

It may be best to speak of congregational worship as a particular expression of the total life-response that is the worship of the new covenant. Inasmuch as we meet to encounter Christ in one another, for the giving and receiving of ministries and for corporate prayer and praise, we meet to worship or engage with God. However, such a description of the church meeting should not be allowed to obscure the centrality of edification to the purpose of the gathering. If the focus of the meeting is on the edification of the church, this should enable God's people to engage with him afresh and to offer themselves to him in the way that he requires and himself makes possible through the Holy Spirit. Thus, the 'vertical' and the 'horizontal' dimensions of what takes place should not be artificially separated. One part of the meeting cannot be 'the worship time' (e.g., prayer and praise) and another part 'the edification time' (e.g., preaching), since Paul's teaching encourages us to view edification and worship occurring together.

The church meeting should not be regarded as a means to an end – a preparation for worship and witness in everyday life – but as 'the focus-point of that whole wider worship which is the continually repeated self-surrender of the Christian in obedience of life'.[122] The church is at the centre of God's redemptive purposes for the universe (cf. Eph. 3:10–11), the earthly and temporal anticipation of the fellowship of the new creation, where God will be served without compromise or hindrance (cf. Rev. 7:15; 22:3). Ministry exercised in love amongst the people of God is a sign of the Spirit's transforming power already at work in those who believe. Yet Christ claims absolute lordship over this whole fallen world and desires that his people should live to the praise of his glory in every context. Thus, the Christian gathering should not simply focus on the spiritual and psychological needs of the participants but on God's purposes for his creation and his intention 'to bring all things on heaven and on earth together under one head, even Christ' (Eph. 1:10).

Christian Assembly in Hebrews

It was noted above that in Hebrews the locus of Christian worship is to be the heavenly sanctuary, where Christ is seated at the right hand of God. Put another way, the goal of the Christian life is to share in the eschatological assembly of God's people, which Christ has made possible by his high-priestly ministry. Meanwhile, there is a need to encourage fellow believers in faith, hope, and love, lest any should fall by the wayside and fail to share in this heavenly inheritance.

The writer does not apply the language of worship specifically to what goes on when Christians meet together on earth. Urging his readers not to forsake the assembling of themselves together, 'as some are in the habit of doing', his emphasis is on the need for *mutual encouragement*, not for corporate worship (10:24–5). The specific terminology of edification is not used but related concepts are found in key contexts. The appeal to 'consider one another' (*katanoōmen allēlous*, 10:24) implies thoughtful reflection on the needs of others in the Christian fellowship and recalls the the challenge of 3:12 for each one to 'take care' (*blepete*) with respect to the spiritual health of the congregation. The following expression (*eis paroxysmon agapēs kai kalōn ergōn*) points to the goal of constantly *rousing or provoking one another to godly living*, no matter how much 'love and good works' may have been demonstrated in the past (cf. 10:32–4)! Such a stimulus to godliness will not simply come by the setting of a good example. The attached clauses in 10:25 indicate that it will mean not forsaking their assembly but positively using every such occasion as a means of mutual encouragement or exhortation. The concept is not that of self protection by staying in the fold but of a positive responsibility to minister to other believers.

It may be appropriate to render *parakalountes* in 10:25 more generally as 'encouraging (one another)', although provoking one another to love and good works clearly demands more than just being present at the church meeting and participating enthusiastically! In a parallel passage ('exhort one another every day, as long as it is called "today", that none of you may be hardened by the deceitfulness of sin', 3:12–13), the RSV rightly translates *parakaleite* 'exhort', since the context demands something stronger than 'encourage' (NEB, NIV). The need for *warning on the basis of Scriptural teaching is on view*, together with the sort of encouragement to persevere suggested by the writer's own exposition of the truths of the gospel.[123]

One of the features of Hebrews is its emphasis on the care that members of the church should have for each other. They should take care lest *any* of their number (3:12) has a sinful, unbelieving heart, and exhort one another lest *any* should be hardened by sin's deceitfulnes (3:13). The writer's desire for *each one* of them to show 'the same earnestness in realizing the full assurance of hope until the end' (6:11) leads him to challenge them to minister to one another again in 10:24–5 and in 12:12–17. 'If there should be a concern of the individual for the community ("exhort one another"), there should also be a concern of the community for the individual ("lest any one of you . . . "), in line with the teaching of Paul that "if one member suffers, all suffer together" (1 Cor. 12:26)'.[124]

The exhortation in 10:24–5 clearly outlines the purpose of the congregational gathering as *mutual ministry with an eschatological focus* ('encourage one another – and all the more as you see the Day approaching'). Faith, hope and love are to be expressed in the fellowship of God's people because that is the way worship is offered to God in every context. However, the church meeting has the special task of enabling believers to *maintain* their confidence in Christ 'firmly to the end' (cf. 3:12–14), no matter what trials they may be enduring. Our writer has nothing of the elaborate teaching of Paul about spiritual gifts but he is no less insistent on the importance of mutual ministry in the congregation so that God's purposes for the church may be fulfilled in the world.

Meeting together with Christians on earth is a way of expressing our participation in that eschatological community, gathered, cleansed and consecrated to God by Messiah's work (cf. 12:22–4). We are to think of drawing near to God as a corporate activity and the Christian assembly as an occasion for realizing together the benefits of the gospel. Looked at another way, we meet to encourage one another to maintain our confidence in Jesus and his promises before unbelievers in everyday life situations (10: 23, 35; 13:15) and to stimulate one another to serve him with gratitude, reverence and awe (12:28–9). All this will happen when Christians exhort one another on the basis of gospel truths and care for one another in other practical ways, engaging with God in prayer and praise, but also in obedient service to others.

The emphasis on mutual exhortation in Hebrews recalls Paul's teaching about the value and importance of spontaneous, verbal ministries of exhortation, comfort or admonition by congregational members (e.g., 1 Cor. 14:26–33; 1 Thes. 4:18; 5:11, 14; Eph. 4:15). Such mutual ministry in our churches today is often confined to the home group, or to times of personal interaction after public services. Why is it not also encouraged in the formal gathering of the whole church? Many Christian traditions rightly emphasize the need for regular and systematic exposition of Scripture and the teaching of 'sound doctrine' by those gifted and appointed for this task (cf. 1 Tim. 4:6, 11, 13; 5:17; 2 Tim. 2:1–2, 14–15; 4:1–5; Tit. 1:9).[125] However, if the balance of New Testament teaching is to be preserved, should there not be some space for the informal contributions of members?

WORSHIP IN THE REVELATION TO JOHN

It is not possible to deal with the theme of worship in every New Testament book, but the Revelation to John certainly cannot be excluded from our study. Visions of the heavenly realm consistently portray the offering of adoration and praise to God and the Lamb and the language of worship pervades the whole document. Most significantly, *proskynein* is used 24 times, in such a way as to suggest that it is a key to unlocking the author's theology of worship. In a sense, the theme of the entire prophecy is the distinction between true worship and idolatry.[126] John's perspective forms a fitting climax to this survey of the theme of worship in the New Testament.

Worship on Earth

It is clear from the general reference in Rev. 9:20 that a large proportion of humanity is envisaged as worshipping 'demons and idols of gold and silver and bronze and stone and wood, which cannot either see or hear or walk'. Participation in the cults of paganism is linked with murders, sorceries, immorality and thefts, as an expression of the rebellion of humanity against the rule of the true and living God. However, the focus in the rest of the Apocalypse is specifically on the worship of 'the beast' which comes up 'out of the sea' (13:4,8,12,15; 14:9,11; 16:2; 19:20; 20:4). Most commentators agree that the primary reference is to the aggressive programme of Caesar – worship being forced upon the population of the Roman Empire in the latter part of the first century.

The imperial cult was a means of maintaining the unity of the Empire: the loyalty of the citizens was fostered by ceremonies taken from religion and focussed on the emperor. Religious, political, social and economic realities were thus linked together. Participation in the imperial cult helped people to affirm the values of their society and 'to express their own interest in the preservation of the world in which they lived.'[127]

From John's point of view, to engage in the imperial cult is to worship 'the dragon' ('that ancient serpent called the devil or Satan, who leads the whole world astray', 12:9), since he gives his authority to the beast (13:4). John sees also a second beast coming up 'out of the earth', 'who exercises all the authority of the first beast on his behalf', and whose task is to make the earth and its inhabitants worship the first beast (13:11–12). Its use of great signs to deceive people suggests that this beast represents 'the role of false religion in effecting the capitulation of mankind to the worship of the secular power'.[128] Those who will not worship the image of the first beast are to be slain (13:15). Only those who worship the first beast receive the mark on the right hand or the forehead, enabling them to buy and sell in the commerce of the empire. Clearly, economic privation or death await those who refuse to participate in the emperor-cult.[129]

John's Apocalypse teaches that 'the conflict between God and Satan takes historical form in the conflict of human allegiances manifest in *worship*.'[130] Satan works through the ordinary structures of society, as well as through the deceits of false religion, to capture the allegiance of people and to turn them from the service of God. John directs his original readers to recognize the religious dimension to their involvement in the Greco-Roman world. While some New Testament writers stress the importance of honouring and obeying the governing authorities (e.g. Rom. 13:1–7; 1 Pet. 2:13–17), John sees the need to warn Christians about rendering to God 'the things that are God's (cf. Mk. 12:17.)

The frightening prophecy of persecution for Christians who refuse to worship the beast and to bear its mark (13:1–18) is followed by a vision of 'the Lamb, standing on Mount Zion, and with him 144,000 who had his name and his Father's name written on their foreheads' (14:1–5). John intersperses glimpses of the final blessedness of God's people among his visions of judgment so as to encourage them to patient endurance and faithfulness in the present. Those who are 'redeemed from the earth' are engaged in the worship of heaven, as they sing a new song before the throne and before the four living creatures and the elders and 'follow the Lamb wherever he goes'. The implication is clear: *only those who abstain from worshipping the beast on earth will share, by God's grace, in the worship of heaven.* John then goes on to give the message of three angels, each of which relates to the conflict of worship previously highlighted.

The first angel summons people from every nation and tribe and tongue to 'fear God and give him glory, because the hour of his judgment has come'. (and to) 'worship (*proskynēsate*) him who made the heavens, the earth, the sea and the springs of water' (14:6–7). This 'eternal gospel' recalls the vision of Revelation 4 and summons the whole creation to acknowledge God as Creator and Lord of history. Notwithstanding the message of God's redeeming grace in Christ which is so prominent in this book, the doctrine of creation, with the consequent notion that every human being is accountable to God, is shown to be the fundamental reason for honouring God as God or worshipping him (cf. Rom. 1:18–25; Acts 14:15–17; 17:22–31). This passage suggests again that evangelism can be viewed from one perspective as a *call to worship God*.

The second angel reinforces the proclamation that 'the hour of his judgment has come' by announcing the fall of 'Babylon the Great' (14:8). The third angel decrees that those who worship the beast and bear his mark suffer a terrible fate *at the hands of God* (14:9–11). When the terrible fury of God is poured out upon them, 'there is no rest day or night for those who worship the beast and his image, or for anyone who receives the mark of his name'. God's wrath against the worshippers of the beast is then portrayed in 16:2 and the punishment of the beast and the false prophet who had persuaded people to worship the beast is recorded in 19:20.

The worship of the beast, which is effectively the worship of Satan, involves literally paying homage to an image in Revelation 13, but more profoundly *giving that allegiance to the State that belongs to God*: a life orientation as well as involvement in the emperor-cult. What, then, is the nature of Christian worship in the earthly sphere, according to John the Seer? The angelic summons to worship God alone (14:6–7;19:10; 22:8–9), broadly calls for *submission and undivided allegiance to the Creator*. However, beyond that, *proskynein* is not specifically applied to what Christians do here and now, even though it is liberally used in the visions of heaven.

Although it is not called worship as such, there is a clear alternative for Christians to the worship of the beast. In 14:12, following the portrayal of the judgment of God on all idolaters, John's call is for 'patient endurance on the part of the saints who obey God's commandments and remain faithful to Jesus' (cf. 13:10). The writer's aim is not simply negative: to warn Christians of the persecution they must endure or of the danger of giving into Satan's demands and becoming apostate. He writes positively to encourage his readers to persevere in their obedience to divine revelation, to continue in their reliance on Jesus and his saving work, and to hold fast to the testimony about the future sent to them by the risen Christ (cf. 22:16–20). Such verses function, in effect, to define Christian worship *as the ongoing expression of Christian faith and obedience in each and every circumstance of life*. By implication, the worship of Christians on earth is the exact opposite to the worship of the beast and involves giving proper allegiance to God and the Lamb in everyday situations. In 22:6–15, the worship of God is closely associated with keeping the words of this prophecy and living in a godly way as the consummation of history is awaited.

Worship in the Heavenly Realm

In the context of this call for Christians to remain faithful to Christ and not to miss out on the joy of serving God and the Lamb in the new Jerusalem, John presents a series of visions featuring the worship of the heavenly assembly. The sense of paying homage to God by some literal act of obeisance in his presence is suggested by the regular coupling of *proskynein* with the verb *piptein*, 'to fall down' (4:10; 5:14; 7:11; 11:16; 19:4) or by the expression 'worship before you' (*proskynēsousin enōpion sou*, 15:4), with respect to God. Nevertheless, the worship envisaged is not simply an act of physical obeisance but *an acknowledgement of God's character and purposes*, as revealed in his righteous acts.

The connection between worship and the revelation of God's character and purposes is made clear by the fact that at strategic points in the Apocalypse, the heavenly host falls down and worships God and the Lamb, ascribing certain characteristics and mighty acts to them. Here it is significant to notice that *verbs of saying and singing are regularly coupled with the verb 'to worship'*. The first vision in Revelation 4 is fundamental to the teaching of the book, since it establishes God's absolute sovereignty over his creation and the fact that all life exists to reflect his glory and honour and power. The honour that is paid to God in the heavenly realm contrasts dramatically with the situation on earth, where few hold fast to his words and serve him faithfully. The same heavenly host sings a 'new song' to Christ as the Lamb in 5:9–10, falling on their faces before him, as he is revealed to be the only one worthy to open the scroll and its seven seals, thus setting in motion the final events of human history. His worthiness has to do with his redemptive work, which is briefly recounted in a credal form addressed directly to Christ:

> You are worthy to take the scroll and to open the seals, because you were slain, and with your blood you purchased men for God from every tribe and language and people and nation. You have made them to be a kingdom and priests to serve our God, and they will reign on the earth.

A further ascription of praise to Christ as the Lamb follows in 5:12, echoing to some extent the language of 4:11 ('Worthy is the Lamb, who was slain, to receive power and wealth and wisdom and strength and honour and glory and praise!'). Indeed the parallels between 4:9–11 and 5:8–12 make it clear that *Christ is being adored on absolutely equal terms with God the Creator!*[131] Christ is not an alternative object of worship but *shares in the glory due to God*.

When the Lamb opens the seals to inaugurate a series of judgments on the earth (6:1–17), those who are redeemed from the nations are pictured as standing before God and the Lamb, crying out with a loud voice, 'Salvation belongs to our God who sits on the throne and to the Lamb' (7:9–10), while the angels, the elders and the four living creatures fall down on their faces and worship God with another hymn of praise (7:11–12). The chapter concludes with an identification of the redeemed as those who have 'come out of the great tribulation; they have washed their robes and made them white in the blood of the Lamb' (v. 14). The victory of Christ in his death and resurrection has become their victory, and now they are 'before the throne of God and serve (*latreuousin*) him day and night in his temple' (v. 15).

With the sounding of the seventh trumpet in 11:15–19, loud voices in heaven proclaim that 'the kingdom of the world has become the kingdom of our Lord and of his Christ, and he will reign for ever and ever'. This provokes the twenty-four elders, who are seated on their thrones before God, to fall on their faces and worship God with an outburst of thanksgiving. They are grateful because God has exercised his power and exercised his reign over rebellious men and women by *inaugurating the final judgment*. The response to the outpouring of God's wrath in 16:5–7 is similar in sentiment. Again, in 19:1–9, after the destruction of 'Babylon the Great', a roar of praise goes up from the great multitude in heaven, glorifying God for his judgments which are 'true and just' and rejoicing that final salvation, here pictured as 'the wedding supper of the Lamb', has come for the benefit all who fear him, 'both small and great'. It would appear from this context that *rejoicing in God, giving him the glory and praising him are all different aspects of homage or worship* (note especially 19:4). Such adoration and praise occurs in the Apocalypse as the events of the End time are unfolded or as the saving work of God in Christ is recalled.

The Link Between Heaven and Earth

The obvious applicability of the doxologies, acclamations and hymns of praise in the Apocalypse to Christian congregational worship has led some scholars to propose that the writer used sentences and phrases taken from pre-existing liturgical sources in the first century.[132] Others have argued that Revelation presupposes a whole pattern of worship in the churches addressed by John, largely influenced by contemporary Jewish practices in temple and synagogue, or by those services together with aspects of the imperial and ruler cults of the Hellenistic world.[133] However, although elements of Christian and Jewish services may have been interwoven in the portrayal of the heavenly worship, it is now impossible to separate the details and see the basic lines of the primitive Christian service.

The elements of the heavenly worship in the Apocalypse have their own special function in the book as a whole: 'They interpret the apocalyptic events, the peculiar meaning of which would not be completely clear without such interpretation. For this reason, they are quite closely linked, as regards their contents at any rate, with the visions of the future.'[134] John has made eschatological drama unfold from a cultic setting: the heavenly liturgy regularly proclaims eschatological realities prior to their presentation in narrative form. In particular it is important to notice that the hymnic material emphasizes the victory already accomplished by Jesus through his death and heavenly exaltation. The scenes of heavenly worship express fundamental theological truths represented in other ways elsewhere in the New Testament. By this means, John leaves his readers in no doubt that *the end has come in the historic events of Jesus of Nazareth.*[135]

If, as I have suggested, the implication of the Apocalypse is that 'worship' here on earth is offered to Christ *in everyday life*, as Christians maintain their faith in him and resist every temptation to idolatry and apostasy, the hymnic material, with its focus on the sovereignty of God and the victory of the Lamb, would have provided every encouragement to honour God, rather than the dragon and the beast. By implication, a theology of the Christian gathering emerges here. In the process of living out their obedience to God, meeting to hear 'the words of the prophecy of this book' (22:18) would be a significant aid to keeping them (22:7). A logical response to the hearing of this prophecy in the congregation would be to acknowledge the kingship of God with acclamations and songs and to echo the praise of the heavenly host for the fulfilment of his redemptive purposes in Christ, even before the final outworking of those events in history.

Against those who have argued that John has made the worship of heaven in some way a reflection of what was going on in the churches of Asia in the first century, it is more reasonable to suggest that the reverse is true. John wrote to encourage his readers *to reflect the pattern of the heavenly assembly in their life on earth*, not only when they gathered but whenever they were faced with any new sign of the dragon's power or with any manifestation of God's wrath. John is not simply concerned that the churches sing the same songs as the heavenly assembly but that they reflect the same confidence in God. With the qualification that Christian worship in the Apocalypse means more than singing hymns in church on Sunday, it is correct to assert that 'in its innermost meaning primitive Christian Worship was intended to be parallel to the Worship of heaven'.[136]

CONCLUSIONS

Apart from references to the Jewish cult or to the practices of paganism, the terminology of worship is consistently used in the New Testament in a way that indicates the fulfilment of the institutions of priesthood, sacrifice and holy place by Jesus in his death, resurrection and heavenly exaltation. In terms of Old Testament prophecy, he has inaugurated the new covenant, with its promise of a renewed relationship with God; he has poured out the Spirit on all God's people, enabling them to serve him as the community of the End time; and he has secured for them the promised inheritance of the kingdom of God. Where the terminology of worship is applied to believers it highlights the nature of the relationship with God which Jesus has made possible. Every sphere of life provides the Christian with the opportunity to glorify and serve God, in grateful response to the work of Jesus. But worship language is used quite specifically in several contexts with reference to gospel preaching and ministries that support gospel work. Submission to Jesus as Lord and Saviour is the fundamental act of worship under the new covenant, and evangelism is the means by which such homage is brought about.

The purpose and function of Christian gatherings is not simply 'worship' but edification of the congregation through the various ministries provided by the Lord himself. Even specifically God-directed activities such as prayer and praise must be for the building up of God's people. However, ministry to one another is clearly a way of serving or worshipping God. In other words, there is a certain overlap between edification and what we may call congregational worship. This review of New Testament priorities for the church meeting suggests that many of our contemporary perspectives and practices ought to be re-assessed. In particular, we need to consider the relationship between what we do 'in church' and the worship of everyday life.

In its meetings 'the peculiar character of the church in the world is disclosed in an exemplary way, just as the indwelling of Christ in his church becomes manifest through the proclamation of the gospel, the observance of the Lord's Supper, the promise given, and the benediction pronounced in his name (cf., e.g., 2 Cor. 1:20; Col. 3:16; 2 Cor. 13:14, *et al.*).'[137] The exposition and application of gospel truths in the congregational meeting should provide a constant reminder of the basis on which it is possible to be in a right relationship with God. Confession, thanksgiving, intercession, self-dedication and praise are the appropriate responses for God's people to make in every context, but especially when they gather together to express their true identity as the eschatological assembly of the Lord. Meeting together as those indwelt by the Spirit, we have the opportunity of meeting and engaging with

God together. In its gathering, the church should thus be *made aware of its own identity and special relationship to God*.

However, this also necessitates a recognition of *the special relationship that believers enjoy with one another* by virtue of their common participation in the saving benefits of Christ's death. The church has a special role in God's redemptive plan for the world and believers must recognize their responsibility to build up the body of Christ by mutual ministry in love for one another. Yet the special relationship of believers as a body to Christ also involves *a priestly and prophetic task in relation to the world* (e.g. Rom. 15:5–6; 16:25–7; Phil. 2:14–16; Col. 4:2–6; 1 Tim. 2:1–8; 1 Pet. 2:9) and the gathering of Christ's people must have this responsibility clearly in view.

Part Two

Reflections on Worship in the Heritage of the Majesterial Reformation

4

The Reformed Liturgy in the Dutch Tradition

KLAAS RUNIA

INTRODUCTION

In his important essay on 'Worship in the New Testament' David Peterson convincingly demonstrates that the concept of worship in the NT is much broader than what happens in the regular church service on Sunday. In the beginning of his essay he proposes the thesis 'that worship in the NT is essentially an engagement with God through faith in Jesus Christ and what he has done for us. Such faith will express itself in daily obedience or service to God in every sphere of life. What we do "in church" must be considered as part of that engagement with God but it is misleading to restrict the notion of worship to the congregational gathering' (p. 52)

He goes on to show that already in the OT the cultic service is set within the broader framework of fearing God, walking in all his ways and obeying all his commands and decrees (p. 54).[1] In the NT this very same emphasis is present everywhere. We encounter it, for instance, in the Gospels and in particular also in the writings of Paul. A very clear instance is what the apostle writes in Rom. 12:1, exhorting the believers in Rome to present themselves as living sacrifices, holy and pleasing to God' (p. 67). Actually these words cover all that is said in the last chapters of the epistle. 'From chapters 12–15 it is clear that acceptable worship involves effective ministry to one another within the body of Christ, love and forgiveness towards those outside the Christian community, right relationships with ruling authorities, living expectantly in the light of Christ's imminent return and expressing love especially towards those with different opinions within the congregation of Christ's people' (pp. 69–70).

This wide concept of worship does not exclude from Paul's theology any place for a 'special' serving of God in the assembly (pp. 77ff), but according to Peterson Paul sees the purpose of such special worship in the pursuit of mutual edification (pp. 77–83). There is therefore a need to re-assess many of our contemporary perspectives and practices and, in particular, to reconsider the relationship between what we do 'in church' and the worship of everyday life (p. 82).

It is interesting to note that from the beginning the Reformed tradition has been aware of this broader concept of worship. We find it already in Calvin's *Institutes*. Discussing the Roman mass he distinguishes two kinds of sacrifice: that of expiation and that of thanksgiving. The former was accomplished by Christ. The latter is our task. It is the sacrifice which the believers give to God by 'paying back to him their whole selves and all their acts' (IV, xviii, 13). It includes 'all the duties of love'. 'When we embrace the brethren with these, we honour the Lord himself in his members. Also included are all our prayers, praises, thanksgivings, and whatever we do in the worship of God. All these things finally depend upon the greater sacrifice, by which we are consecrated in soul and body to be a holy temple to the Lord. For it is not enough for our outward acts to be applied to his service; but first ourselves and then all that is ours ought to be consecrated and dedicated to him, so that all that is in us may serve his glory and may zealously aspire to increase it' (IV, xviii, 16; cf. also IV, xx, 15). It is, furthermore, interesting to note that in this very context Calvin also appeals to Rom. 12:1![2]

In accordance with this broad conception of Calvin is the emphasis on sanctification which we find in the classical Reformed liturgical forms. It is in particular also illustrated by the Heidelberg Catechism, which divides Christian 'knowledge' into three parts (misery, redemption and thankfulness). The last includes both the Ten Commandments and the Lord's Prayer. In other words, the whole life of the Christian is an expression of obedience and worship.[3]

We encounter the same emphasis in the views of Abraham Kuyper, who in the second half of the 19th century tried to revive classical Calvinism in the Netherlands. In his famous Stone-lectures on *Calvinism* he stressed again and again the idea that worship means serving God in the whole arena of life. In the first lecture on 'Calvinism as a life system' he said: 'To praise God in the Church and serve Him in the world became the inspiring impulse, and, in the Church, strength was to be gathered by which to resist temptation and sin in the world.'[4] A 20th century Dutch Reformed scholar, Dr O. Noordmans, once summarized this basic Reformed conviction in the striking words: 'The real liturgy occurs on the street!' And a 20th century Reformed confession says: 'Jesus Christ has given the church preaching and teaching, praise and prayer, and Baptism and the Lord's Supper *as means of fulfilling its service of God among men*'.[5]

THE DUTCH TRADITION

Although I fully agree with this broader concept and do believe that we have to bear this constantly in mind, in this paper I shall focus on the Dutch liturgy in the more specific sense. What happened in the past and what happens today, when Reformed people in the Netherlands meet in their assembly on Sunday? Or to put it in other words: what is characteristic of Reformed liturgy in the Netherlands?

Let me begin by telling you something about the structure of the service as it was when I was a schoolboy. It was a very simple, not to say, barren structure. The service started with the so-called *votum* or *adjutorium* ('Our help is in the name of the Lord who made heaven and earth')[6], followed by the apostolic greeting. Then we sang a psalm (at that time we had only eleven hymns, such as the Songs of Mary, Zechariah and Simeon and hymnodic versions of the Lord's Prayer and the Apostles' Creed). Next, an elder read the Ten Commandments, followed by a psalm of contrition or exhortation. (In the afternoon service the Apostles' Creed was read by the elder.) He then read a portion from Scripture, either from the Old or from the New Testament, depending on the text selected by the minister. Then followed the so-called long prayer, usually including a confession of sin and the inter-cessions. After the singing of another psalm (during which the collection was taken) the sermon followed (usually consisting of three parts, with, after the second part, the singing of another psalm). The closing part of the service consisted of another prayer (quite often a summary or even an additional application of the sermon!), a psalm and the benediction.

Was this kind of service typically *Reformed*? Or was it perhaps typical of the *Dutch* Reformed tradition? This question will occupy us for the greater part of this chapter, but at this moment I must point to the fact that in countries to which Dutch people emigrated and where they established their own church, we always encounter the same liturgy. This is true of the Reformed Church of America and the Dutch Reformed Church in South Africa (both dating from the 17th century), of the Christian Reformed Church in the USA and Canada and of the Reformed Churches in South Africa (both dating from the 19th century), and of the Reformed Churches in Australia and the Reformed Churches in New Zealand (both dating from the period after World War II). In this 'genealogical' sense the tradition as I have outlined it above, most certainly is typical of *Dutch* Reformed Protestantism.[7]

The Dutch Liturgy in the 16th and 17th Centuries

Where did this liturgy originate? Was it a Dutch invention? It is a fact, indeed, that in the 16th and 17th centuries the Dutch Reformed churches used almost an identical liturgy. It is further noteworthy that this liturgy, which was used in all Dutch churches, was never prescribed by any synod. No general or provincial synod ever prepared and imposed a complete liturgy for the worship services. But in so far as they did deal with liturgical matters it is evident that the usual order of service was virtually identical to the one used in my youth.

Some of the earliest synods dealt with specific aspects of the liturgy. The first ecclesiastical assembly, the so-called Convention of Wesel (1568), meeting under the presidency of Petrus Dathenus, recommended the use of his psalter and his translation of the Heidelberg Catechism to the churches, but did not prescribe a fixed liturgy.[8] Apparently these fathers did not want to restrict the liberty and autonomy of the local churches on this score. The Synod of Dort (1574) is sometimes called the 'liturgical synod', because more than any other synod it dealt with liturgical matters. It recommended the use of the liturgical forms of Dathenus and also regulated quite a few details of the liturgical order, but again refrained from imposing a fixed order on the churches.[9] Taking into account the various liturgical details on which this synod took a decision we can reconstruct the following order of service: *votum*, prayer, (psalm), sermon, prayer, creed, benediction. In the afternoon service the reading of the Decalogue preceded the sermon. The collection was taken at the door.[10] A few years later the Synod of Middelburg (1581) declared that a separate absolution was unnecessary. The sermon, containing the forgiveness and retention of sins, should suffice. Small wonder that gradually the confession of sin and the absolution disappeared from the Dutch services.[11] The 'great' Synod of Dort (1618–1619) appointed a committee for the revision of the liturgy, but did not have time to deal with the matter. It did decide, however, that the Decalogue should be read in the morning service, while the Creed was assigned to the catechetical service in the afternoon.[12] For the rest, the final ordering of the service remained in the hands of the local churches.

From these few data it is evident that the fathers of the Dutch Reformed Church in the 17th century were not very liturgically-minded. All they really wanted was to keep their liturgy as simple and sober as possible. Their worship service was virtually little more than a preaching service with a few appendices.[13] Rightly Hageman notes that such a practice must have been 'monotonous to a degree'.[14]

But even now the question remains: Was all this typically *Dutch* Reformed? How did the Dutch fathers arrive at this extremely sober, monotonous, almost rigid liturgy? In order to find the answer we have to go back to the beginnings of the Reformed Reformation. The Dutch churches did not invent their own liturgy, but it had come to them via a rather complicated and tortuous route.

The Beginnings of the Reformed Liturgy

The Reformation itself did not appear out of the blue. On the one hand, it had many deeply embedded historical roots, also *in liturgics*, and can be understood only against the background of developments that had begun long before.[15] On the other hand, the Reformers were deeply convinced that the medieval church had gone astray and therefore they wanted to go back, not only to Scripture itself, but also to the Early Church, which in their opinion had been faithful to the gospel of the Lord. Therefore, they felt committed to a purification of the liturgy. As the Liturgical Committee of the Christian Reformed Church put it in 1968:

> The liturgy was purified inwardly; the theological and spiritual content was transformed. All that smacked of the meritorious sacrifice of Christ in the Mass was cut away. Altar gave way to table; sacrifice made way for communion. The balance between Word and sacrament was restored – not by diminishing the importance of the sacrament but by upgrading the place of the Word. The extraneous extravaganza of pomp and ceremony was all but eliminated – but only to let the essentials of the liturgy become more prominent. The people were restored to their liturgical office as priests at the altar of praise; they were led down from the observer's balcony into the field of liturgical action.[16]

All this is also true of the Reformed Reformation, the beginnings of which we find in some of the Swiss and German cities that joined the new reformation movement and became the breeding places of a new re-formed liturgy. I am thinking in particular of Zurich, Strasbourg and Geneva.

In Zurich Huldrych Zwingly was the leading reformer. In his liturgical approach he closely associated himself with the preaching service (the so-called prone or 'pronaus'[17]) which had come into existence in the latter part of the Middle Ages.[18] In some respects he was rather rationalistic. To him the preaching of the Word was paramount. Actually, he regarded the Lord's Supper as another form of preaching, 'the dramatic re-enactment of what on other occasions had been said from the pulpit'.[19] Without doubt this was also the reason why he (unlike Calvin) did not plead for a weekly celebration of the Lord's Supper but was satisfied with four celebrations a year (Christmas, Easter, Pentecost, and on the Festival of the patron saints of Zurich, September 11). At all other times the service was a preaching service, with a liturgy that was largely derived from Johann Ulrich Surgant (professor at Basle), who in his *Manuale Curatorum* (1502) had already revised the prone.[20] This service had only one focus: the preaching of the Word. The sacrament was 'appended' to it only on special occasions. In addition, even though Zwingli himself was very musical, congregational singing was lacking!

In Strasbourg the main reformer was Martin Bucer. When he came to Strasbourg he already found an existing liturgy, namely, the German Mass, which the Lutheran Diebold Schwarz had prepared for the church at Strasbourg (1524). Schwarz had purified the medieval mass of all objectionable parts and introduced some ancient responses (such as the *Kyrie*, the *Gloria*, the *Sanctus* and the *Benedictus*) and also the Creed and prayers to be said by the people themselves.[21] In doing all this, however, he maintained the basic structure of the ancient liturgy: the preaching of the Word, responses by the people, and the sacrament. Bucer modified the liturgy still further by introducing metrical psalms to be sung by the people and the *lectio continua* (the reading of – and preaching on – whole books of the Bible in succession), instead of the old Roman lectionary. But he, too, retained the basic framework.[22] This was the vast difference between Bucer and Zwingli. While the latter adopted the prone (the medieval preaching service) as his starting point, Bucer retained the basic structure underlying the medieval mass and deriving from the ancient church. Zwingli in effect had only a liturgy of the Word; Bucer had a liturgy of Word, response by people, and sacrament. Because he, in turn, deeply influenced Calvin, he has become particularly important for the further history of the Reformed liturgy.

When in 1536 John Calvin arrived in Geneva, he met Guillaume Farel who had worked in this city since 1533. In the same year Farel had also published a little book of 87 pages, in which he expounded his liturgical views. The long-winded title of the book, consisting of some 70 words (!), clearly indicates that Farel's views were in keeping with those of Zwingli. In the last part of the title we read about 'the manner in which the preaching begins, continues and ends'. For Farel, too, the Sunday service is basically a preaching service.[23]

Calvin himself did not come to Geneva *tabula rasa*. Already in the first edition of his *Institutes*, which was published in March 1536 but had been written in 1535, he had given special attention to the liturgy of the church. He appeared to have some very clear and outspoken ideas. He was of the opinion that the Lord's Super should be celebrated frequently, that is, at least once a week.[24] Since he dealt with the liturgy in the context of his discussion of the sacraments, the emphasis was on the celebration of the Lord's Supper, but even so it is abundantly clear that according to him the complete worship service should consist of both preaching and the celebration of the Lord's Supper, because this was done also in the Early Church.[25] It is evident that he really wanted a re-formation of the medieval liturgy, not by creating an entirely new liturgy but by going back to the custom of the ancient church.[26]

During his first stay in Geneva (1536–1538) he did not immediately try to impose his own views on the church there, but largely adhered to the liturgical directions given by Farel. On the other hand, in 1536 he and Farel had already presented to the city council some Articles relative to the organization of church life. In these Articles or *Ordinances* they stated that the Lord's Supper should actually be celebrated weekly, but that they themselves would be satisfied with a monthly celebration, because of the weakness of the people's faith. The council, however, decided to keep the quarterly celebration.

In 1538 all the ministers of Geneva were dismissed by the city council. Calvin went to Strasbourg and became the minister of the congregation of French exiles there. W.D. Maxwell says of this period: 'Calvin seems to have had a high opinion of the worship then established in Strasbourg, for he adopted it almost word for word.'[27] Calvin himself afterwards wrote: 'I took the form of Strasbourg, and borrowed the greater part of it.'[28] His liturgy consisted of the following elements: *Votum*, confession of sin, words of pardon, pronouncement of absolution, the Decalogue (sung by the congregation), Scripture reading, sermon, offering of alms, intercessions, Lord's Prayer with paraphrase, Creed (sung), words of institution, exhortation, communion, post-communion, *Nunc Dimittis* (sung), benediction.[29] With great pleasure Calvin included congregational singing in his French service.

Already in the Articles of 1537 he had advocated this. 'The Psalms will be able to incite us to lift up our hearts to God and move us to zeal as well as to invoke and exalt the glory of His Name by our praises'. In 1539 he published the first edition of his French psalter, containing eighteen psalms and three canticles, seven of the translations being made by himself. This psalter was the ancestor of the great Genevan Psalter of later years (1562)[30], the tunes of which have been used ever since by most of the Reformed churches in France, Switzerland, the Netherlands, Hungary, Germany, and afterwards also in the USA and South Africa, Australia and New Zealand.

After his return to Geneva in 1541 Calvin succeeded in introducing many of his liturgical ideas into the worship services of the church there. In 1542 he published his liturgy under the title: *The Form of Prayers, according to the customs of the Ancient Church.* Again the frequency of the communion became an issue. The city council still opposed the idea of a weekly celebration of the Lord's Supper and continued to do so during Calvin's life.

Summing up our discussion of the beginnings of Reformed liturgy we cannot but conclude that from the very beginning there were two different liturgical conceptions within the Reformed wing of the Reformation: the Zwinglian and the Calvinian. Hageman rightly points out that both have proved historically viable in the Reformed church. 'With negligible exceptions, all the worship of the Reformed churches can be traced back to one of these two sources.'[31] Zwingli's liturgy, which adopted the more radical pattern, came first. Even though he still used many of the traditional elements and ceremonies, he in actual fact 'completely demolished the traditional liturgical structure'. Calvin, who came later, attempted to keep the worship of the re-formed church within the historical pattern of the Christian church. Even though he almost completely abandoned the elements and ceremonies that had come into existence during the Middle Ages, he 'carefully preserved the traditional shape of the liturgy'.[32]

The Evolution of the Dutch Tradition

It is now time to return to the Dutch tradition. How did it evolve from these early beginnings? What happened? Every one who studies this evolution knows that is it not easy to say how exactly the later Dutch tradition evolved from these beginnings in Zurich, Strasbourg and Geneva.[33] There was definitely not a direct line from Calvin's Geneva to the Netherlands, but in so far as he did influence the Reformed liturgy in the Netherlands, we have to distinguish various historical lines, which at times coincided with and at other times contradicted each other.

I begin with London where in 1553 we find two different congregations of Reformed exiles, one from France, the other from Holland. The minister of the French-speaking congregation was Vallérand Poullain (Pollanus), who was deeply influenced by both Bucer and Calvin. The superintendent of the Dutch-speaking congregation was the Polish nobleman Johannes à Lasco who[34] among other things, introduced catechism preaching and a preparatory service on the Sunday preceding the celebration of the Lord's Supper. He also wrote a book on liturgy, *Forma ac Ratio*, which later on was translated into Dutch by Martin Micron.[35] According to some scholars à Lasco's liturgy clearly shows the influence of Zwingli and of the medieval pronaus.[36] Others regard his liturgy as Calvinian rather than Zwinglian.[37] Be this as it may, à Lasco was not the one who really stamped the Dutch liturgy.

When the Roman Catholic Mary Tudor (afterwards known as Bloody Mary) came to the throne in England, the Dutch refugees left. Some went to Embden, others to Frankfort and subsequently to Frankenthal, in the Palatinate.[38] Their minister was Peter Dathenus, who knew the London liturgy of à Lasco, but was also involved, at the request of the elector Frederick III, in the re-organization of church life in the Palatinate. It was he who largely stamped the further development of the liturgy in the Dutch churches. He not only drew up the main liturgical forms, which were afterwards used by these churches, but also prepared a psalter that was in use in the Netherlands until the second half of the 18th century.

The liturgy that was used in the congregation of Dutch exiles in the Palatinate derived from various sources. Although Dathenus may be regarded as its main author, he did not begin from scratch either, but made use of the Palatinate liturgy, at the back of which in turn lie à Lasco (with the influence of Zwingli?), Calvin and Ursinus, with perhaps a touch of Lutheranism.[39] The liturgy was very simple and consisted of the following elements: Salutation (no *Votum*), prayer before sermon (including a long confession of sin), Scripture reading, sermon, confession of sin and proclamation of the keys (absolution and retention), long prayer (of thanksgiving and intercession), psalm, (Aaronic) benediction.[40]

It was this liturgy that afterwards, largely owing to the influence of Dathenus himself (he was president of several synods), was adopted in the Dutch churches. The main change was that the confession was put before the sermon, being included in the prayer before the sermon. One can hardly say that it was patterned after the Genevan liturgy. In structure it was Zwinglian rather than Calvinian. There was no separate prayer of confession; nor was

there an absolution, pronounced by the minister.[41] There was not a special
prayer for illumination. The Lord's Supper did not have a 'natural' place in
the worship service. The morning service was a preaching service, to which
once every three months the celebration of the Lord's Supper was
'appended'. I believe that Hageman is correct when he characterizes this
liturgy as 'Zwinglian in structure, Calvinist in content, with some Lutheran
overtones'.[42]

At the end of the 16th century this extremely austere liturgy was even
further emaciated. Several elements were transferred to the time prior to the
actual service. First, it was decided that, before the actual service would start,
an elder should read portions from Scripture (a custom also known in the
Scottish churches[43]) and the people sing some psalms, 'lest the church be
disturbed by idle chatter'. Gradually the reading of the Decalogue and of the
Creed was also included in this pre-service assembly. Fortunately, this whole
pre-service idea was afterwards abandoned again and all these elements were
re-introduced into the service proper.

When at this point we look back at the developments and take stock of the
results of our research, we must in all honesty state that the Dutch tradition of
the whole period from the 16th till the 19th century retained little of Calvin's
ideas about the basic structure of the worship service, namely, that of an
ellipse with two foci: the preaching of the Word and the celebration of the
Lord's Supper. In actual fact, Zwingli had won the day in Holland.[44] The
worship service had become a simple 'preaching service', in line with the
medieval pronaus.[45] The Lord's Supper had become a mere 'addendum' that
was 'appended' to the sermon, and that only four times a year. So the
situation remained until the end of the 19th century. In fact, it was still so in
my own church in the thirties of this century!

The Liturgical Movement

Fortunately this is not the whole story. At the end of the 19th and the
beginning of the 20th century we see the emergence of a liturgical movement
within the Reformed churches in the Netherlands. Naturally, it took quite
some time for this movement to bear fruit (I did not notice anything yet, when
I was a boy!), but nevertheless, there were promising intimations of change.
In both the Dutch Reformed Church (the 'Nederlandse Hervormde Kerk',
the formerly established church) and in the Reformed Churches (the
'Gereformeerde Kerken', fruit of two secessions in the 19th century) voices
were heard pleading for a renewal of the liturgy. Three names in particular
must be mentioned here: Prof. J.H. Gunning and J.H. Gerretsen (both
belonging to the Dutch Reformed Church) and Dr Abraham Kuyper
(belonging to the Reformed Churches).[46] In 1920 the 'Liturgical Circle' was
established by a group of Dutch Reformed theologians dedicated to the
renewal of the liturgy in their church. After the Second World War the Dutch
Reformed Church itself looked for renewal of its liturgy. In 'A Specimen
Description', a report issued by two church committees in 1950, ten theses
were propounded, containing the principles by which the renewal should be
guided.[47] We shall mention two. The seventh thesis reads: 'Although . . .
preaching is directed to the whole world and involves all men, as the ministry
of the Word it takes place within the congregation, presupposes Holy
Baptism and always invites to the Table of the Lord. It is never fully heard,

understood, and received without these signs and seal which accompany and confirm it according to Christ's expressed institution. Preaching and sacrament together make a living and powerful Word of God in our midst through the operation of the Holy Spirit.' Here we see the Calvinian emphasis on the unity of preaching and sacrament reappear. In thesis 9 we read: 'In the order of worship the lawful freedom and diversity of the Church is formed and limited by its catholic character and by its Reformation confession. . . .' Here the Catholic and the Reformed aspect are united again! In 1955 a first draft of a Service Book was published, offering many choices, at times quite different in both liturgical construction and theological point of view.

In my own church, the Reformed Churches in the Netherlands, the changes were slow in coming. In 1923 a synodical committee proposed the introduction of the confession of sin and the absolution as well as a prayer for illumination by the Holy Spirit, but synod itself rejected the proposal. Ten years later (1933) the climate had changed little. To be sure, the synod recommended to the churches a fixed order for the liturgy. In actual fact, it was the very first Dutch synod since the Reformation that fixed the entire liturgical order, but unfortunately it simply confirmed the existing traditional order! It was more than thirty years before another synod (Middelburg 1965/6) introduced a really renewed liturgy. According to the committee that prepared it, this liturgy was a return to the classical 'basic pattern for the order in the assembly of the congregating', a pattern that is determined 'by the two ways in which the Lord deals with his people: the preaching of the gospel and the distribution of bread and wine at the Lord's Table'. Some ten years later another synod (Haarlem 1973–75) allowed for more variety in the liturgy. It offered the congregations four choices for the first part of the service, which is then called 'preparation'.[48]

The two Reformed churches in the USA that have a Dutch background, the Reformed Church and the Christian Reformed Church, also tried to renew the traditional liturgy by returning to the original Calvinian pattern of the liturgy. In 1968 the RCA adopted a new *Liturgy and Psalms*, which represents a significant recovery of many of Calvin's insights.[49] In the same year the CRC also adopted a much improved liturgy.[50]

Summarizing the developments during the post-World War II period we see the appearance or re-appearance of the following elements: 1. The morning service is seen as an elliptic structure with two foci: preaching and the Lord's Supper. 2. Confession of sin and absolution have their own independent place and function. 3. The prayer for illumination receives a separate place and function. 4. In some liturgies there is room for responses by the congregation. 5. The intercessory prayer now follows the sermon. 6. Together with the offering and the reciting of the Creed this part is now regarded as the 'service of offerings' by the congregation. In this way several characteristics of the original Reformed worship have been re-introduced and re-emphasized.

CHARACTERISTICS OF THE CALVINIAN/REFORMED LITURGY

Having investigated the intricate historical developments of Reformed liturgy in the Netherlands since the Reformation we shall now attempt to analyze

Reformed liturgy according to its original intentions, giving special attention to the views of Calvin himself.

1. In his approach to liturgy Calvin did not want to break with all existing tradition and begin entirely *ab novo*, but rather, reaching back across the liturgical deformation of the Middle Ages, he wanted to return to the liturgy of the Ancient Church. In other words, he was prepared to carry out extensive surgery, but not wholesale amputation. This is also the reason why he calls his published liturgy: *The Form of Church Prayers and Hymns with the Manner of Administering the Sacraments and Consecrating Marriage According to the Custom of the Ancient Church.*[51]

In his plea for a weekly celebration of the Lord's Supper he likewise appeals to the Ancient Church. He finds this weekly celebration not only in Acts and in the congregation of Corinth, but also in the canons attributed to Anacletus and Calixtus, and in the decisions of the Councils of Antioch and Toledo (*Inst.* IV, xvii, 44). He further appeals to the writings of Augustine and Chrysostom (IV, xvii, 45).

2. Yet Calvin does *not* want to *imitate* the practice of the New Testament or the sub-apostolic church. Undoubtedly, his fundamental principle is: 'I approve only those human constitutions which are founded upon God's authority, drawn from Scripture, and, therefore, wholly divine' (*Inst.* IV, x, 30). This applies in particular to the central elements of the worship service. In the preface to his liturgical book *The Forms of Prayers* he emphatically states that there are *three* holy ordinances of the Lord: the preaching of his Word, the corporate and solemn prayers and the administration of the sacraments. As far as other matters are concerned he wants to safeguard the freedom the divine Lord has given to his people. In the same section of the *Institutes* from which we just quoted, he writes:

> Because he [= the Master] did not will in outward discipline and ceremonies to prescribe in detail what we ought to do (because he foresaw that this depended upon the state of the times, and he did not deem one form suitable for all ages), here we must take refuge in those general rules which he has given, that whatever the necessity of the church will require for order and decorum should be tested against these. [Furthermore,] because he has taught nothing specifically, and because these things are not necessary to salvation, and for the upbuilding of the church ought to be variously accommodated to the customs of each nation and age, it will be fitting (as the advantage of the church will require) to change and abrogate traditional practices and to establish new ones.[52]

But he also warns against rash innovation, without sufficient cause. 'Love will be the best judge what may hurt or edify; and if we let love be our guide, all will be safe.' In the next section we find the same line of thought. Dealing, among other things, with women's headwear in church, he uses the following rules of thumb: custom, humanity, and the rule of modesty (IV, x, 31). From these examples it is quite evident that Calvin does not require 'a servile imitation of the primitive church'.

3. But what he does require is that the Reformed church adhere to those 'three holy ordinances of the Lord'. Hence his insistence that there should be *preaching and celebration of the Lord's Supper in the main service each Sunday*. According to him Acts 2:42 teaches us that 'it became the unvarying

rule that no meeting of the church should take place without the Word, prayers, partaking of the Supper, and almsgiving' (*Inst.* IV, xvii, 44[53]). Thus it was in the entire Ancient Church. Calvin therefore strongly opposes the medieval custom of receiving communion only once a year.[54] He writes: 'It should have been done far differently: the Lord's Table should have been spread at least once a week for the assembly of Christians, and the promises declared in it should feed us spiritually. None is indeed to be forcibly compelled, but all are to be urged and aroused; also the inertia of indolent people is to be rebuked. All, like hungry men, should flock to such a bounteous repast' (*Inst.* IV, xvii, 46). We all know that he did not succeed in introducing this custom into the church of Geneva because of the opposition of the city council.[55] Calvin refused to make it a breaking point, but also adhered to his conviction. As late as in 1561 (three years before his death) he wrote: 'I have taken care to record publicly that our custom is defective, so that those who come after me may be able to correct it more freely and easily.'[56]

4. Like the other Reformers Calvin also insisted on the *corporate* character of worship. 'It was to be the corporate action of the people of God, not something done on their behalf; and something done not by individuals but together.'[57] Undoubtedly this was the reason why the general confession of sin, which in the mass was a private confession of the priest and his assistants when approaching the altar, was moved to the beginning of the service and became a public confession of the whole congregation. Even though it was still said by the minister, it was meant as a corporate act of confession; the minister was speaking on behalf of the entire congregation.[58] The entire congregation knelt at the minister's call, after which he said a fixed prayer known to the entire congregation[59], followed by the absolution. Something similar happened to the Creed. In the Middle Ages the Apostles' Creed was generally used only in the baptismal service and then only in Latin. Calvin wanted it in every Sunday service in the vernacular as a congregational act.[60]

These changes were not private innovations by Calvin, but related to the general conviction of the Reformers that the worship of the congregation must witness to the *priesthood of all believers*. Worship is not a spectacle, executed by a special class of people and watched by an inactive congregation, but it is the corporate task of the entire Christian community, the whole *koinonia*, which is the body of Christ. Hageman says: 'No Reformed liturgy is truly Reformed which does not make a large and adequate place for the exercise of the priesthood of all believers in corporate prayer, praise, and affirmation as the people of God respond to the life-giving Word of their Creator and Redeemer.'[61]

5. This was also the reason why Calvin was such a strong advocate of *congregational singing*. He regarded the psalms as prayers that were sung by the congregation itself. Singing was not unknown in the later Middle Ages, but on the whole it was not very meaningful. Erasmus once complained: 'They chant nowadays in our churches in what is an unknown tongue and nothing else, while you will not hear a sermon once in six months telling people to amend their lives. Modern church music is so constructed that the congregation cannot hear one distinct word . . . If they want music, let them sing psalms like rational beings, and not too many of these.'[62] What Calvin thought of congregational singing we can gather from the prefaces to his 1542 and 1545 editions of the metrical psalter. He tells us that when he arrived at

Strasbourg, he found a singing congregation there. 'For five or six days at the beginning, when I looked at this little company of exiles from all countries, I wept, not for sadness, but for joy to hear them all singing so heartily and as they sang giving thanks to God that he had led them to a place where his name is glorified. No one could believe what joy there is in singing the praises and wonders of the Lord in the mother tongue as they are sung here.'[63] In his *Institutes*, where he deals with singing in the chapter on prayer(!), he points out that it was done already in the apostolic church and also in the days of Augustine (III, xx, 32).

Although it cannot be stated with absolute certainly that Calvin wanted to restrict the singing of the congregation to the Old Testament psalms[64], it cannot be denied that he had great preference for the psalms. Here one was praising God, so to speak, in one's own language.[65] In addition, the psalms are so varied as to content that they are suited for every situation in which the congregation may find itself. And since Calvin, just like the other Reformers, was used to reading them christologically and as prophetic of the life of the church, they were just as suitable for the New Testament congregation as they had been for God's people of old.[66]

Up to the 19th century most Reformed churches all through the world used a metrical version of the psalms, set to the so-called Genevan tunes. On the European continent this is still the case, although in most churches a great number of hymns have been added to the psalter. As to the USA John Hesselink writes that in the first half of this century 'most mainline Presbyterian/Reformed denominations sold out to a hymnody that represented either the ornate, subjectivism and often liberal spirit of the nineteenth century, or the individualistic, Arminian flavor of the American revivals of roughly the same period.'[67] He is obviously very critical of many hymns and quotes Karl Barth who stated in his *Church Dogmatics* (I, 2, 257): 'The secularization of protestantism, in the specific form of modernistic Neo-Protestantism, is only a symptom of the inner secularization visible in the evolution of the hymn . . . In every section of our hymnbooks we can find the hidden heresy involved in the whole development.' If Calvin lived in our day and could read and hear what sometimes is sung in some Reformed churches, he most certainly would be shocked.

6. He would most certainly also be shocked by the many, often meaningless liturgical '*decorations*' he would encounter in many Reformed worship services. On principle he was in favour of *simplicitas* in the worship of the church. He condemned the many ceremonies of the medieval church, 'which, with Christ half buried, cause us to return to Jewish symbols' (*Inst.*, IV, x, 14) and appealed to Augustine, who had written: 'Our Lord Christ has bound the fellowship of the new people together with sacraments, very few in number, very excellent in meaning, very easy to observe'. If the opponents would say that there are now very many as untutored as there were among Israel, his answer is that though we must necessarily be mindful of the infirmity of the brethren, it has to be done in the right way. It is certainly not correct to overwhelm them with great heaps of ceremonies. God dealt with Israel as children who were under custody of the law (Gal. 4:1–2), but Christ said that his own people should worship God in spirit and in truth (John 4:23). This does not mean that Calvin is against all ceremonies. He says: 'I only contend that the means used ought to show Christ, not to hide him . . . It is necessary

to keep fewness in number, ease in observance, dignity in representation, which also includes clarity.'

The Reformed simplicity of worship is not a *testimonium paupertatis*, but a scriptural, a theological, more precisely, a redemption-historical principle![68] The New Testament believers are spiritual adults who should worship their Lord in spirit and truth.

CRITERIA FOR A TRULY REFORMED LITURGY

Is it possible to derive from these characteristics of Reformed liturgy some criteria that should guide a Reformed church in the review and reform of its liturgy? I believe the answer is in the affirmative. In 1965 a synodical liturgical committee of the Reformed Churches in the Netherlands distinguished four motifs that should guide a Reformed church.[69] These motifs were afterwards also adopted by the liturgical committee of the Christian Reformed Church.[70] They neatly summarize what we have found in the characteristics mentioned above. We believe, however, that a fifth motif should be added to them.

1.   The Biblical Motif

Although it is true that the Bible does not prescribe a definite order of worship, it is and remains the basic orientation for Reformed churches. It not only commands us to worship God and tells us who our God is, but it also teaches us in what frame of mind and heart we should worship God, namely, as an act of thanksgiving and self-dedication. Moreover, it mentions many elements that should have a place in our worship. We do not know exactly how the worship service in the New Testament was ordered, but it is generally agreed that it was largely derived from the synagogue worship and from the Lord's own action, when he instituted the Lord's Supper. As to the order of the synagogue worship, during Jesus' own time it most likely contained the following elements: the recitation of the so-called 'Shema' (Deut. 6:4ff.); prayer (concluded by the 'Amen' of the congregation); reading from Law and Prophets; exposition; and the Aaronic benediction.[71] In the New Testament itself we hear of Scripture reading, preaching, celebration of the Lord's Supper, *Agape*-meals, prayers (with the 'Amen'!), confessions of faith, salutations and benedictions, singing and offerings. In Lord's Day 38 the *Heidelberg Catechism* summarizes it very concisely: God's will for me in the fourth commandment is that 'especially on the festive day of rest, I regularly attend the assembly of God's people to learn what God's Word teaches, to participate in the sacraments, to pray to God publicly, and to bring Christian offerings for the poor'.

2.   The Ecumenical Motif

Since the Bible does not prescribe an exact order of worship, the church itself, in the course of the centuries, has taken many decisions concerning the liturgy. A Reformed church should always be willing to listen carefully to what the *church of the past* did and the *other churches of today* do in their liturgy. To the Corinthians Paul writes that they are 'called to be saints together with all those who in every place call on the name of our Lord Jesus Christ, both their Lord and ours' (1 Cor. 1:2), and he tells the Ephesians that they can comprehend 'what is the breadth and length and height and depth' of the love of Gods only '*with all the saints*' (Eph. 3:18). Other Christians, therefore, should be able to recognize in Reformed worship the basic elements of the worship of the universal church of all ages and all places. For whatever deformations and reformations there may have been in the history of liturgy, it remains a fact that, at least formally, there always has been a *basic structure*, which can be recognized in most ecclesiastical traditions.

Naturally, this does not mean that the Reformed church of today should uncritically accept what has been done in the past, either by other churches or by its own spiritual forebears. There have been many deformations in Christian worship, deformations that in some churches are still present. There should be a twofold, reciprocal relationship between a Reformed Church and the church of all ages. On the one hand, a Reformed church should be ready to examine critically the liturgical past of all churches (including its own past!). On the other hand, this same Reformed church should be willing to let the tradition of the Christian Church evaluate and judge its own present liturgy.

Respect for tradition in liturgy is a fence against individualism and sectarianism. It keeps us from trying to improve liturgy through gimmickry and novelty for the sake of novelty. It will keep reminding us of what is essential and what is peripheral. It is also the best teacher of the lesson of flexibility; for it is in the history of liturgy that we observe the constant fluidities along with the underlying stability of the church's liturgy.[72]

3. The Confessional Motif

This motif follows almost naturally from what has been said before. The confessional motif serves as a counterbalance to the ecumenical. Every congregation comes to its worship as a people that is committed to a certain *confessional perspective on God and human beings*. Although confessions do not spell out the form of worship, they do contain the theological decisions that determine worship. Liturgics is not only a historical science, but it is just as much a dogmatic-confessional science. It does make a world of difference, whether we see the eucharist as a repetition (albeit a bloodless repetition) of the sacrifice on the cross, a view that led to the medieval mass, or as the commemoration of the sacrifice, once and for all accomplished on the cross, a view that led to the Reformed way of celebrating the Lord's Supper. It makes a world of difference whether we see baptism as the effectual cause of regeneration or as the seal and sign of God's covenant; and consequently the liturgy of baptism will be formulated quite differently.

Again we can speak of a twofold, reciprocal relationship, this time between liturgy and confession. On the one hand, the liturgy will demonstrate what the church's faith is, what its hope is, and what its life is. On the other hand, this very same liturgy will strengthen the faith and hope and life of the worshipper.

4. The Pastoral Motif

This motif takes into account that the liturgy is always a liturgy *for* people of a *certain time and culture*. As the other motifs emphasize the need for stability, this motif stresses the need for *flexibility*. The liturgy wants to edify the people and build up the congregation (cf. the essay of David Peterson). It can do this only when the church that is responsible for the form of the liturgy bears in mind that people in various times and places have different needs. We refer here again to what Calvin, who so strongly emphasized the biblical motif, said about the liberty of the church. He warned against both traditionalism and rash innovation. His final words on this score were: 'Love will best judge what may hurt or edify; and if we let love be our guide, all will be safe' (*Inst.* IV, x, 30).

5. The 'All of Life is Worship' Motif

In agreement with the tenor of David Peterson's essay in this volume and also with the broader concept of liturgy which we encountered in Calvin, Kuyper and Noordmans, a Reformed church that seeks for the renewal of its liturgy should ask itself: Does the worship in the services on the Lord's Day inspire the members of the congregation to be active in the world and to engage in the service of God and their fellow human beings in society at large? However important the Sunday services may be for the mutual upbuilding of the congregation, their purpose should not be restricted to this mutual edification. The congregation meets also for the adoration of God, which in turn should lead to action in the world, which is another form of worship. To put it the words of Herman Ridderbos:

> All of life is spiritual worship, every believer a priest (Rom. 12:1; cf. Rom. 1:9; Phil. 3:3; 2 Tim. 1:3) . . . The New Testament knows no holy persons who substitionally perform the service of God for the whole people of God, nor holy places and seasons or holy acts, which create a distance between the cultus and the life of every day and every place. All members of the church have access to God (Rom. 5:2) and a share in the Holy Spirit; all of life is service to God; there is no profane area.[73]

Any Reformed church that will heed the five fundamental motifs will remain in the Reformed tradition and at the same time it will be able to renew this tradition. For no Reformed church may forget the famous dictum, which also applies to its liturgy: *Ecclesia reformata semper reformanda*.

5

Presbyterian Worship

EDMUND P. CLOWNEY

If historic Presbyterian worship be judged distinctive today, it is surely not because the Scottish fathers sought to develop innovations in worship that might justify a brand name. Their desire was to reform Christian worship according to Scripture. They understood this to mean the elimination from public worship of all rites and ceremonies without divine warrant and the inclusion of only those elements of worship that God has commanded for his new covenant people. This conviction has not escaped the criticism of those who have viewed its generic, no-name-brand practice of worship as barren and sterile. Of course, streams that began in the Protestant Reformation now flow in a wide delta of divisions and swamps. In the United States, the name Presbyterian is the only vestige of Presbyterian doctrine or practice that survives in some churches. Others may still have some memory of a Scots diet of oatmeal porridge and the Shorter Catechism, but now think of themselves as charismatic churches, or megachurches, or churches in the Willow Creek Community model.[1] The blight of liberalism in the 'mainline' Presbyterian denomination has destroyed not only Presbyterian convictions, but Christian convictions as well.[2] One might conclude that historic Presbyterian worship belongs to past generations.

It is also true that practices in worship do not flow directly from fountainheads of conviction. Cultural contexts provide the medium that may become the message. The medieval church maintained catholic uniformity of a kind in the Latin words of the Mass, but at the sacrifice of all meaningful communication to the peoples of Europe. They became spectators at a remote performance of mysterious magic: 'a spectacle, a sort of *tableau vivant* played before a public which, beyond a few automatic gestures, takes no part in it at all.'[3] Vatican II has now sought to provide for cultural diversity in liturgy:

> Not even in the liturgy does the Church wish to impose a rigid uniformity in matters which do not involve the faith or the good of the whole community; rather does she respect and foster the genius and talents of the various races and peoples.[4]

The Westminster Assembly, with a radically different agenda, also took account of different customs and settings for worship. The Divines clearly

110

recognized an area touching 'some circumstances' of worship 'common to human actions and societies' that may be ordered in the 'light of nature' without express warrant in Scripture.[5] Certainly the circumstances of worship have varied widely in Presbyterian history. Given these changing settings and the freedom of Presbyterian worship from fixed forms, can any worship be defined as distinctively Presbyterian? So loyal a Presbyterian as the late Robert Rayburn subtitled his book on renewal in worship, *Corporate Worship in the Evangelical Church*.[6] It is true that Reformed and Puritan emphases have been a major factor in the development of evangelical worship; it is also true that the practice of worship in evangelical Presbyterian churches may often be broadly evangelical rather than distinctively Reformed. Nevertheless, Reformed and Presbyterian principles of worship have been developed from Scripture and brought to expression in practices that have a clear tradition. Freedom from any required form of worship has not produced chaos in Presbyterian worship; indeed, the Presbyterian churches have often rejected the dictates of king, pope, and bishop only to follow uncritically the dictates of custom.[7] Yet historic Presbyterianism has taken account of the ordering of worship as well as of its freedom. The Westminster Assembly's *Directory for the Public Worship of God* is markedly different from the *Book of Common Prayer*, but it does describe the elements of public worship and it presents an order for the services of the church. Its directions for prayers are not mandatory, but they do model the scriptural richness of the ministry of adoration, confession, and intercession.

What, then, are the foundational convictions that mark Presbyterian worship?

The first is affirmed in the phrase *soli Deo gloria*. Although Luther as well as Calvin taught the sovereignty of God in salvation, it was the Reformed churches that continued to emphasize God's electing grace in Christ. Reformed theology rejoiced to find God's glory central, not only in salvation, but in all the works of the Lord. 'Man's chief end is to glorify God and to enjoy him forever.' This answer to the first question of the Shorter Catechism shapes Presbyterian worship as well as theology. God does not exist for our sake, but we exist for God's sake. Worship ascribes to God the glory due to his name.

All of life is a service of worship; we are to do all to the glory of God, in the name of the Lord Jesus (Col. 3:17; Eph. 5:20; 1 Cor. 10:31). In his chapter on 'Worship in the New Testament', David Peterson shows how totally the Old Testament cultus is fulfilled in Jesus Christ, our great high priest, who is not only the mediator of the new covenant, but the Lord of glory. No longer do we gather at Jerusalem to offer sacrifices; through him we present ourselves to God in the daily sacrifice of living service (Rom. 12:1,2). Presbyterians have cherished this insight of the Protestant Reformation that has sanctified the daily work and witness of the believer.

Does the offering of our whole life to God mean that there is now no point in setting apart a time for devotion as such?[8] We need only recall the habits of Jesus in prayer to answer that question. Although his whole life was a work of worship of the Father, Jesus still went apart to pray, and taught his disciples a model of prayer to direct their own worship. Further, he gave them that prayer in the first person plural. They were to hallow God's name, not only with the door shut in private, but also together, as a company of disciples.

Jesus' participation in the services of the synagogue also provided a pattern for his followers. The apostle Paul regularly taught in synagogue services; when rejected in the synagogue, he continued similar gatherings for believing Jews and Gentiles. As his epistles to the Corinthian church show, Paul was deeply concerned about the worship and discipline of the church when believers gathered in the name of the Lord. Indeed, the very term 'church' (*ekklēsia*) was a term applied to the Old Testament people of God because of the great assembly at Sinai, when they had stood before God to hear his words. The church is named from the assembly, not at Sinai, nor in the earthly Zion, but in the heavenly Zion, where it is joined with the worshipping host of the saints and the angels (Heb. 12:22–24).[9]

When believers meet in the name of the Lord, they set apart their gathering from other meetings. Those who meet in his name call upon his name in prayer; they acknowledge his presence in the midst (1 Cor. 1:2 5:4;). So, too, Paul sets apart the Lord's Supper from ordinary meals. Hungry Corinthians should eat at home, for the supper is the Lord's institution and must be approached with heart-searching reverence. To ignore its holy character would be to sin against the death of Christ and to despise the assembly of God (1 Cor. 11:17–34). The church assembles in God's presence to address him and one another, to hear his Word, to pray, to sing his praise, to celebrate his salvation in the sacraments he has appointed (Acts 2:1; 4:23–31; 5:42; 13:2; 1 Cor. 11:18–34; 14:23–25; Eph. 5:19,20; Col. 3:16; 1 Pet. 3:21). The Book of Revelation describes the final consummation when all creation will sing,

> To him who sits on the throne and to the Lamb be praise and honor and glory and power, for ever and ever! (Rev. 5:13).

The final Hallelujah chorus has already begun for the congregation of God's people. Indeed, by faith we have already come to the heavenly assembly of the saints and the angels, where Christ is, and where spiritual worship may be offered to our God, who is a consuming fire (Heb. 12:28,29).[10] The contrast in Hebrews is not between the elaborate ordinances of Old Testament and no corporate worship at all. Rather, it is between the types and shadows of an imperfect worship and the full reality of worship through Jesus Christ. Through Christ, we too, draw near to God, not in the physical approach to the holy place of the tabernacle, but in the spiritual approach of new covenant worship. We offer that worship as we daily bring the offerings of our lips and our hands in his service, but also as we meet together – which we must not fail to do (Heb. 10:22,25).

The Reformed concern for the glory of God has always focussed on Jesus Christ, through whom God's glory is revealed. The rule of the risen Christ is the starting point for the Westminster Assembly *Form of Government*; Christ's glory marks the Assembly's instruction for prayers in public worship.[11] Christian worship responds to Christ's lordship.

Two other features of Presbyterian worship greatly heightened its doxological character. The singing of the Psalms gave expression to the struggles and suffering of stormy days, but also put praise of the Lord at the heart of worship. So did the scrupulous observance of the Lord's Day as a day of worship.

A second Presbyterian conviction that shaped worship was the Reformation emphasis on the Bible. The Westminster Confession begins with a magnificent statement on Scripture. The revelation of God in his works of creation and providence is sufficient to make us without excuse for sin, but only the Scripture gives that knowledge of God and of his will that is necessary to salvation. Holy Scripture is therefore 'most necessary', particularly since those special revelations from God that gave us Scripture have now ceased.

The recovery of the Bible in the language of the people at the time of the Reformation was even more dramatic than its recovery today in lands where state or church had banned it. Ulrich Zwingli was called to Zurich as the Reformation was just beginning (1519).

> He started out by taking the Gospel of Matthew and preaching through it verse by verse, day after day for a whole year. Every man, woman, and child who could possibly get there crammed into Zurich's Great Minster to hear him.[12]

The churches before the Reformation were not without eloquent preachers. What was new was the systematic preaching of the contents of the Bible. Luther preached biblically from the pericopes of the lectionary (although he also lectured sermonically on whole books of the Bible). Calvin and other Reformed preachers continually preached 'in course,' that is, passage by passage through Bible books. Calvin covered almost the entire Bible.[13] In Reformed services of worship the Bible was read chapter after chapter in sequence, from the Old Testament and from the New. Many of the hearers were illiterate, but for those who could read, Bibles were chained to lecterns in the churches. For the Reformed and Presbyterian churches, preaching has been the central part of worship: the proclaiming and hearing of the Word of God written.

The Westminster Assembly recognized that the divine authority of Scripture was exclusive. Nothing was to be added to the whole counsel of God set down in Scripture 'whether by new revelations of the Spirit, or traditions of men.'[14] From this acknowledgment of the sufficiency of Scripture, a further consequence was drawn. If in doctrine nothing may be added to the teaching of Scripture, so, too, in worship nothing may be added to what God has revealed.[15] A preacher, a church, a pope has no right to require Christians to believe what the Bible does not teach. No more does a preacher, a church, a pope have a right to require practices in worship that God has not required. The argument is carefully stated in the Confession's chapter on Christian Liberty:

> God alone is Lord of the conscience, and hath left it free from the doctrines and commandments of men, which are, in any thing, contrary to His Word; or beside it, if matters of faith, or worship. So that, to believe such doctrines, or to obey such commands, out of conscience, is to betray true liberty of conscience: and the requiring of an implicit faith, and an absolute and blind obedience, is to destroy liberty of conscience, and reason also.[16]

This principle is applied specifically to worship in the next chapter of the Confession:

But the acceptable way of worshipping the true God is instituted by Himself, and so limited by His own revealed will, that He may not be worshipped according to the imaginations and devices of men, or the suggestions of Satan, under any visible representation, or any other way not prescribed in the holy Scripture.[17]

In worship, therefore, anything that God has not commanded is forbidden. The Shorter Catechism puts this most succinctly: 'The second commandment forbiddeth the worshipping of God by images, or any other way not appointed in his word.'

The Westminster Divines saw the issue respecting worship in terms of liberty of conscience. First, since God is Lord of my conscience, no one can compel me to believe or do anything *contrary* to God's Word. This freedom applies precisely where conscientious obedience is required of us by the Lord himself, who has instituted the church, the family, the state. Second, in addition to this general rule that applies to all spheres of life, there is a more specific rule that applies to faith and worship. In these matters of religion the conscience is free not only from demands contrary to God's Word, but from any that add to it. The first principle would apply if the state should command population control by abortion or infanticide. My conscience is then free to disobey the state; indeed I am obliged to disobey when the doomed child is mine. But if the state sets a highway speed limit, I am not free in conscience to disobey, for that ordinance does not run contrary to God's Word.[18] In two areas, however, liberty of conscience is even greater. No one – no state, church, or individual – may bind my conscience to *believe* what God has not revealed in Scripture. Neither may anyone require me to *practise* in worship what God has not required.

This principle is strongly presented to Israel in God's law. Israel is commanded to worship as God has commanded, avoiding the idolatry that was universal in the surrounding culture. Israel must also obey the ordinances God appointed for the worship of the tabernacle and the temple. The sin of Nadab and Abihu was to offer 'strange fire' before the Lord, that is, to use censers kindled by their own means rather than with fire taken from God's altar, as he commanded (Lev. 10:1–3; cf. 16:12). The severity of God's judgment on these sons of Aaron, coming as it did at the very beginning of the priestly ministry, showed how seriously God took any departure from his word.

The Lord warns Israel against imitating the worship of the Canaanites when they enter the land, not only because the Canaanites in worship 'do all kinds of detestable things that the LORD hates', but also because such innovations go beyond the command of God: 'See that you do all I command you; do not add to it or take away from it' (Deut. 12:32).

Does this principle also continue in the New Testament, or does the freedom of new convenant worship remove the need for divine revelation to legitimatize worship? Is everything permissible in Christian worship that has not been forbidden in the New Testament? James I. Packer argues for this position:

> The idea that direct biblical warrant, in the form of precept or precedent, is required to sanction every item included in the public worship of God was in fact a Puritan innovation, which crystallised out in the course of the prolonged debates that followed the Elizabethan settlement.[19]

That there was amplification of this principle, as well as an unduly legalistic development of it in the Puritan reformation may be recognized, but to describe it as an innovation fails to take sufficient account of its advocacy by John Calvin and John Knox. Calvin was ready to say bluntly, 'First, whatever is not commanded, we are not free to choose.'[20] Indeed, in the *Institutes* Calvin carefully develops the argument regarding Christian liberty of conscience to which the Westminster Confession appeals. He completely rejects the power of the church to make new ordinances respecting worship beyond what God has commanded. He acknowledges the authority of the church to order worship so that all things may be done decently, and in a fitting way, but he rejects any claim to introduce new elements in worship beyond what God has commanded. Appealing to Colossians 2:16–23, he says of the apostle Paul:

> But at the end of the chapter he condemns with greater confidence all self-made religion, that is, all feigned worship, which men have devised for themselves or received from others, and all precepts they of themselves dare promulgate concerning the worship of God.[21]

Discussion of this so-called 'regulative principle' sometimes leaves out of account the context assumed by Calvin and the Westminster Divines: the regulation of worship by the church (or, indeed, the state). Liberty of conscience is the issue. 'All arbitrary lordship is an encroachment upon God's Kingdom.'[22] Calvin protests this encroachment by the Roman Church; its ecclesiastical constitutions have required in worship what God has not required. 'He [God] alone (when we seek the way to worship him aright and fitly) has authority over our souls, him we ought to obey, and upon his will we ought to wait.'[23] The liberty that Calvin defends does not deny, but assumes church authority in the ordering of worship. Any concerted activity requires direction, and worship is no exception.[24] The apostolic direction that all things be done 'decently, and in order' must be observed (1 Cor. 14:40). God has not given detailed instructions for the order of service, but some order must be followed to secure the unity and peace that corporate worship requires.[25] Under the rubric of 'decorum' – good order in worship – Calvin contrasts 'theatrical props' with ceremonies as exercises of piety, that lead straight to Christ.[26] By 'ceremonies' he has in view such things as kneeling in prayer, maintaining dignity at the Lord's Table, and using 'some decency' in burying the dead. He outlines other circumstances that the church may order: set hours for services, appointed places, unison singing. All must be done to edify: 'If we let love be our guide all will be safe.'[27] Calvin's irenic spirit would minimize conflict over non-essential issues, but while his conception of 'circumstances' of worship was broader than that of many who have adhered to the regulative principle, his commitment to it should not be questioned.[28]

John Knox, in arguing against the celebration of the Mass, presented this syllogism:

> All worshipping, honoring or service invented by the brain of man in the religion of God, without his own express commandment is idolatry. The Mass is invented by the brain of men, without any commandment of God; therefore it is idolatry.[29]

Knox develops the premise of his argument by appealing to the scriptural account of Saul's rejection by God for offering sacrifices although he was not a priest, and for sparing Agag, the king of the Amalekites (1 Sam. 15). Says Knox:

> Disobedience to God's voice is not only when man does wickedly contrary to the precepts of God, but also when of good zeal, or good intent (as we commonly speak), man does anything to the honor or service of God not commanded by the express Word of God . . .[30]

Knox summarizes Old Testament evidence for the regulative principle, asks when God ever set it aside, and then proceeds to support the same principle from New Testament texts. He appeals to the Lordship of Christ over his church, to the inspiration of the apostles in delivering to the church the Word of God, and to Paul's statement concerning the Lord's Supper: 'I have received and learned of the Lord that which I have taught to you'.[31]

Packer objects that the regulative principle is not a necessary implication of the *authority* and *sufficiency* of Scripture, but that it is a question of the *contents* and *interpretation* of Scripture. The mere fact that God has spoken in his Word, and that the Word of God is to be obeyed in all things, does not in itself exclude the possibility that God may have withheld a liberty of conscience such as the Westminster Confession describes. He may, for example, have licensed the church to determine how divine worship was to be offered. But suppose such a possibility were allowed with respect to doctrine. Could the Reformed doctrine of the *sufficiency* of Scripture then be maintained? If the church can promulgate new doctrines that bind the conscience (that *must* be believed for salvation), then the Scripture is not a sufficient revelation. But is the case different when worship is in view? Suppose the church does have the authority to determine what it will do in worship, apart from any particular teaching in God's Word, would the worshipper's conscience be left free, nevertheless, if the church did not make these practices binding? In the case of the Roman Mass, of course, the answer is clear, because that church *requires* participation in the Mass for salvation. But even if such a claim were not made, the problem remains. God does require participation in corporate as well as private worship. For this reason, public worship is not an optional exercise; to require attendance and participation, as it must, the church needs to be able to appeal to God's authority. If it must then go beyond Scripture to determine what worship is acceptable to God, Scripture cannot be a sufficient rule for public worship.

When describing the proper observance of the Lord's Supper, the apostle Paul appeals to the positive institution of the sacrament by the Lord himself (1 Cor. 11:23). In providing further instructions for the worship of the church at Corinth, Paul does not hesitate to claim the authority of the Lord's commandment (1 Cor. 14:37,38).

The New Testament does not repeat a categorical ban on worship that God has not shown to be acceptable to him; there is no precise New Testament equivalent to Deuteronomy 12:29–32. The term that Paul apparently coined (*ethelothrēskeia*) expresses his endorsement of the principle, however.[32] He condemns the 'self-imposed worship' of the false teachers at Colosse.[33] Such worship, apparently connected with ascetic practices, is valueless and disregards the apostolic ordering of worship in Christ's church.

It is true that the New Testament contains no Book of Leviticus, nor is there a Book of Discipline like that which ordered the life and worship of the

Dead Sea community. Calvin acknowledged the divine wisdom in *not* providing a directory of worship, so that the church in various times and places could order its worship appropriately.[34] The proper ordering of corporate worship cannot be extended, however, to include the introduction of new *elements* of worship.

The New Testament indicates, by precept and example, what the elements of worship are. As in the synagogue, corporate prayer is offered (Acts 2:42; 1 Tim. 2:1; 1 Cor. 14:16); Scripture is read (1 Tim. 4:13; 1 Th. 5:27; 2 Th. 3:14; Col. 4:15,16; 2 Pet. 3:15,16) and expounded in preaching (1 Tim 4:13; cf. Lk. 4:20; 2 Tim. 3:15–17; 4:2). There is a direct shift from the synagogue to the gathering of the church (Acts 18:7,11; cf. 19:8–10). The teaching of the word is also linked with table fellowship (Acts 2:42; 20:7, cf. vv. 20,25,28). The songs of the new covenant people both praise God and encourage one another (Eph. 5:19; Col. 3:15; 1 Cor. 14:15,26; cf 1 Tim. 3:16; Rev. 5:9–13; 11:17f; 15:3,4). Giving to the poor is recognized as a spiritual service to God and a Christian form of 'sacrifice' (2 Cor. 9:11–15; Phil. 4:18; Heb. 13:16). The reception and distribution of gifts is related to the office of the deacon (Acts 6:1–6; Rom. 12:8,13; cf. Rom. 16:1,2; 2 Cor. 8:19–21; Acts 20:4; 1 Cor. 16:1–4) and to the gathering of believers (Acts 2:42; 5:2; 1 Cor. 16:2). The faith is also publicly confessed (1 Tim. 6:12; 1 Pet. 3:21; Heb. 13:15; cf. 1 Cor. 15:1–3. The people receive God's blessing (2 Cor. 13:14; Lk. 24:50; cf. Num. 6:22–27. The holy kiss of salutation is also commanded (Rom. 16:16; 1 Cor. 16:20; 2 Cor. 13:12; 1 Th. 5:26; 1 Pet. 5:14). The people respond to praise and prayer with the saying of 'Amen' (1 Cor. 14:16; Rev. 5:14; cf. Rom. 1:25; 9:5; Eph. 3:21 etc.). The sacraments of baptism and the Lord's Supper are explicitly provided for. Confession is linked with baptism (1 Pet. 3:21); and a prayer of thanksgiving with the breaking of the bread (1 Cor. 11:24).

The Presbyterian regulative principle for worship does maintain a New Testament freedom. What it opposes is the introduction of new *observances* in worship; it has no quarrel with any culturally appropriate arrangement of the *circumstances* of worship. The long controversy over the use of instrumental accompaniment in singing seems to arise from a failure to grasp the implications of the Westminster Confession definition of a 'circumstance'. If the use of instruments to accompany and support singing is a circumstance 'common to human actions and societies', it does not require New Testament authorization, for it is not in itself a religious observance, but only a culturally conditioned way of supporting singing.[35]

The issue is different in connection with another distinctive emphasis of Presbyterian worship, the singing of Psalms. Along with the exposition of Scripture, the singing of Psalms was characteristic of the Reformation. Corporate song on the part of the congregation was the chief form of their participation in the service of worship. Calvin wrote French metrical versions of a number of Psalms himself, and used the versions of Clement Marot, the foremost French poet of his day.[36] Psalm singing became the mark of the persecuted Huguenots. A man condemned to the galleys for attending a service of worship in the open fields might manage to preserve with him his most precious possession: a copy of the Psalms.[37] Later Protestant martyrs sang at the stake when the flames burned away their gags. Only the cutting out of their tongues would silence them.

The Reformation church did not sing Psalms exclusively. The Synod of

Montpellier (1598) authorized the use of hymns composed by Theodore Beza.[38] The use of Psalms in metrical versions became the standard, however. The regulative principle was later invoked to require the exclusive use of the Psalms in worship. The two major passages that speak directly of song in worship are Ephesians 5:18–21 and Colossians 3:16, 17. Since the terms used for 'psalms, hymns, and spiritual songs' are found in the initial annotations that form part of the text of the Old Testament Book of Psalms, it has been argued that the three terms are used in the Pauline passages to describe the Psalms of the Old Testament. The two passages, however, when taken together, describe teaching, exhortation, and praise in song that is the product of the filling of the Holy Spirit and the richly indwelling Word of Christ. In particular, it is the wisdom that flows from Christ's Word and Spirit that finds expression in these 'spiritual' songs (see the Spirit-given wisdom of Col. 1:9). Paul surely would not have so described the production of spiritual songs if he had been speaking about the Psalms of the Old Testament.

The close connection in Scottish Presbyterian conviction between the regulative principle and the exclusive use of Psalms did keep worship focussed on the glory of God, and undergirded it with a deep solemnity and earnestness. The richness of the God-centered piety of the Psalms shaped Presbyterian devotion.

There was, however, loss as well as gain. Although preaching sought to show the Messianic thrust of the Psalms, there remained an Old Testament stamp on Presbyterian piety. Psalm-singing Presbyterians readily understood the church as the people of God, but this understanding overshadowed their grasp of the church as the body of Christ and the fellowship of the Spirit. The Presbyterian emphasis well and truly maintained the unity of God's covenant people in the old covenant and the new. If there was weakness, it was in the need to take fuller account of the transformation of covenant renewal and fulfilment in Christ.

Yet another distinctive of Presbyterian worship is its reflection of the covenant theology of Scripture. Presbyterian doctrine appreciated the corporate character of God's dealings with his people. It perceived that in Christ the promise of God was fulfilled: 'I will be your God, and you shall be my people.' Christ is the Alpha and Omega of salvation. The reformers were disciples of the apostle Paul in understanding that Christ represented us in his obedience as well as in his atoning sufferings. The bold assurance by which the new people of God may approach him in worship is drawn from confidence in Christ, the covenant Head. The doctrine of the covenant, grounded in God's election of his people in Christ, provided a sense of the community of the people of God. Presbyterian doctrine taught the perseverance of the saints: that those who persevere to the end as believers will be saved, but that God gives to his own the grace of perseverance.[39] This biblical doctrine increased the emphasis on the means of grace, the Word and the sacraments, and therefore on the services of worship in which these means of grace were provided.

In particular, Presbyterian doctrine taught the solidarity of the people of God in its claim for the children of the covenant. On the one hand, it was recognized that children are born in sin through the fall of the race in its first head, Adam. On the other hand, God made his covenant, not just with isolated individuals, but with heads of families: 'the promise is to you and to your children' (Acts 2:39; Isa. 44:3; 54:13). Circumcision, the sign of faith in the old covenant (Rom. 4:11) was performed on the male children as a sign of God's claim on them. Jesus blessed the little children, pronouncing the name of his heavenly Father upon them. Jesus' blessing showed that under the new covenant, too, children may be named with God's name, as belonging to the family of God.[40] As God's instructions to Aaron show, the pronouncing of blessing on God's people means putting his name upon them (Num. 6:23–27). If children are blessed they are blessed in the divine name. To have God's name placed upon them requires the sign of cleansing: in the new covenant, the sign of baptism. Baptism into the triune name of God is a naming ceremony as well as a sacrament of cleansing (Matt. 28:19). It does not convey salvation (to a child or a professing adult), but it claims God's possession, and the fulfilment of his promise.

To claim the promises of God's mercy for his little ones requires faithfulness on the part of parents. Children must be brought up in the nurture and admonition of the Lord – not simply the nurture of which he approves, but the nurture that the Lord himself directs (Eph. 6:4). This understanding of the covenant led to two major emphases in Presbyterian worship: the importance of family worship and of catechizing. Although the Westminster *Directory* is for public worship, it notes the obligation to sing Psalms 'also privately in the family'. Parents and youth alike were to be instructed in Sunday afternoon services, and parents were held accountable for the teaching of their children. As the Reformed churches became established, systems of house visitation were developed, in which pastors and elders would inquire into the practices of family worship and catechizing. The rise of a literate middle-class laity in the seventeenth century led, in the Puritan movement, to a widespread use of catechisms and devotional literature in the homes.[41] Richard Baxter expected 'the Christian parent to lead family prayers twice daily and to catechize on Sunday, in addition to his private prayer'.[42] The development of family prayers replaced public morning and evening prayers for the community.

Presbyterian doctrine of the covenant also required discipline in the church. Calvin and Knox alike struggled for the independence of church discipline from state control. Particularly at the Lord's Table the keys of the kingdom were to be exercised. Zwingli's original teaching that would regard the Supper as merely symbolical was found inadequate to the sacramental significance of the Lord's institution. Under Calvin's teaching, the Reformed churches emphasized the spiritual presence of Christ in the sacrament. It was a seal as well as a sign, a means of grace when received in faith. This high view of the Supper required careful administration to guard against the dangers of unworthy participation. The confessional of the Roman church was not continued because of the claim of the priesthood to forgive sins. But Reformed services included the confession of sin in prayer, and the pronouncing of God's forgiveness for those who put their penitent trust in Christ. Calvin sought a unified weekly service of worship culminating in the Lord's Supper.[43] He wished to celebrate the sacrament each Lord's Day. His desire was never granted by the elders of Geneva; in the Reformed churches communion was rarely celebrated more often than quarterly. Part of the reason was the desire to prepare adequately for so solemn a service. A preparatory service preceded communion. It was held on Saturday; later, in

American Presbyterian churches of the last generation, on Friday evening. In Scotland and on the Continent, communion tokens were issued to those who had been examined and admitted to the supper. (In the Huguenot churches during the century of persecution, these tokens also served to identify bona fide worshippers in contrast to informers.)

The exercise of discipline in relation to the Lord's Supper was not an isolated aspect of Presbyterian practice. Presbyterians were the heirs of Reformation and of Puritan practice in the cure of souls. Richard Baxter's encyclopaedic *Directory* gives monumental expression to the Puritan concern with individual counselling. The bulk of discipline was carried on by faithful pastors and elders, laboring for the restoration and growth of the flock of Christ.

Presbyterian worship was anchored in the Presbyterian doctrine of the Lord's Day as the Christian Sabbath. It was held that since the Sabbath command is part of the Decalogue, it should be regarded as part of the moral law, not merely an element in the sabbatical system of days and years that was part of the ceremonial law. It was noted that in prophetic passages where mere ceremonialism is denounced, the Sabbath is appealed to in the interests of spiritual worship (Isa. 58). Further, the rationale for the Sabbath, contained in the Ten Commandments, grounds it in God's rest after the six days of creation. The day, to be sure, has been changed, from the seventh to the first, in celebration of Christ's resurrection, but the sabbath principle of one day of rest in seven is still maintained in the observance of the Lord's Day.

Discussions continue in conservative Presbyterian circles as to the exegesis of Colossians 2:16,17, and as to the sense in which the Lord's Day can be regarded as a Sabbath. It is to be feared, however, that the decline in Sunday observance, even in Presbyterian churches, is to be traced, not to any shifts in conviction, but rather to the eroding effects of contemporary culture. Surely the practice of Lord's Day observance in historic Presbyterianism not only underwrote morning and evening services as well as Sabbath school, but also preserved time for family teaching and catechizing. In spite of the adverse effects of a kind of enforced idleness in many homes, the observance of the day brought a deep awareness of the worship of God by those who claimed his covenant.

A final characteristic of Presbyterian worship has been the place given to the care of the poor. The Protestant Reformation brought a revolution in deaconal ministry. Beggars besieged the doors of medieval churches, but cities that adopted the Reformation organized charitable structures to care for them. Nuremberg and Strasbourg took the lead in this. There was no collection taken in the Reformed service in Strasbourg, but a chest for alms was placed at the back of the church, and the people were exhorted to remember the poor. Calvin, in his study of office in New Testament church, recovered the significance of the office of the deacon, which had become just a step in ecclesiastical orders in the medieval church. Geneva became a model of deaconal ministry with its hospice, gardens, and kitchen for the relief of the poor, and its French Refugee Fund for the thousands who fled persecution to take refuge in the city.[44] The Westminster *Directory* urges care for the poor as a Sabbath duty, and links collections for the poor with the communion service and seasons of thanksgiving.

It might seem that even a brief article on Presbyterian worship should discuss the history of the order of service in Reformed and Presbyterian history. This task has been often undertaken, making it evident that a fixed order of service has deep roots in the Reformed branch of the Reformation.[45] Charles W. Baird's book, *Eutaxia*, published in 1855, created a stir in Presbyterian circles at that time by presenting the orders of service with accompanying prayers from Reformed sources, including Calvin's Geneva, Knox's Scotland, and Baxter's England.[46]

Yet it would run contrary to the Presbyterian theology of liberty in worship to seek to develop a fixed liturgy. Even principles of ordering liturgy would have to be given Scriptural support before they could be made mandatory. One such principle, often stated in Reformed circles, is that the order of worship must alternate between God's address to his people and their response to God. That the elements of worship include both cannot be disputed: God does address his people through the Scriptures, in preaching, in the blessing. The people also respond to God in prayer and praise. They say, 'Amen' to what God says (1 Cor. 14:16). But nowhere does the Bible require that worship must proceed with a fixed alternation of God's address and response. Further, Scripture constantly blends the worship of God with the edification of his people. When God's people meet in his name, they meet with each other even as they stand before him. It would be not only arbitrary but unscriptural to exclude from a service of worship the means by which Christians may encourage one another as they draw near to God (Heb. 10:25; Col. 3:16).[47] We do not seek first to benefit the saints when we hallow God's name, but hallowing God's name does benefit the saints.

At the same time, Paul's careful guarding of worship at Corinth makes clear that worship is not a human-centered social occasion, arranged for entertainment and conviviality, so that only the golden calf is missing. The goal of worship is met when the stranger, rebuked for his sin, falls down, and says, 'God is really among you!' (1 Cor. 14:25). So are the Old Testament promises fulfilled in the New (Isa. 45:14) as the people of God draw near to the heavenly festival, to Jesus, the Lord of glory, and to our God, a consuming fire. True evangelism and nurture are not impeded, but mightily advanced when the worshipping church sees with awe the Christ of the lampstands and the glory of the throne (Rev. 1:17).

PRESBYTERIAN WORSHIP: A BRIEF BIBLIOGRAPHY

Baird, Charles W., *Presbyterian Liturgies: Historical Sketches* (Grand Rapids: Baker Book House reprint, 1967).

Barkley, John M., *Worship of the Reformed Church*, Ecumenical Studies in Worship 15 (Atlanta: John Knox Press, 1967).

Baxter, Richard, 'The Ordinary Public Worship on the Lord's Day' in *The Practical Works of Richard Baxter*, vol. 1 (Ligonier, Pa.: Soli Deo Gloria Publications, reprint, 1990)

Bogue, Carl W., *The Scriptural Law of Worship* (Dallas: Presbyterian Heritage Publications, 1988).

Benoit, J. D., *Liturgical Renewal: Studies in Catholic and Protestant Developments on the Continent* (London: SCM, 1958).

Dennison, James T., Jr., *The Market Day of the Soul: The Puritan Doctrine of the Sabbath in England, 1532–1700* (Lanham, Md.: University Press of America, 1983).

Forrester, Duncan & Murray, Douglas, eds., *Studies in the History of Worship in Scotland* (Edinburgh: T & T Clark, 1984).

Knox, John, *True and False Worship* (Reprinted from David Laing, ed., *The Works of John Knox* (Edinburgh: James Thin, 1895), vol. 3, pp. 29–70.) (Dallas: Presbyterian Heritage Publications, 1988).

Macleod, Donald, *Presbyterian Worship: Its Meaning and Method* (Atlanta: John Knox Press, 1965)

Martin, Ralph P., *The Worship of God* (Grand Rapids: Eerdmans, 1982).

Maxwell, William D., *John Knox's Genevan Service Book, 1556: the Liturgical Portions* (Edinburgh: Oliver & Boyd, 1931).

Maxwell, William D., *An Outline of Christian Worship* (London: Oxford University Press, 1955).

Murray, Iain, ed., *The Reformation of the Church* (London: Banner of Truth Trust, 1965).

Nichols, James Hastings, *Corporate Worship in the Reformed Tradition* (Philadelphia: Westminster Press, 1968).

Old, Hughes Oliphant, *Worship* (Guides to the Reformed Tradition) (Atlanta: John Knox Press, 1984).

Rayburn, Robert G., *O Come, Let Us Worship: Corporate Worship in the Evangelical Church* (Grand Rapids: Baker Book House, 1980).

Robson, Edward A., ed. *The Biblical Doctrine of Worship: A Symposium* (Beaver Falls: Reformed Presbyterian Church of North America, 1974).

Shepherd, Massey H., Jr. *The Paschal Liturgy in the Apocalypse* (Ecumenical Studies in Worship, 6) (Atlanta: John Knox Press, 1960).

Thompson, Bard, *Liturgies of the Western Church* (Cleveland: World Publishing, 1965).

Wegman, Herman A. J. trans. Lathrop, Gordon W., *Christian Worship in East and West* (New York: Pueblo Publishing, 1985).

White, James F., *Introduction to Christian Worship* (Nashville: Abingdon Press, 1980).

6

Worship in Anglicanism

ROGER BECKWITH

The outstanding characteristic of Anglicanism is its tradition of congregational worship. The *Book of Common Prayer*, drawn up in 1549 by the leading Reformer of the Church of England, Archbishop Thomas Cranmer (1489–1556), and revised by him in 1552, was its first vernacular service book, but such was the quality of this first attempt that it has never been superseded, and (with some revision) is still in use today. 'Our incomparable liturgy', as Robert Southey boldly called it, has found many admirers in the reformed churches abroad, and even in the Free Churches in England, despite their non-liturgical traditions.[1] Only since the Second World War have rivals to it sprung up in the Anglican Churches: how long their challenge will last is as yet uncertain. With a little more modernization, the Prayer Book would probably outlast them all.

ANGLICAN CHRISTIANITY

Anglicanism is a pattern of Christianity which arose in England, Wales and Ireland under the influence of the sixteenth-century Reformation, and was afterwards carried by emigrants and missionaries to the British possessions abroad, and to some extent beyond them. Like the other traditions of the Reformation, it aimed at a restoration of biblical doctrine, which it embodied in a confession of faith, the *Thirty-Nine Articles of Religion* (1553, brought to its present form in 1571). This is generally Lutheran in character, but Calvinistic on the divisive points of sacramental doctrine (the same doctrinal standpoint being evident in the Holy Communion service of the Prayer Book).[2] In his reform of church practice, Cranmer sympathized with the more conservative among the continental Reformers. The Church of England therefore remained episcopal, paedo-baptist, national and liturgical. Like Luther, and unlike Zwingli or the Anabaptists, he followed the policy of changing what, in the light of Scripture, needed changing, but not of beginning afresh. The *Book of Common Prayer* is an example of this policy. Cranmer defended the policy as minimising disputes among Christians and hurt to the conscience of the weaker brother.

THE ANGLICAN LITURGY

Like the continental Reformers, Cranmer maintained the practice of liturgical prayer for corporate worship. Liturgy is a set form of prayer, particularly suited to universal and permanent topics, and uniquely capable of safeguarding biblical doctrine. Although highly formal if led or approached in an unspiritual state of mind, and although inviting supplementation by free prayer, perhaps on other occasions, to cover local and temporary topics, good liturgy has a proven capacity to sustain and deepen the spiritual life, to which many great Christians bear witness.[3] The liturgy Cranmer produced is a far-reaching revision, in the vernacular, of the Latin Sarum liturgy (the most influential of the local British uses of the Roman liturgy, taking its name from the cathedral of Sarum or Salisbury). It consists of services for daily use (Morning and Evening Prayer), services for use on Sundays and holy days (these plus Holy Communion) and services for use on special occasions (Baptism, Confirmation, Marriage, Burial, Ordination etc). It also includes a reformed and simplified church Calendar; a new Lectionary, designed to ensure that most of the Bible is publicly read, in an orderly fashion, once a year (and the New Testament more than once); and a Catechism for the instruction of enquirers and the young. The sources Cranmer drew upon, apart from Sarum and the Bible, are the early Fathers and continental revisers of the liturgy, notably Francis Quignon and Hermann von Wied. Much of the added material, and the English style of the whole, is of his own composition.

An exhortation introducing Morning and Evening Prayer, and another introducing the second half of the Holy Communion service, outline the structure of these services, and show how carefully they were planned to include all the elements of biblical worship in an orderly development. As an example of Cranmer's skill in embodying biblical teaching in a graceful liturgical style, one may take his newly-composed collect for the Second Sunday in Advent:

> Blessed Lord, who hast caused all holy Scriptures to be written for our learning; Grant that we may in such wise hear them, read, mark, learn, and inwardly digest them, that by patience, and comfort of thy holy Word, we may embrace, and ever hold fast the blessed hope of everlasting life, which thou hast given us in our Saviour Jesus Christ. *Amen.*

Cranmer's general liturgical aims are clear from his Prayer Book itself, and especially from his two prefatory statements 'Concerning the Service of the Church' (as it is now called) and 'Of Ceremonies'. These reveal many of the concerns common to the Reformers, noted also in Klaas Runia's chapter on reformed worship in Holland. As I have written elsewhere, Cranmer

> seeks to attain intelligibility, edification, and corporateness, by producing, for regular use, a single, simple liturgy in the vernacular, in which the Scriptures are read and expounded in an orderly way, biblical teaching is incorporated throughout, all that is misleading or meaningless is excluded, words are audible, actions visible, and congregational participation in speaking, singing, and reception of the sacrament (in both kinds) is encouraged. In pursuing these aims, there were limits to what he achieved. Like other students of the Bible, he had his blind spots. Being

confronted with a largely illiterate Church, and longstanding habits of infrequent lay communion, he was not able to implement his principle of congregational worship as fully as he wished, and he had to carry simplicity to lengths which restricted variety and freedom, and sacrificed some of the riches of the pre-Reformation liturgy. He curbed music and ceremonial to an extent which may have been necessary at the time, but was not permanently desirable. He made rather too much use of exhortations. Yet, when all necessary deductions have been made, his achievement remains extraordinary. When compared with the state of the liturgy at the beginning of Henry VIII's reign, Cranmer's Prayer Books show the following significant changes: the language has been altered from Latin to English; a many-volume service book has been reduced to one; a number of regional uses has been reduced to one national use; the rubrics have been pruned (even to excess), simplified, and fully integrated with the liturgical texts; the lectionary has been reformed; preaching has been revived; the congregation has been given a considerable part in the service; the cup has been restored to the laity, and the rule of receiving the sacrament once a year has been increased threefold; an impressive new structure has been given to the Communion service; the eight daily offices have been combined into two; the biblical content of most services has been greatly increased; and traditional doctrines and practices which Cranmer judged to be in conflict with biblical theology (notably the sacrifice of the Mass, transubstantiation, reservation, the confessional, petition for the departed and the invocation of saints), have been reformed or entirely removed. The fact that his second Prayer Book received only minor revisions in 1559, 1604, and 1662, and in its 1662 form is still widely used in England and other parts of the world, is a tribute to his achievement which is not easy to gainsay.[4]

'Spiritual sacrifices', such as link worship with the whole Christian life, are prominent in Prayer Book worship, especially in the Holy Communion service, where the sacrifices of alms, of praise and thanksgiving, and of ourselves, our souls and bodies, alike feature; but the New Testament principle that corporate worship should 'edify' the worshipper is even more prominent. Cranmer makes this point in both of his prefatory statements, quoting 1 Cor. 14. Edification should be the aim of all that takes place in the congregation, he says. For this reason he has abolished the use of Latin and of meaningless or misleading ceremonies. The ample provision which the Prayer Book makes for the public reading of Scripture, and its revival of preaching, are in the same interest, and so is its inclusion of explanatory exhortations in the services. For the Reformers, the test of 'edification' (or of building one another up through the understanding, as it is interpreted in 1 Cor. 14) is Scripture, and Cranmer evidently aimed to ensure that the text of his services did not merely avoid any conflict with Scripture, but positively expressed the ideas of Scripture, and often in the very language of Scripture. So successful was he in this, that a book used to be in circulation which listed parallel passages from the Bible for every page of the spoken text of the Prayer Book.[5]

PRAYER BOOK REVISION

Like other confessional families, the Anglican Communion has been influenced by new movements of theological thought since Reformation times, and these have sometimes affected the way the Prayer Book has been revised. Cranmer's first Prayer Book was an interim stage in his work of reform,[6] and was therefore more like mediaeval liturgy, which meant in turn that (externally at least) it was more like patristic liturgy, than his second. Cranmer's attitude to the Fathers was selective, recognising that some of their practices had become misleading owing to mediaeval theological developments, and only restoring their practices (if no longer in use) where there was need for change and where it was they that provided the best model. In the seventeenth and eighteenth centuries, however, an ardent antiquarianism arose, which sought to restore patristic liturgy for its own sake, and this made Cranmer's first Prayer Book seem preferable to his second. A move back in that direction was therefore made in the Scottish and American Prayer Books of the period. In the nineteenth century, the traditionalism of the Anglo-Catholic movement tended to revive pre-Reformation doctrine as well as pre-Reformation practice, which made pre-Reformation liturgy seem even more attractive; while the rationalism of the Broad Church movement tended to throw doubt on tradition, and even to undermine the biblical basis on which the Anglican liturgy rests. Since that time, Prayer Book revision has frequently been influenced by these two conflicting tendencies. Some pre-Reformation practices have been restored, usually as options, and some biblical features have been made optional or omitted. On the whole, this has been done with restraint, but not in accordance with a consistent theological purpose. The 1662 revision, which is uninfluenced by these developments, is the most satisfactory edition of the Prayer Book currently in use, though it of course lays no claim to perfection.

NEW TENDENCIES IN LITURGICAL REVISION

Since the Second World War, partly under the influence of the radical Anglo-Catholic liturgiologist Gregory Dix,[7] and partly in deference to expected ecumenical developments which look less and less likely as time goes on, the Anglican churches have tended to set the Prayer Book aside as a starting-point for liturgical revision. The same theological trends as have influenced revision of the Prayer Book since the nineteenth century are still at work, generally speaking, but the new liturgies which have been produced are taken directly from patristic models, and are worded in a contemporary idiom of language. The deeply biblical content of Cranmer's text, and the classic beauty of its expressive style, which were such a powerful influence on all revisions which took his liturgy as their starting-point, thus cease to play any significant part. Congregational participation is rightly stressed, but doctrinal clarity is abandoned in favour of studied ambiguity. In the worst cases, all penitential material and all credal material are made optional, and only modern fads such as feminism are given obligatory expression. Though some of these new service books borrow the name of the *Book of Common Prayer* (e.g. those produced in the U.S.A. and Wales), they are really quite distinct from it, and the names used in England and Canada (*Alternative Service Book, Book of Alternative Services*) give a much clearer indication of their character.

An exception deserves to be made in favour of those Anglican churches, notably that of Australia, which have consciously attempted to maintain the doctrine of the existing liturgy in their revision, and have included modernizations of Prayer Book services as well as services newly composed.[8]

THE CONTEXT OF THE LITURGY

Liturgical texts are not, of course, the sum-total of corporate worship, even in liturgical churches. Hymns have for more than two centuries been a popular and powerful adjunct, though it is left to the officiant to see that they are appropriately chosen. The ordering of church buildings and their furnishings plays a significant part in worship; and the Liturgical Movement, which began in the Church of Rome at the turn of the century and has since spread to other liturgical churches, has done much to restore a simple and corporate pattern of worship, which had previously been restored by the Reformers but had been to some degree lost since, even among their followers. Frequency of receiving the sacrament has increased, owing to the joint influence of the Evangelical and Anglo-Catholic movements of the eighteenth and nineteenth centuries, and this has made Holy Communion more prominent among the regular services. The advent of universal literacy in this century has led to more congregational participation in saying and singing, and a greater degree of prescribed variety, than older liturgies, with their strict rubrics, provide for. This is one of the reasons why the Prayer Book tends today to be used with some freedom. The new service books, in reaction against strict rubrics, provide very lax ones, and since these are used with equal freedom, there are many congregations where liturgical worship is in danger of giving way to impromptu worship directed by the minister. This is particularly the case, of course, in congregations where the Charismatic Movement has taken control. Anglican services today range from the precise musical renderings of the liturgy in cathedrals to the very informal imitations of Nonconformist worship practised in some parish churches. It is evangelicals in particular who seem at present to show the least grasp of the value of liturgy, but there are some signs that a renewed appreciation of it is beginning to emerge.

BIBLIOGRAPHY

G. W. O. Addleshaw and F. Etchells, *The Architectural Setting of Anglican Worship* (London: Faber, 1948).

S. Brook, *The Language of the Book of Common Prayer* (London: Deutsch, 1965).

J. Dowden, *The Workmanship of the Prayer Book* (London: Methuen, 1901).

C. Jones, G. Wainwright and E. Yarnold, ed., *The Study of Liturgy* (London: SPCK, 1978, new ed. 1992).

C. Neil and J. M. Willoughby, ed., *The Tutorial Prayer Book* (London: Harrison Trust, 1912, new ed. forthcoming).

7

Worship in Lutheranism

NORVALD YRI

I. INTRODUCTION

Robert D. Preus concludes an article on 'Lutheranism and Lutheran Theology' with these words: *'The highest worship of God is to believe in Christ.* Thus the entire Christian life flows from the theology of the cross, and all the articles of faith proceed from this central article of faith of the Christian.'[1]

J. Atkinson, writing about Martin Luther (1483–1546), points out how Luther's spiritual experience was at the centre of the Reformation:

> Luther rediscovered the original gospel – the truth of Eph. 2:8. As he expressed it: 'The door of paradise was flung open to me and I entered.' This discovery meant the unqualified centrality of Christ, the proclamation of the original gospel message, and the restoration of biblical, evangelical thinking. Here lay the source of Luther's Reformation theology, as he felt driven by God to re-form what had been deformed . . . He set *Christ and his work at the centre* rather than humanity and its works. He put the *common man* on his theological feet by restoring the doctrine of the *priesthood of all believers.*[2]

Faith in Jesus Christ, then, is the highest worship of God. Such a conclusion is implicit in the lengthy biblical essays in this collection. Y. Hattori, dealing with worship in the OT, argues that 'the truth of the covenant of redemption must be at the core of all aspect related to worship' – and at the same time insists that many of the OT cultic themes drive toward God's self-disclosure under the new covenant.[3] Discussing worship in the NT, D. Peterson, writes, 'It will be argued below that worship in the NT is essentially an engagement with God through faith in Jesus Christ and what he had done for us. Such faith will express itself in daily obedience or service to God in every sphere of life.'[4]

Without discussing the theology of worship presented in the book, *Ten Worshipping Churches*, this comment drawn from its Introduction is surely right:

> In the midst of our contemporary debates about forms, styles, traditions and different interpretations of scriptural commands about worship, often the last question to be considered is what God might be looking for. Jesus declared Jn. 4: 'Believe me, woman, a time is coming when you will worship the Father neither on

this mountain nor in Jerusalem . . . A time is coming and has now come when the true worshippers will worship the Father in Spirit and truth, for they are the kind of worshippers the Father seeks. God is spirit, and his worshippers must worship in spirit and in truth; (*Jn. 4:21–24*) The measure of the true worshipper that the Father seeks is not the length of his historical tradition or the height of his hands above his head . . . It has more to do with integrity – 'in truth' – than pedigree.[5]

II. THE CONTEXT OF LUTHERANISM

It is impossible to understand the Protestant world, including the Lutheran, without being aware of the historical and ecclesiastical context in which Protestantism as such, was born. Worship theology in the Lutheran tradition will also be left hanging in the air unless we recognize the main issues of fundamental importance at the time when Protestant churches came into being.

Martin Luther was born into a German Catholic family. He entered the monastery of the Augustinian Hermits in Erfurt (1505), and was ordained a priest in 1507. In 1511 he became Doctor of Theology and then professor of biblical studies at the University of Wittenberg until his death. Luther lectured on Genesis, Psalms, Romans and Galatians. In his *Disputation against Scholastic Theology* (1517) Luther challenged the prevailing philosophical theology and favoured the Augustinian/biblical theology. On October 31, 1517, Luther posted his Ninety-five Theses condemning the abuses of the system of indulgences within the Catholic Church. The posting of theses was an ordinary way of discussing theological questions, but the issues at stake were in this case massive and sensitive.

What was the background for this theological debate? Let us look at it in Luther's own words:

It happened in the year 1517, that a preaching monk called John Tetzel, a great ranter, made his appearance . . . with indulgences, selling grace for money as clearly and cheaply as he could . . . the same grace (he said) as that by which a man is reconciled to God. Again that it was not necessary to have remorse, sorrow, or repentance for sin, if one brought (I ought to say, acquired) an indulgence or a dispensation, indeed he (Tetzel) sold also for future sins . . . He showed regard for neither the truth nor the salvation of men's souls . . . This is the first, real, fundamental beginning of the Lutheran rumpus . . . The other cause for the beginning of this rumpus was the most holy father, Pope Leo, with his untimely ban (*Exurge Domine*, 1520).[6]

It is possible to articulate a variety of political and social factors that provide a frame of reference for the Protestant Reformation. For instance, we might mention the growing tensions between the Pope's influence in both political and ecclesiastical realms, and the growing development in the German state of the political principle *cuius regio eius religio*: the one who has the political power has the right to decide what kind of 'religion' [understood to be Christianity] this region should have. Thus we acknowledge that the German political outlook was strongly stirred up by the Reformation ideas that were freeing the German people from the authority of the Pope in Rome.

However, the basic issue in the Reformation was theological. It was a re-discovery of the biblical message of salvation by faith for the sake of Jesus Christ. This re-discovery came as Martin Luther sought to discover how a sinner can ever find God to be gracious, as he recognized how the Catholic Church had left the teaching of Scripture, as he reacted to Tetzel's ministry, and as he re-studied the Psalms in the light of justification by faith as he found it in Romans. For several years Luther hoped that the Pope and the Catholic Church as a whole would see and understand the need for a true Reformation from within the Church. However, when this failed schism became inevitable.

It is important to remember that Luther did not come with a new teaching or a new theology; he did not intend to establish a new denomination. Luther's concern was the theology of Holy Scripture, and he argued that he belonged to the church of the apostles and of the church fathers such as Ambrose and Augustine. However, Luther was forced to separate from the Roman Church system as the only way to advance a reform that would give room for the true gospel. The Diet of Augsburg was held in 1530 where the Augsburg Confession was presented, an official publication of those who wanted the classical Christian faith. In the meantime Luther had written a reformed Mass (1523) and a popular, *German Mass* (1526), the *Great Catechism* and the *Short Catechism* (1529), as well as a variety of other publications. The various confessional writings of the Lutheran Church are found in the so-called *Book of Concord* (1580), a complete statement of Protestant theology that would differentiate it from Catholic theology. The book also contains the three great universal creeds of the early church.

Luther did not want his name to be part of the title of this rising evangelical church. The confessional writings do not speak of the 'Lutheran Church' but of 'our congregations', 'the Church among us', 'the pure evangelical Church', 'our reformed Church', etc. Many called themselves 'the evangelicals'. However, as the Calvinists began to call themselves 'the Reformed', the 'Lutheran' rubric appeared to distinguish then from the Calvinists.[7]

III. HOLY SCRIPTURE AND WORSHIP

Classic Lutheran theology constantly stresses the truthfulness of Scripture. In fact, the truthfulness of the Old and New Testaments is the basis for worship – a theme that goes through all the writings of Luther. It is an underlying issue in all the Lutheran confessional documents, particularly clear in the Formula of Concord (1577). Holy Scripture is the foundation of Christian worship, and Holy Scripture gives the understanding of Christian worship. All other writings and all teachers are to be judged by Holy Scripture; the Scripture is the highest authority in all questions dealing with Christian faith and conduct. Luther and the confessional Lutheran documents did not accept as Christian teaching that which was absent from Scripture, even though it had been approved by popes, church councils, church-tradition, theologians or bishops.[8]

However, this principle of *norma normans* – the basic norm of all true theology and worship – is today endangered by a variety of philosophical movements that tend to regard human reason, feelings or religious experience of higher authority than God's Word. This has created a variety of crises, not only in the Lutheran churches, but in other Protestant churches as well. Similarly, Roman Catholic Christianity has been influenced by this erosion of biblical authority. These theological and philosophical movements sometimes combine with conciliar pressure that tends to be quiet on the *sola scriptura* principle. All this has led much Lutheran theology to ask whether or not we have the right to argue for a particular Christian ministry and worship.

The Lutheran World Federation, a fellowship in which most of the Churches representing the 70 million Lutherans are members, has struggled with the question of *sola scriptura* since the general assembly at Helsinki, Finland in 1963 (primarily to discuss the theme of justification by faith alone). Today the dominant Lutheran theology tends to doubt the possibility of arguing for *sola scriptura* in the terms in which it is expounded in Luther's theology and in the Lutheran confessions. Here and there, however, there have been restatements of the classical Lutheran theology of Scripture among Lutherans.[9]

IV. THE THEOLOGY OF THE CROSS AT THE CENTRE OF WORSHIP

As we have seen, Peterson defines New Testament worship as 'an engagement with God through faith in Jesus Christ and what he had done for us'. One of his central themes is that in the New Testament Jesus Christ is the fulfilment of the Old Testament sacrificial institutions, and thus Christ is the only atoning sacrifice for our sins, recognized and accepted by God. Peterson's theological explanations are very much in line with Luther's writings and the Lutheran confessional documents on these points.

The main issue in this context is the question of how to be saved. Is the sacrifice of Jesus Christ sufficient, or is something more needed? Is the vicarious atonement of Jesus the only foundation for a person's redemption, or is something also required from the human side? The theology of worship has here its focal point.

Martin Luther was brought up in a Church that had developed its theology into a system that insisted on human co-operation with God for salvation. The Catholic Mass, as an institution, placed extraordinary power into human hands. The Catholic priest has the authority to offer sacrifice. What is he sacrificing? He presents Jesus Christ to God in an unbloody way.

Lutheran worship theology is deeply influenced by the Reformation break with the Mass as the presentation of Christ to God in an unbloody way. This is often not understood today, even by many contemporary Catholics. According to Roman Catholic theology the Lord's Supper is both a sacrament and a sacrifice. It is not only given to the participants, but it is also offered to God. This sacrifice of Christ is being brought to the Father by means of the hands of the priest. What God has given to us, a person takes and gives to God as a sacrifice: 'The priests fulfil their most important ministry in the eucharistic mystery of the sacrifice, in which our redemption is continuously fulfilled'.[10]

Luther was himself a sacrificing priest, but stopped reading mass in 1521. Luther preferred the term 'Abendmahl' (lit. 'evening meal') to refer to the Lord's Supper, and avoided terms like 'Eucharist', 'Missa' 'the sacrament of the altar', etc. Today when conservative Catholic priests say that Christ has to be offered in sacrifice, it is hard to avoid the conclusion that the sacrifice of Christ at Calvary was not sufficient. The Son of God is presented to the Father again, but now in an unbloody way.

But the Lord's Supper is not a sacrifice for our sins. *That* sacrifice was offered once and for all by our Lord Jesus Christ. The Augsburg Confession (1530) rightly insists that the sin and lostness of humankind go so deep that it is impossible for fallen people to co-operate with God in their salvation. In the theological context of the day, this cannot mean less than that a man is not able to co-operate with God by changing the Lord's Supper into a sacrificial act.

The centrality of Christ in Lutheran worship flows from this strong reaction against Roman Catholic teaching. On the critical issues of the nature of the Lord's Supper and the inability of human beings to contribute redemptively in their own salvation, Luther himself said:

> I can say 'Thus my teaching stands, and so it is correct; it is a good teaching. This is evident from the fact that it builds upon the Lord Christ, it lets God be our God, and it gives God the glory. This teaching is correct, and it cannot go wrong . . . We have to sacrifice nothing else to God than to trust and hope in him (by Christ).'[11]

Thus Lutheran worship-theology is Christ-centered and it is established on the basis of the unity of Scripture. We have to study the Old Testament, Luther said, 'The OT is the cradle where Christ was lying.'

As is obvious from Luther's writings (e.g. Weimer Ausgabe) as well as from the *Book of Concord* (the Lutheran confessional writings), the centrality of Christ as mediator, as the only sacrifice for us and as the only high priest of the new covenant, is strongly stated.

Luther translated the word *hilastērion* in Rom. 3:25 with the German word *Gnadestuhl* ('mercy seat'). John Calvin adopted the same rendering. D. Peterson in his article in this book apparently prefers the rendering 'means of atonement' or 'sacrifice of atonement'.

However, both Luther and Calvin aligned themselves with a tradition of interpretation where the unity of Scripture and 'fulfilment' themes were rather strong. For both of them, Christians participate in the reality that was given to Jesus as a shadow (to use the language of the epistle to the Hebrews).

The text in Rom. 3:24–25 says, literally, 'being justified freely by his grace through the redemption that is in Christ Jesus, whom God set forth as *hilastērion* by his blood through faith . . .' The word *hilastērion* comes from the verb *hilaskomai* – 'to propitiate', and thus more generally to 'atone'; the cognate noun, on this reading, means 'that which atones'. In the corresponding Hebrew the word is *kapporeth* – and this word denotes the place above the ark in the Most Holy Place of the Tabernacle. This 'mercy-seat' is rendered *hilastērion* in the LXX. It is important to remember that the *kapporeth* was *the place* where the high priest sprinkled blood on the Day of Atonement (*Yom Kippur*, from the verb *kipper*, 'to atone' cf. Exod. 25:17f.; Lev. 16:2, 13f.; comp. Heb. 9:5). It has often been pointed out that the Jewish Targum (Aramaic paraphrases of the Hebrew Bible) translates *kapporeth* with the expression 'the *place* of atonement'. The meaning is not abstract but concrete, a technical expression for the 'mercy-seat' (or 'throne') where God revealed himself to Israel (Exod. 25:22); he revealed his glory, and smoke covered the mercy-seat on the Day of Atonement when the high priest went in with blood (Lev. 16:13). Further, it has been argued that the abstract meaning of *hilastērion* is absent from the profane Greek of the Hellenistic period, as well as from the LXX in particular. Nor is the meaning 'sacrifice of atonement' found.[12]

Both Luther and Calvin, then, are in a tradition of interpretation that includes the LXX, the Targum and various church fathers. There is also strong support for interpreting Heb. 9:5 as referring to the 'mercy-seat', a concrete place (cf. Exod. 25:17–18; 31:7; 35:12; 37:1, 6; Lev.16:14, 19; Num.7. 89).

God himself gave the prescription for the Jewish Tabernacle, the ark and the mercy-seat. And it was God himself who presented Jesus in his own blood as the fulfilment of that to which the mercy-seat in the OT pointed forward. Under the mercy-seat were the two tablets of the law, the ten commandments. The requirements of the law are covered by Jesus Christ as the mercy-seat sacrifice and high priest. This is the classical Lutheran interpretation of this reality, and is at the very core of classic Lutheran worship.

V.   FAITH IN JESUS

Reacting against the worship theology of the Roman Catholic Church, Lutheran theology has emphasized that Christian worship is only by faith in Jesus Christ.

As Luther said: 'We are to sacrifice nothing else to God than trust and hope in him . . . The forgiveness of sins and grace are greater than the whole world's act of worship . . . The best and most appropriate worship of God is to trust and believe. And he demands nothing more than a heart that believes in him' . . . 'To attribute glory to God is to believe in him and to regard him as truthful, wise, righteous, merciful, and almighty, in short, to acknowledge him as the source and donor of every good' . . . 'To glorify God is nothing else than to believe in him, to hope in him, and to love him, for whoever believes him treats him as true and through this ascribes truth to him'.[13] Of course, this is not to neglect the variety of other issues connected with Christian worship to which we shall shortly turn.

However, it is crucial to be aware of the importance of faith! Faith is not a product of a person's spiritual ability; it is not a good work, but it is created in the heart of a person by the word of the cross, by listening to the message about Jesus Christ as Saviour and Mediator. Further, this faith is *alone* (*sola fide*) in the sense that God's righteousness and forgiveness of sins are given as gifts solely for the sake of Jesus Christ, and appropriated solely by the means of faith. Good works, understood as something contributed by human beings to add to faith as a gift from God, are contrary to God's Word.

VI.   LAW AND GOSPEL IN WORSHIP

Various components in Lutheran theology must be clarified in order to make clear the differences between the pre-Reformation Catholic theology of worship and the Reformation theology of worship.

The classical Catholic worship theology tended to hold worshippers under a variety of spiritual demands that had no foundation in Scripture, but nevertheless represented pressing ecclesiastical authority. This theological and ecclesiastical slavery was both internal and external; it had to do with both content and forms in Catholic worship.

Luther, as he struggled to find out how to find a gracious God, began by assuming that the righteousness of God was necessarily and exclusively a judging, punishing righteousness. Eventually he came to see that God gives in Christ the righteousness Luther needed. This experience, however, was closely related to his growing understanding of the difference between God's law and his gospel. As a monk and as a sacrificing priest he had confused the two. Now he came to recognize that God's law will always accuse sinful human beings. The absoluteness of God's holy law means that all are lost under God's holy demand. But now Luther came to see that the gospel, the message about Jesus Christ, his vicarious life and atoning death and resurrection, fulfil everything God demands of sinners. This fulfilment is God's righteousness in Christ given as a gift by God's grace to the sinner. This righteousness that is accepted by God is solely that of Christ; as Luther so often stated, our righteousness is a person (1 Cor. 1:30), and must be differentiated from the believers' empirical righteousness of life.

Thus while classic Catholic theology thinks of righteousness in terms of a healing process (*sanatio*), classic Lutheran theology points to the biblical understanding of 'justification' with the forensic meaning. It is God in heaven who is the Judge in the court, and he has pronounced his judgment that every person who believes in Jesus is recognized as having in him all his righteousness, and is forgiven all sins by God.

This message, the message of the gospel, creates faith in the heart of men and women, so that they trust in Jesus.

VII. THE PRIESTHOOD OF ALL BELIEVERS IN WORSHIP

Out of this background we more readily grasp the Lutheran emphasis on the priesthood of all believers (of. esp. 1 Pet. 2:5–9).

While the Catholic Church posited two priesthoods (the priest who offered sacrifice [*sacerdos*] and the priesthood of all believers), Lutheran theology teaches that there is only one priesthood under the new covenant: all believers. Thus the servant leaders of the congregations are chosen from among the priesthood of all believers.

We have only one mediator between us and God, Jesus Christ the high priest, who remains forever on our behalf before God. Every believer in Christ has direct access to God through him. All true believers, themselves priests, are the only true worshippers in the whole world. This has been a revolutionary idea throughout the Protestant world.

In principle, then, the whole worship of the Christian Church is connected with, and springs from, the priesthood of all believers. Such elements, as preaching, the administration of baptism and the Lord's Supper, emerge from the fact that all believers have direct access to God by Christ; he alone is the Mediator. All believers have the right to pray for others, the right to test and judge the preaching and teaching, because true believers will listen to the Shepherd's voice (John 10:27f).[14]

VIII. LUTHERAN WORSHIP AND THE MEANS OF GRACE

'Outside the church is no salvation': so wrote Cyprian. Luther said something similar. Outside Christianity there is no salvation, no forgiveness of sins, but only eternal death and condemnation.[15] But while Cyprian by 'church' understood the 'catholic' church of his day, Luther argued that salvation is bound up with the Christian gospel, and that this message exists only within Christianity.[16]

Christian worship understood in terms of faith in Jesus Christ, is not created out of thin air. It depends utterly upon the means of salvation God has given to us. No priesthood of believers, no true worshippers, are created apart from God's grace. This grace God gives by three principal means; the word, the baptism, and the Lord's Supper. Lutheran theology calls two of these sacraments: a word of Jesus is bound to visible elements, which are therefore called visible words. Thus, the Word together with water is baptism and the Word together with bread and wine is the Lord's Supper.

(A)   Worship and the Word

The main means of grace is God's Word. Baptism and the Lord's Supper are nothing without the Word, but the Word of God can be without baptism and the Lord's Supper, according to Lutheran worship theology.

For the gospel is the unique, the most certain, and the most noble sign of the church – more even than the bread and baptism, for it is through the gospel alone that the church is conceived, formed, nourished, born, trained, fed, clothed, cared for, strengthened, armed, and preserved – in short the entire life and substance of the church is in the Word of God.[17]

This gospel, however, is present in more than one way. God knows our weakness, so he offers us his grace in more than one way. God gives us the gospel from God's Word to be preached; from his hand, we have also received baptism and the Lord's Supper.

A sacrament is understood as a visible sign that has been connected with Christ's divine promise of grace. The Word is added to the element (water or bread and wine) and it becomes a sacrament.

(B)   Worship and Baptism

There is of course a variety of theological interpretations of baptism within the Protestant world. It is not my task to debate these traditions. My task here is to delineate the main point in Lutheran theology of worship as they relate to the means of grace.

Baptism is Jesus' word of promise together with water (Matt 28: 16–20). According to the *Short Catechism* (a confessional document in the Lutheran church), baptism effects forgiveness of sins, delivers from death and the Devil, and grants eternal salvation to all who believe. This is not effected by the water as such, but by the Word of God together with the water; it is a 'washing of regeneration' (Tit.3). In baptism we are buried and raised with Christ (Rom. 6:4).

All who are baptized in the name of the Father, the Son and the Holy Spirit have received a valid baptism (Eph. 4). But they are not born again without faith. A hypocrite or one who resists Christian faith does not receive new birth even though he or she is baptized. But if the sinner repents and is converted, no new baptism is needed.

The Lutheran Church did not break with the traditional Catholic practice of baptizing small children. This must be seen in the historical context of the

European state-churches and of the principle, already mentioned, of *cuius regio eius religio*: the one who has the political power rules on religious questions.

However, this worship practice is based on biblical convictions. Lutheran theology often refers to circumcision in the OT as a parallel to the baptism that was instituted under the new covenant (cf. Col. 2). Often reference is made to Matt.28 and the expression 'all nations': children are among 'all nations' and should therefore be baptized. Lutherans also refer to Acts 16 and related passages to justify the baptism of families. The underlying theological perspective is that baptism is a means of grace, and that subjective faith is not the *foundation* of the sacrament.

Faith is nevertheless necessary for salvation. God works faith in the children as the adults who bring them to Christ pray and hope that God will give faith and that the children will come to know Christ as they grow up. There is no denial that all children are sinners, inheriting a sinful nature (Ps. 51: John 3; Rom. 5:12).

One problem in the Lutheran Church has been that many dogmaticians teach that, on principle, regeneration is found only in the sacrament of baptism. This view, however, is not held by other Lutheran theologians, who insist that the Word gives new birth (1 Pet. 2:23f). If this is so, then it is necessary to preach repentance and conversion to the many unbelieving baptized people. The word of God must give sinners new birth.

The practice of baptism in churches like the Church of Norway, where around 90% of the nation's population is baptized, raises many questions – especially among believers who do not understand the context and the history of state churches. For example: in Norway, one traditional justification for this practice is the 'people's church' (what the German refer to as *Volks Kirche*) thinking and the constitutional system of the church. All who belong to the state church are obliged 'to educate their children in the Christian faith'. Thus Christian teaching is provided in all governmental-supported primary schools. Obviously there are weaknesses in our system. Without doubt many baptize their children for merely traditional reasons, and many neglect Christian teaching.

On the other hand evangelical Lutherans are given outstanding opportunities to engage in evangelical ministries within the national Lutheran Church. People do not need to leave the Church; they are not asked to break with their society and culture in order to be saved. And we can ask men and women to recognize the truth about him in whose name they were baptized. Sadly, the situation today is that many do not want to have *any* contact with a Christian church whatsoever.

Many Lutheran churches in other parts of the world, even though not state churches, have the same mixture of baptized believers and baptized people who openly live as unbelievers. Ministries aiming at conversion and new birth are needed. It has to be said that the same is also the case in many 'free' churches of other denominations.[18]

(C) Worship and the Lord's Supper

The Lord's Supper is also regarded as a sacrament in the Lutheran Church. In the *Short Catechism* Luther stated:

It is the true body and blood of our Lord Jesus Christ under the bread and wine, given unto us Christians to eat and drink, as it was instituted by Christ himself . . . This sacrament, then, is the body and blood of Jesus under bread and wine. We are asked to eat and drink it.

We have seen that Luther strongly opposed the Roman theology of making the Lord's Supper an unbloody sacrifice of Christ presented to God. Luther also abandoned the view that the substance (material) of bread and wine was transformed into the substance (material) of the body and blood of Jesus. He also broke with the Catholic practice of giving only the bread to the participants.

Nevertheless Luther emphasized the words of Jesus: 'This is my body', 'This is my blood'. The body and blood of Jesus are present under the bread and the wine. There is no transformation of the elements, but we receive Christ with our mouth and believe his promise in our heart that this is given for forgiveness of sins. Where there is forgiveness of sins, there is also life and salvation ('blessedness').

Without faith, however, the Lord's Supper is of no advantage to us. Faith is the right receiving of it; the words 'given for you' require believing hearts. In addition, the Lutheran Church recognizes in the Lord's Supper the value of remembering the once-for-all death and resurrection of Jesus Christ.

The practice of the Lord's Supper within Lutheranism varies according to different traditions. For example, the administration of the Lord's Supper in the Church of Norway was tied to the state-church minister until around 1900. At that time it was more clearly recognized that the administration of the sacrament cannot be restricted to a group of persons, such as the ministers. Christ instituted the Lord's Supper for believers. A governmental decree in 1913 stated that the Lord's Supper is for all believers. The decree came at a time when some among the Lutheran awakening had started to share the Lord's Supper in their homes and in prayer and mission houses. They find biblical warrant for this practice in Acts.[19]

We have seen, then, that Christian worship in classic Lutheranism is basically understood as faith in Jesus Christ, based upon Holy Scripture and its teaching about Jesus Christ as our only Mediator, and that it is only by this message that true faith is created so that the sinner is given God's righteousness in Christ and the forgiveness of all sins. A fellowship of believers is created by the good news that God gives us by his means of grace: the Word, baptism and the Lord's Supper.

IX.   WORSHIP AND THE UNDERSTANDING OF THE CHURCH

The priesthood of all believers comes into existence; or to word it differently, God's church is founded. But what is 'the church'?

The nature of the church is very crucial in Lutheran theology of worship. When Luther challenged the Roman Church, its councils, leaders and theologians, he was asked how he could dare to oppose the institutional church and its authority.

'Church' is a blind word, said Luther; it is unclear, because the word directs attention to the church-building and the clergy. But when we confess our faith in 'one, holy, common church' then we are dealing with something quite different.[20]

A child may know what the church is, namely the holy, believing people, the sheep who recognize the voice of their shepherd (John 10:27). By such a definition it is clear that the church is primarily *personal*, not *institutional*. The church is the assembly of believers; I believe in the holy, apostolic church – the fellowship of the holy. The Holy Spirit calls, gathers and sanctifies the whole Christian body on earth, and the Holy Spirit keeps it connected with Jesus Christ in the one true faith. Where the Word of Christ is being preached, there also will some believe. This Church is spread all over the world. The Christian body, the community of believers, consists, by definition, of believing persons.[21]

Two basic perspectives in Lutheran worship theology as it relates to the church are that the church is invisible, and that it is faith that recognizes the church.

Only God himself knows all the true believers. The true church cannot be aligned with the external church, with particular denominations. We can see the clergy and church-members, but we cannot see the church as we confess it in the Apostle's Creed.

Faith asks first and foremost for the main sign of the church, viz. the Word of God, the true sign of the true church. Other signs include baptism, the Lord's Supper, the ministry of the word, prayer, praise, and a variety of other activities connected with Christian ministries.

The main sign is not the mere possession of the Bible, but that the true gospel is being preached: 'For the gospel is the unique, the most certain and the most noble sign of the church – more so even than the bread and baptism; for it is through the gospel alone that the church is conceived . . .'.[22]

The gospel, then, is the true sign of the Church that creates worship in the human heart, true worship by faith in Jesus Christ.

People are easily drawn away from the true sign of the church, Luther said. When God is building his Church, immediately Satan builds his chapel. God gives us the Word and sacraments, the Devil calls attention to external things by which he wants to deceive people; holy water, bells, amulets blessed by the priest, garments believed to be more holy. Satan has humankind's natural reason and religious feelings on his side as sinful men and women prefer external splendour above the invisible grace of God. Believers committed to true worship must look to the Word of God and keep constantly to it.[23]

Nevertheless the church is visible in the sense that it is a concrete reality of believers in this world – those who listen to the true gospel of Christ. The Church is there where the true gospel is preached. The assembly of God is nothing other than those people who listen to the voice of the good shepherd. The true gospel constitutes the true church.

Thus in answering the question, 'What is the church?' Luther and classic Lutheran theology answer that in principle there are only two churches in the world, viz. the false and the true. The difference between these two churches does not coincide with lines of various 'churches' or denominations. Right teaching, for example, does not guarantee that all of a 'church's' members constitute the true church.

Ecclesia (church) is the Christian people in whom Christ lives and rules for redemption, by grace and the forgiveness of sins. The Holy Spirit gives the true church daily cleansing of sins and renewal of spiritual life.

The false church, in principle, consists of false Christians, members of denominations who have no saving faith. The difference between the true and the false church is seen from the time of Cain and Abel. The false church will all the time attack the true church (cf. Gal. 4:21–31). The true church is not to accept the false church and its false prophets coming in sheep's clothing, who inwardly are ravenous wolves (Matt. 7).

Lutheran churches do not have many detailed regulations about church order. Congregational worships is marked by great flexibility. Many elements come under the terms *adiaphora*, 'things that are between' in the sense that one has freedom to arrange such elements in different ways according to the local or national situation.

But always the centrality of the preaching of the gospel lies at the heart of all classic Lutheran church ministries. The same point is made in the Augsburg Confession: the unity of the church does not depend on common external rules and regulations, but is constituted by the Word and the sacraments. The gospel gives freedom, yet at the same time certain foundational principles are emphasized.[24]

X. WORSHIP AND CHRISTIAN MINISTRY

Once again, classic Lutheranism has defined itself, in part, over against Roman Catholic tradition. The ministry of the Lutheran Church must be seen in connection with the priesthood of all believers. Catholic theology of worship, even today, takes its starting-point in a sacrificial understanding of the Lord's Supper (the 'Mass') and in the priest as one who offers sacrifices. The Catholic priest has received power and authority to consecrate the bread and wine and to offer the sacrifice of Christ afresh for the benefit of the living and the dead. He has an authority and power that cannot be taken from him as he is a member of the priesthood that is different from the priesthood of all believers.[25] Every Catholic priest is obliged to read mass every day, even though no congregation is present.

Lutheran theology of worship has no place for such a priesthood. In the New Testament there is no continuation of a mediating priesthood from Old Testament times, orchestrating or controlling Christian congregational worship. There is only one priesthood in the new covenant, that of all believers (1 Pet. 2:9; Rev. 5:10 and 20:6). All believers are under the obligation 'to declare the wonderful deeds of him who called them . . .' (1 Pet. 2:9). This is the priestly ministry of the New Testament, while Jesus Christ alone serves as mediating high priest (Heb. 7; cf. 1 Tim. 2:5–6).

However, the Lutheran Church recognizes the biblical teaching about elders, leaders and preachers in the congregations of Christians. But these have no part in any other priesthood than that of all believers. Some persons are chosen to be servants, 'ministers', of the congregations.[26]

The minister of the congregation needs a calling from the Christian community. To ordain is to call out of the priesthood of all believers and give a person a ministry on behalf of all believers. If the church has the system of bishops, these bishops ask a person to minister on behalf of all the others.

There have been periods in the history of the Lutheran Church when there were attempts to argue for two different, separate priesthoods (as in the Catholic Church) – that of all believers and another one comprising the ordained ministers of congregations (especially in the period of the neo-lutheran theology, 1800–1900). This theology however, is contrary to the classical Lutheran theology of worship. We have only one priesthood, that of all believers.

The Roman Catholic Church reacted against the thinking of the Reformers by arguing, in part, that according to this teaching woman as well as men could be called into the pastoral ministries. Here, too, Luther and the other Reformers attempted to provide an answer on the basis of Scripture. Much of the modern Lutheran theology is in this question marked by the contemporary historical-critical theology that is not willing to take the Scripture at its face value. Modern arguments tend to discuss the creation accounts as myth, with the result that we do need to reckon with New Testament's arguments based on the order of creation. Many Lutheran scholars argue that the apostle Paul did not understand the consequences of Christian freedom that he himself had affirmed in Gal. 3:28, and consequently he failed in the epistles to the Ephesians and the Corinthians to live up to his own insights. Some argue that passages dealing with men and women in 1. Cor. 11 and 14 and in 1 Tim. 2, are secondary, and therefore cannot claim authority over us today. Much modern theology, without doubt, is afraid of the liberation movements, or at least cherishes keeping up with them, so that many theologians try to adjust their findings to popular views of our own time.

Luther himself referred to the creation order, to the consequences of the fall and to the authority of the apostle Paul when he was discussing and answering questions regarding leadership in the church. From this study Luther came to the conclusion that the leadership of the Christian congregations should be in the hands of believing men. However, if no man was present, the believing woman has responsibility.[27]

Believers have the responsibility to judge the teaching and the teachers of the assembly. They are supposed to decide whether or not the voice of the good shepherd, the Lord Jesus, is heard in the teaching and preaching of bishops, pastors and other teachers. The true church is supposed to follow only the voice of the good shepherd, not the voice of strangers, false teachers. The believing community will stay away from all authorities who teach what is contrary to the Word of God. If the ecclesiastical authorities are not willing to send true preachers, the believers themselves must call and place into ministry some who are suited for serving others with the Word of God.[28]

XI.   *ECCLESIA* AND *ECCLESIOLA* IN SERVICE

The Lutheran Sunday-morning service builds upon the tradition of the Catholic mass. The Lutheran service is cleansed from elements regarded as not evangelical and is re-arranged into a worship-service for the community.

The Lutheran service normally includes the following elements and explanations:

1. The Lord's Supper takes the place of the unbloody sacrifice of Christ in the Mass.

2. The service is conducted in the language of the people (which was not the case in the Mass of Luther's day, but is increasingly the case today, even in Roman Catholicism).
3. Preaching is a necessary element in the service, not so in the Catholic Mass. The Lutheran service is strongly marked by the preached Word.
4. Singing is an important element in the service. A Lutheran service without singing is unthinkable (cf. the fact that as early as the Deutsche Messe of 1526, 'Credo' and 'Agnus Dei' were edited in German for congregational singing).
5. Typical of the Lutheran service in the mainline contexts is an arranged liturgical order, but there is no liturgical uniformity in all Lutheran services. In many Lutheran churches there are fixed texts for reading and preaching. However, in some Lutheran 'free' churches and in various Lutheran societies for home and foreign mission (functioning like 'free churches'), patterns of congregational worship may be freer.

By *ecclesiolas* we refer to the various smaller devotional groups within national Lutheran Churches; we also have in mind the various mission agencies within Lutheran Christendom. These various groups represent in Scandinavia and other places in Europe very much the same ethos as some Lutheran 'free' churches in the United States, for example. In Norway this movement is often called the lay-movement, representing around 25 voluntary organizations for home and foreign missions. These societies still remain within the formal body of the Lutheran National church. These movements tend to display a much wider range of worship practices than do the mainline branches.

In the 17th century, the age of Lutheran orthodoxy, there was no room for '*ecclesiolas in ecclesia*'. However, some time before the English Revolution in 1689 there was a growing appreciation of a deeper and more personal spiritual life in worship and service. The *ecclesiolas*-movement in Lutheranism developed in particular after 1730 in the *Herrnhutische* societies: they came together for prayer, testimonies, etc. at the same time as they kept membership of national churches (cf. the *collegia pietatis* and Philipp J. Spener, 1635–1705). The revivals and awakenings of the 18th and 19th centuries created the background for the modern *ecclesiolas* in Lutheran Churches, a movement that today is finding its way into Lutheran Christendom worldwide.

In Sweden, for example, many of the revival-movements broke off from the National Church, something that tended to empty the state church of spiritual life. In Norway the revival movement for the most part remained inside the state church and established its structures – in freedom – within the state church.

The main feature of these movements was first of all a strong spirit-filled preaching that urged the baptized Lutheran to be converted or born again to personal faith in Jesus Christ. This preaching created *ecclesiolas* within the church – often gathering in homes until the time came when the revival people built a variety of mission and prayer houses where they conducted their services. These people called one another 'brothers' and 'sisters' in the Lord. They had broken with sinful living and agreed to live according to the teaching of the Bible. These people were not satisfied with a 'Christian' life that was simply tied to the official national church – a 'Christian' life often termed 'religious' but without personal understanding of what it means to be a believer.

In Norway a young farmer called Hans Nielsen Hauge is regarded as the father of the lay-movement (from around 1800). Because of his preaching he was thrown into prison where he languished for 14 years, owing to orthodox laws and regulations and pressure from the clergy of the state church. Today this revival-movement has grown to embrace most of the Christian activities prompted by strong spiritual conviction within the Church, as well as the mission outreach from the Church to peoples and tribes worldwide. It is surely interesting to learn that all the missionaries from within the Church of Norway are sent and supported by voluntary mission agencies.

My own mission, Norwegian Lutheran Mission, is said to be the largest in Europe, with more than 600 missionaries, hundreds of mission or prayer houses (like 'free' church buildings), a variety of schools, kindergartens, etc. The constituency of this mission is approximately 4000 *ecclesiolas* within the national church – mission groups that come together for worship several evenings every month. Most of the meetings are in homes where there is singing, praying, testimonies, eating, often the Lord's Supper, preaching, reading mission magazines, and giving offerings to support home and foreign mission activities. The understanding of worship and service is built upon the priesthood of all believers and the conviction that every believer has his or her spiritual gift. Every year a variety of these groups come together in a mission or prayer house for a series of meetings with an evangelist or a lay-preacher (educated or not, farmer or theologian), the aim being to revive the believers but also to win believers (usually members of the state church) by conversion to personal faith. People who come to Norway in order to study the Church of Norway without meeting or seeing this movement have no real understanding of Lutheran service and life in Norway. All in all there are approximately 20,000 groups within a variety of Lutheran agencies within the national church.

Various streams of the charismatic movement also create varied forms of worship and service within the more rigid structures of national churches in Scandinavia. Both among pastors and other church members there is a growing recognition of the need for more freedom within the framework of public Christian services. An important question to be faced is the direction in which this liberalization of the forms of congregational worship is going. On the one hand, there is the possibility of real spiritual renewal on the basis of clear understanding of the saving message in the Bible. On the other, we can also discern the tendency to believe that spiritual renewal first and foremost has its focal point in external forms of activities that often are no more than 'horizontal' relationships among the members of the body.

Many Lutheran churches have people today who are aware of the need for spiritual renewal – indeed, that the many baptized people need to hear the gospel in such a way that they come to personal understanding of salvation in the Lord Jesus Christ. We may mention places like Ethiopia, Tanzania, Japan, Nigeria, Eastern Europe, Finland, Norway, etc.

I recently visited the Lutheran Church of Tanzania, where I have been teaching and preaching for about six years. Tanzania has the largest Lutheran church in Africa with about 1.3 million baptized members. Some years ago a variety of revivals and awakenings touched the Church. Many pastors and other church members were afraid. They labelled the movement a 'Pentecostal movement', and without doubt many Lutherans were influenced by various 'charismatic' preachers and groups. However, little by little, bishops, pastors and others began to adjust to the revivals and the new forms of worship being developed. They had to take the new spiritual needs and perceptions into consideration and give place for *ecclesiolas* in the Christian communities. Where this was not done, many Lutherans left the church and joined smaller Pentecostal congregations. Alternatively, they established new ones. I myself recognized that we had to find forms and functions for the new life within the Church, with sufficient freedom that the *ecclesiola*-movement could grow and prosper for the good of the whole church.

One main question I met was this: Is it possible to be a true believer without leaving the Lutheran church to attend (for example) a Pentecostal church? Eventually more and more Lutherans in Tanzania understood that it is possible to keep their membership in the Lutheran church, and at the same time be part of 'born again' groups that come together in churches and houses for spiritual worship and service, and where room is given for evangelistic preaching, testimonies, healing, speaking in tongues, helping people who are demon-possessed, planning for outreach among church members who are still unconverted, and for outreach among the unreached.

During a mission we had at Kilimanjaro it became quite clear that many Lutheran church members still worship the spirits of the dead, many still sacrifice animals to get freedom from demons – all this because they are afraid and have not truly heard the gospel in such a way that they are redeemed from the powers of darkness. But the gospel is again penetrating the various peoples of Tanzania to set sinners free.[29]

Part Three

Reflections on Worship in some 'Free' Church Traditions

8

'Free Church' Worship in Britain

PETER LEWIS

The 'Free Church' tradition in Britain can hardly be understood apart from the history of the Free (or non-Established) Churches themselves. They began in the 17th century with the Presbyterian, Congregational/Independent, and Baptist Churches.[1] These had their roots in the Reformation and Puritan movements. They came to include the Methodist Churches with their roots in the great 18th century revival.[2] The character of Free Church life and worship, its emphases and complexion have been for centuries self-consciously affected by these historical origins.

HISTORICAL BACKGROUND

In the 16th century the continental Protestant Reformation made its way into England, Scotland, Wales and Ireland. In Scotland, under leaders like John Knox (d. 1572) and Andrew Melville (1545–1622) it became the official religion of the state and the community with its own distinctive Presbyterian worship, church-government and organization. From 1564 to 1645 the Scottish Presbyterians used *The Book of Common Order*, often known as Knox's Liturgy.

In England after Henry the Eighth, the short, six-year reign of his son Edward 1 saw England take decisive steps toward Protestantism with Cranmer's First and Second Prayer Books (1549 and 1552). Only the second of these satisfied the more thorough-going Protestants but, after six years of Mary's Catholic monarchy, Edward's other sister, the Protestant Elizabeth, re-established Protestantism on a less radical basis than before, bringing back Cranmer's First Prayer Book in her 'Elizabethan Settlement' of 1559. This 'Settlement' established the English church on a distinctive Anglican model that stood mid-way between the old Catholicism of Elizabeth's father Henry and the Geneva-Protestantism of John Calvin.

While the Reformation Church in Scotland was largely united in its Calvinistic/Knoxian Protestantism, the church in England was not. From the beginning there were leaders (and a majority of concerned people) who wanted continuing Reformation of worship and discipline in the English churches, bringing church government and worship more in line with the simplicities of the New Testament and the 'Primitive Church' model. These became known as the Puritans. Opposing them were those who wanted a distinctive and, to them, more moderately reformed English church. These were the Anglicans. These two important parties or factions, while sharing a basic evangelical theology in regard to the fundamentals of the faith including the distinctive Protestant doctrine of justification by faith only, leaned in very different directions in a number of important areas including the area of worship.[3]

Both Anglican and Puritan regarded the Bible as the Word of God. But while the Anglicans, after Luther, saw it as authoritative in matters of doctrine and behaviour, the Puritans, after Calvin, went further and maintained that it also contained the pattern for ecclesiastical government, church-discipline and congregational worship. Richard Hooker, the great apologist for Anglicanism, in his *Laws of Ecclesiastical Polity*, defended the 'Normative Principle,' which meant that while Scripture laid down the ground rules and basics, yet in regard to the 'accidentals' of worship (such as liturgical form, clerical dress, etc.), whatever was not positively forbidden in Scripture and was suitable to it was allowable in church worship if it seemed good and desirable and suitable to the church's leaders; indeed, it might be commanded and enforced by such authorities. The Puritans on the other hand developed The 'Regulative Principle' by which every significant ingredient in worship had to have clear warrant in Scripture. For instance, the Westminster Confession (formulated as a result of the call by Parliament in 1643 to impose a creed suitable for the English and Scottish churches), states that '. . . the acceptable way of worshipping the true God is instituted by himself, and so limited by his own revealed will that he may not be worshipped according to the imaginations and devices of men . . . or any other way not prescribed in the Holy Scripture'. The Puritan doctrine of the human race is reflected here with its stress on the fallenness of all people in every part of their natures and the danger arising from indwelling sin even in believers and from their imperfect compatibility with the standards and will of God. Worship was considered far too important and people far too wayward for mere human additions.

It was this conviction that had strengthened Puritan resistance to Anglican impositions for nearly a century, since 1559. They maintained their refusal to conform to those ceremonies and requirements of the Prayer Book which they deemed unscriptural (hence the term 'Non-Conformists' and later on, 'Dissenters'). For this they suffered much persecution especially in and after the 'Great Ejection' of nearly 2,000 clergy in 1662. They had also developed either Presbyterian or Independent convictions about church-government and fathered the first Free Church congregations of the 17th century.

Michael Watts observes that in practice the Dissenters of the late 17th century and after 'inherited two rather different traditions of worship, the Separatist and the Puritan, and the resultant pattern of worship was an amalgam of the two.' (The Separatists were a more radical part of the Puritan movement in the late 16th century. While the Puritans generally stayed in the established Church of England hoping to reform it, the Separatists withdrew insisting on 'Reformation without tarrying for any'). Watts continues: 'From the Separatists the Dissenters inherited their opposition to set forms of prayer, an attitude which had not been shared either by the Puritans of the

16th century or the Presbyterians of the Westminster Assembly'. However, (he informs us) 'In the case of preaching the reverse happened, and it was the Puritan rather than the Separatist tradition which proved more durable.'[3a]

The result of all this in the Presbyterian and Independent churches of the middle and late 17th century, and in the new proliferating Baptist churches too, was a congregational worship without ecclesiastical architecture, without a professional priesthood and without an enforced liturgy; where prayer and preaching predominated and where psalm-singing was only gradually supplemented with hymns among the Congregational and Calvinistic Baptist Churches.

The English Puritans and Dissenters, and also their Scottish Covenanter counterparts, were renowned for their strong Sabbatarianism. It is true that this was sometimes taken to unnecessary and legalistic extremes. However, the recognition of a weekly day of rest was in itself important in regard to the social needs and personal dignity of men and women. Their concept of 'the market-day of the soul' was given rich illustration in the Puritan preaching and in the Puritan devotional writings. Whatever criticisms might be made of sacralising time and blurring the distinction between old and new covenants, the congregational services in the Puritan churches were a powerful and attractive force in the land: potently evangelistic, deeply biblical, and, in the Puritan 'practical' preaching, engaging with everyday life in ways that affected every level of national as well as private existence.

No religion was more 'worldly' (in the best sense of the word) than Puritan religion. Its entire ethos and its *raison d'être* were to integrate every area of life as a priestly offering, a real liturgy to God. Puritan religion was about living: 'Divinity is the doctrine of living to God', wrote William Ames in the first sentence of his celebrated *Marrow of Divinity*. The saints were no longer celibates behind monastery walls but ordinary men and women working out extraordinary grace in daily tasks. They were a royal priesthood whose daily work was a holy calling, whose lives were a pilgrim's progress and whose place in the world was as the elect of God, destined for glory. Thus there could be no divorce between 'worship' and 'life' since all of life was to be an act of worship: for the farm labourer or the housewife no less than for the preacher or the parliamentarian. The Puritans recognized the importance and uniqueness of congregational worship, not in any cultic or escapist sense but as a necessary part, and indeed a focal part, of a life lived 'to glorify God and to enjoy him for ever'.

This was reinforced in preaching that had a central place in all Puritan congregational worship. It has been said that for the Anglican, worship was man's approach to God; for the Puritan worship was God's speech to man. This may need to be qualified – as all one-liners do! – but it rightly stresses the prophetic element in puritan worship. Preaching was the exposition of the mind of God: his way of salvation and his will for the saved. By it the Holy Spirit worked in a unique way and to a unique degree confirming, edifying and directing the believer. It was the climax of congregational worship, a chief means of grace, and Christ's great converting ordinance. And generally puritan practice seems to have been as good as its theory. Certainly in their heyday puritan preachers like William Perkins, Richard Sibbes, Richard Baxter, Thomas Brooks and Thomas Watson had the largest and most enthusiastic as well as the most devout congregations. Even if the length of the prayers and the depth and discursiveness of the sermons astonish the modern observer, they certainly satisfied and motivated their 17th century counterparts.

It is however a fact of life that our strengths can also be our weaknesses, and it is a fact of history that the descendants of the Puritans lost something of the vibrant, spiritual life of earlier Puritanism. The Presbyterians in England, in particular, suffered, becoming intellectualized and formal, drifting into a fatal Unitarianism, losing both the theology and the life of evangelical Puritanism. At this period too the Church of England was in the grip of Deism, Latitudinarianism, and formal Spirit-less religion. Even the Independents, the Congregationalists, who remained true to their doctrinal roots, were not unaffected by the correctness and formality of the day which feared 'enthusiasm' in any department of religion. Scotland, too, was thirsty soil for spiritual renewal.

Then came the Great Awakening of the 1730s and '40s and its aftermath. An international phenomenon, rising almost simultaneously from several sources, it touched New England Congregationalism, Scottish Presbyterianism and Anglican and Free Church life in England and Wales. It profoundly affected the historic denominations and brought into being both Calvinistic and Arminian brands of Methodism. In Britain it began with a group of young Anglican(!) clergy including George Whitefield and the brothers John and Charles Wesley, and transformed the spiritual scene in England, Scotland and Wales with its Spirit-anointed stress on new birth, full assurance and 'experimental' (ie. experiential) religion.

Although this movement began, in England, with clergy of the established church, it was largely opposed by the Establishment, and the leaders found most of their support among their new converts and in their own 'societies'. Wesley himself, always a strong churchman, resisted throughout his long life any suggestion of leaving the Church of England and timed his Methodist meetings so that they never clashed with attendance at parish church services or rivalled its sacramental worship. However, soon after his death his Methodists more explicitly separated from the Church of England, thus bringing practice into line with reality. In the following century, one of great growth and expansion for the Methodists, various movements in turn grew up in and separated from the original 'Wesleyan' Methodist connection, some of the largest returning to full union only in our own century. Their worship developed too, growing out of their earliest roots and developing their own tradition of unread prayers and famous hymns as well as class meetings and open testimony to personal blessing.

As later Puritanism had its shadow-side in over-strictness and intellectualising so Methodism in revival had its shadow-side in the dangers of pietism: subjectivism, fanaticism, division and the loss of important traditional doctrines. Still, like the Puritans, no one was more 'worldly' than John Wesley in his Christianity, and in Methodism as much as in Puritanism the call was 'to present your bodies a living sacrifice' (AV). The people called Methodists were to be as interested in social needs and compassionate ministries as they were in church purity and spiritual life. No study of Wesley's Methodism fails to give attention to this.

This rich and potent history affected the self-perception, vision and church life of the English Free Churches to a very considerable extent in the ensuing generations. However, new experiences and influences were to prove potent too. Nineteenth century Non-Conformity saw a huge rise in its numbers and faced both the exhilaration and the dangers of becoming a social and political force in the land[4]. Its old fashioned 'meeting houses' became stately and even cathedral-like places of worship as Non-Conformists showed their affluence, status and sense of destiny, perhaps in conscious rivalry with their Anglican neighbours. Its music became more elaborate, its sacred songs more 'culti-vated', and its preaching more socially and politically 'aware', less doctrinal and expository and more ethical and oratorical – except of course where the old doctrinal and evangelistic emphases continued as in ministries like that of C. H. Spurgeon and denominational groupings such as the Strict and Particular Baptists.

In this century too an entirely new spiritual force was to grow: proliferating groups of people called 'the Plymouth Brethren'. Led by talented seceders from the Church of England such as J. N. Darby and A. N. Groves, they gathered together weekly for 'the breaking of bread' (their name for the Lord's Supper of Non-conformity and the Eucharist of Anglicanism) and for mutual edification in which thanksgiving, prayer and the ministry of the Word was supplied, not by an ordained order of clergymen, but by as many (men only!) in the meeting as had such ministry to share. In these and other ways they sought to return to the simplicity of apostolic days and worship. They grew and divided dramatically into Closed (exclusive) and Open Brethren. The latter grew yet further, becoming, in the following century, a main bastion for biblical faith and fundamentals in England and promoting a zealous and effective missionary outreach.[4a]

TWENTIETH CENTURY CHALLENGES AND CHANGES

The real sea-changes in the Free Churches during the last 100 years or more have been produced by two very different movements, one of them very recent: they are the 'higher-critical' approach to biblical study, and the charismatic movement.

The theological liberalism that began to affect the Free Churches in the 19th century rose like a flood in the first half of the twentieth. The 'higher criticism' left people unable to rely as they had done on the Bible as the unerring, reliable, authority for faith and life. Evolutionary theories seemed to push God farther and farther to the background or even the sidelines. The human race stood alone at the beginning of all thinking and at the end of all evolutionary progress. The biblicism of Puritan and Methodist beginnings was widely abandoned to be replaced by a conscience more concerned with social causes in the nation and abroad than with doctrinal standards in the church or denomination. As doctrine lost its importance and evangelism its urgency, preaching lost its primacy.[5] Under the influence of the ecumenical movement union between denominations became an overriding goal for many; doctrinal divisions were seen only in that light, and therefore as undesirable and unnecessary. Schemes for church-union emerged and marked the central and later decades of the 20th century. The three main branches of Methodism had united by the 1920s and in 1972 the Presbyterian and Congregational groupings largely merged to form the United Reformed Church.

Changes in Free Church worship became notable: liturgies and set-forms began to appear. Directories and service books were officially issued by the various Free Church denominations. The English Presbyterians published their *Directory of Public Worship* in 1898 (revised and re-issued in 1921). The Congregationalists published *A Book of Congregational Worship* (1921) and *A Manual for Ministers* (1936) and the Methodists issued *Divine Worship*, also in 1936. A new stress on the sacraments became observable, and ordination became more elaborate. By many these were welcomed as providing a much needed balance in Non-conformity and an enriching of her life and worship. To others they seemed a poor substitute for what had largely been lost in Free Church life: the doctrine of the Puritans and the fire of the early Methodists.[6]

Meantime from unnoticed and unremarkable beginnings a 20th century movement was developing which would, in a couple of generations, out-number any of its non-episcopal fellows – the Pentecostal Movement.[7] Historically its roots are in Wesley's Methodism, the Primitive Methodist's revivalism and the 19th-century holiness movement, but it has always seen itself as a Bible-based, Spirit-anointed movement which has recovered a long-lost New Testament emphasis on the baptism in the Holy Spirit and the place of spiritual gifts, including tongues, prophecy and healings – gifts regarded as being scattered throughout the body of the church's membership for its common and corporate edification, worship and witness. Its fundamental evangelicalism, its spirituality and its evangelistic zeal made Pentecostalism the phenomenal missionary power it has been throughout the twentieth century. In America and Britain it was in its earlier days suspected and even despised by the older 'Free Churches', yet it made undeniable headway among the working classes and the disadvantaged, and in many countries (e.g. in Latin America) its growth has been phenomenal.

In the 1960s another, though similar, movement emerged and gathered strength with incredible swiftness: the charismatic movement[8]. Unlike its Pentecostal look-alike the charismatic movement has made its way chiefly within the historic denominations except in regard to the 'New Churches', also called 'Restoration Churches'. These have emphasized the on-going place of 'apostolic ministry' with its charismatic church-planting and super-intending gift as integral to the well-being of the church in every age (Eph. 4:11–13). Strongly pietistic but with a genuine love of Scripture, the charismatic movement emphasised the experiential side of Christianity: the presence, the baptism and the gifts of the Holy Spirit in the church; congregational worship as a celebration of God's grace in salvation and as an adoration of his Son; and also the place of small groups for mutual encouragement and 'body-ministry'. Its extraordinary effects and growth touched almost all the major denominations, Catholic and Protestant.

The Pentecostal and charismatic movements have brought to the Christian church many blessings and not a few problems. Their people have been both the subject and the channels of a renewing movement of God's Spirit in the 20th century which is staggering by any standards and of truly historic significance. Undoubtedly the Holy Spirit had become the neglected Person of the Godhead for many in the older churches. Liberalism was content with the Fatherhood of God; evangelicalism had largely become a 'Jesus only' movement; and except in those circles where the classic view of revivals was prominent, the outpouring of the Holy Spirit was scarcely thought about. The rise of modern Pentecostalism and neo-Pentecostalism challenged all that!

The traditional churches[9] have been forced to face neglected Scriptures, invited to seek and use forgotten gifts, and encouraged to meet its surrounding culture on more contemporary and familiar terms. The Roman Catholic and Anglican communions world-wide have managed to embrace the charismatic movement within their comprehensiveness. In England among the Free Churches there has been a general, if cautious, acceptance of charismatic insights and styles of worship among the evangelicals of the Methodist Church, and in the Baptist Union (now said to be overwhelmingly evangelical in its leadership and church life). More liberal groupings such as the United Reformed Church and more traditional groupings such as the Fellowship of Independent Evangelical Churches and the Reformed, Grace Baptist Churches have tended to be more critical or even hostile. In Scotland and Ireland a more traditional culture as well as strong doctrinal emphases have been more generally resistant to new movements and trends in worship. In Wales, a strongly conservative 'chapel' culture, combined with an evangelical appreciation of historic revivals (especially in the Principality), have given little room to charismatic styles of worship. In general, however, the British evangelical scene is not so polarised on this matter as their North American counterparts appear to be, and with most of our parachurch organizations and missions it is not allowed to be, in itself, an issue.

Problems, however, remain. The movement's track record on healing is nowhere near as good as it claims; its 'prophecies' are often little more than 'blessed thoughts' dressed up and its stress on tongues is sometimes more Corinthian than scriptural! Yet who among those who have any close fellowship with these fellow Christians will deny the integrity of their joyful worship, their unquenchable love, and their working faith? Who can fail to see God's blessing on them and use of them? And are we not challenged even in our professed biblicism to take all Scripture with all seriousness and not by a theological sleight of hand to dispensationalize whole chapters of the New Testament or to neutralise Scripture with 'the Fathers' of our particular tradition?

ABIDING PRIORITIES

When every *caveat* has been sounded the church does meet to worship and does worship in its assemblies. In worship, as in everything else, the church as community has a very special place in New Testament teaching. Baptism is into the church, sanctification is with the church, gifts are for the church; the experience of the Holy Spirit himself is a shared and not only an individual experience. In congregational worship, the *koinonia*, the fellowship of believers, becomes a fresh supernatural experience lifting them up in a common *participation* in Christ as they engage in praise and prayer, as they share the sacrament (some would prefer 'ordinance') of bread and wine 'until he comes' and as the Word of God is taught in their midst. In congregational worship the separate life of the individual and the collective life of the church meet. Indeed it is inevitable that this should be so, and that worship should be (in C. E. B. Cranfield's words, quoted earlier by David Peterson) 'the focus point of that whole wider worship which is the continually repeated self-surrender of the Christian in obedience and of life'. This in itself will mean that adoration, confession, thanksgiving and supplication will rise to unique heights when the people of God come together into the presence of God.

The sense of being in the presence of God in a special way in the Christian congregation has been precious to the Christian worshipper across the centuries. (It is not of course that God is seen as static so that we literally enter and leave his presence. I think it was the 12th-century Bernard of Clairvaux who said, 'I never come to Thee but by Thee; I never go from Thee without Thee.') The 17th-century Puritan, David Clarkson, preached a celebrated sermon entitled 'Public Worship to be Preferred before Private', offering in typical puritan style twelve major reasons in defence of the statement in the title,[10] the second of which was that 'There is more sense of the Lord's presence'. A modern preacher, Dr. D. M. Lloyd Jones, in his book *Preaching and Preachers*[11], asks the question: 'What is the chief end of preaching?' and replies, 'It is to give men and women a sense of God and His presence.'

Siegfried Grossmann, in a perceptive study and application of charismatic movements and its insights, quotes Ernst Benz in regard to this matter: 'Every genuine religious experience is in essence an experience of the *presence* of God . . . of contact in the here and now with the overwhelming, joy-bringing, terrifying, saving and judging power of the transcendent.'[12] He observes the Protestant church's long-time stress on the preaching of the Word of God as mediating this but protests that 'the word which is meant to mediate the presence of God has been reduced to the level of colourless information'. What is now needed, argues Siegfried Grossmann fairly, 'is a healthy balance between theology and church-tradition and present experience, between intellect and emotion'.

In recent years, one question that has been asked with increasing frequency is, 'What part do the people of God in general play in being channels of God's love, word and power when the church gathers for congregational worship?' In Protestantism it has been largely the preacher who is the channel of blessing. Today much more stress is laid on an 'every member ministry' where everybody has something and nobody has everything and where the 'body-life' of the local church, of which Paul speaks in Romans 12 and 1 Corinthians 12, is given larger recognition.

Much of this emphasis was needed, even in the Free Churches that prided themselves on recovering and holding to what became known as 'the priesthood of all believers'. Gradually a non-people symbolism had become prominent in church gatherings. Speaking people had been replaced by silent objects. In the Catholic tradition the 'silent objects' were cathedrals, crucifixes and altars. But Non-Conformity developed certain equivalents in this respect: the communion table with open Bible on stand, empty cross, chalices and collection plates! All these ended up speaking more eloquently of God and salvation than the people silent in their pews could except of course in their hymn singing. The people were silenced and only the objects allowed to speak.

All this was and is a far cry from the New Testament.[13] There, to be sure, we have surprisingly little information about the church gatherings of the earliest Christians. This holds good even with respect to Corinthians. Two expressions of worship that do emerge are the Lord's Supper (11:17–34) and vocal worship (14:26). In both cases, writes Fee, 'Paul emphasises the truly corporate nature of such worship.'[14] Fee continues, 'The purpose of worship is two-fold. On the one hand, singing, praying and thanksgiving are directed toward God (11:13; 14:14–17); on the other hand utterances of various kinds are directed toward the community so that it may be built up.' While the evidence elsewhere points to the pre-eminence of the teaching office given to certain individuals who lead the church (e.g. Acts 13:1; Eph. 4:11–13; 1 Tim. 3:2; Titus 1:7–10), contributions also come from a wide variety of people.

In responding to and correcting the abuses of worship in Corinth, Paul stresses both an underlying unity and a harmonious and effective diversity:[15] 'There are different kinds of gifts, but the same Spirit . . . All these are the work of one and the same Spirit, and he gives them to each one, just as he determines' (1 Cor. 12:4,11). How this worked out in church meetings must largely be a matter for conjecture. However we do have 1 Corinthians 14:26, doubtless neither woodenly *prescriptive* nor merely *descriptive* but a glimpse into congregational worship in the first generation(s): 'When you come together, everyone has a hymn, or a word of instruction, a revelation, a tongue or an interpretation. All of these must be done for the strengthening of the church' (1 Cor. 14:26; cf. Col. 3:15,16) The democratising of ministry has, strangely, been resisted longer in some congregational churches than in many episcopal ones. Especially at first, a professional – and often liberal – ministry felt that itself and the church under its care was threatened by an uncritical fundamentalism and an unbridled emotionalism. However, the proper answer was a biblical fundamentalism and a right integration of the emotional and intellectual components of worship and a proper use of spiritual gifts in the membership. Evangelical church leaders often encountered, and still encounter, an over-realized eschatology among many charismatics, an eschatology that cannot cope with the realities of life in a fallen world and in a 'not yet' situation; and which needs to be confronted by the correctives of a far more experienced 'charismatic' – the apostle Paul (1 Cor. 1:4–7; 4:8,10; 2 Cor. 1:3–4; 12:1–10).

For Paul two controlling factors are vital in permitting the exercise of spiritual gifts in the assembly: they are *order* and *intelligibility* (1 Cor. 14:39,40). The tendency in the churches to transgress these rules is not to be countered by the imposition of silence (1 Cor. 14:39; 1 Thess. 5:19) but by due recognition of gifting (1 Cor. 1:4–7; 12:1–31) coupled with the testing and regulating of every contribution (1 Cor. 14:1–40; 1 Thess. 5:17–22). These are lessons all the churches are having to learn with their leaders since it has been found that the wrong response to abuses often simply adds another abuse and further confuses or disintegrates a tense and fragile situation.

A common criticism of the 'new worship' is that it owes more to the Old Testament than the New and is obsessed with elements belonging to the 'church' in its infancy, thus betraying its immaturity. Questions related to the continuity and discontinuity between the Testaments are tied to some of our most persistent disagreements – e.g. over such matters as baptism and worship. In regard to the latter we should, I think, distinguish within the Mosaic economy between elements essential to the Levitical and Aaronic order ('see to it that you make everything according to the pattern shown you on the mountain' Heb. 8:5; cf. Exod. 25:40) and elements added later that were adventitious to it, such as David's organization of temple singers

(1 Chron. 15:16) and the use of such psalms as the psalms of ascent (Psalms 120–134). These latter elements surely include some forms of corporate worship that might also be adventitious under the new covenant. The Puritan fathers of the Free Churches who eschewed the 'trappings and baubles' of the Aaronic economic never surrendered the psalms of Israel but rather sang them within a new covenant framework and against a background of salvation. If their evangelical grand children choose to sing David's psalms to a different tempo they may in that particular be nearer to David (1 Chron. 15:16; Pss. 149, 150) without necessarily being nearer to Moses. What matters most, whether they sing or shout (Ps. 95:1), kneel or bow down, is that they do so with clean hands and a pure heart (Ps. 24:3–6), the worship of the lips being one with the consecration of the life (Rom. 6:11–14; 12:1–2).

In every generation there needs to be a fresh appraisal before God of the church by the church, and a sustained attempt to seek both *reformation* and *renewal* at all levels of her life, including the level of congregational worship. Such reformation however, must acknowledge Scripture to be the authoritative standard and test of the church's life in every respect. By this standard all our traditions and innovations must be tried. We cannot be wiser than Scripture either in the one or in the other.

Scripture is never redundant and it is never to be left behind or on the sidelines. Nor is the ongoing work of the Spirit to be regarded as in some way superseding the Spirit's own inspired Word given for the church in all generations. Today we see Christians of almost every theological complexion and church tradition renewed by a fresh work of the Spirit of God. Some therefore rush to the conclusion that our theological differences do not matter to God. But the Holy Spirit's blessing on men and women is no seal of approval on all their doctrine, nor is it a statement of divine indifference with regard to their doctrinal beliefs or teaching. Certain 'spiritual' experiences may encourage them to feel still wedded – indeed even more wedded – to former beliefs, and these beliefs may still be quite wrong and unbiblical. The truth seems to be that much spiritual experience is often more like varnish than paint: it brightens up what is already there without basically changing the colour of it. Spiritual experience does not of itself automatically alter a person's doctrine. It needs the Word of Scripture to do that. So if someone holds to, say, liberal Protestant or sacramental Catholic ideas, however 'devoutly' he or she adheres to them, these beliefs (and all others!) need to be brought to the bar of Scripture. And if a believer or a church or a movement does not allow itself to be informed and reformed by the Word of God, they can on the one hand expect chastisement from the Spirit who first inspired that Word, and on the other confusion and disarray from Satan who opposes it, obscures it and distorts it.

It is here too that we locate the importance of preaching and of the systematic exposition and application of Scripture to the world scene, to the wider church and to the personal and corporate lives of those listening. The dearth of good expository and doctrinal preaching has been the weakness of the Free Churches in our century as the abundance of it was the strength of the Free Churches at their beginnings. The charismatic movement has not recovered this. Even where churches are 'renewed' they still need to be 'reformed' to the biblical standard by giving space to the public reading of the Scriptures (e.g. Col. 4:16; 1 Thess. 5:27; 1 Tim. 4:13) and by developing the regular and systematic exposition of them (e.g. Act 13:1; 20:7,11,20; 2 Tim. 3:16,17; 4:1–5).

At its best the Free Church tradition has always believed in preaching as the climax of worship and not merely as an adjunct to it. And at its best preaching is itself an act of *congregational participation* in which the hearts of the people rise in adoration or confession or thanksgiving as the words of the preacher become in Calvin's phrase 'the voice of God resounding in them'.[16] Preaching is not merely lecturing or moralising or speech-making: it is, as P. T. Forsyth put it, 'a prophetic act', a 'deed charged with blessing or with judgement'; it is 'the Spirit spreading to the churches. It is the past Church speaking to the present, the whole Church to the single Church, the ripe Church to the unripe, the faithful Church to the faltering Church, the ideal Church to the actual, the unseen to the seen'; it is in its proclamation and celebration of divine truth 'the organised Hallelujah of an ordered community'.[17]

Unbiblical omissions or practices in the church meetings are not the only danger in the matter of worship. Even where a person is reconciled to God by the death of his Son, justified by faith in him, and able to please God as never before in worship, the temptation because of remaining corruption is to separate worship and life, to attempt to affirm God in the one while neglecting or even denying him in the other, to sing 'psalms, hymns and spiritual songs' on Sundays while marching to a different drummer in the working week that follows. David Peterson has shown what a contradiction and even a destruction of true worship this is. Orthodoxy without ethic is empty; doctrine without life is dead; worship 'in spirit and in truth' is a matter of the total life and the whole heart.

In the New Testament Jesus Christ is the great Worshipper in his obedience, priesthood and offering, summing up the old and modelling the new worship of God. He once for all offered himself for us, an unblemished and uniquely suitable sacrifice for sin. This was his unique and supreme act of worship (Heb. 8–10), and it calls forth from us a response to his finished work in terms both of celebration and dedication. The celebration includes proclamation, exploration, doxology, preaching, teaching and praise. The dedication involves the proper imitation of Christ (1 Cor. 11:1; Phil. 2:5), the consecration of our bodily life in this fallen world (Rom. 12:1–3), as well as the aspiration of our spirits toward the world to come (Phil. 2:20–26).

Love so amazing, so divine
Demands my soul, my life, my all.

9

Some Reflections on the Meaning and Practice of Worship from inside South America

FELICITY B. HOUGHTON

INTRODUCTION

One of the privileges I enjoy in travelling within Latin America in order to minister to the student movements affiliated to the International Fellowship of Evangelical Students in this continent, is that of being able to gather with God's people in a variety of places and denominational settings. What I share now is the fruit of what I have seen and experienced in Argentina, Chile, Ecuador, Peru, and Bolivia which is my homeland for the time being. I have tried to be a careful observer of some of the church services in which I have taken part on my travels, as well as here in La Paz, Bolivia, and to note down my observations during the course of the service, putting on one side subjective reactions.

However, before describing what I have seen, it is necessary to refer to the historical and cultural context of which the evangelical church in Latin America is an integral part.

THE HISTORICAL BACKGROUND

Compared with China, or the countries of the Middle East or of Europe, Latin America is a young continent. Her documented history is not longer than 500 years, a period which divides approximately into 330 years of Spanish colonial rule, and 170 of existence as independent republics. Though these had broken free from the Spanish yoke politically, they did not seek to uproot the Roman Catholic Church which had been planted in Latin American soil three centuries before. So profound and dominant is the influence of Roman Catholicism in Latin America that it is not possible to understand the continent apart from the religion that has shaped its life and moulded its outlook. Politics, education, art and architecture all bear an imprint that is unmistakably Roman Catholic.

In contrast with these deep religious roots, Protestant missionary work has a relatively short history. It has nevertheless produced effects that are far from shallow. Its beginnings go back between 100 and 150 years, that is, a few decades after the birth of the independent republics, and were marked by powerful opposition from the official church. As time went on, more missionaries from Britain and a few other European countries, and many from the United States, came to this continent to evangelize and to plant churches.

From its small and harsh beginnings, this mountain spring – the evangelical church – has become a wide and fast-flowing river. Evangelical Christians in Latin America now number between 50 and 60 millions, and it is calculated that by the next century this figure will have swollen to between 135 and 137 millions. These many millions of Christians are members of many hundreds of different denominations, the multi-denominational character of the church being due to the following factors: the variety of denominational backgrounds represented by the foreign missionaries who came to Latin America, the growth of indigenous churches as an offshoot of the work done by the missionaries, and the tendency to fragmentation in both streams already mentioned – a fragmentation that has led to further multiplication of congregations, groups and denominations.

If it is necessary to understand Roman Catholicism in order to understand Latin America, it is equally necessary to understand Pentecostalism in order to understand the growth of the evangelical churches in this continent. The movement in Chile began with an outpouring of God's Spirit in the year 1909 on the members of the Methodist Episcopal Church in Valparaíso, Chile. The pastor was the Rev. William C. Hoover, who with his wife had arrived from the United States in Chile in the year 1889. The fire that fell from heaven then spread further and further in the decades that followed, and far from being put out, continues to grow. I heard an Argentinian pastor affirm in conversation earlier this year that Pentecostalism goes hand in hand with the idiosyncrasy of the Latin American peoples; to put it another way, I would say that it is the expression of the Latin American soul. God has been pleased to use Pentecostalism to give his gospel a Latin American face.

In the early 1970s, some of the non-Pentecostal denominations in Argentina, Chile and Bolivia received the impact of a movement of spiritual and charismatic renewal. The effects of this movement were sometimes helpfully challenging and refreshing and sometimes divisive and disturbing. At the same time the charismatic movement within the Roman Catholic church in these countries was growing fast. For Roman Catholics, it was a period of unprecedented openness to the experiential reality of the Holy Spirit and to his power to make Christ real in the life of those who believe in him. For evangelicals, there was a return to the biblical emphasis on the Lordship of Christ, a fresh attention given to the church as the body of Christ equipped with the gifts of the Holy Spirit, but also an unbiblical concentration on 'the baptism of the Spirit' as an essential post-conversion experience, accompanied by speaking with tongues.

One further comment must be made before I move on to the cultural context of the evangelical churches in Latin America, a comment that concerns the political and economic situations of these republics. Exactly how these realities affect the church at any given period of her history, and how she affects them is, I think, something understood fully only by God. On the one hand we observe that military dictatorships and irresponsible democracy, terrorism and violence, poverty, inflation and economic instability, the strangling foreign debt, corruption, illiteracy, drug traffic and the abuse of natural resources are the milieu in which the churches carry on their work and witness. They are unavoidable realities that entail suffering and could lead to despair. On the other hand, we can see these things as means God may use to instruct his people concerning what he requires of them as the salt and the light of the world. What is clear is that the worship of Jesus Christ cannot be genuine if we shut our eyes and ears to the cry of our neighbour and the groaning of our nation.

THE CULTURAL CONTEXT

I shall refer to a few characteristics that impinge on the practice of worship. First, the attitude to time. At the risk of exaggeration, I would say that the Latin American wears a watch because it is a modern habit to do so, and in order to know the time. But the watch is not consulted as a way of finding out if there is time to do something, or if one ought to be at a certain place, or stop one activity and pass on to another. The clock marks the passing of the hours, but it is one's internal, subjective rhythm that determines the pace of life. Hence, church meetings may or may not begin on time, are generally speaking long and often open-ended, and no one is worried.

Second, it is normal to express one's emotions openly, not only with words that describe them frankly, but also with gestures of the face and hands, tears, embraces and bodily movements. Hence, the raising of arms and hands in church, or clapping, or moving with the music, or a kind of dancing, or greeting with a kiss on the cheek, are all part of normal and expected behaviour in the churches I am describing.

Third, it is an obvious fact, and therefore could easily be overlooked, that the language of all communication is Spanish, a language that is extraordinarily rich in resources to reach the mind and the heart by many paths. Dr Pablo Deiros, an Argentinian pastor and theologian, has pointed out that Latin American culture sets great store by the word, but particularly by the well-spoken word, the elegant turn of phrase, the eloquent flow of sound. The content and the truthfulness of what is said are of secondary importance; what matters is that it should be well said and sound impressive. But we are taught by the apostle Paul that in Christian preaching the values are reversed: that truth is all, and wise and persuasive words are not the secret of efficacy and power (1 Cor. 2:4,5). This inclination towards the word and the sound and their immediate effect may be one of the factors that account for impromptu messages from the pulpit and a widespread lack of serious biblical exposition.

Fourth, modernity has come to Latin America. Os Guinness, speaking on this subject at Lausanne II in Manila, said:

> It is my prayer that we will put modernity on our agenda for mission. And that we will analyze its impact at our local levels in our countries, our cities, our audiencies, our ministries. And I pray that we will seek to reform the church where the impact of modernity has already been damaging. For example, the loss of truth; sweatless,

long-distance evangelism without incarnation; technique without spiritual warfare; a reliance on images until they are coming out of our ears without a trust in the power of words in general, *and the Word* in particular. I pray we will also abandon our easy excuses.[1]

The danger I see in some churches here is that of a TV show mentality: on the high platform where the lights and the movement engage the attention of the audience, there must be variety, there must be good entertainment, and above all, there must be not only sound but volume, not only volume but noise to shut out thought and shut in feeling. And in the midst of so much 'music', musicality has fled like a shy fairy before the approach of the giants.

In the fifth place, I want to say something about church buildings. Part of the cultural heritage received from Spain is the presence of many Roman Catholic church buildings, of which a large number date back to colonial times. These are often imposing in size, elaborate in style, sombre and dark in their interior, and characterized by the presence of images of Christ, Mary and the saints, and confessionals. Here Mass is celebrated frequently, and from time to time, baptisms, weddings, funerals, and ecclesiastical festivals. Here at any time the individual may slip in alone to pray before a statue or light a candle. Here the weight of tradition and the familiarity of religious custom offer a certain security.

On the other hand, the evangelical understands the church building as a place where he or she meets with God and fellow Christians. Often the buildings themselves are architecturally nondescript, utilitarian, humble in the extreme, and yet 'holy ground'. Sometimes they are cinemas hired for use on Sundays and filled more than once, and sometimes they are elegant buildings raised brick by brick by the sole effort and faith and costly giving of the congregation. In other cases, generous financial help for building is received from overseas. In general, their beauty is in their lightness and simplicity; with no images and no candles, they are truly 'houses of prayer'.

THE CHURCH AT ITS BEST

Shaped by its historical background and reflecting its own culture, the evangelical church has developed under the mercy of God. At its best, I see it as Paul, faithful in the practice of love as he himself expounds it in 1 Cor. 13:7, saw the church in Corinth. At the outset of his first letter to them, knowing that he must expose the things that needed to be reproved and corrected, he nevertheless wrote them these words of gratitude, appreciation and wholehearted confidence:

I always thank God for you because of his grace given you in Christ Jesus. For in him you have been enriched in every way – in all your speaking and in all your knowledge – because our testimony about Christ was confirmed in you. Therefore you do not lack any spiritual gift as you eagerly wait for our Lord Jesus Christ to be revealed. He will keep you strong to the end, so that you will be blameless on the day of our Lord Jesus Christ. God, who has called you into fellowship with his Son Jesus Christ our Lord, is faithful (1 Cor. 1:4–9).

So I see it as a church made up of redeemed men and women, of people from a variety of class backgrounds, who have had a firsthand experience of conversion. They have been rescued from drunkenness, marriage break-down, drug addiction, disillusionment with religion, superstition, unbelief, ignorance and misery, and transferred into the kingdom of God's beloved Son. They love the Word, and are open and sensitive to the Holy Spirit. They are a people actively engaged in spreading God's kingdom on the streets, in hospitals and prisons, in homes and schools and universities, for they know that the work of ministry is the work of all the saints. Among them, the Christian woman finds ample scope for service and is respected and appre-ciated. As there is boldness in witness, so there is growth and expansion in the number of baptised believers and new congregations. They are joyful and musical, and concerned that the gospel and its power should meet the needs of the whole person within his or her community.

ROOM FOR GROWTH

At the same time, I see this same people of God needing to become more theologically rooted, more serious in its study of the Word, better instructed concerning how to contextualize the Christian faith, more able to reflect on political and social concerns from the standpoint of the Scriptures. This in turn would lead to more effective social and political involvement. One perceives the need for greater awareness of world mission and for orientation for those who are called to take part in it beyond their national frontiers. Likewise there is a need for greater awareness of church history and for people well equipped in the field of Christian apologetics to discern the dangers lurking within liberation theologies and current philosophical trends. The church needs to become more responsible for providing her pastors and workers with adequate financial support, better supplied with good Christian literature written in Spanish and not translated from the English, and eager to use these resources for growth in character and understanding. Within herself, the church needs to grow in maturity and unity, a unity grounded on the foundation of the Word, the gospel and the evangelical heritage, and to be accepting of diversity in matters that are not essential.

A CATALOGUE OF CONGREGATIONAL WORSHIP EXPERIENCES

In speaking of the church at her best, as also of her need for growth, it has been necessary to generalise. With some relief, therefore, I now turn to the description of some services in which I have taken part, and so move from the general to the particular.

Argentina

Jujuy is a small city in the far northwest of the country, not many hours from the Bolivian border. On two consecutive Sunday evenings I attended a church belonging to the 'Movimiento Cristiano Misionero' (the Christian Missionary Movement). The building is made of stone; on the wall behind the platform, the name JESUS, drawn in bricks which jut out from the wall, is the only adornment. The pastor directed the singing, to the accompaniment of an electronic piano; we sang a few songs several times over. Other elements in the two services were prayer, testimonies from young people in discipleship training, notices,[2] the offering, and the sermon.

Here is the gist of the sermon on the first Sunday that I was present: It is a tremendous thing to draw near to God; he is near and he is holy. We are to deny ourselves the pleasure of giving way to our bad temper. It is time to begin to trust in God. The preacher referred to John 14:30 and Matt. 23:27. He had consulted a Bible dictionary on the meaning of 'hypocrite'. Obedience to God: this is the difference between religion and the way of Jesus Christ. It's a matter of whether I am doing the will of God. The more we obey God, the more blessing we receive from him. But you need faith in order to obey. Our disobedience creates a resistance to the way of faith. In the times we live in now, all we can do is to lay hold of God. But we wriggle away and look for a place where we won't have to do the will of God. To obey is the most difficult thing for us to do. What is hypocrisy? How difficult it is to be a Christian! What is your obedience like before God? In Argentina we are going through the crisis of hyperinflation. When are we going to start obeying God? Our obedience to a God who is real must be concrete and evident. He is wiser than we are and corrects us because he loves us. He must conquer me by the strength of his love. God says to me: 'You have got to change.'

The preaching began at 8.55 p.m. and went on for about an hour. Though the two Sundays I have referred to were Palm Sunday and Easter Day, there was no reference made to the meaning of Christ's passion and resurrection in the life of God's people, nor to these special days.

When, on another occasion, I asked the pastor of a very large congregation in the industrial city of Córdoba, Argentina, what he considered to be the reasons for God's people to gather together, he replied that it is in order to thank and praise God, to bring our petitions to him, and to preach to those who do not know him.

Bolivia

One of the Assemblies of God congregations in the Ciudad El Alto, near the city of La Paz, holds a Sunday morning service in a cinema that faces onto a public square. On the occasion on which I was present, the singing of eleven choruses and one hymn occupied the longest space of time, to the accompaniment of two electric guitars. Other elements were prayer, the reading of Ps.40, words from the pastor addressed to the regular congregation and to possible visitors, an offering, and then the preaching of a young man who referred to Num. 21:4–9 and to his own experience of conversion. When the congregation was asked, 'Who is our God?' all replied, 'Jesus Christ'. Later on there was a round of applause 'for Jesus Christ'. Towards the close there was a prayer for physical healing for the sick, and those who desired to receive Jesus Christ as Saviour were invited to go forward.

In the centre of La Paz a large congregation has recently bought an unused cinema. On the Sunday morning that I went, it was filled to overflowing with people from a variety of social backgrounds. On the platform were two electronic pianos, two drums, two electric guitars, and two singers. Two men between them led the service and the singing; it was long, informal and enthusiastic. Reference was made to three psalms at different moments. One of the leaders gave a long explanation of the financial situation of the congregation in relation to the payment of the building and to God's provision. There was no sermon as such. One of the leaders spoke 'a word of prophecy', followed by a song and a prayer of confession. Many people responded to the invitation to go forward in repentance. They were exhorted to believe and confess and to read the Bible. 'You haven't changed your religion, but rather have found the Lord of Life.' Later on there was prayer for healing, testimonies, prayer for parents and their young children who went up on the platform, and a round of grateful applause to the Lord. The service concluded at 12.30 p.m., having begun at 8.30 a.m.

A few months later, I talked with a friend who had visited this same congregation. Her comment was that she had been frightened by the lack of respect for the person, and felt that psychological manipulation was used. I asked her how she understood worship; she answered: 'To worship is to pour out our hearts to God. We must worship him, no matter how we feel, for he is worthy of all honour. We practise worship by praise.' I asked then, 'What is praise?' 'Praise is to sing songs which exalt the name of God.' The praise time in her congregation lasts an hour, during which a few songs are sung, each one being repeated a number of times. My friend is aware of the danger of the blank mind during the singing.

'In what other ways do you worship?' I asked. 'Singing in tongues, and praying,' she said. 'Is the Bible read in public in your services?' 'No, we don't have that custom.' I asked her what changes she would like to see in the Sunday service, and she replied that she would like the leaders to explain what it means to worship God, to create an awareness of this in the congregation, to give more intellectual content to the message, and then to contextualize it for the people now.

Chile

Surrounded by the Atacama Desert, Calama is at one and the same time an oasis and a small town. A friend and I arrived at the 'Church of God' on a housing estate for 7 p.m. It was the last day of their 'Women's Week'; on the platform were five women dressed in black skirts, white blouses, and a red carnation pinned on the blouse. Behind the pulpit on the wall was a painting, a feature typical of Chilean Pentecostal churches. An open Bible occupied the centre, with rays of light falling on it from above. In the background was a river and waterfall, trees and a snow-covered peak. Pss. 19:1 and 24:1 were written on either side of the scene.

On this special occasion, the whole service was conducted by the five women on the platform, two of whom read the Scripture passage to which the pastor was later to refer in his sermon on Matt. 25:1–13. Two offerings were taken, one near the beginning and the other at the close of the service. There was a prayer of thanksgiving, and a time of joyful singing to the accompani-ment of an accordian, an electric guitar, and a group of young girls whirling their tambourines with flowing streamers hanging from them. The music was melodious and simple, typically Chilean, and all the words were known by heart by the congregation.

There was a sense of expectation as the pastor began to preach. It was obvious that he had carefully prepared what he was going to say, and had borne in mind that this was the last day of 'Women's Week' in the church. The Lord is coming for his church, not for any denomination in particular (Matt. 25:1–13). In Luke 8:1–3 we learn of women who served Jesus, and in Luke 7:36–50 we see that love is not something to be talked about, but to be demonstrated. The women who watched Jesus die on the cross, from a distance (Matt. 27:55,56), were grateful women, and we who are now cleansed by his blood should be much more grateful than they.

Here the pastor referred to his own conversion, and to how God had healed and rescued him from misery. In his zeal for us to understand the message, he left the pulpit and the microphone for a few minutes and came down among the congregation, appealing fervently to us. He went on to mention Anna, the prophetess, Rahab the harlot, Ruth the Moabitess. Jesus requires us to love him with all our heart and soul; let us serve him and recognize all the mercies we have received from him. We have been forgiven great sins, and therefore we must assume our responsibility to serve him. Let us serve him with much love for we know what he has done for us.

Ecuador

Standing opposite the buildings of the radio station HCJB in Quito, the capital of Ecuador, is a church named after the district where it is found, Iñaquito. On Sunday mornings they celebrate three services, one after another, in order to give opportunity for all who desire to gather there for worship. The words of the songs were projected onto the wall at the back of the platform where the music group of five members played their instruments. Piano, trumpet and saxophone also made their contribution at different moments. The songs, some of whose words were based on Bible stories, were neither announced nor repeated. Passages of Scripture were read in between the singing of them; often clapping accompanied the rhythm of the music. There was a prayer of intercession before the offering was taken. Then came the sermon, based on 2 Sam. 7, part of which was read. Many of those present had their Bibles with them. Later a member of the pastoral team of this church told me that he had been responsible for introducing changes into the singing habits of the congregation a year ago; the changes involved combining traditional hymns with songs, and eliminating songs that have no theological content.

Peru

In the capital city of Lima I attended a Sunday morning service in a congregation now associated with the Assemblies of God. The structure of the service was straightforward: from 10 a.m. until 10.45 there was congregational singing alternating with prayer led by the man who led the singing. Then came the notices, given by the pastor, after which he preached from 11 to 12 noon. He closed his message with a long evangelistic invitation, which was followed by the taking up of the tithes and offerings. The pastor informed us about the work of construction going on, we sang again and then little by little the 300-strong congregation on that morning slowly left the building, chatting with one another as they did so.

The songs in this case were projected onto the wall and accompanied by an orchestra made up of an electronic piano, an electric guitar, trumpet and drums.

Reflections

In a continent nurtured on religious liturgy, it is noteworthy that by and large the structure of evangelical church services is very far removed from that liturgy. Public reading of the Word is absent; prayers of intercession for the nation are rare; baptism of adults receives prominence but the sacrament of the Lord's Supper is not given a central place, except in the Brethren assemblies. The Lord's prayer and the Apostles' Creed are not used. There is an emphasis on corporate praise, but on the whole I venture to think that this 'praise' is the response to the music and words of a song, rather than to a fresh contemplation of God in Jesus Christ arising from an understanding of the Word. I have already mentioned the dearth of biblical exposition, a situation that opens the door to 'worship' being practised as a 'trip', divorced from daily life and national and cultural situations.

In one city, characterised by violence and poverty, fear and danger, during the course of the church service I attended, the fire brigade with loud sirens twice raced past the church building where we were gathered, but we had been encouraged by the leader, as the service began, to forget the news we had heard and the things which were happening 'outside'. We did not pray for 'the peace of Jerusalem'.

Genuine worship can only be offered to God by his people within two contexts: the context which he has provided for us in his Word, and the context he has provided for us by creation and providence. He is the God of both, and if we alienate ourselves from either, we lose touch with him. 'For we are the true circumcision, who worship God in spirit [or worship by the Spirit of God], and glory in Christ Jesus, and put no confidence in the flesh' (Phil. 3:3). Worship of the one true God has been made possible for us through the coming of his Spirit and the gift of his Son; nevertheless it does not happen automatically. God must regenerate our hearts so that we become the 'true circumcision', and we must ourselves worship and serve him, abandoning all confidence in self and other idols and glorying only in Christ Jesus.

Worship is a term that describes the total relationship of the Christian man and woman, and the Christian community, to the living and triune God. It is a relationship involving love, exclusive loyalty, service, holy fear, obedience, a constant recalling to mind of God's words and deeds, and a renunciation of all other gods and idols. Worship is impossible without faith, the revelation of the Word and the enlightenment of the Holy Spirit. The fact that the forms of congregational worship vary from place to place, from time to time and from culture to culture, in no way affects its essential nature, but underlines the fact that it is mortal beings, creatures of change, time and place, who are responding to the living God from their own situations.

Both Old and New Testaments make it clear that God requires both the surrender of our whole life to him and also the practice of coming together to worship him. The gathering of Christians for this purpose is not, of course, confined to set times and consecrated buildings, but our meeting on Sundays, for example, makes visible this commitment of the whole life and at the same time serves to deepen and strengthen it.

A corporate time of worship can be called 'good' only if it is good both for God and for the church at the same time – in other words, if God receives from his people what is his right – their love, praise, thanksgiving, adoration, and trust – and if his people receive the edification they constantly need, using the means he has supplied – the Word, the sacraments, prayer, song, the gifts of his Spirit and mutual fellowship (see, for example, Heb. 10:24,25).

It is true that only God knows when he is being truly worshipped in the daily lives of his people and in their corporate times of praise, but his Holy Spirit requires our spirit to know whether we are obeying him, loving him, seeking and serving him. It is we who must be aware if there is repentance towards God and forgiveness towards others in our hearts when we approach God. Our conscience knows if we have opened ourselves to the Holy Spirit, if the leading of the worship has been authentic and helpful and carefully thought out, if we have heard God speak, if the words we have sung have challenged us with the truth and have enabled us to express it.

All this being the case, it is inevitable that when genuine worship occurs in the gathering of Christians it is the fruit of the genuine worship of their daily lives. However loud the music, or fervent the preaching, or correct the liturgy, these outward things can never of themselves create worship in human hearts. Hence repentance needs to be unfailingly present in our worship, for as we come together we need to recognize and confess our sins, the sins that have marred the worship of God in our daily lives when we are a scattered community, and that will likewise make unacceptable to God the worship we offer him as a gathered community unless we are first cleansed of them.

The first half of Psalm 95 makes it clear that community worship needs a time and a place and someone to lead or call the gathering; that such worship is expressed in music, song, shouts and thanksgiving; that the contemplation of God on the basis of his revelation leads us to recognize who he is and who we are. And then we are pulled up abruptly by the words: 'Today, if you hear his voice, do not harden your hearts' (v. 7). We are being called to repent; we are being warned of the unbelief that lurks in our hearts; we are being challenged to abandon our resistance to the Word, and to become docile, obedient and believing.

If one of the purposes for which John recorded what he saw through the open door in heaven in Rev. 4 and 5 is, as David Peterson says, 'to encourage his readers to reflect the pattern of the heavenly assembly in their life on earth' (p. 89), we do well to ask what light these chapters throw on the subject of repentance in worship. The answer is to be found in the Lamb, 'looking as if it had been slain, standing in the centre of the throne, encircled by the four living creatures and the elders' (Rev. 5:6). He is the object of all praise from creation and the church, but it is also he who makes all praise possible, for he has 'purchased men for God' and 'made them to be a kingdom and priests to serve our God, and they will reign on the earth' (vv. 9, 10). Here praise is the fruit of repentance, the result of the exultant joy of having been redeemed and forgiven.

God is not seeking worship in the abstract, but worshippers. The difference is significant. He seeks not only worshipping individuals, but a worshipping community, a universal community that worships the Lamb.

BIBLIOGRAPHY OF WORSHIP IN LATIN AMERICA
(compiled by Samuel Escobar)

Background and Life of Evangelical Churches in Latin America

Esther and Mortimer Arias, *The Cry of My People* (New York: Friendship Press, 1981).
— *El clamor de mi pueblo* (Mexico: Casa Unida de Publicaciones, 1981).
Juan A. Mackay, *El otro Cristo español* (Mexico: Casa Unida de Publicaciones, 1988 [2a. ed.]).
David Martin, *Tongues of Fire* (Oxford: Basil Blackwell, 1990).
Emilio A. Núñez and William D. Taylor, *Crisis in Latin America* (Chicago: Moody Press, 1989).
Hans Jürgen Prien, *Historia del cristianismo en América Latina* (Salamanca: Sígueme, 1985).
Varios, *En tierra extraña. Itinerario del pueblo pentecostal chileno* (Santiago de Chile: Amerinda, 1988).

Worship

Rubem Martins Amorese, *Celebração do evangelho*. (Brasilia: Sião, 1987).
Caio Fábio D'Araújo Filho *Um projeto de espiritualidade integral*. Brasilia: Sião, 1988.
Bonhoeffer Dietrich *Vida en comunidad* (Buenos Aires: La Aurora, 1966).
E. M. Bounds, *Orad sin cesar* (Miami: Editorial Vida, 1983).
Centro de Estudios Cristianos, *Culto: crítica y búsqueda* (Buenos Aires: CEC, 1972).
Francisco E. Estrello, *En comunión con lo eterno* (Mexico: Casa Unida de Publicaciones, 1975 [3ra. ed.]).
David Evans, *Diálogo con Dios* (Buenos Aires: Ediciones Certeza, 1976).
Richard Foster, *La oración personal* (Buenos Aires: Ediciones Certeza, 1989).
Francisco Lacueva, *Espiritualidad trinitaria* (Barcelona: CLIE, 1983).
Roberto Lazear, *El maestro de dolores* (Miami: Editorial Caribe, 1979).
José M. Martinez y otros, *Los cristianos en el mundo de hoy* (Barcelona: CLIE – Alianza Evangélica Española, 1987).
José M. Martínez y Pablo Martínez Vila, *Abba, Padre. Teología y psicología de la oración* (Barcelona: GBU, 1990).
Emilio A. Núñez, *Caminos de renovación* (Grand Rapids: Portavoz, 1975).
Rodolfo G. Turnbull, Ed., *Diccionario de la teología práctica: culto* (Grand Rapids: Subcomisión de Litearatura Cristiana, 1977).
Varios, *El culto es fiesta* (Mexico: El Faro, 1985).
Varios, *Ser evangélico hoy* (Barcelona: GBU, 1988).

10

Worship in the Independent/Free Church/ Congregational Tradition: A View from the Two-Thirds World

GUILLERMO W. MENDEZ

INTRODUCTION

Stereotypes are powerful tools of communication. Granted that they are far from accurate, they still have a message. Don Juan, Sor Juana Inés de la Cruz and Don Quixote serve as types of the Latin American. Thus it is said that the Latin American is enamoured of love, is deeply religious and a supporter of causes doomed to failure.[1]

There is no room for disclaimers. The idealism, religiosity and romanticism of Latin Americans are inextricably intertwined with the history of their land.[2] But from a historical perspective, what does it mean to say that the Latin American is deeply religious? What are the effects of Roman Catholic Christianity on the Philippines, Japan, and some African countries influenced by Catholicism? What shape did Protestantism take in all those countries sharing a Catholic background? How do the cultural and religious grids determine today what becomes of Protestantism in each land?[3]

These are crucial questions for understanding the shape that worship has taken in every culture, though we cannot deal with all of them in a comprehensive manner. To do this would require a much longer paper, and might also change the subject from worship to a social and historical study of the founding of the Christian church in these countries. To follow a more modest approach, in this paper I have decided to explore the historical antecedents of worship against the backdrop of Roman Catholic Christianity, which has so powerfully moulded Latin American culture. I shall also consider the relationship between the charismatic forms of worship and those of the independent, Free Churches. Finally, I shall point to some theological areas of concern that need further study. This approach will touch upon social and historical considerations, but will have worship as its primary theological focus. In this way, I hope also to communicate something of the religious context where worship takes place.

To narrow down this ambitious subject even more I shall take as a starting point three basic presuppositions that undergird what follows:

1. Medieval religion resulted in a separation between faith and life, and this perspective was inherited by Latin America from Spanish medieval Catholicism. Such understanding contradicts Scripture's larger view, that life in general and multiform service in the church must also be worship. The medieval understanding, however, not only contributes to the dichotomy between church and 'real' life, but also fails to recognize worship as a far broader endeavour than mere church attendance or a church programme.[4]

2. Colonial North American Protestant religion was transplanted to Latin America in a quite segmented fashion. This reality is seen not only in our church institutions, but also in our manner of doing things and in our alignments. One example is the resulting strife between charismatic and non-charismatic modes of worship.[5]

3. There are social and cultural factors that shape our understanding of worship in and outside the church.[6]

This essay does not pretend to be a comprehensive representation of the role of worship in the independent tradition in the Two-Thirds World. Written material on this subject is scarce, and where the subject is treated, it is often done from a one-sided perspective and from a practical point of view, leaving out very important theoretical questions. The literary heritage is so small that using experience and cultural observations more than literary sources as guide to the historical role of worship could lead to serious errors of interpretation.[7] At best, I can communicate my impressions on this subject, based on the history and culture of the Latin American church, but there is no room for dogmatism.

In the next section I shall touch upon the historical origins of Christian worship in our lands. The main thesis is that Catholic religion christianized Latin America in a way that failed to teach the full relation between faith and life.

HISTORICAL ROOTS OF WORSHIP

As far as the Latin American scene is concerned, the old Roman Catholic tradition and doctrine communicated a conception of religion that resulted in a virtual separation between spiritual life and ethics. This has a bearing on the interpretation of worship as a total commitment to God.

A variety of Indian religions were practised before the arrival of Christianity on the shores of Latin America. None of them survived intact the impact of colonial Spanish Catholicism.[8] But it soon became evident that between those antecedents and the new religion there was room for much interplay. In some places the ancient traditions have been mingled with Roman Christianity.[9] This means that worship as the life lived before the true God, serving and properly relating to him, through faith in his crucified and resurrected Son, did not find a new and radical expression within Spanish Catholicism, which tended to point to Christ without fully introducing him.

Roman Catholicism brought from Spain Christianity blended with an ideology compounded of the Roman legal manner of reasoning, Greek medieval philosophy and medieval chivalry traditions.[10] In particular, the heroes of the Spanish novel, based on the ideals of the chivalry traditions, were clever enough to get around ethical principles and practices. But this was far more than fictional tradition. In fact, even the prototype of religious people, the clergyman, was a cunning glutton and drunkard who had violated his vows to God. This amounted to a virtual separation between ethics and religion. The character of this kind of religion is masterfully portrayed by the old Dutch historian Johann Huizinga in his *The Autumn of the Middle Ages*.[11]

Against this backdrop, biblical Protestant preaching from its inception has demanded that the secular and the sacred be integrated in the believer's life in a holistic pattern of obedience to the faith.[12] This is a sort of Copernican revolution in religion which has fought not only against dominant Catholic religious structures, but against the entire religious culture of Latin America, where beliefs and practices are inherently opposed to this very integration, if not for philosophical reasons, then for the indulgent lifestyle it allows.[13]

But Protestant preaching has not always been effective. These cultural tides explain the reason why some ideas are tolerated even in some Two-Thirds World Protestant churches. These include: (1) Since worship is mainly for a church situation, daily life has little to do with worshipping God. (2) It follows that whereas church events are of first importance to God ethics rate second or third. (3) Christianity does not require obedience or total commitment but merely intellectual assent. (4) Cultural beliefs and practices do not have to be affected by religion.[14]

Liberation theology with its holistic approach has not enhanced the place and function of worship and spiritual life as a total commitment of the total person to the total self-disclosure of God.[15] It has merely shifted the locus of interest from the sacred to the secular in the name of God. One does not have to be very perceptive to realize that in the attempt to integrate both realities the latter overrides the former.[16] This shift might on occasion be helpful if liberation theology had a stronger theological and metaphysical base (Scriptures, Church teachings, sacraments, etc.),[17] but it leaves many metaphysical matters open to reinterpretation by 'the people', 'the thinking elite', or 'praxis'.

These are some of the historical and ideological influences in our religious scene. Another will be articulated in the next section. It has to do with the arrival in Latin America of the Protestant (both non-charismatic and Pentecostal) traditions from North America.

THE DIVIDED MIND OF CONGREGATIONAL WORSHIP

By 'worship' we understand that engagement with God through faith in Jesus Christ expressed in daily obedience to God in every aspect of life, or service to him on all planes of human existence. This we shall call worship in a broader sense. The development of a broader concept of worship as it was defined above has never been central in the independent-congregational traditions. What relationship exists between our insistence on daily obedience and worship in the local church has not yet been explored. Today, the centrality of worship, in general, is drawn from the interaction between the traditional Protestant concepts of worship and the Pentecostal/charismatic type of worship.[18] Why assign such importance to the specifically charismatic type of worship? Because more and more we see a general spread of this type of worship throughout the independent Protestant camps.[19]

In Latin America, the criticism that says, 'Protestantism is a foreign religion' is a double-edged sword, since in one sense all forms of Christianity are not indigenous wherever one goes in the world – except Palestine. In that sense, Christianity, including biblical Protestantism, is as alien as all other forms, but for the same reason can become part and parcel of the civilization where it takes root.[20] In its different garments, Christianity has been one of the most active missionary religions. In the last two centuries, Two-Thirds World countries have been invaded by a form of Christianity that some would label as a white man's religion.[21]

The foreign nature of Protestantism has greatly influenced the shape Christianity has taken in our lands. It is no secret that whoever sponsors the missionary enterprise sets the pace for important items such as the content of the church's message and the format of its congregational worship.

North American Protestant religion was transplanted to Latin America through many efforts quite independent of one another. As a result there is great diversity in the character of evangelical Christianity in Latin America. As I have already suggested, this diversity surfaces, for instance, in the charismatic vs. congregational strife over modes of worship.[22] The thesis of this section is that in all Latin American independent church traditions there is a critical interaction with charismatic worship styles and that the former are shaped to a certain extent by the position taken for or against charismatic-type practices.[23] A by-product of this is that often the biblical data are not seriously considered in the formulation of Latin American Independent and Baptist worship styles.

From the perspective of some groups, congregational worship has come down as a cold, structured protocol to meet with the dignitaries of heaven.[24] Others hold to an ecclesiastical tradition that sees worship as a frenetic spontaneous response of an emotional body to a God interested in promoting religious experiences in exchange for faithful church attendance. These two extremes have always needed a thorough biblical response. Scripture, common sense and experience teach us that, when it comes to congregational worship, truth does not belong exclusively to either camp.

Yet the styles of worship in the independent church tradition move within these extremes. There are some fallacies that encourage the independent tradition to reproduce these extremes. The fallacies concerning the more traditional worship are: (1) Awe, admiration and quiet pondering are the only possible human responses to God's majesty. That means that all non-silent responses are less spiritual, or at least, less pleasing to God. (2) Cognitive handling of Scripture is more pleasing to God than praise. The concept often involves the importance of total obedience in regard to worldly issues in daily Christian living, but its incarnation is based solely on knowledge; the impression left is that knowledge has devoured experience.[25] (3) Any corporeal (bodily-expressed) religious experience is influenced by charismatism and therefore must be avoided.

But the fallacies in the charismatic camp must also be considered, since their impact on the independent tradition is so great. The following are some of their presuppositions: (1) In the New Testament church there were no transitions and there was no variety. The transitory nature of the history told in Acts should not be overstated. Nevertheless Acts does not present itself as a homogeneous historical setting where God intends to do exactly the same things all the time. Even a superficial study of Acts reveals that there is not always the same response to demons, death or deity. Failure to recognize this may put us into an interpretative straight-jacket as we try to reproduce 'the things that the early church did'. To imitate their practices in the best sense, it is important to reproduce the life of the early church.[26] (2) What is practised today in charismatic-type churches is exactly what took place in the early church. But is it? This is assumed without question. Leaving aside doctrines like healing and tongues, can we sustain such a belief based solely on the format of worship we suspect that the early church used?[27] (3) Freedom of the spirit and planned worship are mutually exclusive. Of course, if all church business were conducted with this philosophy, people would not even know when to come to church, or at least would come only when they felt Spirit-led.[28]

The concept of spiritual life is obviously twisted in both sets of false presuppositions. The independent tradition rightly seeks to instill in its followers a sense that worship requires our whole being to be fleshed out in the market place. But there seems to be a downplaying of our emotions as a valid part of our human response to God. On the other hand, there seems to be a conviction that spiritual life must be objective and that the subjectivity that feelings may bring into this experience is not safe. Thus worshippers crave greater knowledge to increase their objectivity.[29]

It seems that the dichotomy between emotions and knowledge owes much to the idealization of apostolic doctrine as the *only* true mark of a New Testament church. The lost balance needs a remedy. Should we not delineate more clearly the relationship between a life of faith, love and hope, and congregational worship? A strong prayer life will prove to be a corrective to any conception of church assembly that does not long for a sense of God's presence. Indeed, prayer should form a greater part of the churches' agenda than it does today. By and large, contemporary Christians do not pray enough, or with adequate biblical knowledge and fervour, and therefore our *congregational* meetings seem so barren[30]. Prayer will bring these business-like worship meetings closer to a lively interaction with the living God.

The charismatic set of presuppositions has in its favour the idea that once the church is gathered together to celebrate God the whole being must be involved. But in daily life, the value of biblical knowledge and the importance of addressing earthly concerns can be left out.[31] There seems to be an unspoken assumption that spiritual life and worship are mainly church-assembly affairs. This conception drives worshippers back to church day after day to 'recharge spiritual batteries'.[32]

Why does this dichotomy take place? Perhaps in part because of the idealization of early church practices as the only true marks of a New Testament church. Could it be that recovering discipleship as part and parcel of the church's life will not only transform the concept of worship from a church assembly affair to a market place affair, but will also put in better perspective a whole range of other earthly concerns? This will unite both the apostolic doctrine and the apostolic life of the church as true marks of a New Testament church.

A plea for balance is needed in the charistmatic camp. Scripture is loved and shared among charismatics. The question is, whether there is a truly scriptural basis for our Christian experience or whether we are repeating a twentieth-century tradition as it was handed down to us by the missionary who worked in our midst. To have a Scriptural basis is far more than proof-texting Scripture. We all know too well what that methodology has done for Jehovah's Witnesses.

A cross-pollenation is greatly needed. Charismatics usually demonstrate a spirit of worship that is often missing in the independent free church congregational traditions. I do not mean to belittle Christian experience of most believers within either camp. My concern, rather, is to insist that biblical worship is a far greater endeavour than church attendance or a church program or a charismatic experience. In the next section I want to deal with some broader areas of concern related to worship in the independent free church tradition.

THEOLOGICAL CONCERNS RELATED TO WORSHIP

There is in the Two-Thirds World independent church tradition a rediscovery of 'worship', but the theological definition of what true worship is has been left out. Churches and denominations are far more interested in the practical side of worship than in its serious exegetical underpinnings. This is not only a reflection of our lively emotional culture, but also of our theological bankruptcy. To a certain extent, as we have already said, this renewed interest in worship has emerged out of the phenomenal growth of Pentecostal/charismatic churches.

David Peterson has well said that 'the most pressing reason for exploring this issue is the confusion that exists today about the content and meaning of Sunday services and their role within the total life of the congregation and of individuals who belong to our churches. I believe that the Charismatic movement is in some measure responsible for the confusion that exists, though sociological factors . . . seem to have contributed significantly to a changed perception about the value and importance of church services.'[33]

What are some of the results in our church meetings of not having a proper sense of God's presence?

Confusing Reverent Fear with Wrath

In much of the modern world the theological theme of the fear of God is unknown. What is worse, there is little fear of God in any sense. 'The fear of the Lord is the beginning of knowledge' (Prov. 1:7): there is surely a sense in which Christians must fear God, not entirely unlike the way a child rightly ought at one level to fear his or her parent, regardless of the great love that parent might have for the child. In the Latin American culture, however, the fear of the Lord easily degenerates into cringing fear before the wrath of God, where wrath is something akin to bad temper. This is a familiar feeling for those of us who come from a Latin culture, with its roots in Medieval forms of Catholicism. In such contexts, where God is viewed as a 'sovereign bully', we need to emphasize his goodness.

It is true that a proper vision of God's glory brings men and women to their knees, but not out of cringing fear. Confusing God's majesty with his wrath does not permit a responsive and responsible worship. Certainly, God is not an 'associate' we can address any way we wish. But worship language is not stiff language. When we confuse the response to God's character with the response to his anger that can destroy, we are bound to forget that worship language is full of joy, as well as feelings of reverent fear. There is a need for both quiet pondering and joyful celebration.

Exalting Reverent Fear over Joy

There are parts of our world where joy seems to be contagious. Those of us who live in this kind of culture want to say that a loud and outgoing worship is what lies behind the Psalms. In Latin America many view the quiet pondering taught to us by the foreign missionary as a betrayal of our culture. We are therefore prone to experiment with new forms of worship. For better or worse, this 'wave' of a more expressive worship has also been imported from North America, but, in Latin soil, the popular sentiment is that we are 'returning' to a more indigenous worship.

This pattern is also occurring within Roman Catholicism, where winds of renewal have started to blow. In the Roman Catholic charismatic movement this renewal has implied a revision in pneumatology, so in this sense it is more than a cosmetic change, and is unlike what has happened in evangelical non-charismatic worship, where theology stays the same even as externals seem to be changing. This latter phenomenon is worth studying in depth, since it used to be that, in evangelical non-charismatic circles, a change in liturgy necessarily involved a change in theology.

This same mistake arises when we respond to God with reverent silence at the expense of other forms of response to God. The favourite verse of those who hold this position is to be found in Habakkuk 2:20: 'The Lord is in his holy temple; let all the earth be silent before him.' But then what shall we make of the most exuberant psalms (e.g. Pss. 149, 150)? We can celebrate how great he is in different ways.

Exalting Old Testament Format over New Covenant Praise

Some believers seem to be more concerned with detailed format than with freedom. Perhaps we have inherited a good deal of the Old Testament worldview where the priest, in order to offer anything to God, must first comply with several laws and regulations in order to avoid death. Our response can be to celebrate in worship services with the meticulous Old Testament priestly format of presenting sacrifices in the proper order so that God's wrath is not brought upon us. We emphasize the Law and forget the Psalms.

Maybe one of the most difficult things is to define what freedom means in worship. It's easier to say what it does not mean. It does not mean that we can do away with programmes. Neither does it refer to 100% spontaneity. Perhaps an analogy from daily life is helpful. We do not deny or oppose the order or pattern of life that gives it regularity, structure, even meaning, but neither do we deny the spontaneity and warmth and empathy required from us in daily situations. We live openly before one another. When it comes to worship it seems that many of us cannot respond unless there is a blueprint telling us exactly what to do. This is a denial of psalmodic openness to God.

Ignoring Revelation and Preferring Safe Programmes

Does not God really want to fellowship with us? Does he not want us to offer him praise? Is not this one of the lessons to be learned from the hymnic literature in the Bible? But this is easily forgotten as we substitute safe programmes or symbol-laden techniques. This is a blatant denial of the biblical revelation that reminds us how pleasing it is for God to hear our praises.

These errors are common in both the charismatic and the non-charismatic camps. In the former, the error turns, in Latin American charismatic experience, on Old Testament and temple symbolism; in the latter it is often subtle – a matter of following a traditional 'blue print'. In both cases, it is a product of biblical and theological imbalance.

The failure is tied to the the preeminence of physical symbols and traditional practices in worship. Yet are the physical and visible symbols the precondition for defining what is sacred? How important are they for worship? Our culture in our part of the Two-Thirds World has had a strong tradition of images as useful objects in worship. In our ancestral religions and later in Roman Catholic Christianity, symbolism and the culture of images have served as important didactic tools. This, of course, reminds us of the importance of symbolism in Old Testament times. However, does not this need a full revision in the light of the message of, say, the book of Hebrews? Does not our tradition need some qualification in view of the New Testament replacement of the physical by the spiritual?

What do Jesus' words mean: 'Believe me, woman, a time is coming when you will worship the Father neither on this mountain nor in Jerusalem . . . yet a time is coming and has now come when the true worshippers will worship the Father in spirit and in truth . . . God is Spirit, and his worshippers must worship in spirit and in truth' (John 4: 21; 23–24)? This is an important question for us in the independent tradition as we are enamoured with the charismatic tendency to stress visible symbolism in worship. We have decided to quarrel, as the Samaritan woman did, on the issues of place and modes of worship. This has partly resulted from a revival of visible symbols in charismatic worship. Despite our cultural heritage, perhaps even because of it, must we not ask ourselves whether our concentration on the external teaches us to overlook what is important, that is, our life and ethics – something that was also raised by Jesus to a point of importance when he interrogated the Samaritan woman about her marital status?

The Catholic Church discovered long ago that worship is linked to culture. Even though the Mass took a long time to be adapted to new situations, in Latin America popular religion and imagery have long been intertwined with cultural expressions. Today in Latin American evangelicalism the use of Old Testament figures and symbols is what is at stake.[34] We must ask some questions here: Does a relevant definition of worship require a consideration of the role of visible symbols within the church? Do symbols contribute to, enhance, or sever worship from, daily life? In places where there has been so much paganism, even within Christianity, what is the real balance between symbols as, on the one hand, teaching tools and appropriate worship incentives and, on the other, marks of superficiality or even syncretism? Are symbolism in general and art in particular helpful to establish a continum between worship in daily life and worship in the church, or do they hinder it?

There is no question that symbolism and images *can* serve as a didactic tool, but do they need some qualification in the light of the N T replacement of O T symbols? These are some of the questions that must be answered before we jump too quickly and too easily into the use of Old Testament visible symbols in a worship tradition that has been imageless.

OPENING OURSELVES TO GOD

We started this paper by assuming that the Latin American is deeply religious. That popular pietistic sentiment has not necessarily always had an orthodox substance nor a definite Christian content. As it has been said of Africans and Asians, the old pre-Columbian tribes of South America were deeply religious.[35] This seems to have left a deep impression on the general population, with the result that religion is a widespread phenomenon.

If, as is true in Latin America, there are cultures in which piety and devotion are part of the entire conception of life, and if these cultural biases are then shaped by truly biblical content, they can be a powerful expression of love for God, and have something to teach other cultures as well. Tokunbo Adeyemo has expressed it well: 'There are important contributions that the Third World church can make to the body of Christ universally. Prime among them is the joy and exuberance of worship, that we can be abandoned in the presence of the Lord in Worship.'[36]

11

Charismatically-orientated Worship

ALISTAIR BROWN

Two aspects valued by those who worship in a free, charismatically-orientated church are variety and the absence of prescribed forms. Desirable though these features may be, they increase the difficulty of evaluating the principles and practice of worship in this setting. Add to that the fact that while charismatics the world over may have the same roots, they flower in very varying colours. I consider some of the British charismatics I know are occasionally a little wild, but many American charismatics would think them hardly off first base, and might want to deliver them from the demon of reserve. Bring in variations from South America, Asia, Africa and many other areas, and the extravagant and diverse splendour of charismatic foliage is magnificent. It is inevitable that most of my observations reflect the sample I know best.

Nevertheless charismatics have assumptions, goals and distinctive practices about worship, many of them near universal. These will provide considerable grounds for analysis, before finishing with brief comments on some problems of a free style of worship.

GOALS FOR WORSHIP

There are key ideas in the minds of charismatic worshippers, and these determine what they do and how they do it. Foundational is the belief that they are part of God's 'new wine' people,[1] or, as Peterson describes the consciousness of the first Christians, 'an awareness of being the community of the End time . . .'.[2]

Some think it right to try to reproduce the New Testament church today, believing it was God's blueprint for his church in all ages. Whether that view is held or not, all charismatics would accept that the positive examples of New Testament worship ought to be practised still.[3] That would certainly give the following goals.

Fulfilling God's Command

The description of Christians as a chosen people, royal priesthood, holy nation, a people belonging to God, goes on to describe their central purpose:

'. . . that you may declare the praises of him who called you out of darkness into his wonderful light'(1 Pet. 2:9). That verse involves more than worship, but certainly includes it. It builds on several Old Testament passages which also stress that worship is not optional: 'You who fear him, praise the Lord'; 'The Lord, who brought you up out of Egypt with mighty power and outstretched arm, is the one you must worship. To him you shall bow down and to him offer sacrifices' (Ps. 135:20; 2 Kings 17:36).

Charismatic Christians reject an attitude not uncommon in some traditions which designates all that precedes the sermon as the preliminaries. Such demeaning terminology is wrong. The worship time matters.[4] Worship is an essential, required goal of private and corporate Christian life.

To Honour God

Out of a recognition of God's greatness and goodness, there is a sincere desire to 'give God the place he deserves'. To do that would be a fundamental and sufficient reason for coming together.

Peterson says: 'The purpose and function of Christian gatherings is not simply "worship" but edification of the congregation through the various ministries provided by the Lord himself. Even specifically God-directed activities such [as] prayer and praise must be for the building up of God's people.'[5] While not outrightly disagreeing with that, many charismatics would feel uncomfortable with the emphasis on the essential benefit to the congregation of meeting. Could there not be worship for the sake of God alone? Just as the individual believer is to 'worship' God in all of life, for the sake of God himself, can we not say that the corporate meeting of many Christians embraces the same transcendent aim?

Charismatics would be more likely to note Hattori's description of Old Testament altar building in connection with worship,[6] do some judicious spiritualizing, and regard their 'worship time' as an altar building activity to enable them to bring a sacrifice of praise (cf. Heb. 13:15). They would consider that as needful as any of the literal altar-building of Old Testament worshippers.

Alternative imagery is offered by passages such as Ps. 22:3: 'Yet thou art holy, enthroned on the praises of Israel' (RSV; NIVmg is similar). From altar building we've moved to throne building, and that is reflected in songs like 'Jesus we enthrone you' with the lines: 'And as we worship build a throne . . . Come Lord Jesus and take Your place'. God is ruler of all. Worship is acknowledgment of that fact.

The desire is to honour God; the belief is that as his people sincerely worship, God's rightful position as Lord and King is recognized and declared.

To Bring Acceptable Worship

The emphasis here is on the adjective 'acceptable', and the fundamental intention is to make worship acceptable and even meaningful for God,[7] not the worshippers (though hopefully also for them).

There is more than a little criticism of what some other traditions offer. The unvarying ritual of a fixed liturgy is considered to be mindless repetition and therefore unacceptable to God.[8] Equally, evangelical enthusiasm, with its encouragement to 'sing louder – let's raise the roof', incurs scepticism about how important extra energy and volume are to God, unless the worshippers think him to be deaf.

Instead of these, charismatics seek to worship 'in spirit and in truth' (John 4:24), believing that can be done only with the energizing power of the Holy Spirit. Ideally nothing is done in charismatic worship without the leading of the Spirit. The mood and content of praise, plus the gifts and ministry offered, are all at the Spirit's prompting.[9] When that is true, by implication the worship must be acceptable and meaningful to God.

To Offer the Worshipper to God

If worship involves the recognition of God's lordship, then part of worship involves submission of the worshipper's life to that Lord for correction and direction. Peterson notes the offering of self to God in Rom. 12:1.[10] Charismatics would look also to the use of spiritual gifts specifically intended to draw disciples' lives into line with God's will. Paul teaches at length along these lines in 1 Corinthians, especially with his emphasis on the value of prophecy (1 Cor. 14:1). That gift, or tongues plus interpretation, is a principal way of edifying the church (1 Cor. 14:5). Other supernatural gifts such as wisdom, a message of knowledge, or the ability to distinguish between spirits, might also be used (cf. 1 Cor. 12:8–10).

Emphasis on these revelatory gifts is not intended to denigrate preaching or teaching (however one distinguishes between them). Preaching, after all, is precisely what Peter, newly baptised in the Spirit, was immediately inspired to do on the Day of Pentecost. Teaching is listed in Eph. 4:11 among ministries gifted by God for the upbuilding of the church. The desire is that by all the means God provides, the lives of Christians should be open to the Holy Spirit and that his word should be heard and obeyed. That too is worship.

Judgment needs to be suspended temporarily regarding how successful charismatics are in achieving these goals. Even if some criticism is valid, credit must be given that it is no small thing to have goals that seek to obey God's command, honour him, give him meaningful praise, and submit the worshipper's life before God. On the whole there is a serious and thoughtful attempt to achieve these. If there is any shortcoming it is not for the lack of trying.

From that basis of understanding some aims of charismatic worship, we move now to a summary of distinctive features.

DISTINCTIVES OF CHARISMATIC WORSHIP

There are key distinctives of charismatic worship. Some are visible, and a wandering stranger with theological and ecclesiological awareness would soon know he or she had stumbled into a charismatic worship service rather than into any other. Other distinctives are in the heart or mind of the worshipper, and are therefore less readily discerned or described.

Sense of the Presence of God

Charismatics are rather notorious for evaluating their worship in a manner similar to the way in which Christians of other traditions will analyze a sermon.

At the least thoughtful level, someone will say, 'I didn't get much out of the worship time today.' Such a comment betrays an immature and self-indulgent approach to worship, but – more positively – it also reveals a search for a depth to worship that involves more than merely singing upbeat or expressive songs. While some Christians might assume they had worshipped because they had sung or prayed words that express God's glory, the charismatic will look also for some personal sense of having made contact with God. That is a matter of feeling – hopefully not merely of emotions but also of spiritual awareness.

There are specific moments in worship at which this sense of God might be especially strong, though one person's experience may differ from another's. Some will find it in the excitement of expressive singing (perhaps dancing), others in the comparative quietness of a very intimate song of love to God. Many identify God's presence in a 'powerful' word of prophecy or message brought in tongues, or even in the silence that may follow such a gift. Singing in tongues, a harmonizing of many different words and tunes, can create music some equate with the sound of a heavenly choir. While it is not difficult to see how a worship leader can create some of these events,[11] he cannot manufacture the sense of God's presence. There is a difference between human striving for a 'special moment' and an atmosphere pregnant with the power of God, and most thinking charismatics are sensitive to it.

Every good charismatic will insist that sense of power comes because the Holy Spirit is moving among his people as they worship. That being so, when someone says he or she didn't get much from the worship, does this mean the Spirit didn't come that day? Actually, some might answer 'Yes' to that question, not because they believe God is ever absent from his people, but because their understanding of the Spirit's work is so dynamic that they think of his presence in terms of what he does. Sometimes he chooses not to do much, in which case they would not feel inclined to say the power of the Spirit was there on that occasion.[12]

Release of the Spirit-filled Life

A story is told among charismatics of a little boy buying a glass of lemonade in a self-service cafeteria. A generous counter assistant filled his glass to the brim, but her kindness gave the lad problems as he tried to carry his drink back to his seat without spilling any. In fact, since it was so full it was harder to keep the contents in than it was to let them overflow.

The analogy, of course, is with the person filled with the Spirit, who cannot contain the life of Jesus. There is a natural and inevitable overflow into all areas of life, and certainly into worship.

So the charismatic would be unlikely to value the repetition of liturgy, probably regarding it as mere mouthing of words. Nor would charismatics be helped by listening to a choral rendering of some great anthem, nor by gazing at stained glass windows.[13] The charismatics' real desire is to allow the Holy Spirit to lead them in expressive and (usually) joyful praise. The Spirit is not merely an external stimulus to the worshippers: the Spirit is in them (John 14:17), and offers up perfect praise to God from them.[14]

The results of the coming of the Spirit initially at Pentecost to the apostles, and subsequently to Cornelius and others, are examples of this. Acts 2 describes a sudden experience of the Spirit which seemed to lead immediately to only marginally controlled expressions of praise.[15] Acts 10 finds Peter only half way through a very respectable sermon when his congregation is filled with the Spirit and bursts out in praise (10:44ff). Verse 46 says 'they heard them speaking in tongues and praising God'. Quite an interruption!

If worship was the response back then to the presence of the Spirit, it is not unreasonable that those today who are aware of the Spirit's infilling on an ongoing basis should want to let out the praise which wells up inside them. Of course they may be guilty at times of spiritualizing (almost divinizing) the source of their own ordinary need to release pent up energy. Moreover, their conviction of God's inner leading makes them vulnerable to those skilled at manipulating feelings and desires. As more and more charismatics grow out of the naivety of spiritual infancy, however, they become increasingly aware of these dangers.

Nevertheless, especially where a private life of worship is combined with an appreciation of the extra dimensions of worship possible for a group, people arrive for a church meeting feeling like a bottle of champagne already shaken and only needing the cork taken off to let the contents out. The result can be as dramatic and unpredictable as uncorking the bottle.

Emotional Expression of Worship Allowed, Even Encouraged

No-one could miss the excitement of charismatic worship. A leader will positively encourage his congregation to 'let the Lord see that you love him' and probably a forest of hands will be raised heavenwards. Others may simply gaze upwards, eyes tight closed in concentration, a beatific expression on their faces. When the mood is appropriate, some will step out into an aisle and dance before the Lord, not always with grace to match their devotion.

Most charismatics would see this as a wonderful freedom, much more to be desired than the spiritual frigidity (as they perceive it) to be found in many other traditions, where a smile might be regarded as a major and suspect event. They regard their emotional and physical expressions of worship as desirable and biblical.

They are desirable in the sense of being the natural response of people in love with and in awe of their God. Arm raising could be seen as a very rough parallel to the embrace of a couple or the handwaving and clapping accorded to the famous. Neither of these types of behaviour is considered inappropriate in those contexts; why should they be so with God? He may be spirit, but he made us of flesh. It is not unreasonable to assume that he takes pleasure in the use of the physical bodies he gave us to worship him.

As far as biblical support is concerned, charismatics wonder how others find it possible to ignore the instructions and encouragements to enter joyfully and enthusiastically into the worship of the Lord. The Psalmist says: 'Lift up your hands in the sanctuary and praise the Lord' (Ps. 134:2), and Paul wants 'men everywhere to lift up holy hands in prayer . . .' (1Tim. 2:8). Hand clapping and shouts of joy to God are invited, perhaps even commanded (Ps. 47:1). Heaven itself is portrayed as a place of very physical expressions of worship as elders fall down before God (Rev. 4:10; 5:8–14). Perhaps least acceptable of all to some, the Old Testament Scriptures even commend praising God with dancing (Ps. 149:3; 150:4). David dancing before the Lord (2 Sam. 6:14)[16] caused controversy in his own day, but criticism of him appears to have brought infertility on Michal, daughter of Saul (2 Sam. 6:23).

Some argue with charismatics that these exuberant expressions of worship belong only among Old Testament people. However, we've already noted the New Testament instruction on hand-lifting in prayer, and the prostration before God included in John's vision of heaven. It seems more than a little arbitrary to preach everything else in (for example) the Psalms but omit references to the manner of worship. Those who wish to edit out these sections must surely find hermeneutical or theological justification for removing them; the onus is not on charismatics for leaving them in. Others say that extrovert behaviour was natural to Middle Eastern culture and cannot be commanded for others. In response, charismatics point out that not all cultural variations are negotiable. Our reserve may be wrong, and we need to learn how to 'let go' of our inhibitions before the Lord.

Nevertheless, since it is a fundamental of charismatic worship that nothing and no-one is forced, but people are free to worship as they feel led, there is liberty *not* to raise hands or engage in any of the other expressive modes of worship. But the non-participative worshipper would be thought to be the loser.

Worship that is Varied and Unpredictable

Hattori draws attention to David's use of various musical instruments for praising God with his people. The passages he cites make reference to harps, lyres, tambourines, sistrums, cymbals, and trumpets.[17] What he does not mention is the variety of sound and experience such a range must have contributed to worship. Psalm 150 adds strings and flute to the list of instruments to be used for praise, thus extending the 'orchestra's' resources and (along with the harp) bringing softer sounds. A flute produces a very different note from a trumpet, and a lyre a distinct alternative to cymbals, and so on. When all were played together, the end result must have been . . . impressive!

On the whole charismatics welcome such diversity, a pot-pourri of more or less melodious sound. So worship bands are common, with a miscellany of instruments according to the abilities of the particular congregation. While some form of keyboard is normal, a guitar-playing worship leader is also common. Of course a worship band strives for excellence, and some have achieved professional standards, performing in front of thousands at large Christian gatherings. But when it comes to leading congregational worship, the excitement and 'drive' of the music have a higher priority than technical precision.

The variety is not confined to instruments. It is unusual for a congregation to have the same worship leader each week. Songs also have a rapid turnover. What is 'top of the spiritual pops' one month may well have slipped down the 'charts' by the next. That partly explains why so many congregations now use an overhead projector to display songs, rather than purchase expensive song books whose contents will rapidly become redundant.[18] The mood of worship will also vary. One week the 'flow' may be upbeat, with loud singing and dancing. The next may be decidedly downbeat, with meditative music, and several long silences. Another time there may be constant interruptions as spiritual gifts are used, principally the bringing of words of prophecy or knowledge.

This amount of variety usually equals unpredictability. While most charismatic worship leaders have a sense of 'direction' as they start a worship session, it's unlikely they will have a detailed plan and even more unlikely that if they do it will be fulfilled. Where congregational participation is allowed, and the Holy Spirit invited to 'move', the content of worship will probably follow unexpected lines.

Is that wrong? Peterson cites 1 Cor. 14:33: 'God is not a God of disorder but of peace', and comments, 'Order and not disorder will be a sign of the Spirit's presence and control . . .'[19] However, no-one should confuse order with predictability. Paul's concern was that a worship time should not degenerate into chaos by everyone practising his or her gift at the same time. Therefore he wanted good order. But that did not exclude congregational participation, at least some of which could not have been pre-planned since it consisted of 'revelation' from God (1 Cor. 14:30).

The best of charismatic worship services are always under firm control. Far from restricting worship such responsible control enables the worshipper to relax and participate with a feeling of peace and security. Nevertheless, no-one can know how the Spirit will lead his people, or what words may be spoken that will entirely change the mood or affect the purpose of that meeting. One elderly member of a congregation that had become at least partially charismatic complained that she could no longer bring even her Christian friends along to a church service 'because you could never tell what might happen'. She meant it as criticism. Her leader took it as encouragement.

Worship that Includes Direct Ministry to Each Other

Adrian Plass caused considerable mirth when he began his 'Sacred Diary' by recounting a tale of accidentally dropping his fruit-gums when the preacher shouted 'LUST!'. He bent down to retrieve his property, 'then couldn't get up because Doreen Cook pressed her hands down on the back of my head. She prayed that "our despairing brother would move from darkness to light".' He adds: 'Everyone thinks I've got a big lust problem now.'[20]

The best humour is rooted in partial truth, though hopefully most charismatic congregations are not so keen to lay hands on people that they fail to check first if they really need ministry. Nonetheless, churches do seek to meet the spiritual needs of worshippers in this direct way.

Peterson finds such ministry a recurring emphasis of the New Testament.[21] In respect of Eph. 4:12–16 he says that edification occurs 'when Christians *minister to one another in word and deed*, seeking to express and encourage a Christ-centred faith, hope and love. Clearly this ought to take place when the congregation meets together but also as individuals have the opportunity to minister to one another in everyday life situations (cf. 1 Cor. 8:1, 10; 10:23).'[22] Charismatics would readily agree with that.

In line with their view that the Holy Spirit is dynamically at work whenever Christians come before God, it follows that God will highlight areas of sin or weakness in the lives of at least some. These people may choose to deal privately with their sense of conviction or need, but there is usually an invitation to seek help from others.

Because it will involve an admission of failure or difficulty, a response requires considerable humility. But the Bible teaches precisely that kind of honesty. For example, the instructions of James are well known that a sick person should call for the church elders to pray over him. That is direct ministry to an individual struggling with poor health. What is not so often noted is that this personal ministry is to be preceded by confession of sin to each other (Jas. 5:16), presumably a necessary prerequisite for healing. The Bible shows scant respect for a person's pride, and charismatics are no more generous. 'You can have your pride or you can have your deliverance' was the stark choice put before one troubled person.

Nevertheless, individual prayer is often found to be very effective. The act of asking for help is in itself usually a huge step forward for someone, and the time and love shown in prayer (plus the efficacy of the prayer) make a deep impression. The vulnerability of baring a soul before another also bonds Christian to Christian quite deeply.[23]

So valued is this ministry that many congregations will always finish their meetings with some opportunity for people to seek prayer or counsel. It will not necessarily be an invitation to 'come forward now', but an offer of a specific room to go to or a person to contact. Those with particularly deep needs may be prayed for by appointment at other times. Others will seek private help from trusted friends.

Emphasis on the 'Now' Experience of God

Most charismatics do not consider that the church exists either to remember the past or to anticipate the future. Both of these activities happen, but fundamentally the church is called to experience God now.

That experience will vary according to the purposes God has for his people at any one moment: conversion; maturity; service; worship; witness; or some other encounter between God and human beings. Of course, each individual Christian lives constantly with the divine presence (Matt. 28:20), but most also believe God's nearness has an extra reality when the church gathers. Many find biblical basis for this view in a dubious exegesis of Matt. 18:20, 'For where two or three come together in my name, there am I with them'. Peterson sees it legitimately in Cor. 14:24–25[24] where prophecy will convict an unbeliever of his sin and make him realize 'God is really among you!'

Whatever the biblical basis, charismatics would lose almost everything distinctive about them if they had to abandon their consciousness of an active God in the midst of his people. Some Christian traditions seem happy to reflect constantly on the cross and the wonderful cleansing from sin achieved there by Jesus. Or they may be forever looking into millennial mysteries, discussing which signs have come and which have not. Classic Pentecostals are known for some fascination with the latter subject, but the cutting edge for most charismatics would revolve around such questions as: 'What is God saying to us today?' 'What does God want to do next among us?' 'What ministry is God leading us to undertake now?' The answers to these questions are shaped back and front by the atonement and parousia respectively, but their centre rests on the present work of the Spirit.

Such an emphasis fosters the danger of neglecting serious study: of Scripture, history, prophecy. Some may become unhealthily dependent on today's 'kick', the need for constantly new experiences.

However, charismatics are not noted for avoiding risk. Safety can equal stuffiness.

Instead, the conviction that colours and directs worship is the belief that God is always ready to speak and act. Today – every day – he longs to receive his people's worship, and right now he wants to work with and among them. Believe that and every act of worship becomes immensely important, and liable to redirect the worshipper's life for evermore. Worship of a 'now' God can never be safe.

PROBLEMS IN CHARISMATIC WORSHIP

No worshippers are perfect, and certainly not charismatic ones. They have their strengths and their weaknesses, and a final but brief summary of some difficulties will balance the generally positive points already made.

Sometimes the very thing that is such a strength leads charismatics to a weakness: their concentration on worship as a major, commanded, and meaningful activity. That priority certainly used to lead to a neglect of teaching, and in many parts of the world still does. 'We just spent our time before the Lord. . . . There was no need for a sermon.' Such a statement may sound wonderfully spiritual, but the long term consequence is immature Christians.

Even a cursory glance over Ps.119 reveals its heavily pedagogic emphasis. It would be simpler to note the few verses that do not refer to God's precepts, statutes, laws or judgments than list those that do. No-one could doubt the Psalmist's appreciation of learning God's will. Equally Peterson notes the priority of word ministries in the listing of Eph. 4:11 and says the use of *oikodomē* in passages like 2 Cor. 10:8; 12:19; 13:10, 'suggests that edification involves also a process of teaching and encouragement beyond the initial task of evangelism'.[25] Sometimes that emphasis has been missing, or teaching is done so superficially or badly,[26] that little progress is made in the Christian life by church members.

It is only fair to say that in many cases that state of affairs has changed. Some charismatic congregations are noted now for the *length* of their sermons. Nothing is done by halves.

Another strength that can become a weakness is the stress on experience of God. While it wonderfully avoids a casual approach to worship ('Oh well, that's us done our duty by being in church for another week . . .'), it can degenerate to extreme self-centredness and dependence on feelings. God is not to be sought merely to make the worshipper feel better, nor is his presence to be assessed on the basis of fluttering eyelids or trembling body.[27] What of worshipping God for his own sake? What of the great indicatives of the faith that should be proclaimed whether or not accompanied by supernatural signs? There is a temptation to evaluate worship according to personal experience.

Ministry to one another carries a similar risk. Other traditions may fail by not offering it, but charismatics can become self-indulgent. The same people may seek prayer week after week, perhaps looking for some spiritual boost or failing to take responsibility for their discipleship. Sometimes the help being sought reveals too great a focus on personal desires, with a lack of interest regarding the needs of others. Well ordered fellowships try to spot and resist these problems, perhaps by diverting such people to private counselling, but the danger may be intrinsic. By virtue of offering individual ministry for personal needs, church members are invited to have an inward focus on their own problems and wishes. That tendency may be inevitable no matter how many attempts are made to make people more 'outward' in their orientation. Even so, it is a price most congregations are willing to pay in order to deal lovingly and meaningfully with real hurts.

Probably all churches have people who believe that the only time they can worship is when they gather with others at a Sunday service. The charismatic emphasis on being caught up together by the Spirit may aggravate that danger. More than most, charismatics need Peterson's reminder that 'sharing the gospel with unbelievers, supporting gospel work, offering material help to those in need, and serving God in the workplace or wider community is no less important than prayer, praise or participating in the Lord's Supper!'[28] All too easily, charismatics make the mistake of looking forward to Sunday as the day when next they can glorify God meaningfully. They would benefit from Peterson's wish to use worship terminology for 'a Christ-centred, gospel-serving, life-orientation'.[29] The 'now' experience of God needs to be lived out Monday to Saturday as well as on Sundays.

Real questions must also be asked regarding whether charismatic worship is really as free as is claimed. While almost all of nature drifts into chaos if left alone,[30] much charismatic worship eventually drifts towards more and more order.[31]

Of course that's because worship is not left alone. Worship leaders increasingly find a need to organize the pattern of a service. That may be to prevent monotony; the tendency to keep going down the same well-worn lines is considerable. Or they may have found that some of the congregational contributions to worship are less than edifying, and stricter control is necessary. Or it may simply be that there are not too many options when it comes to an order of service. There must be singing, praying, perhaps an opportunity for spiritual gifts to be used, preaching, and the inevitable 'notices' and offering. While a little tinkering with sequence can be done, too much of that merely annoys people, so worship services usually settle into distinct blocks. It may not be too outrageous to speak of a charismatic liturgy.

Such predictability does not need to be seen as failure, even though it undermines claims of complete freedom, since a good structure helps fulfil the 'fitting and orderly' requirement of 1 Cor. 14:40. Just as people usually don't object to a safety fence along a cliff-top, worshippers find that some restrictions give a feeling of security. They are not fearful of what is coming next, and that promotes proper concentration on worship.

There are problems and weaknesses with charismatically-orientated worship. But few who have made the change would go back to what they feel were dull and empty forms of worship. They value highly the strengths highlighted earlier as goals and distinctives of charismatic worship. They would never want to lose the sensitivity to God that they now find in worship, conscious that their words and actions have no meaning without the Holy

Spirit's energizing. The Spirit has been rescued from being no more than a theoretical third person of the Trinity, and is now the One who fills lives and inspires worship from grateful and enthusiastic Christians.

If that last statement is even partly true, then the charismatic style of worship is not only useful but inevitable.

12

Patterns of Worship Among Students Worldwide

SUE BROWN*

'Do your students think of worship as the response of their whole lives to God?' I asked the staffworker of one Continental European student movement. 'No,' he replied, 'although they do think their whole lives should be lived to God's praise, so this doesn't worry me.'

His answer well expresses the ambiguity that surrounds the term 'worship' in many people's minds. Students, like most other Christians, are deeply influenced by the churches to which they belong and in which, one suspects, the same ambiguity about 'worship' prevails. As David Peterson rightly points out, the term 'worship' is often narrowly applied to what we do 'in church', or in the Christian meeting. Sometimes, indeed, the focus is even narrower: 'worship' is that part of the meeting or service that precedes or follows the sermon.

But the concept of worship that students hold may be much broader, encompassing not only the expression of praise to God in song, thanksgiving and adoration, but witness to non-Christian friends, attitude to studies, stances on social and ethical questions – in short, all aspects of life. As one Australian student defined it, 'Worship is doing everything for God. It isn't something limited and restricted to Sundays and church but rather a whole lifestyle. It is a reflection back to God of thankfulness in every area of your life for what he is worth.'

At the risk of over-simplification, then, it seems fair to say that the majority of students hold a concept of 'worship' in these two senses. Jonathan Lamb, in a booklet entitled *Draw Near to God: Worship in the Christian Union*, defines them like this: 'There is worship in the specific sense of individual and corporate response in thanksgiving, praise, prayer and preaching. But there is also worship in the generic sense – the devotion we owe to God in the whole

* The author is indebted to numerous staff of IFES member movements who have contributed insights from their experience. In particular she is grateful to Chua Wee Hian, Pete Lowman, Mike Adegbile, Jenny Petersen, Jill Goddard and Julia Cameron for reading and commenting on the original text. She asks the reader to bear in mind that her own origins are in the British student movement and that, while she has tried to give an international perspective, the above inevitably reflects some of her personal preoccupations.

of life, which will be reflected in the way we serve him in our work, our witness, our behaviour and our relationships. True worship acknowledges that every part of our life comes under God's control.'[1]

However, if you ask a student today what he or she understands by the *word* 'worship' the narrower definition will come immediately to mind because this seems to be the current common usage: the classic phrase runs 'And now let's move into a time of worship.' In the following pages, therefore, I propose to consider, first, how the aims and emphases of IFES mesh with the insights of Drs. Hattori and Peterson on the biblical understanding of worship. I shall then proceed to an analysis of the specific worship patterns of students around the world today. Finally, I shall consider some of the particular features of modern youth culture and campus life that pose a threat to a fully biblical understanding of Christian worship.

Worship . . . by any other name

In IFES circles, the fuller or generic definition of worship has usually been classified under the heading of 'discipleship' or 'living under the Lordship of Christ'. Thus, FOCUS-Zimbabwe speaks of its objectives in terms of godly discipleship that embraces both the specific and the generic definitions of worship: 'A godly disciple is a person under God's authority-Lordship.' He or she is a person of Scripture; a person of prayer, worship and faith.[2] Whatever terminology we use, the essential point is the same, for what is worship if not living as a godly disciple in submission to the Lord Jesus Christ? It has ever been the concern of IFES and its constituent national movements that students and graduates should understand worship in the comprehensive sense given by the apostle Paul in Romans 12:1,2 and helpfully elaborated by Peterson.[3] And IFES has emphasized the importance of a renewed mind as the basis of all true worship. Many Christian graduates can echo the testimony of Gottfried Osei-Mensah: 'Through IFES I developed a Christian mind, submissive to the Lord and confident to find in his word relevant principles of conduct for every situation in life.'[4]

The three main aims of a Christian Union can be summed up as evangelism, discipleship and mission. The CU exists to present the claims of Christ to fellow members of the university or college, to unite and strengthen those who thus desire to serve him, and to promote members' concern for, and participation in, the worldwide accomplishment of God's purposes. An evangelical Statement of Faith forms the basis on which Christian students of different denominations can unite to bear witness to Christ on campus. So Christian Unions see their identity, in distinction to the other student societies around them, very much in the terms that Peterson uses: 'not an ordinary association like a club, where people simply meet together because of common interests or ideals: it is a gathering that arises out of sharing together in the benefits of Christ's saving work'.[5] On becoming a member (in German, a 'co-worker', in French and Spanish a 'responsible'), a student would ordinarily express his or her commitment by assenting to some such statement as 'I acknowledge Jesus Christ as my Lord and Saviour and the Bible as my authority in all matters of faith and conduct.' Leaders of groups and officers of the national movement are further expected to indicate their wholehearted agreement with the full Doctrinal Basis. The atoning work of

Christ was the key theological issue that led to the original breakaway of evangelical students from the then much more liberal Student Christian Movement.[6] It is the atoning work of Christ that brings Christian students together today and motivates them for evangelism. 'The Love of Christ Moves us' was the bold title of the IFES European Evangelism Conference held in Würzburg, Germany, in 1988.

Evangelism among students at home and concern for God's mission overseas are two of the main aims of IFES movements worldwide. The third is discipleship. Recognizing that it is not enough simply to proclaim the gospel on campus, student groups take seriously the need to establish new converts in the faith, particularly in countries where the evangelical churches are not many or particularly strong. The Colombian student movement has seen this as a pressing need and has developed a very carefully thought out and effective discipleship training programme that grounds young believers in the faith and prepares them for leadership. UCU-Colombia has seen a steady stream of graduates moving into cross-cultural mission. If, as Peterson suggests, 'those who are concerned about God-honouring worship will be pre-occupied with bringing people to Christ',[7] then – in theory at any rate – this is what Christian students are about. IFES in the 1990s can legitimately call itself a movement of 'students reaching students' and increasingly these students are from all nations to all nations.

Edification, which is another way of describing discipleship, is very much at the heart of the corporate life of the Christian Union. However, the teaching and learning that goes on in the campus context should not be thought of as being in competition with the ministry of local churches. The CU sees itself not as an alternative to the local church (though it does often serve as a bridge for those students converted from a totally unchurched background), but as 'the missionary arm of the church on campus'.[8] The essential purpose of its central teaching programme and small group Bible study meetings is to introduce non-Christian students to Christ, establish believers in the faith and encourage them to live their lives in glad submission to their Lord and Master. The atmosphere is informal as students meet weekly in a lecture hall or private room to study the Bible together inductively, to share and sing and pray.

Hospitality, especially towards international students, informal fellowship over meals (or at least a cup of coffee), serving one another in everyday contexts and sharing material possessions are also common features of CU life and activity. It was heartening for me recently to listen in on a discussion about financial support for IFES at a meeting of TSCF-New Zealand's student leaders. With clear recognition of their own material privileges, these young men and women pledged themselves and their groups to raise thousands of dollars for poorer student movements in Central and East Asia. Nor is such service confined to fellow Christians. At the university of Temuco in Southern Chile, the student group runs a daily 'mini-restaurant' at lunchtime for those students who can't afford proper meals. Their only outside help is the cook and caterer; students organize a rota for shopping, setting tables, serving meals and clearing up afterwards.

From all of the above it will be obvious that the university campus lends itself to the practice of living out the Christian life in an everyday context. While the relative informality, mutuality and fellowship of Christian corporate life on campus can sometimes make it difficult for students (especially those converted during their student days) and graduates to integrate into local churches (especially those where traditions seem to be set in concrete), the CU is nevertheless a great training ground for future service in the church and in the world. Furthermore, in the inter-denominational context of the CU, students rub shoulders with those from other church backgrounds and learn to test their own traditions and cultural preferences against the yardstick of Scripture. For those who are open to learn, this can be a deeply challenging and enriching experience which, in the grace of God, may also prove subsequently to be of great benefit to the church.

One word, finally, about the celebration of the Lord's Supper and the exercise of spiritual gifts in the CU. Of a representative sample of 20 IFES-affiliated student movements more than half do not celebrate the Lord's Supper in the CU context out of deference to local churches who might disapprove. A further five might have an informal communion service at the end of a weekend houseparty, regional or national camp, as a fitting conclusion to their time together. Only one movement (heavily influenced by the Brethren tradition) was happy to celebrate the Lord's supper with or without a pastor present.[9]

The reasons for proceeding cautiously in this matter are not hard to find. Quite apart from local church sensitivities, the CU needs to be sensitive to the scruples of an inter-denominational membership, some of whom might not approve of celebrating the sacrament (some might prefer 'ordinance') outside the local church context and others of whom would only find the practice acceptable if there were an ordained minister or recognized elder to officiate. Furthermore, students recognize that the CU is not a church but exists for the limited purpose of bearing witness to Christ on campus. For all its inter-denominational variety, it is in every other way an homogeneous group of people: of roughly the same age and experience, from a similar educational background. It lacks the social breadth, the age range, the spiritual maturity and the continuity of the average local congregation, hence the need to exercise caution and restraint in such areas as the exercise of pastoral discipline, use of spiritual gifts and the administration of the sacraments. (These constraints apply particularly to those parts of the world where students are young. There are parts of Africa and Latin America where students study longer and are generally older; some indeed are married and already serving as elders in their local church.)

From the foregoing it will be apparent that the CU has some advantages over the local church when it comes to understanding and practising worship in the generic sense. Its *fellowship* is very clearly a fellowship in Christ, overriding denominational differences on secondary matters; its *aims* are evangelism, edification and mission; its *basis* the fundamental truths of Scripture; its *sphere of service* is right in the middle of its workaday world; and its *scope* is truly international.

The question remains as to how far students themselves actually understand and practise what has been described in the foregoing paragraphs. And how far do they see their corporate life and witness as rendering homage to Christ? It is impossible to generalize and there are certain built-in factors (e.g. the rapid student turnover in many CUs) that militate against ever being able to state categorically that this is how Christian students understand their own discipleship and the corporate life of their group. The challenge facing every staffworker with every new generation of Christian students and student leaders is to communicate and deepen such an understanding and to encourage a wholehearted response to Christ so that students may serve his purposes in their generation.

How far they are succeeding and what pressures and obstacles they are up against will be the subject of the concluding sections. We turn next, therefore, to a consideration of worship patterns, not now in the generic but in the specific sense, among students.

SPECIFIC WORSHIP PATTERNS AMONG STUDENTS

'We have almost stamped out singing (= "worship") as part of our public meetings on campus, and to some extent in prayer and Bible study groups. In the last five years we have been teaching that ECU meetings are for outsiders and for systematic, expository Bible teaching. Our main groups have grasped this and have adopted this style. In our annual national conferences we have a daily diet of three teaching sessions and two hours of training sessions. Each session is preceded by the singing of 3–5 songs (led by a trained leader) generally avoiding the ones that are specifically designed to do nothing but send tingles up your spine.' The Australian student movement sees its campus meetings as being part of its witness and has abandoned specific 'times of worship' as being inappropriate in an essentially evangelistic context.

'You arrive at the [CU] meeting, primed to speak . . . And you wait. The last time we waited for an hour (after the meeting started), singing chorus after chorus to the accompaniment of an assortment of instruments definitely unknown to the pre-Beatles. There was also a considerable amount of (presumably spiritual) clapping of the hands. Then suddenly, and for no very apparent reason, you are asked to speak. Usually on sin or hell or predestination. . . . Is it not remarkable how Charismatics simply take it for granted that everyone will have to conform to their way of worshipping God? From Manila to St Andrews the chorus has replaced the psalm and the raised hand the bent knee, as the new spiritual totalitarianism sweeps all before it.' The wry comment of an older speaker on his experience as the invited guest of a British CU records another meeting format, with a strong emphasis on praise and no immediate connection between the opening 'time of worship' and the subject of the Bible reading.

'I was recently at the *Sendforth* programme of one of our key campus groups', writes Femi Adeleye of the Nigerian Fellowship of Evangelical Students. 'It was a bright Sunday morning and there was something contagious about the atmosphere of worship. We all worshipped, danced heartily and when the choir sang, it was, whao, Hallelujah! But what thrilled me were the close to 300 students being sent forth . . . Those graduating were not being sent off or away from the Fellowship, but *forth* into the world as instruments of the Holy Spirit. They were being commissioned to go and change the world with the Gospel. The years they'd spent on campus were years of training and preparation as disciples. Now it was time to infiltrate society as salt and light.'[10]

These three quotations convey something of the range of worship patterns across the IFES world today. At one end of the spectrum, there is the CU meeting where the main emphasis falls on Bible exposition and study. At the other, the 'time of worship' may be longer than the time allocated to the speaker. The majority of student meetings, however, will contain an opening 'time of worship' (varying in length) followed by a Bible exposition, topical talk or inductive study and ending with discussion and/or prayer. Some might include a sketch by a drama team. Smaller CUs might also follow their meeting with an informal meal together.

However well or badly students may understand the close relationship between 'worship' and the Word (and those who fail to see the connection should not necessarily be blamed, for many churches also drive asunder what God has joined together), IFES has always been at pains to emphasize the centrality of the Word of God in its corporate life. 'Whenever we meet together, the main ingredient which will provoke worship will be our appreciation of God's Word – whether this is a group Bible study or the more formal exposition of a Bible passage by an invited speaker. In the case of a main CU meeting we should see the teaching of God's word as central to our worship.'[11] With the growing tendency to include 'times of worship' in CU meetings, staffworkers devote considerable time and energy to equipping student leaders for the task of leading meetings thoughtfully and well. It was out of such a concern that Jonathan Lamb wrote the booklet just quoted. What we aim for is a CU meeting that combines listening to God through the exposition of his Word with a deep and true response in praise, adoration and the obedience of surrendered lives.

But if worship (in the specific sense) is more in evidence today than hitherto, what exactly do students today sing in their 'times of worship'? It is probably fair to say that, by and large, the chorus has replaced the traditional hymn. The preference of today's students is for the shorter chorus, often repeated, invariably in the popular music mode, sometimes in the folk style of a particular culture, be it traditional African rhythms, Caribbean reggae or European soft rock. Settings of the psalms – or, more usually, small sections or single verses of the psalms – are popular with students because they give opportunity to praise God directly or to voice personal feelings. The significant difference, however, between today's choruses lifted from the psalter and the metrical psalms of an earlier day, is that the former tend to focus on the command to praise the Lord while often omitting all the reasons the psalmist gives for so doing! Of course, where the full psalm is read beforehand or the chorus thoughtfully introduced, there is no reason why such short and direct expressions of praise to God should not be sung, and indeed sung more than once as long as it is not mindless repetition. (The psalmists themselves are not averse to repetition.)

Similarly with the choruses that express personal feelings: 'I love you, Lord, and I lift my voice'[12] captures for many students the essence of what they want to say to God in simple, personal devotion. True, it omits the crucial biblical truth that 'we love because he first loved us' (1 Jn 4:19) and so needs to be complemented by hymns that encourage us to 'sing of his love'[13] and by Scripture readings that speak of it. There is much appeal and merit in such simple expressions of personal feeling and direct praise to God, but if this kind of material becomes the staple hymnody of students or is divorced from other aspects of worship that feed our understanding of who God is and what he has done for us in Christ, it will quickly lead to spiritual impoverishment, for what we habitually sing conditions what we believe. Erik Routley's point is well taken: 'A congregation's disposition towards right belief or away from it is subtly influenced by the habitual use of hymns. No single influence in public worship can so surely condition a congregation to self-deception, to fugitive follies, to religious perversities, as thoughtlessly chosen hymns. The singing congregation is uncritical; but it matters very much what it sings, for it comes to believe its hymns. Wrong doctrine in preaching would be noticed; in hymns it may come to be believed.'[14]

The reviewer of a recently published Christian songbook in Britain pointed out the virtual absence of the Cross, Christ, the Holy Spirit and God the Creator in the song collection. 'Bible echoes float through the flowing music,' he wrote 'but the grand theme is Ourselves . . . All you need for lyrics is a pastiche of code words currently popular . . . These are arranged like wallpaper patterns to create an effect with no attempt to explore their biblical meaning. But one by one some of the songs will drip feed their way into the lifeblood of mainstream churches by way of further exciting and indispensable new collections: look out. . . .'[15] The problem is not just a Western one: a Bolivian staffworker notes that in the choruses Bolivian students sing there is much repetition of refrains and a lack of coherent development of theological truth. There are, of course, modern Christian songwriters, very popular in student circles, who wonderfully combine contemporaneity with deep biblical content. It wasn't only British students who loved singing the songs of Graham Kendrick at their Manchester '90 national conference; European students also enjoy singing his songs (albeit in English).

IFES has always been aware of the importance of good hymnody. IVCF-USA produced *Hymns* and *Hymns II* in 1947 and 1976 respectively. IVF (UCCF) published *Christian Praise* in 1957, and a shorter booklet to meet subsequent needs, called *Declare His Glory*, in the early '80s. Selection criteria for hymns included were their fidelity to biblical truth and their artistic quality (words and music). Following in the footsteps of IVCF and IVF, the IFES team in Latin America translated and popularized hymns with biblical content and good music in the late '60s. IFES movements have also spawned hymnwriters: Margaret Clarkson, who wrote hymns for IVCF-Canada, and David Burt, former staffworker of GBU-Spain, come immediately to mind. Today many student movements produce their own songbooks, but tend to be more passive as regards creating new material, allowing others (Graham Kendrick is a good example) to set the pace and preferring rather to concentrate on musical execution. Worship bands are the order of the day in many CUs.

Has the 'raised hand' replaced the 'bent knee' in student circles? Is celebration more prominent than intercession? It is broadly true that more lively and 'charismatic' styles of worship are currently very popular. The youth culture in general is more exuberant than the culture of its parents. In some countries there is a huge gulf between the preferred informal and spontaneous worship style of young people and the more formal and often liturgical style of the church service. The charismatic movement has undoubtedly had a tremendous effect on the conduct and content of worship, and in countries where Pentecostalism is strong or the charismatic renewal has made an impact, this is of course reflected in the way students worship. The gain has been in the vitality and immediacy of worship, in the participation of all and in the strengthening of fellowship. In some instances there may have been an accompanying loss in the area of theological understanding and coherence, especially where the hymn has given way to the chorus and the 'word of knowledge' is greeted with more interest than the reading of Scripture. Certainly one could level charges of triumphalism, superficiality and a too casual approach to God against some gatherings of Christian students (especially, but not only, in the West). As the General Secretary of the Nigerian movement wisely commented on the 21st anniversary of NIFES, 'We must continually sift through the ecstasy of new ways and styles that lead to superficiality and shallow commitments, and move on to spiritual depths. The times we live in demand a level of Christian maturity that can stand the storms of life.'[16] On the other hand, those of us who are older and regret the passing of earlier styles of worship must beware lest we disparage what today's young people genuinely find meaningful.

As regards Africa and Latin America, missionaries introduced hymns in the more ponderous rhythms of Western hymnody which simply do not excite exuberant young Christian believers to express their heart-felt emotions. Unwittingly, some missionaries and conservative national pastors have given students the impression that existing hymns translated from the West are almost as sacred as the Scriptures. When charismatics, Pentecostals and Independent African churches use drums, cymbals, tambourines and guitars, young people flock to their meetings. Once again the challenge is to combine sound theology with appropriate contemporary musical forms if we are to have a hymnody that truly edifies and is worthy of the God we worship.

But many students are also exploring the dimensions of a quiet and reflective approach to God, as witnessed by the popularity of books by Joyce Huggett, Richard Foster and Henri Nouwen. A colleague in East Asia wrote recently of the effect of morning meditations on Scripture at a student discipleship training camp in Japan: 'One morning . . . many were broken down in tears, confessing sins and committing themselves to Christ afresh. I was reminded of the power of God's word. Even when it was read by a humble heart and meditated upon without any word of explanation it moved and touched the hearts and minds of students in such an impressive way.'

Western students look at me in amazement when I tell of the prayer life of their peers in some African countries. It is not unknown for some student 'prayer warriors' in the SCM of South Africa to commit themselves to intercessory prayer, not once but four times daily for an hour at a time.

In Nigerian universities, up to 500 Christian students will gather for the main weekly evening prayer meeting, and the General Secretary of NIFES reckons that some Christian students in his country spend up to four hours daily on their knees. 'Prayer bands', a selected number of volunteers who meet to pray right through the night once a week or a month, are another feature of Nigerian Christian student life. In the University of Ibadan, the 'prayer band' at one stage grew to 120 strong out of a CU of around 800.

Granted that there are always exceptions to the rule, it seems fair to say in conclusion that students currently place greater emphasis on their 'times of worship' in the CU than was the case twenty or thirty years ago. They also prefer the more spontaneous 'charismatic' style of worship. This is partly because of the communications explosion that has enabled musical styles to 'travel' more easily: the songs of the Vineyard Fellowship, for example, have travelled as widely as John Wimber himself. It is partly because of the growth of parachurch youth organizations and the increased interaction between young people. The Youth With a Mission Songbook *J'aime l'Eternel*, for example, is widely known and used among the Francophone countries of Europe. Nor should we underestimate the conditioning power of mega-events like *Spring Harvest*[17] in Britain, the *Urbana* missions convention[18] in the USA and the *Katoomba* youth convention[19] in Sydney, Australia, to influence the musical tastes of the Christian public. Interestingly, a press release concerning *Urbana '90* announced that 'Music will be more contemporary than in the past, with about 70% contemporary hymnody . . . Music is a powerful means of communication for this generation of students.'[20]

There is no doubt that music is the major feature of the youth sub-culture (and that includes the specifically Christian youth sub-culture) worldwide. Allan Bloom has a provocative chapter on this in *The Closing of the American Mind*,[21] and it is also well documented in relation to Canada's young people.[22] Erik Routley astutely observes: 'If you know what hymns a person loves most, or what hymns a congregation is most addicted to, you'll be able to infer what, in Christianity, means most to that person or that church.' He continues, 'You are entitled to say that when people sing hymns they don't pay much attention to the words they sing, and that their satisfaction is usually generated by the tune rather than the text. In as much as that is true, it is a degeneration . . . from an earlier state of things. . . . But the fact is that words still mean a good deal; or if they don't, once the music has carried them past the critical faculty into the affections, they do a certain amount of good or harm.'[23]

SOME DANGERS

Routley's perceptive comment helps me to pinpoint, in closing, what I consider to be the greatest danger facing Christian students today (at least in the Western world). At its simplest it is the danger of falling into a shallow, superficial understanding of worship and therefore of what it means to be a Christian.

Consider the following features of modern society, especially influential on young people today, which militate against what Peterson translates as 'understanding worship', that is, 'the worship which is consonant with the truth of the gospel'.[24]

Firstly there is the challenge to the very concept of absolute truth, as noted in America at least, by Allan Bloom. The title of his controversial and provocative book is significantly, *The Closing of the American Mind*. In the late Middle Ages, when the church founded the oldest universities of Europe, it was presupposed that faith and knowledge were intrinsically related. Theology, with its basic conviction that it was dealing with God-given revelation, was known as 'the queen of the sciences' because of its unifying role in the field of knowledge. From the Age of Enlightenment onwards, however, the truth claims of the Christian faith have been progressively banished from the arena of public discourse into the realm of private belief, and Reason has been centre-stage as the arbiter of what is true. Lesslie

Newbigin, in *Foolishness to the Greeks*, gives a penetrating analysis of the changes that have taken place in the Western world as a result of this paradigm shift in the area of establishing what is true.[25]

Bloom argues that American higher education is now undergoing a further paradigm shift from the rationalist tradition of the Enlightenment. 'There is one thing a professor can be absolutely certain of: almost every student entering the university believes, or says he believes, that truth is relative . . . Openness – and the relativism that makes it the only plausible stance in the face of various claims to truth and various ways of life and kinds of human beings – is the great insight of our times.'[26]

The new tendency is to replace objective knowledge of the truth with 'perspectives' on reality, and the rational knowledge of 'good and evil' with purely subjective 'values'. If Bloom is accurate in his analysis, the consequences are extremely serious for young people entering the American university today. It is not just that the truth of Christianity is being undermined by their experience of higher education, but more disastrously, that their confidence in knowing the truth about anything is being eroded. The search is no longer for answers to fundamental questions like 'What is true?' and 'What is good?'. Rather, 'the good life' is defined now not in intellectual or moral terms but in terms of what is enjoyable or lucrative or what will guarantee a good career. In other words, the so-called open mind of relativism degenerates into the narrowly closed mind of mere self-interest.

Christian students are not immune to these trends which pose a great threat to the development of a truly Christian mind. But if they are to survive as Christians on campus and to engage meaningfully with their peers, Christian students must be helped to bring all the powers of a renewed Christian mind to bear on their university experience: to recognize idolatry and false worship and to challenge it in the name of the one true God, as Paul did in the once great 'university' city of Athens (Acts 17).

Of course, it is especially important in the context of the university that Christian students should learn to think (and therefore to act) biblically. In the words of Bobby Sng of FES-Singapore, 'The campus is an ideological battleground where Christian students themselves have to learn to think through their own faith. Confronted by various systems of thought – liberal, secular, scientific, religious, humanistic etc – these students must learn to ground themselves in the Word of God and to "destroy arguments and every proud obstacle to the knowledge of God, and take every thought captive and make it obey Christ." '[27]

Of San Marcos, the oldest university in Latin America, Ian Darke of the Peruvian student movement writes: 'I believe that the university is fundamental in the transformation of society. Much more so than in my home country of Britain, the university is at the centre of political reflection. Because students are that much older – many don't finish until they are in their thirties – the political life is maturer and more serious. For 25 years AGEUP has been working, witnessing and praying in this context. . . . The Christian students who are involved are known as "militants", because it requires guts to stand for Christ among mocking class-mates. Christian witness is spiritual warfare.'[28]

Elsewhere the challenge has been not so much from other ideologies as from a certain anti-intellectualism that can also affect Christian students. It was in such a climate that John Stott, then President of the British IVF (now UCCF), addressed the subject of the Christian mind in 1972. His first point of application was in the area of worship. 'All Christian worship, public and private, should be an intelligent response to God's self-revelation in his words and works recorded in Scripture.'[29] UCCF has always stressed the necessity of developing a Christian mind as the basis for a true and full-orbed worship of God, expressed in word and life.[30]

A recent interview published in the magazine of the Union of Evangelical Students of India suggests that John Stott still sees the danger of anti-intellectualism among students today. IFES has been committed 'from the beginning to believe in the proper use of the mind, glorifying God', he says. 'We can't come to terms with anti-intellectualism.'[31]

At the same time, students, by virtue of their calling, may also fall prey to arid hyper-intellectualism, an equally unbiblical if admittedly much rarer phenomenon these days. For all its stress on the importance of loving God with all our mind, IFES is equally strong on the necessity of loving him with heart, soul and strength. The East Asian student movements have their own terminology for this full-orbed response to the gospel issuing in a life of submission to the Lordship of Christ. They speak of 'holistic discipleship'. Thus Goh Keat-Peng of FES-Malaysia: 'It is possible to be highly competent intellectually and yet unable to handle emotions properly. When we speak of holistic growth in discipleship, we are speaking of integrated growth in every aspect of our personal lives.'[32]

For many East Asian students today, as for those in Eastern Europe, to live under the Lordship of Christ of necessity involves thinking through and taking a stance on the social and political issues affecting their nations. I remember seeing the text of Amos 5:24 ('But let justice roll on like a river, righteousness like a never-failing stream!') on the back of a tee-shirt worn by a Filipino student shortly after the overthrow of the Marcos dictatorship. This was no mere slogan, for that young student had actually been prepared, with countless other Christians in his country, to give his life, if necessary, for values he believed to be biblical and right. Christian students in Peru at present know what it is to be the possible target of guerrilla activity, but they maintain their witness to Christ as Lord, refusing to be intimidated by the possible danger to their lives. In all of these instances, one is reminded of Daniel and his friends, those Jewish post-graduate students in the alien environment of Babylon University who refused to give allegiance to any other than the Most High God.

Secondly there are powerful factors at work to undermine what Routley calls 'the critical faculty'. Jacques Ellul, in his compelling critique of modern society, *The Humiliation of the Word*,[33] documents the pernicious effects of the domination and displacement of the word by the visual image, especially on our reasoning powers. As a result of TV and other visual media, argues Ellul, 'The word, although prevalent in our day, has lost its *reasoning value*, and has value only as an accessory to images.'[34] As a consequence of constant exposure to visual media, people today 'are arriving at a purely emotional stage of thinking. . . . When we jump from image to image, we are really going from emotion to emotion'[35]. People move in their mind not by analysis and reflection but by association and intuition: this issues in intensity of conviction but incoherence in argument. People assimilate images and mistakenly think that in so doing they have really understood what is being presented, whereas in actual fact what has happened is what another writer has termed a process of brainwashing or 'cerebral bypass'.[36]

Thirdly, if the image has replaced the word, music has replaced the book. Young people watch and listen more than they read (although – gratifyingly – Christian students, certainly in some of the less visual-media oriented societies, still do read). Music appeals primarily to the emotions and does precisely what Routley says, it carries words past the critical faculty into the affections where they may do either good or harm.

Music and the image, then, the two most potent influences on young people today, conspire to bypass the reasoning powers of the mind and to encourage thinking by association rather than by analysis. The relationship between this trend and the emotional orientation of modern young people is too complex a subject to enter into here, but it should give us pause for thought whenever we discern signs of spiritual shallowness (only let us be sure we are judging aright) among student Christians.

There is much to rejoice in as we look at the vitality and exuberance and zeal of Christian students around the world today. They have much to teach some of us who are older. But we need to be alert to the dangers of zeal without knowledge and to help them to be sensitive to the pressures of the world in which they live so that they may be 'transformed in their minds'. We need to be aware of the dangers of the media, too, as well as of their great potential, if rightly harnessed and intelligently used, to influence for good. The challenge before those of us engaged in student ministry or youth work is to seek truly to understand the youth culture, to endorse and build on the genuine and good (whether it happens to suit our taste or not); to be pastorally sensitive to the baneful influences (and not merely throw up our hands in horror when we encounter superficiality among young people) and to counter them with positive means; to nurture a love of the Word and of good books, and to pray that God will raise up more hymn writers and communicators in the Christian world who can express the historic faith in verbal and musical language which combine spiritual integrity, artistic merit and contemporary appeal.

Part Four

Reflections on Worship from a Systematic Perspective

13

Worship as Adoration and Action: Reflections on a Christian Way of Being-in-the World

MIROSLAV VOLF

I

One of the most significant accomplishments of the Protestant reformation was overcoming the monastic understanding of the relation between the life of contemplation (*vita contemplativa*) and life of action (*vita activa*). Almost five centuries later, some important segments of Protestant Christianity (especially of the evangelical brand) are still caught in the false dichotomy between the sacred and the secular and are operating with a pre-reformation understanding of the relation between (what they term) spiritual worship and secular work. In the context of the reflection on the Christian understanding of worship, it is important therefore to recall Luther's rediscovery of the Christian calling to active service of God in the world and to reflect on its biblical roots.

The monastic understanding of the relationship between contemplation and action is rooted in the Greek philosophical tradition. Contemplation of the unchangeable order of things and of its divine origin was the highest possible human activity; it was considered the activity of the divine in human beings. Practical involvement in the world, though important, was inferior to contemplation.[1] The influences of Greek reflection on this issue on Christian spirituality and theology were strong and are easily observable, for instance, in Thomas Aquinas (though he was not the Christian theologian who adhered most slavishly to the Greek tradition on this point). For him, practical involvement in the world had no intrinsic value.[2] The ultimate reason for secular work lies in making the contemplation of God possible. Work keeps people alive by providing 'for the necessities of the present life' so that they are able to contemplate God and it 'quiets' and 'directs' the internal passions of the soul thus making human beings more 'apt for contemplation'.[3] Like Mary, those who can devote themselves to a life of contemplation of God (monks and nuns) have chosen 'the good portion'; like Martha, the rest who work for the maintenance of earthly existence must settle for the second best.

Martha's work is not bad because it is a means to a good end. But Mary's contemplation is much better, because it is good in and of itself.

Together with the discovery of the merciful God who justifies sinners through faith alone, Luther overcame the medieval bias in favour of the contemplative life. This can be best seen in his views on Christian vocation. He came to believe that all Christians (and not only monks as was thought before him) have a vocation and that this vocation is twofold. The one vocation he called *spiritual*. It consists of the call of God through the proclamation of the gospel to enter the kingdom of God. The other vocation he called *external*. It consists in the call of God to serve God and fellow human beings in the world. For Luther, work in every profession – growing potatoes, proclaiming the gospel, governing a state – rests on a divine call. And if God calls to every type of work, there can be no hierarchy of human activities. Contemplation and action are fundamentally of equal value, because God calls to both.[4] Once Luther dismantled the hierarchy of activities, the way was open for the belief that one can equally honour God in all dimensions of one's life, provided that one obediently does the will of God.

Luther's understanding of Christians' active life in the world is no less biblical than his teaching on justification by faith.[5] He acquired both beliefs in the school of the Apostle Paul. On the basis of his message of justification by faith, Paul wrote in Rom 12:1f: 'Therefore I urge you, brothers, in view of God's mercy, to offer your bodies as living sacrifices, holy and pleasing to God – this is your spiritual act of worship. Do not be conformed any longer to the pattern of this world, but be transformed by the renewing of your mind. Then you will be able to test and approve what God's will is – his good, pleasing and perfect will.' As J. D. G. Dunn points out, Paul here transports the notion of worship 'across a double line – from cultic ritual to everyday life, from previous epoch characterized by daily offering of animals to one characterized by a whole-person commitment lived out in daily existence'.[6] There is no space in which worship should not take place, no time when it should not occur, and no activity through which it should not happen. All dimensions of human life are the 'temples' in which Christians should honour their God – the God who created the whole reality, and the God who desires to redeem it.[7] In his essay in this book David Peterson has rightly emphasized that the understanding of worship as 'daily obedience or service to God in every sphere of life' is not peculiar to Paul but permeates the whole New Testament.[8]

The liberation of worship from the cultic constraints of sacred space and time was, of course, not an accomplishment of the New Testament writers. They inherited and radicalized the Old Testament perspectives on worship in the light of the salvific work of Jesus Christ. As is well known, Hebrew has a single word to denote activities we have come to designate as work, service, and worship.[9] In the first chapters of Genesis we read that God created human beings in order for them to serve God, not simply in the realm of the cult, but explicitly in the realm of the *culture*. Human beings serve God by doing 'worldly' things, like tilling and keeping the garden of Eden (see Gen. 2:15).[10] Correspondingly in the proclamation of the prophets we encounter the stress on worship in the sphere of ethical responsibility. They stressed that the true worship consists not simply in the participation in cultic activities but in *doing justice*: 'Is not this the kind of fasting I have chosen: to loose the chains of injustice and untie the cords of the yoke, to set the oppressed free and to break every yoke? Is it not to share your food with the hungry, and to provide the poor wanderer with shelter – when you see the naked, to clothe him, and not to run away from your own flesh and blood?' (Isa. 58:6–7; see Amos 5:21–24; James 1:27).

II

Luther's rejection of the monastic hierarchy of contemplative and active life was a result of a profound spiritual and theological insight. The new perspectives on involvement in the world were, however, not acquired in a social vacuum but were closely tied to a larger cultural movement of his time. It will suffice for my purposes here to enumerate some of the striking features of this transitional period in European history (without analyzing in detail each of them separately and their interrelations). In economic life, feudalism was in a state of collapse and a new, much more dynamic social order was being formed in which craftsmen and merchants would play the dominant role. In the political arena, the givenness of social structures was being called into question and the insight was emerging that these structures had been made by human beings and could therefore be altered by them. In relation to general culture, the Renaissance humanists were closing the gap between the sacred and the profane. In the sphere of intellectual pursuits, philosophers had boldly proclaimed the new experimental philosophy in which the researcher, who actively forced nature to reveal its truths, replaced the speculative scholar, who was satisfied to contemplate the truth.[11] Together with the affirmations of *sola scriptura* and of the priesthood of all believers, Luther's critique of monastic contemplative life and the rediscovery that God's calling pertains also to secular forms of activity is part and parcel of the one cultural movement infecting economics, politics, science, and theology alike. The movement marked the birth of modernity.

There is much talk today about the economically developed societies entering into a phase of post-modernity. The future will decide whether an epoch-making cultural shift is in fact taking place. In any case, activistic modernity still has a firm grip on our social and private lives. Despite a chorus of voices critical of Western culture the dominant goal of this culture still remains 'to know everything in order to predict everything in order to control everything.'[12] And although we are increasingly aware that technological rationality is incapable of steering the powers unleashed by technological advances, our technological successes ensure that the altar flame in honour of the god of technology is kept burning.

In this situation, it is increasingly difficult for Christians to hold seriously to the belief that God governs history and that the salvation of the world can, let alone must, come from God. And the more God is pushed out of our world – out of the spheres of nature, of society, and of individual human beings – the more difficult it will be to address this loving God in prayer and thanksgiving, and to stand before this holy God in awe and reverence. 'When the modernizing reason has harnessed all the facts, figures and forces . . . prayer, worship and reliance on the Holy Spirit, along with humility and the sanctity of things, are out of place. Technique is all.'[13] Technological culture does not deny God (it is not atheistic), but it makes God superfluous (it is a-theistic) and thus cuts off the worship of God at its roots. For adoration of a superfluous God is a religious impossibility. Where technique reigns, talking to God gives way to talking about God (or even to talking about talking about God!), reverence is replaced by manipulation, and joyous celebration of God's acts and God's character degenerates either into self-congratulatory praises of human vain-glory or into oppressive demands for better and greater deeds.

Some modern theologians seem to think that it is their task to make a virtue out of our cultural predicaments. It is to be expected that the modern suppression of the contemplative life would be given a theological version too. Summarizing the argument developed in *Marx and the Bible*,[14] J. P. Miranda – who is in this respect *not* typical of liberation theologians – claims that 'God can *only* be known and approached through moral conscience.'[15] This is the case, claims Miranda, because 'God is God solely *in* the nonobjectifiable interpellation through which God's commandment is enjoined.'[16] To claim to know or to be able to approach God directly would mean reducing God to an object. From this it seems to follow that every supplication and every thanksgiving turns God into an idol, that every liturgy is idolatry. Miranda absolutizes the prophetic critique of the cult, and proclaims the ethically responsible (social) action as the only true worship of God.[17] The monastic hierarchy in the relation between contemplation and action has been inverted: the subordination of the active life to the contemplative life has given way to a total suppression of the contemplative life by the active life.

There is an important truth in Miranda's position. A person cannot worship God and oppress his/her neighbour at the same time. Cult without justice is no worship of the true God but detestable idolatry (see Isa. 1:11–17); true worship is impossible without doing justice, indeed it consists partly in doing justice. But can worship be reduced to action – whether that action is ethical, evangelistic or both? The biblical tradition affirms clearly the independent significance of adoration of God as a form of worship. I am not thinking here so much of the fact that the prophets do not call into question the cult as such but its misuse as justification of social oppression. For Christian theology this is of limited significance, because the New Testament clearly states that the ministry of Christ is the fulfilment of the priesthood and cult associated with the old covenant. But the songs of exuberant praise to God in the Psalter are certainly a model for Christian worship. The hymnal of the old covenant people of God remained the hymnal of the Christian church. As Hattori states, the grand symphony of praise to God in Psalm 150 is a very appropriate finale for all the praises of God in the whole Psalter.[18] The Psalm is the call to the whole creation – to everything that has breath – to give praise to God for God's mighty deeds and exceeding greatness.

In the New Testament we find the new people of God adoring God with psalms, hymns, and spiritual songs (see Eph. 5:18f.). The early Christians worshipped God not only through their obedient service in the church and the world, but by their celebration in response to God's mighty deeds of salvation as well. Luke portrays the earliest Christian community as full of joy, with lips full of praises to God (see Lk 24:52–53; Acts 2:26–47). Throughout the Revelation the heavenly beings and the heavenly church are portrayed as worshipping God and the Lamb (Rev. 4:8ff. 5:9–10; 7:10; 15:3ff. 16:5–7; 19:1–9). The different aspects of worship mentioned in Revelation – 'rejoicing in God, giving him the glory and praising him'[19] – are clearly meant to be paradigmatic for the churches on the earth as they are facing godless economic and political powers desiring to crush them.

III

Christian worship consists both in obedient service to God and in the joyful praise of God. Both of these elements are brought together in Hebrews 13:15–16, a passage that comes close to giving a definition of Christian worship: 'Through Jesus, therefore, let us continually offer to God a sacrifice of praise – the fruit of lips that confess his name. And do not forget to do good and to share with others, for with such sacrifices God is pleased.' The sacrifice of praise and the sacrifice of good works are two fundamental aspects of the Christian way of being-in-the-world. They are at the same time the two constitutive elements of Christian worship: *authentic Christian worship takes place in a rhythm of adoration and action.*

Why does Christian worship need to branch out into action and adoration? What is the reason for this biformity of worship? In what follows I will try to answer these questions.

First, why cannot worship consist simply in active life in the world? Why does adoration need to take place as a distinct activity beside action? Because God did not create human beings to be merely God's servants but above all to be God's children and friends. As much as they need to do God's will in the world, they also need to enjoy God's presence. The centre of Christian life consists in personal *fellowship* of human beings with the Son of God through faith. Adoration is a time when this personal fellowship, which determines the whole life of Christians – their relation to themselves, to their neighbours and nature – is nurtured, either privately or corporately.[20] This is the reason why human beings 'need periodic moments of time in which God's commands concerning their work will disappear from the forefront of their consciousness as they adore the God of loving holiness and to thank and pray to the God of holy love.'[21]

Second, why can we not make the adoration of God our supreme goal, and be satisfied to consider action in the world simply a necessary consequence of adoration? Because the world is God's creation and the object of God's redemptive purposes. Christian hope is not for the liberation of souls from the evil world, but for the redemption of human beings together *with* the world with which they comprise the good creation of God. The material creation is not a scaffolding that will be discarded once it has helped in the construction of the pure spiritual community of souls with one another and with their God; material creation represents the building materials from which, after they are transfigured, the glorified world will be made. This is why worship can never be an event taking place simply between the naked soul and its God. It must always include active striving to bring the eschatological new creation to bear on this world through proclamation of the good news, nurture of the community of faith and socio-economic action. Fellowship with God is not possible without cooperation with God in the world; indeed cooperation with God is a dimension of fellowship with God.

As Christians worship God in adoration and action they anticipate the conditions of this world as God's new creation. Through action they seek to anticipate a world in which Satan will no longer 'deceive the nations', a world in which God will 'wipe away every tear' from the eyes of God's people, a world in which peace will reign between human beings and nature. Through their adoration they anticipate the enjoyment of God in the new creation where they will communally dwell in the triune God and the triune God will dwell among them (see Rev. 21–22). The eschatological bliss of God's people in the presence of their God and the eschatological *shalom* of God's world are two inseparable dimensions of Christian eschatological hope. It is this two-dimensional hope that makes Christian worship into a two-dimensional reality.

Adoration and action are two distinct aspects of Christian worship, each of which is valuable in its own right. The purpose of action is not merely to provide material support for the life of adoration. The purpose of adoration is not simply to provide spiritual strength for the life of action. When we adore God, we worship God by enjoying God's presence and by celebrating God's mighty deeds of liberation. When we are involved in the world, we worship God by announcing God's liberation, and we cooperate with God by the power of the Spirit through loving action.

Christian worship is bivalent. But do its two components stand merely side by side or are they also positively related to one another? I will return to this question after I consider the relation between adoration of God and seclusion from the world.

IV

I have argued that adoration is an activity distinct from involvement in the world. It would seem that as a distinct activity adoration requires distinct space and distinct time. If that is the case, are we not then back at the notions of sacred space and sacred time, which I have discarded earlier?

Does adoration need to take place in seclusion from the world? The answer to this question depends on where God is to be found. It is a consistent teaching of the Bible that God's presence is not limited to a particular locale. God is present in the whole created reality. No segment of it is secular in the sense that the transcendent God is absent from it. All dimensions of life in the world have what one might call a sacramental dimension: they *can* be places of meeting God in gratitude and adoration.[22] This is why the New Testament can ascribe redemptive significance to such an ordinary event as the table fellowship amongst Jesus' disciples: a meal can be an occasion for an encounter with the risen Lord.[23] Furthermore, if God is present in all of the created reality, then the soul ceases to be the privileged place for meeting

God. We do not need to turn away from the world and search into the depths of our soul to find God there. Adoration does not require seclusion; indeed it is provoked by the apprehension of God's presence and activity in the world.

Still the New Testament does speak of taking time to go to a 'secret' place (Matt. 6:6). The 'secret' place should not be confused with 'sacred space', however. It stands for the cessation of active involvement in the world, not for the exclusion of the profane reality. Every place can be a 'secret space', and every moment a time reserved for God. But if we want to escape the tendency to dissolve the holy into the secular, which seems to be the danger of affirmation that the holy is not restricted to particular places,[24] then we need to reserve special time for the adoration of God, whether it means going to the 'secret place' (as Jesus advised), spending a night in the mountains (as Jesus practised), or gathering together in Jesus' name as a community of believers. The point of the talk about the *rhythm* of adoration and action is to *preserve profane reality as a meeting-place with the holy God*, not to reintroduce the division between the sacred and the profane.

But does not the very act of adoring God, wherever it takes place, involve turning away from the world toward God? Even if we affirm the possibility of meeting God in the profane reality, do we not reduce this reality to a mere vehicle for encountering God? I will start answering these questions by noting the distinction between adoration and contemplation. As distinct from the modern way of knowing by which we manipulate things in order to grasp them, contemplation is a passive way of knowing by which we behold things as they present themselves to us (*theoria*). Its passivity notwithstanding, contemplation is a way of knowing *things and truths*, not persons. You can contemplate the works of a person, but you do not contemplate persons themselves; you know them by talking to them and letting them talk to you, by doing things with them. Seeing the persons (and touching them) is important, but only as a part of this conversation and cooperation which constitute our common history.

Since God is neither an a-personal truth nor anaesthetic shape, contemplation is not appropriate as a way of relating to God. Adoration is. To adore God is not simply to behold the truth, goodness, and beauty of God in a disinterested way, but to affirm one's allegiance to God by praising God for his deeds in creation and redemption. The contemplation of God's works (like beholding the grandeur of creation or meditating on the passion of Christ) is a presupposition of adoration. But to adore is not to look at God, but to talk about God and to God inspired by God's works in the world. This, however, means that *turning to God in adoration does not entail turning away from the world; it entails perceiving God in relation to the world and the world in relation to God*. The songs of praise to God are at the same time the songs about the world as God's creation and a place which God will transform into a new creation. And the songs about creation and redemption can be nothing else but songs about God the Creator and Redeemer.

Authentic Christian adoration cannot take place in isolation from the world. Because the God Christians adore is engaged in the world, adoration of God leads to action in the world and action in the world leads to adoration of God. Adoration and action are distinct, but nevertheless *interdependent* activities. So we need to investigate further the positive relationship they have to each other.

V

What is the significance of adoration of God for action in the world? We can answer this question best if we reflect on the nature of doxological language. At one level, in adoration a person is stating what is the case; he or she is describing God's action (e.g. 'he has condemned the great prostitute [economic and political power of Babylon] who corrupted the earth by her adulteries') and God's character (e.g. 'true and just are his judgments' [Rev. 19: 2]). There is no adoration without such description. But the actual point of adoration lies deeper than description. In thanking, blessing or praising God, a person expresses his or own relation toward the God he or she is adoring: joyous *gratitude* for what God has done and reverent *alignment* with God's character from which God's actions spring forth.

It is here that the significance of adoration for action becomes visible. First, by aligning with God's character and purposes in adoration one aligns oneself also with God's projects in the world. By praising God who renews the face of the earth and redeems the peoples one affirms at the same time one's desire to be a cooperator with God in the world. Adoration is the well-spring of action. Second, in adoration a person names and celebrates the context of meaning that gives significance to his or her action in the world and indicates the highest value that gives that action binding direction. In the pantheon of the modern world, adoration identifies the God in whose name one engages in action. Without adoration action is blind and easily degenerates into a hit-or-miss activism.

The dependence of action in the world on the adoration of God shows that the frequent disjunction found in cerebral and activistic Protestant circles between adoration and edification is inadmissible. As Psalm 119 shows, instruction in Torah could take place in doxological language. For Paul too, psalms, hymns, and spiritual songs were simultaneously expressions of adoration and a means of instruction and admonition.[25] Every authentic adoration is instruction, because it celebrates God's deeds and God's character, and expresses at the same time commitment to the God it celebrates. The inverse is also true. Every authentic Christian instruction is adoration. Instruction in faith which does not include (at least implicitly) adoration is deficient: it communicates knowledge without transmitting corresponding allegiance. Protestant theology (evangelical theology included!) on this point needs to learn from Eastern Orthodoxy which, in addition to maintaining that there is 'no mysticism without theology', has stressed 'above all' that there is 'no theology without mysticism'.[26]

What is the significance of action for adoration? In order to answer this question we need to look briefly at the nature and the purpose of Christian involvement in the world. Christian action is nothing less than cooperation with God. As Genesis 2 vividly portrays, there is a partnership between the creating God and working human beings.[27] Just as in Genesis a farmer is a co-operator of God, so Paul thinks of missionaries as 'fellow workers of God' in God's field (1 Cor. 3:9).[28] Whether it consists in evangelism or mundane work, human activity is a means by which God accomplishes God's purposes in the world. If God's deeds in the world open the hearts and mouths of people to praise God, then human action, which God uses to accomplish God's purposes, must do the same: the purpose of evangelism and good works is the well-being of the people and of God's whole creation. And the integral well-being of God's world is the occasion for praise (see 2 Cor. 4:15; Matt. 5:16; 1 Pet. 2:11). Christian action in the world leads to adoration of God. Action establishes conditions in which adoration of God surges out of the human heart.

But there is also another sense in which action is a precondition to adoration. There is something profoundly hypocritical about praising God for God's mighty deeds of salvation and cooperating at the same time with the demons of destruction, whether by neglecting to do good or by actively doing evil. Only those who help the Jews may sing the Gregorian chant, Dietrich Bonhoeffer rightly said, in the context of Nazi Germany. Only those who are actively concerned with the victims of economic, political, racial or sexual oppression – who are doing 'the significant something' – can genuinely worship God. Without action in the world, the adoration of God is empty and hypocritical, and degenerates into irresponsible and godless quietism.

VI

The distinction between action and adoration (just like the old distinction between action and contemplation[29]) is not a distinction between activity and passivity, but a distinction between two forms of human activity. Action designates deeds that are directed toward the world, adoration designates words and symbolic actions that are directed toward God. This is why the writer of Hebrews can describe both the action and the adoration as 'sacrifices': the one is a sacrifice of good works, the other a sacrifice of praise (see Heb. 13:15–16). As sacrifices, action and adoration are something human beings give God. This is why both can properly be called 'worship.' For worship is something human beings owe God: in worship they are the givers, and God is the receiver.

But our arms are lifeless and our mouths dumb if God does not give them strength and facility of speech. We can give God only what we have first received from God. Reception is, therefore, a third dimension of Christian life that is even more fundamental then action and adoration. In distinction to the traditional two-dimensional understanding of Christian existence (*vita activa* and *vita contemplativa*), Luther rightly stressed that *vita passiva* is an additional dimension of Christian life, which underlies both Christian theory and practice.[30] At the foundation of Christian life lies passivity. Christians are receivers at the point when the beginning of the rebirth of the whole cosmos takes place in their new birth by the Holy Spirit (see John 3:3; Matt. 19:28; 2 Cor. 5:17). And the new life is sustained and flourishes only if they continue to be receivers throughout their Christian life. The rhythm of adoration and action must be embedded in the larger rhythmic phrase consisting of Christian passivity and activity.

The passivity of Christian existence can be described as receiving the Spirit by faith (which marks the beginning of Christian life: see Gal. 3:2) and being continually filled by the Spirit (which marks its continuation: see Eph. 5:18ff.). The secret of the whole Christian life is passivity in relation to the Spirit of God. For the Spirit is the source both of adoration (5:18–20) and of action (5:21–6:20).

Notes to Chapters

NOTES TO CHAPTER ONE

1. George Swinnock, *Works* (Edinburgh: James Nichols, 1868) 1.31.
2. Waco: Word, 1987.
3. John Owen, *Works* (ed. William Goold; Edinburgh: Johnstone and Hunter, 1850–53) 9.53–84; cited by J. I. Packer, 'The Puritan Approach to Worship', *Antithesis* 2 (Jan/Feb 1991) 15.
4. Stephen Charnock, *Works* (Edinburgh: James Nichols, 1864) 1.298; cited in J. I. Packer, 'Puritan', 15–16.

NOTES TO CHAPTER TWO

1. Hebrew word is *'ābad* which may be translated 'to serve' or 'to work', even 'to worship'. Cf. *infra*, n.31.
2. Ronald Allen and Gordon Borror, *Worship, Rediscovering the Missing Jewel* (Portland, OR: Multnomah, 1982) 16.
3. 'It extends to every domain of life. God must be served on all planes of human existence, as biblical legislation testifies. It is significant that Hebrew has one word to denote *work, service* and *worship*; in biblical thought there is no watertight division between daily work and the adoration of God; in the very first page of Scripture manual activity and the service of the Creator are inseparably linked' (R. Martin-Achard, 'Worship', *A Companion to the Bible*, ed. J.-J. von Allmen (New York: OUP, 1958) 472.
4. A concise history and nature of various Protestant churches' worship traditions may be seen in James F. White, *Protestant Worship Traditions in Transition* (Louisville, KY: Westminster/John Knox, 1989).
5. The larger part of this book deals with the application of the biblical principles of worship to our present-day practices and priorities. 'To be sure, modern worship must reflect the idiom and life-style of the day we live in, and there is no virtue in a mindless repetition of archaic forms and language that carry no meaning to our contemporaries' Ralph P. Martin, *The Worship of God* (Grand Rapids: Eerdmans, 1982) 16.
6. The word used for 'offering' in the narrative of the offerings of Cain and Abel is *minḥāh*, often translated 'gift', and may refer either to an animal or to produce of the land. In ancient times there was a general preference for animal offerings over vegetable offerings (see John Skinner, *A Critical and Exegetical Commentary on*

Genesis, ICC [Edinburgh: T. & T. Clark, 1930] 105–106; cf. also Saul Levin, 'The More Savory Offering: A Key to the Problem of Gen.4:3–5', *JBL* 98 [1979] 85). Some hold that, quite apart from God's preference for Abel's character over against that of Cain, whose worship is feigned (see Bruce K. Waltke, 'Cain and His Offering', *WTJ* 48 [1986] 363–372), this account is to be understood in terms of a redemptive or messianic motif that anticipates the course of progressive revelation (see Basil F. C. Atkinson, *The Book of Genesis* [Chicago: Moody, 1957] 57–58; J. Barton Payne, *Encyclopedia of Biblical Prophecy*, [Grand Rapids: Baker, 1973] 158). Others caution against this understanding (see Derek Kidner, *Genesis*, TOTC [London: Tyndale, 1968] 75; Gerhard von Rad, *Genesis* OTL, [London: SCM, 1963] 101).

7. See J. H. Kurtz *Sacrificial Worship of the Old Testament*, trans. J. Martin (Minneapolis: Klock & Klock, reprint 1980 [1868] 51. 'The use of the normal sacrificial verb *hēbi'* and the reference to 'the fat' (vs.4), makes it plain that a sacrifice is being described, but whether an altar or a burnt offering is to be understood is left uncertain. What is important is, that the sacrifice is a *minhāh*, not *zebah*, and no sacrificial meal follows' (R. J. Thompson, *Penitence and Sacrifice in Early Israel Outside the Levitical Law* [Leiden: Brill, 1963] 50.

8. *'āz hûhal liqrō' bᵉšēm YHWH* This could be literally: 'Then, to call the name of the Lord was commenced.'

9. LXX renders in the singular.

10. 'Worship in the patriarchal age, then, was simple and individual, and its known forms were sacrifice and prayer. Yet it rose to the heights of fellowship with God seldom surpassed, and worship and life were closely related. It lacked the corporate element which we so often think of as the essential element of worship because the conditions under which the patriarchs lived made corporate worship of that kind impossible. I find it hard to think they mingled in the social worship of the Canaanite shrines of their day, just because the atmosphere of worship reflected in the traditions preserved in Genesis is so completely alien to all we know of the Canaanite shrine' (H. H. Rowley, *Worship in Ancient Israel: Its Forms and Meaning* [London: SPCK, 1976] 36; cf. also pp. 24, 37). Of course, Rowley does not argue this point on the basis of the form of the text, but from his understanding of culture and religion during that period.

11. C. F. Keil and F. Delitzsch, *Biblical Commentary on the Old Testament: The Pentateuch* (Vol. I), trans. by J. Martin (Grand Rapids: Eerdmans, n.d. reprint) 120. Cf. also J. Skinner, 127. However, E. W. Bullinger interprets this expression 'calling the divine name') as referring to the rise of a blasphemous heathen idolatry (cf. Atkinson, *Genesis*, 65), while von Rad recognizes at least some Yahwihstic worship elements in it, saying: 'Our notice does not intend to answer the question about the pre-Mosaic worship of Yahweh in detail, but rather to indicate generally Yahweh-worship as the primeval religion of mankind in general' (von Rad, *Genesis* 109).

12. Commenting on the burnt offerings here, Kidner says, 'Homage, dedication and atonement are all expressed in the "burnt offering": the new earth is to be God's, if He will have it' (Kidner, *Genesis* 93).

13. 'The altar is an essential element in a sanctuary; and in the stories about the Patriarchs, the phrase "setting up an altar" means, in effect, founding a sanctuary (Gen.12:7, 8, 13:18, 26:25, 33:20)' (Roland de Vaux, *Ancient Israel: Its Life and Institutions*, trans. by J. McHugh [New York: McGraw-Hill, 1961] 406; cf. also p. 413).

14. 'Sacrifice is any offering, animal or vegetable, which is wholly or partially destroyed upon an altar as a token of homage to God' (*ibid.* 415).

15. J. H. Kurtz says in the opening section of his book, 'By worship (cultus) we mean the worship of *God*; and from the very act that the sacrifices of which we are speaking formed an essential ingredient in the Old Testament worship, they also formed a part of that service which Israel was required to render to its *God*' (Kurtz, *Sacrificial Worship* 17).

16. On the unique significance of Passover sacrifice, cf. Rowley, *Worship* 115–116. On the later development of sacrifice in Israel, E. A. Martens says, 'Sacrifice, an early cult form, was connected to an act of deliverance. This deliverance from the angel of death was commemorated in worship rituals; each year Israel was required to observe the Passover' (Elmer A. Martens, *God's Design: A Focus on Old Testament Theology* (Grand Rapids: Baker, 1986) 47.

17. Some have suggested that many of these sites were used as sanctuaries by the people who lived before the settlement of the patriarchs and of the Israelites. Thus R. de Vaux says, 'Sanctuaries were erected where nature manifested the presence of the God of Abraham, Isaac and Jacob – near a tree, for example, or on a natural height, or by a water-source; but they were erected principally in places where God had shown himself in a theophany. Sanctuaries of this kind are found all along the route the patriarchs travelled' (*Ancient Israel* 289; cf. also pp. 293–294).

18. 'But the all-important significance of circumcision, in the O.T., appears in the narrative of its institution ordered by God to Abraham (Gen.17:9–14 and 23–27): it is a covenant rite which is the sign of belonging to a family, a race or a people.' 'Henceforward, circumcision will be the mark of the true Israelites, sons of Abraham, and will distinguish them from foreigner and heathen.' So F. Michaeli, 'Circumcision', *A Companion to the Bible*, ed. J.-J. von Allen (New York: Oxford, 1958) 56. Cf. also William H. Dumbrell, *Covenant and Creation: A Theology of Old Testament Covenant* (Nashville/Camden/New York: Thomas Nelson, 1984) 74–75. In some Christian traditions circumcision is typologically related to baptism in New Testament, and tied to the new relationship made possible between human beings and God. Cf. Leonhard Goppelt, *Typos: The Typological Interpretation of the Old Testament in the New*, trans. D. H. Madvig (Grand Rapids: Eerdmans, 1982) 137, 141, 144.

19. R. Martin (*The Worship of God* 22) sees the call to praise God in terms of covenantal response, saying, 'God's faithfulness to Israel persisted in spite of the people's fickleness and perversity (this is the theme of Hosea); and running through all her history is this confidence, even if some times distorted and misplaced, as Jeremiah was to expose, that Israel was bound to Yahweh by covenant ties and pledges. Hence the call to praise God for his covenant fidelity is often heard.'

20. For the older derivation, cf. Robert B. Girdlestone, *Synonyms of the Old Testament* (Grand Rapids: Eerdmans, repr. from 2nd ed. of 1894) 215. But it has been shown that the root is *ḥ-w-y*: cf. M. I. Gruber, *Aspects of Nonverbal Communication in the Ancient Near East*, Studia Pohl 12/1 (Rome: Biblical Institute Press, 1980) 90–5; and H. D. Preuss, *TDOT*, 4. 249–250.

21. In a context of worshipping God, qāḏaḏ ('to incline' or 'to bow') is used in Genesis (24:26, 48).

22. Three words qāḏaḏ 'to bow', ḥ-w-y, 'to worship', bārak 'to bless') are used in this verse (24:48), and the verse is translated in the NIV: 'And I bowed down and worshipped the Lord. I praised the Lord, the God of my master Abraham, who had led me on the right road to get the granddaughter of my master's brother for his son.'

23. The word used here is pālal and translated 'to pray' (NIV).

24. The word used here is ʿātar but translated 'to pray' in this context (NIV).

25. NIV renders the word 'to bless' in 9:26 and 14:20 but 'to praise' in 24:27.

26. NIV renders the word 'to praise'.

27a. This might be later developed into the idea of 'sanctuary' in the history of the people of Israel.

27b. E. W. Nicholson, *Exodus* and *Sinai in the History and Tradition* (Oxford: Basil Blackwell, 1973) 83.

28. Cf. W. H. Gispen, *Exodus* (Bible Student's Commentary), trans. Ed. van der Maas (Grand Rapids: Zondervan, 1982) 29–30; U. Cassuto, *A Commentary on the Book of Exodus*, trans. I. Abrahams (Jerusalem: Magnes, 1967) 7–9; George Bush, *Notes on Exodus*, Vol. 1 (Minneapolis, MN: James & Klock, repr. 1976) 10–11; cf. also Martin Noth, Exodus: *A Commentary* (OTL), trans. J. S. Bowden (London: SCM, 1966) 20.

29. Moses' life in the land of the Midianites and God's appearance to Moses were a basic source for the so-called 'Kenite hypothesis', which insists that Moses was influenced by the concept of Midianite deity. Cf. J. Kenneth Kuntz, *The People of Ancient Israel: An Introduction to Old Testament Literature, History, and Thought* (New York/Evanston/San Francisco/London: Harper & Row, 1974) 104–105; cf. also G. M. Landes, 'Kenites', *IDB* 3. 6–7; J. Philip Hyatt, *Exodus* NCB (Grand Rapids: Eerdmans, 1980 [revised ed.]) 78–79.

30. D. Lys, 'Fear – O.T.', *A Companion to the Bible* (New York: Oxford Univ. Press, 1958) 115–116; R. Earle, 'Fear', *EDT* 409; G. A. Lee, 'Fear', ISBE 2. 287. For a recent and detailed study on the concept of 'fear' in the OT, from a linguistic perspective, cf. Mayer I. Gruber, 'Fear, Anxiety and Reverence in Akkadian, Biblical Hebrew and Other North-west Semitic Languages', *VT* 40 (1990) 411–422.

31. The word used here is *ʿābad*, *supra* n. 1.

32. The word used here is also *zābaḥ* (cf. Exo. 5:3; 8:8 [Hebrew 8:4], 10:25).

33. Other terms used in the context of 'worship' in these chapters of the book of Exodus are: *ʿātar* 'to pray' (8:8 [Hebrew 8:4]; 8:29 [Hebrew 8:25]; 8:30 [Hebrew 8:26]; 9:28; 10:18); *ṣāʿaq* 'to cry' (8:12 [Hebrew 8:8]); *ḥāgag* 'to keep festival' (5:1; 10:9).

34. Only *zābaḥ* 'to sacrifice' is used in 3:18 and 8:27 [Hebrew 8:23].

35. *ḥ-w-y* 'to worship' is used in 4:31.

36. The word 'to redeem' (*gāʾal*) is used here in connection with the event of the Exodus: '. . . I am the Lord and I will bring you out from under the yoke of the Egyptians. I will free you from being slaves to them and will *redeem* you with an outstretched arm and with mighty acts of judgment' (Exod. 6:6). This is the second occurrence of this verb in the OT; the first is in Gen. 48:16.

37. Cf. Keil-Delitzsch 1.485–486, Gispen, *Exodus* 93–94; Alan Cole, *Exodus*, TOTC (London: Tyndale, 1973) 95; J. P. Hyatt, *Exodus* 112. Cf. also R. J. Thompson *Penitence and Sacrifice* 58.

38. As to the origin of the Passover rite, there has been much discussion. Similar rites were doubtless known among some nomadic peoples around the time of Moses or even earlier (cf. Hyatt, *Exodus* 144–146; J. B. Segal, *The Hebrew Passover from the Earliest Times* to A.D. 70, London Oriental Series 12 [London: Oxford Univ. Press, 1963] 78–106). However, the structure of the text (Exod. 12:1–36) argues that God has given this [Passover] rite a new covenantal meaning along with its redemptive implication. As displayed in the text, it is not just a commemoration of an event that took place in the past, but is a 'covenant' which in the first instance *looks forward* to the redemptive event it commemorates. J. B. Segal says, 'The Exodus did not take place in order to celebrate the festival; but the festival was celebrated, and the Exodus followed' (ibid. 46); cf. also Keil-Delitzsch, 2:9. Of course, critical views that adopt a negative attitude toward the Mosaic origin of all the Pentateuch hold that most of this section (chaps. 12–13) is exilic or post-exilic, assigning it to the so-called P-document.

39. The feast of the Passover and the feast of Unleavened Bread have been celebrated, in most cases, in combined form. 'Earlier, in the O.T., and into the N.T. as well, "Passover" and "Feast of Unleavened Bread" (Mark 14:1) were both used with reference to the rites. Now one and now the other covered the entire sequence. But basically the Passover referred to the eve of the first day, the fourteenth day of the month (Lev.23:5, etc.), on which the sacrifice of the Passover lamb took place, while the Feast of Unleavened Bread (Lev.23:6, etc.) applied to the seven days following' (J. C. Ryaarsdam, 'Passover and Feast of Unleavened Bread', *IDB* 664). For a detailed defence of the view that the Passover lamb was for sacrifice to God as an act of worship and not just a celebratory meal for the occasion, cf. Kurtz, *Sacrificial Worship* 360–369.

40. Cf. Charles F. Pfeiffer, 'Passover', *BDT* 395.

41. Dewey M. Beegle, 'Exodus', *BDT* 206.

42. Ronald S. Wallace, 'Lord's Supper', *BDT* 330. For more typological understanding, cf. Goppelt, *Typos* 112–113. Taking the biblical narrative as an interpre-

tation of general custom of Bedouin sacrifice, S. Herrmann says, 'In the case of the passover in Ex. 12, this Bedouin sacrificial custom found a unique historical explanation, it was given a historical basis through a particular event in the history of Israel. It is directly bound up as closely as possible with God's saving action on behalf of Israel in Egypt, and is aetiologically anchored in that act' (Siegried Herrmann, *Israel in Egypt*, Studies in Biblical Theology 27 [Naperville: Allenson, 1973] 55).

43. Exegetically speaking, there are four important concepts that are introduced: two (completion of the work of creating the physical world, and resting from the work) in v.2, and another two (blessing upon the seventh day, and sanctifying the seventh day) in v.3.

44. Walter C. Kaiser, Jr., *Toward An Old Testament Theology* (Grand Rapids: Zondervan, 1978) 76–77. Referring to Delitzsch's expression, D. Kidner says, 'The formula that rounded off each of the six days with the onset of evening and morning is noticeably absent, as if to imply the "infinite perspective" (Delitzsch) of God's sabbath' (Kidner, *Genesis* 53).

45. 'In connection with the gift of manna there now follows the "revelation" of the divine requirement of the sabbath rest. The word "sabbath" here occurs for the first time in the Old Testament' (Noth, *Exodus* 135).

46. 'YHWH has given you the sabbath. On the basis of this, and the breach of the sabbath reported, some suggest that the Israelites had not kept the sabbath while in Egypt, but that it was by way of being a novel observance. Perhaps their condition as slaves would account for this failure to observe it, even if some such had been known (in embryo at least) to their patriarchal ancestors' (Cole, *Exodus*, 132–133). For a somewhat different view, cf. Keil-Delitzsch, *op. cit.*, 2:68–69, 119; also J. P. Lange, *Exodus*, trans. by C. M. Mead (Grand Rapids: Zondervan, reprint n.d.) 64–65. Noth (*Exodus* 136–137) treats the issue from the perspective that distinguishes two different sources (J and P) in the text.

47. Cole, *Exodus* 157–158. Niels-Erik Andreasen ('Recent Studies of the Old Testament Sabbath, Some Observations', *ZAW* 86 [1974] 453–469) sees four aspects in the significance of OT sabbath: (1) rest from work, (2) freedom/redeeming qualities, (3) the idea of worship/celebration/joy, (4) covenantal bond.

48. 'The first recorded mention of singing on the part of men and women comes at the passage of the Sea of Reeds (Exod.15:1, 21) when the antiphonal refrain praised Yahweh's deliverance . . .' (Martin, *Worship* 48).

49. The structure of these verses is important. God's work (v.1b) – praise for God (vv.2–3); God's work (vv.4–5) – praise for God (vv.6–8); God's work (v.9–10) – praise for God (vv.11–12).

50. Cole, *Exodus* 123; Kaiser, *Theology* 106. For a critical form-analytical view of this song, cf. Hyatt, *Exodus* 162–163. On the other hand, Gispen (*Exodus* 146) says of the later usage of this song by the Israelites as well as by Christians: 'The song was transmitted orally and was very popular in Israel, as is evident from the fact that it is frequently quoted in the Psalms (v.1, cf. Pss.66:6; 68:18; 106:12; v.2, cf. Ps.118:14, 21, 28; v.3, cf. Ps.24:8; v.4, cf. Ps.136:15; vv.5–17, cf. Ps.78:52–54; vv.5–13, cf. Ps.77: 14–21; vv.5–10, cf.Ps.106:11; v.7, cf. Ps.78:49; v.8, cf.78:13; v.11, cf. Pss.66:3, 5; 78:4, 12; 86:8, vv.13–17, cf. Pss.44:2, 4; 74:2; v.17, cf. Ps.80:9, 16; v.18, cf. Ps.146:10). This is all the more proof that the crossing of the Red Sea was considered the fundamental fact of Israel's history. Moses sang the song by way of confirmation and remembrance. For the Christian church this song, and the Israelites standing victoriously at the Red Sea, are a prophecy of those who will have been victorious over Satan and the Antichrist and who will then sing "the song of Moses the servant of God and of the Lamb" (cf. Rev.15:1–4). For them the song is an expression of the true background of their struggle or "wilderness journey" seen in the light of Golgotha and the victories over Satan and his instruments that God has granted His people.'

51. Brevard S. Childs (*Old Testament Theology in Canonical Context* [London: SCM, 1985] 53) presents an accurate perspective on the structure of the Pentateuch, and on the Sinai event in particular: 'The fullest and most direct expression of the will

of God in the Old Testament is found in the revelation of the Law at Sinai. In a real sense the book of Genesis is its prologue and the book of Deuteronomy its epilogue, but the heart of the Pentateuch lies in the tradition of Sinai contained in the middle books of Exodus, Leviticus and Numbers.' Of course, this is not to deny the progress of redemptive history within the Pentateuch.

52. n.29, *supra*.

53. Cole, *Exodus* 139.

54. Gispen, *Exodus* 181–182. Further, referring to the Reformer, Gispen says, 'Calvin points out that, although these external cleansings are no longer prescribed for us, their truth and essence remain necessary for us: if we want to be admitted to and participate in the heavenly doctrine, we must cleanse ourselves of all contamination of flesh and spirit (cf. Jude 23)' (p. 182).

55. Cole (*Exodus* 146) takes the expression 'on the third day' (vv.11, 16) as an indication of 'the completeness of the process of purification.'

56. For the location of Mt. Sinai, cf. G. E. Wright, 'Sinai, Mount', *IDB* 376–378; Hyatt, *Exodus* 203–207 ('Excursus: The Location of Mount Sinai').

57. For a similar understanding, cf. Dumbrell, *Covenant and Creation* 88.

58. Cf. n.1, *supra*; n.31, *supra*.

59. Aaron is considered to be the first priest and the founder of the priesthood. However, Nadab and Abihu, who were Aaron's first two sons, were judged and died (Num.3:4; 26:61; Lev.10:1–2). Cf. T. M. Mauch, 'Aaron', *IDB* 1. also Cole, *Exodus* 184.

60. The word 'worship' here is from the *ḥ-w-y* root.

61. Gispen, *Exodus* 237.

62. 'WORDS would be categorical law (like the "ten words") while ORDINANCES (better "judicial decisions") would be "case-law". Since the book of the covenant contains both, the distinction is not important' (Cole, *Exodus* 185).

63. Exod.32–34 is to be understood as the narrative that deals with the rebellion of the Israelites, the theme of the 'unfaithfulness of the Israelites to the covenant', and their renewal of that covenant. For a detailed discussion of Exod.32–34, cf. R. W. L. Moberly, *At the Mountain of God: Story and Theology in Exodus 32–34* (JSOTS 22; Sheffield: JSOT Press, 1983).

64. 'The tabernacle, then, was the localization of God's presence with his people, a visible symbol that he was their God. Here Israel was to worship and stone for breaches of the covenant stipulations' (William Sanford LaSor, David Allen Hubbard, Frederic Wm. Bush, *Old Testament Survey: The Message, Form, and Background of the Old Testament* [Grand Rapids: Eerdmans, 1982] 147). As for its symbolism J. G. S. S. Thomson writes, '(1) Standing in the center of the camp it symbolized the presence of God in Israel. (2) It symbolized the divinely appointed means by which sinful man could approach God, of otherwise unapproachable holiness, ineffable majesty, perfect unity' ('Tabernacle', *BDT* 510).

65. *Contra* H. H. Rowley, *Worship* 50–51, who writes: 'All this is in the Priestly document, and while it is agreed that many things in the ritual were of great antiquity, it is not to be doubted that the whole conception of the Tabernacle and its ministry was a projection into the past of the Temple and its ministry.'

66. Cf. Thomson, 'Tabernacle', 511, for more detailed discussion.

67. The book of Leviticus ends with laws concerning vows (chap. 27).

68. 'Numbers covers a period of thirty-eight years and nine months, referred to as the period of wilderness wonderings.' 'No effort will be made to press these date formulas, for Numbers makes no theological significance of them other than a general reference to the "forty years" in the wilderness (cf. 14:33f.). However, it is highly unlikely that they were mere fictions of post-exilic editors. It is not unreasonable to suppose that in addition to the written log of the stages of journeyings (33:2) Moses also kept a record of the dates – at least those preserved in the account' LaSor/Hubbard/Bush, *Old Testament Survey* 163.

69. 'Deuteronomy is a treasure chest of theological concepts that have influenced the religious thought and life of Israelites, Jews, and Christians' (*ibid.*, 180).

70. The *Shema* (Deut.6:4–5) has confessional elements and is applicable and relevant to us in our worship today. 'These words were to be upon the hearts of the Israelites, who were to teach them diligently to their children. The words were to be bound 'as a sign' on the hand and 'as frontlets' between the eyes. They were to be written on the doorposts of the house and on the gates. These instructions, immediately following the Shema, have become part of the Jews' daily religious rituals. Jesus took the words of vs.5 as the first and greatest commandment (Matt.22:37)' (*ibid.*, 180–181).

71. Commenting on the situation in the days of Joshua, Rowley (*Worship* 57) writes: 'We therefore learn of much fighting, but little worship.'

72. Martin H. Woudstra, *The Book of Joshua* (NICOT; Grand Rapids: Eerdmans, 1983) 90.

73. Some other elements of the exodus-motif may be observed in the expression of v.14: 'That day the Lord exalted Joshua in the sight of all Israel; and they revered him all the days of his life, just as they revered Moses' (NIV). Of course, such is very much evident in v.23.

74. Apart from the question of the exact geographical site of Gilgal, the cultic element of Gilgal has been widely discussed, especially because of Josh., 5:10–12 in particular. R. J. Thompson (*Penitence and Law* 80–81) says, 'Various elements of Kraus' theory have been challenged, but the basic assumption of the antiquity of the three main elements – the circumcision (5:2–9), the Passover (5:10–12), and the appearance (5:13–15) – seems sound. The suggestion of the narrative, that a preparation for the Passover by circumcision was required, is significant for the solemn view.' Woudstra (*Joshua* 94–95) argues: 'Henceforth the commemoration of the first passover will therefore coincide with the commemoration of the entry into the promised land.' Referring to the age of Joshua and the Judges, Rowley (*Worship* 57) says, '. . . it is probable that a Yahweh shrine was established there at this time.'

75. In addition to those in chap. 4, discussed above already.

76. E.g., cf. Edward J. Young, *An Introduction to the Old Testament* (Grand Rapids: Eerdmans, 1954) 160, 166; Gleason L. Archer, Jr., *A Survey of Old Testament Introduction* (Chicago: Moody, 1964) 251, 262; Werner H. Schmidt, *Old Testament Introduction* (trans. M. J. O.'Connell; New York: Crossroad, 1984) 148; etc.

77. These instances appear to be not so much the regular calling to the Lord by the Israelites, as their seeking after help to escape the hardships and tragedies the Lord had given then as divine judgments.

78. Rowley, *Worship* 58.

79. *Ibid.*, 58–64; George W. Ramsey, *The Quest for the Historical Israel* (Atlanta: John Knox, 1981) 89–90; Arthur E. Cundall and L. Morris *Judges, Ruth* (TOTC; London: Tyndale, 1969) 35–37; etc.

80. This 'annual festival (*ḥāg*) of the Lord' could be either the Passover or the Feast of Tabernacles. Cf. Cundall and Morris, 212. Cundall says further, 'This particular pilgrimage, therefore, may have been of a local character, having its origins in the pre-Israelite worship of the locality. Such an explanation could ease the problem of accounting for the absence of any representative from Shiloh in the council of the eleven tribes which hatched this scheme to deprive them of two hundred of their maidens!' (*Ibid.*)

81. There might have been some structure or building for worship at the time of Eli. H. P. Smith says on 1 Sam.1:9, 'The structure seems to have been a solid building, otherwise it could not be called "a temple"; the same word is afterwards applied to the temple of Solomon, I K.6:5' (Henry P. Smith, *A Critical and Exegetical Commentary on the Books of Samuel* [ICC; Edinburgh: T. & T. Clark 1951] 9). Cf. also F. F. Bruce, *Israel and the Nations from the Exodus to the Fall of the Second Temple* (Exeter: Paternoster, 1965) 22. The word used here is *hêkal*, but John R. Kohlenberger III

(*The NIV Triglot Old Testament* [Grand Rapids: Zondervan, 1981]) renders it 'tabernacle' in the margin here in 1:9 and also 3:3.

82. C. F. Keil and F. Delitzsch, *Biblical Commentary on the Old Testament: The Books of Samuel* (trans. J. Martin; Grand Rapids: Eerdmans, 1967) 23. For a detailed discussion, cf. Smith, *Samuel* 8–10.

83. Joseph Gutmann, 'The History of the Ark', *ZAW* 83 (1971) 24.

84. On the importance of the role of Shiloh with respect to the Tent of Meeting, considered in connection with standard Pentateuchal 'sources', cf. Manahem Haran, 'The Nature of the "'OHEL MO'EDH" in Pentateuchal sources', *JSS* 5 (1960) 50–65, esp. 63–65.

85. Of this aspect, cf. also *ibid.* 64–65. 1 Sam.2:27–36 might be understood as a prophetic critique.

86. 'Samuel expostulated with them, telling them that their request marked a lack of faith to raise them up a champion of His choice in time of need heretofore' (Bruce, *Israel and the Nations* 24). Similarly Keil/Delitzsch, *Samuel* 83f: 'This mistrust was founded upon mistrust in the Lord and His guidance. In the person of Samuel they rejected the Lord and his rule; they wanted a king, because they imagined that Jehovah their God-king was not able to secure their constant prosperity . . . In such a state of mind as this, their desire for a king was a contempt and rejection of the kingly government of Jehovah, and was nothing more than forsaking Jehovah to serve other gods.'

87. 'There is nothing in the word itself which gives any indication of its meaning, since no satisfactory derivation of the word can be found in Hebrew' (Patrick H. Vaughan, *The Meaning of 'bāmâ'* in the Old Testament [SOTSMS 3; Cambridge: University Press, 1974] 3).

88. For more detail, cf. G. Henton Davies, 'High Place, Sanctuary', *IDB* 2.

89. 'Nebel and Kinnor are stringed instruments which were used after David's time in connection with the psalmody of divine worship (I Chron.13:8, 15:20-21, Psa.33:2, 43:4, etc.' (Keil/Delitzsch, *Samuel* 99).

90. 'By saying this, Samuel did not reject sacrifices as worthless; he did not say that God took no pleasure in burnt-offerings and slain-offerings, but simply compared sacrifice with obedience to the command of God, and pronounced the latter of greater worth than the former. "It was as much as to say that the sum and substance of divine worship consisted in obedience, with which it should always begin, and that sacrifices were, so to speak, simple appendices, the force and worth of which were not so great as of obedience to the precepts of God" (Calvin). But it necessarily follows that sacrifices without obedience to the commandments of God are utterly worthless; in fact, are displeasing to God, as Ps.1.8 sqq., Isa.i.ll sqq., lxvi.3, Jer. vi.20, and all the prophets, distinctly affirm' (Keil/Delitzsch, *Samuel* 155-156). H. P. Smith, in more critical perspective (*Samuel* 137-139), takes this as 'a summary of later Jewish theology'.

91. The song continues on in the chapter (2 Sam.22:4-51).

92. 'The Tent of Meeting' is sometimes rendered 'Tabernacle' (cf. G. Henton Davies, 'Tabernacle', *IDB* 4. 498-506).

93. On various understandings of the ark of Yahweh, cf. G. Henton Davies, 'Ark of the Covenant', *IDB* 1. 222-226.

94. 'Whether the sacrifices were of dedication, or of fellowship, and whether an eating and rejoicing followed is not certain' (R. J. Thompson, *Penitence and Sacrifice* 126).

95. For cloud as a visible token of Yahweh's presence, cf. Exod. 16:10; 20:21; Lev.16:2; Ezek.10:4. Cf. R. B. Y. Scott, 'Cloud', *IDB* 1. 655.

96. For a different view, cf. James A. Montgomery, *A Critical and Exegetical Commentary on the Books of Kings* (ICC; Edinburgh: T. & T. Clark, 1959) 189: 'The note that "there was nothing in the ark except the two tables of stone" is the remark of an anxious commentator, who may have wished to dissipate false rumours to the

contrary'. John Gray, *I and II Kings* (OTL; 2nd edn; London: SCM, 1970) 203, remarks, 'The compiler, however, has left his own mark on the narrative, indicated by his characteristic phraseology and theology, e.g. "the ark of the covenant of Yahweh", i.e. not as a symbol of the divine presence, but, as is stated explicitly and at length in v.9, as a mere receptacle of the tablets of the law of God, who was above such local limitation.'

97. At the very beginning of v.12, the Hebrew text has a conjunctive particle *'az*.

98. James Muilenburg (*The Way of Israel: Biblical Faith and Ethics* [London: Routledge and Kegan Paul, 1962] 109), says, 'But, in contrast to the religions of other Near Eastern peoples, the place bore no sanctity in and of itself. What made it holy or sacred was the event in time. This leads us to a major reflection upon Israel's faith: it is not bound to the world of space. Yahweh is never limited to any locality, however holy. He is not confined to the sanctuary (II Sam.7:5-7; Eze.10:18ff.).'

99. To a question like 'What made Jerusalem significant for Israel – her connection with the Davidids or the presence of the ark?', M. Noth 'concludes that it was the latter, as much as the former which hallowed Jerusalem as the Holy Mount for Israel. The ark as the central shrine of the Israelite amphictyony, had no less significance on Mt. Zion and must have hallowed the temple also for every Israelite' (Thompson, *Penitence* 120).

100. On this expression 'Let your heart be completely with the Lord', there are various understandings as well as translations: 'in friendship with God' (Gesenius); 'be submissive to God' (de Wette), 'be upright with God' (Luther), 'wholly, undividedly devoted to the Lord' (Keil), 'must be fully committed to the Lord' (NIV), etc. Cf. Bahr, *The Book of the Kings* (Lange's Commentary; ET Grand Rapids: Zondervan, n.d.) 101; C. F. Keil, *Biblical Commentary on the Old Testament: The Books of the Kings* (trans. J. Martin; Grand Rapids: Eerdmans, 1965) 135.

101. Cf. Thompson, *Penitence and Sacrifice* 126.

102. This could be either 14 days or 7 days for the dedication and 7 days for the festival. Cf. de Vaux, *Ancient Israel* 496-497; Gray, *I and II Kings* 232-234.

103. Rowley lists 'joy' in going to the Temple as the top element in the context of worship (*Worship* 256).

104. Cf. nn.87 and 88, *supra*.

105. In contemporary missiological discussion of inter-cultural communication, this term must be dealt with carefully. Morton H. Smith says of 'syncretism': 'It is a term currently used to describe both efforts to unite branches of Christianity, and attempts to harmonize Christianity with non-Christian thought' ('Syncretism', *BDT* 150).

106. 'The sacrificial act without moral living is rejected by God' (S. M. Lehrman, *Hosea* [The Twelve Prophets – Soncino Books of the Bible; London: Soncino, 1965] 23).

107. 'Steadfast love' (RSV), 'loyalty' (NASB). '(For it is love that I delight in, and not sacrifice). The mistake of the people consisted in their notion that sacrifices were sufficient to gain Yahweh's favor. What Yahweh delights in, i.e. that which will gain his favor, is love; I Sam.15:22, in which obedience is emphasized. This love is not love for God as distinguished from love for one's fellowmen, but both' (William R. Harper, *A Critical and Exegetical Commentary on Amos and Hosea* [ICC; Edinburgh: T. & T. Clark, 1960] 286). Cf. especially Francis I. Andersen, 'Yahweh, the kind and sensitive God', in *God who is Rich in Mercy* (*Fs.* D. B. Knox; ed. Peter T. O'Brien and David G. Peterson; Homebush West: Anzea, 1986) 41–88.

108. NIV renders the word *hesed* 'love' in Hos.4:1, while it renders the same word 'mercy' in 6:6.

109. On these verses, Leslie C. Allen says, 'Micah borrows from the entrance liturgy, of which examples survive in Pss.15 and 24 and in another prophetic borrowing at Isa.33:14–16. It is characterized by question and answer, and sets out the requirements for would-be worshippers which they must meet before they can enter the sanctuary. Here the questioner is inquiring what sacrifices he should bring with

him as he comes to worship. He is quite prepared to give whatever is required of him' (*The Books of Joel, Obadiah, Jonah and Micah* [NICOT; Grand Rapids: Eerdmans, 1976] 369).

110. For prophetic criticism, especially about priestly ritualism, Henderson cites some more references, saying, 'The present is one of several passages in the Old Testament, in which the comparative worthlessness of ceremonial observances is taught. See Isa.1:11–17; Ps.40:7–9, 50:8–23, Mic.4:6–8. Comp. Matt. 9:13; 12:7' (Ebenezer Henderson, *The Twelve Minor Prophets* [Thornapple Commentaries; Grand Rapids: Baker, repr. 1980] 36).

111. As to the identity of this expression 'the Book of the Law', some, such as Keil and Slotki, take it to refer to the Pentateuch, while others, such as Montgomery and Schmidt, Deuteronomy or a part of Deuteronomy. Keil, *Biblical Commentary on the Old Testament: The Books of the Kings* 477–478; I. W. Slotki, *Kings* (Soncino Books of the Bible; London: Soncino, 1964) 299; Montgomery, *The Books of Kings* 543–546; Werner H. Schmidt, *Old Testament Introduction* (trans. M. J. O'Connell; New York: Crossroad, 1984) 123–129.

112. Acknowledging the cultic use of the Psalms, Mowinckel says of the 'psalm', 'In any case, it means a poem which arises from, or is related to, that experience which is expressed in worship, a worship which expresses the ideas and sentiments of the worshippers and their common attitude to the Godhead; such a poem therefore makes a more or less marked use of language which has already been shaped by worship'. (Sigmund Mowinckel, *The Psalms in Israel's Worship* [trans. D. R. Ap.-Thomas; New York/Nashville: Abingdon 1962] 1.2.

113. For a more detailed discussion, cf. Hans-Joachim Kraus, *Psalms 1–59, A Commentary* (trans. H. C. Oswald; Minneapolis: Augsburg, 1988) 68–69.

114. Martin, *Worship* 49.

115. Cf. 1 Kings 8:46–53; Deut.28:36–37. Of course, how one understands these biblical references is dependent upon whether they are taken as genuine prophecies or *post eventu* 'prophecies'. Those who follow the latter course think of such passages as 'judgment' rather than prophecy: cf. Peter R. Ackroyd, *Exile and Restoration* (OTL; London: SCM, 1968) 43–48.

116. Such as the Mosaic origin (H. Grotius), the Babylonian exilic origin (C. Sigonius) and the Persian/Ezra origin (Vitringa). For more details, cf. Isaiah Sonne, 'Synagogue' *IDB* 4. 478–479; Charles F. Pfeiffer, *Between the Testaments* (Grand Rapids: Baker, 1959) 59; R. E. Clements, *God and Temple* (Philadelphia: Fortress, 1965) 130; Harold H. Rowley, *The Biblical Doctrine of Election* (London: Lutterworth, 1950) 85–86.

117. 'To the humiliating allegation of the inhabitants of Jerusalem that the exiles, being far removed from the Temple, forfeited the Fatherhood and protection of God, comes the Divine retort that they still preserve their relationship to Him by means of their Houses of Worship and Houses of Learning, each of them serving the purpose of a miniature Temple in which the Spirit of God was present (*Meg.* 29a). The Synagogue is even now called "a little sanctuary" in allusion to this verse' (Solomon Fisch, *Ezekiel* [Soncino Books of the Bible; London: Soncino, 1960] 60).

118. The psalm is considered to be exilic or post-exilic: cf. Hans-Joachim Kraus, *Psalms 60–150, A Commentary* (trans. H. C. Oswald; Minneapolis: Augsburg/Fortress, 1989) 412.

119. Cf. Martin Noth, *The History of Israel* (trans. S. Godman; London: Black, 1958) 294–295; Bruce, *Israel* 101; cf. also Yoshiaki Hattori, *The Prophet Ezekiel and His Idea of the Remnant* (unpublished doctoral dissertation, Westminster Theological Seminary, 1968) 335–337.

120. When this date is compared with the date in 1:1, one must conclude that less than two months had elapsed since the beginning of the rebuilding of the new Temple. Cf. Hinckley G. Mitchell, *A Critical and Exegetical Commentary on Haggai, Zechariah, Malachi and Jonah* (ICC; Edinburgh: T. &. T. Clark, 1951) 58.

121. 'At the two termini we have God and the people. God would speak to the people, and this He did by means of His mouth, the prophets. We conclude, then, that upon the basis of the Old Testament usage, the *nabhi* was a speaker who declared the word that God had given him.' Edward J. Young, *My Servants the Prophets* (Grand Rapids: Eerdmans, 1961) 60; cf. also pp.65–66.

122. The position of Athnah is here taken into consideration. In comparison with the similar expression in 1:1, the expression 'and to the remnant of the people' needs to be understood in its relationship with the question of the following verse (v.3): 'Who of you is left who saw this house in its former glory?'

123. An example of this may be seen in Ezra 3:9–13. Eli Cashdam, *The Twelve Prophets* (Soncino Books of the Bible; London: Soncino, 1965, 253, 259), thinks it possible that Haggai himself was one of those who had seen the first Temple of Solomon.

124. We ought to recognize that although many psalms were in *cultic use* in the second temple after the exile, this does not mean that they necessarily *originated* in the post-exilic period. 'It is quite clear that many psalms in the Psalter have been USED in the cult of the Second Temple. Scholars have often called the Psalter "the hymnbook of the second Temple" meaning that it was collected just for this purpose. In this form the thesis is not quite correct: The Psalter may have BECOME the cultic hymnbook, but was scarcely made with that end in view. Of the cultic use of many psalms, however, there is much evidence' (Mowinckel, *Psalms* 2; cf. also pp. 4, 12). For further discussion, cf. Rowley, *Worship* 176–182, 276.

125. 'The eschatological application, however, transcends the empirical significance of "this house", and must be evaluated first in terms of the contribution of God himself and second in terms of the context of the Day of the Lord, and therefore as a reality of faith. In essence the O.T. temple finds its ultimate fulfilment in the "Lord of the Temple," who is greater than the temple (Matt.12:6), namely, Jesus Christ (cf. John 2:13–22).' Pieter A. Verhoef, *The Books of Haggai and Malachi* (NICOT; Grand Rapids: Eerdmans, 1987) 106; cf. also Joyce G. Baldwin, Haggai, *Zechariah, Malachi* (TOTC; London: Tyndale, 1972) 49.

126. For a detailed discussion on the unity of these chapters (40–48) within the Book of Ezekiel and on the interpretation, cf. Yoshiaki Hattori, *A Study on Ezekiel 40–48* (unpub. Master's Thesis: Westminster Theological Seminary, 1963) 39–50, 59–90), pp. 39–50, 59–90; also Hattori, *The Prophet Ezekiel and His Idea of the Remnant*, 305–326.

127. Cf. James Orr, *The Problem of the Old Testament* (London: James Nisbet, 1906) 307; Young, *Introduction* 264–265. J. Hoschander, a Jewish scholar, considers that these predictions were of a conditional character and that the exiles failed in meeting the expectation of the prophet because the larger and best part of them had not the least desire to return to their homeland, leaving the task of rebuilding the state to the poorer classes. Cf. Jacob Hoschander, *The Priests and Prophets* (New York: Jewish Theological Seminary of America, 1938) 167–168. But J. Klausner, also a Jewish scholar, says, 'In its entirety this ideal was never realized, but in its essentials it was realized in the period of the Second Temple, when the high priests ruled' (Joseph Klausner, *The Messianic Idea in Israel from Its Beginning to the Completion of the Mishnah* [trans. W. F. Stinespring; New York: Macmillan, 1955] 131).

128. Klausner does not consider the priestly background of Ezekiel to be the reason for the ritualistic descriptions. Cf. Klausner, *The Messianic Idea* 123.

129. 'Uncleanness had thus a greater infectious power than holiness', says S. R. Driver, quoted in Cashdam, *The Twelve Prophets* 262.

130. David R. Hildebrand, 'Temple Ritual: A Paradigm for Moral Holiness in Haggai II 10–19', *VT* 39 (1989) 155.

131. Dumbrell, *Covenant and Creation* 11.

132. Gerhardus Vos, *Biblical Theology: Old and New Testaments* (Grand Rapids: Eerdmans, repr. 1959).

133. Quoting the words of Mowinckel, Thompson says, 'This is what one would expect from a writer with so profound an understanding of sin as Yahwist. Mowinckel rightly says that the early chapters of Genesis show that "the sinfulness of man is a fact which must be taken into account in real life" and enable the readers to see "why the latter temple rites of expiation are necessary." This does not prove, of course, that sacrifices for the expiation of sin were offered in the time of the Yahwist, but the above investigation makes it probable that they were, or at least that the fellowship theory is a too simple explanation of early Israelite sacrifice' (Thomson, 'Tabernacle', 62).

134. Several elements of worship are listed by Rowley, *Worship* 256–271.

135. On this, cf. *ibid.* 84–86.

136. On this, cf. Moshe Greenberg, *Biblical Prose Prayer* (Berkeley/Los Angeles/London: Univ. of California Press, 1983) 5.

137. Cf. Rowley, *Worship* 113, 119, 138, etc.

138. de Vaux, *Ancient Israel* 271.

139. *Ibid.* 271–273.

NOTES TO CHAPTER THREE

1. R. Allen and G. Borror, *Worship: Rediscovering the Missing Jewel* (Portland: Multnomah, 1982). The idea that 'worship is the missing jewel of the evangelical church' was first expressed by A. W. Tozer.

2. W. Nicholls, *Jacob's Ladder: The Meaning of Worship* (Ecumenical Studies in Worship No. 4; London: Lutterworth, 1958) 9.

3. R. P. Martin, *The Worship of God: Some Theological, Pastoral and Practical Reflections* (Grand Rapids: Eerdmans, 1982) 4.

4. J. E. Burkhart, *Worship. A Searching Examination of the Liturgical Experience* (Philadelphia: Westminister, 1982) 17.

5. This point is made quite strongly by I. H. Marshall, 'How far did the early Christians *worship* God?' *Churchman* 99 (1985) 216–229 and A. Boyd Luter Jr., ' "Worship" as service: the New Testament Usage of *latreuo*', *Criswell Theological Review* 2 (1988) 335–344.

6. P. W. Hoon, *The Integrity of Worship* (Nashville: Abingdon, 1971) 17. Cf. also pp. 31–2. Nevertheless, his own study proceeds on the basis of the traditional understanding because he admits that a radical new mind-set is required to deal effectively with such biblical insights in relation to liturgical thinking! The aim of this chapter is to encourage and develop such a mind-set with regard to this vitally important topic.

7. Cf. H. Greeven, *TDNT* 6.758–763 for a brief discussion of the etymology of this word and its usage prior to New Testament times. I have explored the use of such terminology in Old and New Testaments more fully in *Engaging with God: A Biblical Theology of Worship* (Leicester: Apollos, 1992/Grand Rapids: Eerdmans, 1993), chapter 2.

8. The root is *h-w-y* ('curl up'), rather than *š-h-w* ('sink down, subside'), as older scholars supposed. Cf. M. I. Gruber, *Aspects of Nonverbal Communication in the Ancient Near East* (Studia Pohl 12/1; Rome: Biblical Institute, 1980) 90–5, and H. D. Preuss, *TDOT* 4.249–250. The other Hebrew verbs rendered by *proskynein* are noted by H. Greeven, *TDNT* 6.760.

9. When other verbs denoting bowing or kneeling are absent from the context and there are no adverbial phrases suggesting physical movement, the more general and abstract sense of 'worship' may be understood. In such cases the offering of sacrifice regularly appears to be the means by which homage is paid to God (e.g., Gen. 22:5 [compare v. 2]; 1 Sam. 15:25, 30 and Jer. 7:2 [compare v. 21]).

10. A number of psalms contain the promise that *the nations* will one day acknowledge the Lord and will come *together* and bow down before him (e.g. Pss. 22:28, 30 [EVV 22:27, 29]; 86:9). This reflects the prophetic view of the future, with its

focus on Jerusalem as the divine sanctuary to which the nations must come in pilgrimage (e.g., Isa. 2:1–3): the Lord will gather the remnant of Israel together as one, to honour him on his holy mountain in Jerusalem (Isa. 27:12–13) and all humankind will come and 'bend over' before him and thus submit to him (Isa. 66:23; cf. 45:23).

11. Cf. G. Kendrick, *Worship* (Eastbourne: Kingsway, 1984), 23–4, who follows the misleading argument of H. Schönweiss and C. Brown, *NIDNTT* 2.875–6. Whether or not the compound verb ever meant 'to come towards to kiss (the hand)' remains a matter of scholarly debate. Old Testament usage, rather than any supposed etymology, must be the interpreter's guide.

12. The term basically meant serving for a wage (*latron*) or for a reward. However, in non-biblical literature the word group was more often than not used in connection with slavery, rather than hired employment. Cf. H. Strathmann, *TDNT* 4. 58–62.

13. There are about ninety occasions when *latreuein* is employed in the LXX, seventy of which are in Exodus, Deuteronomy, Joshua and Judges. In each case, religious service is implied by the context and it is this usage that is mostly followed and adapted by New Testament writers. The verb *douleuein* is generally employed in these books where the reference is to a master-servant relationship in the human sphere. In the rest of the Old Testament, where *latreuein* occurs very rarely, *douleuein* does double service for both the religious and non-religious applications of the same Hebrew verb.

14. W. Eichrodt, *Theology of the Old Testament* (ET, London: SCM, 1961) 1.98.

15. Serving the Lord is a comprehensive term for Israel's relationship with God in Deuteronomy (10:12, 20; 11:13). Bowing down and serving aspects of the creation or other gods is strictly forbidden (Deut. 4:19, 28; 5:9; 7:4, 16; 8:19; 11:16, 28; 28:14) and provisions are made for the removal of every temptation to indulge in idolatry (12:2; 13:1–18; 16:21–17:7; 29:18).

16. As a rule, this verb translates the Hebrew *šērēt* (Piel, 'to minister, serve') when the reference is cultic. When other services or relations are on view, different Greek words are mostly used to render this Hebrew word. Later Jewish literature indicates some movement towards a general figurative application of *leitourgein*. Cf. H. Strathmann, *TDNT* 4. 219–221.

17. The older form of the word is *leitourgein*, indicating that it is a combination of *lēitos* 'concerning the people or national community', and the root *erg*. Cf. H. Strathmann, *TDNT* 4. 215–219, and N. Lewis, '*Leitourgia* and Related Terms', *Greek, Roman & Byzantine Studies* 3 (1960) 175–84, and 6 (1965) 227–30.

18. R. Banks, *Jesus and the Law in the Synoptic Tradition* (SNTS MS 28; Cambridge: University Press, 1975) 107 (my emphasis). Note particularly his conclusions (pp 237–263). D. J. Moo ('Jesus and the Authority of the Mosaic Law', *JSNT* 20 [1984] 5–6) rightly observes that, although Jesus appears to be faithful to the written law, it is impossible to infer from this that he wished his followers to observe it equally faithfully: 'Jesus' adherence to the written law *could* simply reflect an aspect of the old age which was destined to pass away in the new age.'

19. Cf. R. N. Longenecker, 'The Obedience of Christ in the Theology of the Early Church', in *Reconciliation and Hope* (Fs. L. L. Morris; ed. R. J. Banks; Exeter: Paternoster, 1974) 142–152; S. K. Williams, 'The "Righteousness of God" in Romans', *JBL* 99 (1980) 270–8, and S. K. Williams, 'Again *Pistis Christou*', *CBQ* 49 (1987) 431–7.

20. The word *lytron*, meaning 'payment for loosing' or 'ransom price', does not occur in the Greek translation of Isa. 53:10, but is a possible rendering of the Hebrew word *āšām* in that text; *āšām* can mean 'guilt offering', with or without sacrifice (cf. 1 Sam. 6:3–4, 8, 17), or simply 'payment' (cf. 2 Ki. 12:16 [MT 17]). The Greek noun *lytron* never translates *āšām* in the LXX but is not far from equivalent to the latter meaning. Cf. R. T. France, *Jesus and the Old Testament* (London: Tyndale, 1971) 119–120.

21. The link between Isa. 43:3–4 and 53:10–12 is helpfully argued by S. Kim, *'The "Son of Man"'* *as the Son of God* (WUNT 30: Tübingen: Mohr, 1983) 52–8.

22. I. H. Marshall (*Last Supper and Lord's Supper* [Exeter: Paternoster, 1980] 57–75) reviews the arguments for and against the conclusion that the meal was a Passover celebration, particularly noting the problem of the chronology of John's Gospel. He concludes that 'Jesus held a Passover meal earlier than the official Jewish date, and that he was able to do so as the result of calendar differences among the Jews' (75). For another assessment of the differences between John and the Synoptics at this point cf. W. L. Lane, *The Gospel According to Mark* (London/Grand Rapids: Marshall, Morgan & Scott/Eerdmans, 1974) 498 (especially note 33).

23. Cf. J. Jeremias, *The Eucharistic Words of Jesus* (ET, London: SCM, 1966), 225–6.

24. *Ibid.* 252, 256–62.

25. Although the command to 'do this in remembrance of me' is found only in Lk. 22:19 (after the bread-saying) and in 1 Cor. 11:24–5 (after both sayings), the Passover context certainly suggests the inauguration of a new rite, with a focus on remembering the redemption accomplished by Jesus and rejoicing together in its benefits. Yet if the Passover analogy is to be followed at all, the remembrance meal instituted by Jesus was to be a celebration in a home, loosed entirely from any preliminary ritual at the temple and taking its meaning from his death on the cross. Indeed, in a sense, Jesus' reinterpretation of familiar parts of the ancient paschal liturgy gave a redemptive and eschatological significance to *every future experience of table-fellowship amongst his disciples*.

26. On the basis of Jesus' death, the apostle Paul exhorted the Corinthians 'to keep an ongoing feast of the celebration of God's forgiveness *by holy living*' (G. D. Fee, *The First Epistle to the Corinthians* [NICNT; Grand Rapids: Eerdmans, 1987] 218–219, my emphasis).

27. J. Jeremias, 'This is My Body . . .', *ExpT* 83 (1972) 203.

28. I. H. Marshall, *Last Supper and Lord's Supper* 87. Cf. J. Jeremias, *Eucharistic Words* 198–201, 221–2 and Marshall's critique.

29. I. H. Marshall ('The Development of the Concept of Redemption in the New Testament', in *Reconciliation and Hope*, ed. R. J. Banks, 163) highlights the paradox that redemption terminology can be used to express a 'cost' borne by God and an offering made or 'price' paid to God.

30. RSV and NEB rightly indicate that *en tŏ autou haimati* is to be connected with *hilastērion*, showing that it was by means of his blood/death that Christ was a sacrifice of atonement, rather than with *dia pisteōs* ('through faith in his blood', as in KJV and NIV). Cf. C. E. B. Cranfield, *A Critical and Exegetical Commentary on the Epistle to the Romans* (ICC; Edinburgh: Clark, 1975–9) 1.210–211.

31. Cf. Cranfield, *Romans* 1.214–218, for a helpful discussion of the issues. He suggests that the absence of the definite article before *hilastērion* in Rom. 3:25 is an argument against identifying Christ as the anti-type of the mercy seat. Furthermore, 'the mercy-seat would surely be more appropriately regarded as a type of the Cross' (215).

32. Translation of M. Barth, *Ephesians 4–6* (AB 34A; Garden City, NY: Doubleday, 1974) 557–560. Even though *thysia* regularly denoted animal sacrifices and *prosphora* other types of offerings, it is possible that *prosphoran kai thysian* is a hendiadys ('sacrificial offering'), with the second term defining more specifically the meaning of the first.

33. J. R. Schaefer, 'The Relationship between Priestly and Servant Messianism in the Epistle to the Hebrews', *CBQ* 30 (1968) 382. He shows how Hebrews goes beyond Jewish hopes for the ideal priest to come.

34. Cf. D. G. Peterson, *Hebrews and Perfection* (SNTSMS 47; Cambridge: University Press, 1982) 113–116. G. Schrenk (*TDNT* 3.276) rightly observes that in Hebrews 'the crucifixion belongs to the high-priestly office of Christ as well as his

present rule in the sanctuary. His office comprises both the penetrating movement of his saving action and the lofty calm of his constant giving.'

35. Despite the attempt of various commentators to draw parallels here with Platonic idealism, particularly as it is expressed in the writings of Philo of Alexandria, our writer's distinction between the earthly and heavenly is *eschatologically controlled*, rather than philosophically inspiried. Cf. D. G. Peterson, *Hebrews and Perfection* 131–2. The heavenly sanctuary is not a part of the heavenly topography but a way of describing the presence of God (cf. 9:24).

36. The neuter *meizon* in Matt. 12:6 is best taken as a reference to the *person* of Jesus, since that is the meaning of the neuter expressions in the comparisons with Jonah and Solomon in 12:41–2. For a discussion of alternative interpretations see D. A. Carson, 'Matthew', *EBC* 8.281–2.

37. Despite the fact that the gathering of the whole community (*ekklēsia*) to make judgments in such matters is mentioned in v. 17, it is the agreement of two or three that assures the presence of Christ in vv. 19–20. Cf. J. D. M. Derrett, ' "Where two or three are convened in my name . . .": a sad misunderstanding', *ExpT* 91 (1979–80) 83–6.

38. See above, n.10.

39. For a different way of expressing the fulfilment of that same Old Testament hope see Rev. 21:3. In the symbolism of the new Jerusalem, 'coming down out of heaven from God', the point is made that God will locate himself personally and corporately in believers and the community of the new age.

40. Jesus' rebuke to those who sold doves recalls the prophecy of Zech. 14:21 ('there shall no longer be a trader in the house of the Lord of hosts on that day') and suggests that Jesus was taking action to bring about the fulfilment of that prophetic vision, in which God would be glorified by the pure worship of his people. Cf. R. H. Hiers, 'The Purification of the Temple: Preparation for the Kingdom of God', *JBL* 90 (1971) 82–90.

41. John 5–10 is dominated by Jesus' actions and discourses on the occasion of several Jewish feasts, suggesting that in some way he offers a replacement to them all.

42. R. Bultmann (*The Gospel of John: A Commentary* [ET, Oxford: Blackwell, 1971] 127–8. 6) rightly argues that it is impossible that the body of Christ in Jn. 2:19 should refer to the community of believers in a Pauline sense, since the object of the two verbs 'destroy' and 'raise' must be one and the same.

43. R. Bultmann (*John* 190, cf. n. 4) rightly argues that 'neither Jews nor Greeks were in need of enlightenment about the superiority of a spiritual form of worship over a cultic form of worship.' Cf. n. 64 below.

44. When Jesus says here literally 'an hour is coming and now is' the meaning is that the anticipated effects of Jesus' 'hour' upon his disciples are beginning to be felt (cf. 5:25; 16:32). Cf. R. E. Brown, *The Gospel According to John I-XII* (AB 29: Garden City, NY: Doubleday, 1966) 517–518.

45. The word *alēthinos* is used in the Fourth Gospel to contrast OT types with NT realities. Thus Jesus is the '*true* light' (1:9), 'the *true* bread' (6:32) and 'the *true* vine' (15:1). Cf. R. E. Brown, *John I-XII*, 500–1.

46. R. E. Brown, *John I-XII*, 178–9. However, G. R. Beasley-Murray (*John* [WBC 36; Waco: Word, 1987] 60) rightly suggests that we should interpret Jesus as 'both the living water and he who *gives* water of life to believers.'

47. The expression 'God is Spirit' in Jn. 4:24 does not define God's essential nature but his mode of action and working with us (so Bultmann, *John*, 191–2). Consequently, there can be no true relationship between man and God 'unless it first be grounded in God's dealing with man.'

48. The prostration of the Magi appears from the context to be *homage paid to royalty* rather than the worship of deity. Presumably the evangelist intended his readers to discern that this homage had a greater significance than the visitors from the East could have imagined.

49. Against R. H. Gundry (*Matthew: A Commentary on his Literary and Theological Art* [Grand Rapids: Eerdmans, 1982] 139), it is reading too much into the terminology at this stage of the Gospel to suggest that Matthew views this as worship. The developing recognition of Jesus' divine sonship in Matthew's presentation comes at certain obvious and significant moments.

50. The words 'but some doubted' in 28:17 indicate that there were still some for whom the move from unbelief and fear to faith and joy was a hesitant one. Cf. the discussion of alternatives by D. A. Carson, 'Matthew', 593–4. On the significance of obeisance to Jesus for Christology see C. F. D. Moule, *The Origin of Christology* (Cambridge: University Press, 1977) 175–6.

51. Note, however, the significant response of Simon to Jesus in the call narrative of Lk 5:1–11, where he 'fell down at Jesus' knees' (v. 8), acknowledging himself to be a sinner in the presence of an extraordinary manifestation of the power and presence of God. However, in the progression of Luke's narrative this is not yet a confession of the divinity of Christ.

52. G. W. H. Lampe, 'The Holy Spirit in the Writings of St Luke', in *Studies in the Gospels: Essays in Memory of R. H. Lightfoot* (ed. D. E. Nineham; Oxford: Blackwell, 1957) 162. Lampe gives further references to show how the bestowal of the Spirit was a primary characteristic of the age of final redemption in Jewish expectation.

53. On the preaching of the resurrected Christ as the centre of true worship for the nations, cf. R. F. O'Toole, 'Paul at Athens and Luke's Notion of Worship', *RB* 89 (1982) 185–197.

54. Since calling upon the name of the Lord Jesus brings salvation (e.g. Acts 22:16), it is not surprising that Christians can be virtually defined as those who call on this name (Acts 9:14,21; cf. 1 Cor. 1:2). Furthermore, it is not surprising to discover that those who call upon the name of the Lord Jesus for salvation continue to call upon him in prayer (e.g., Acts 7:59–60; 9:10–17 [where v.17 shows that Jesus is the Lord addressed]; cf. 2 Cor. 12:8–10; 1 Thess. 3:11–13; 2 Thess. 2:16–17). Cf. R. P. Martin, 'Some Reflections on New Testament Hymns', in *Christ the Lord: Studies in Christology Presented to Donald Guthrie* (ed. H. H. Rowdon; IVP: Leicester, 1982) 37–49; and R. T. France, 'The Worship of Jesus: a Neglected Factor in Christological Debate?', *ibid.* 17–36.

55. Josephus (*Antiquities* 14.4.3) indicates that public sacrifices were offered in the temple 'twice daily, in the early morning and *about the ninth hour*.' It is specious to argue that the early Christians used the temple only for prayer and not for sacrifice, considering the close connection between the two aspects of this daily ritual at the temple. If they had wanted to make a complete break with the Jewish sacrificial system they would have had to absent themselves from the afternoon sacrifice completely. Cf. Acts 21:20–6.

56. E. Franklin (*Christ the Lord: A Study in the Purpose and Theology of Luke-Acts* [London: SPCK, 1975] 78) rightly comments that, for Luke, 'the remade Israel does not turn aside from the old which still has claims upon her. The relationship is still open-ended. Though there may be little positive hope that Israel as a whole will repent, the relationship is not closed and Christianity has not turned aside from its source.'

57. *Ibid.* 102–3.

58. Luke has the Jews at Corinth charge Paul with 'persuading the people to worship God (*sebesthai ton theon*) in ways contrary to the law' (Acts 18:13), referring not only to what went on in Christian meetings but also to the whole way in which Paul taught that the Gentiles could be related to God. Similarly, he has Paul describing his Christian life and ministry in broad terms as a way of worshipping or serving the God of Israel (24:14; 27:23, using the verb *latreuein*). However, these references do not justify the widespread contemporary practice of restricting the notion of worship to what goes on in church.

59. So E. Haenchen, *The Acts of the Apostles* (ET, Oxford: Blackwell, 1971) 395f.,

Bo Reicke, 'Some Reflections on Worship in the New Testament', in *New Testament Esays–Studies in Memory of T. W. Manson* (ed. A. J. B. Higgins; Manchester: University Press, 1959) 195; and I. H. Marshall, *Acts* (TNTC; Leicester: IVP, 1980) 215.

60. F. F. Bruce, *The Book of the Acts* (NICNT, 3rd ed.; London/Edinburgh: Marshall, Morgan & Scott, 1962) 261 (my emphasis). Cf. 1 Clement 44:3 and Didache 15:1.

61. This is my own translation, adapting NIV.

62. Cf. B. Reicke and G. Bertram, *TDNT* 5.837–841. Note the use of the same verb in Rom. 6:13,16,19.

63. J. D. G. Dunn, *Romans 9–16* (WBC 38B; Dallas: Word, 1988) 710. Dunn rightly observes that the subsequent dominance of *thysia* in reference to the Eucharist or Lord's Supper in the writings of the Church Fathers represents 'something of a regression from Paul's eschatological perspective.'

64. G. Kittel, *TDNT* 4.142. Note the helpful analysis of relevant texts from various religious and philosophical traditions by E. Ferguson, 'Spiritual Sacrifice in Early Christianity and its Environment', *ANRW* II 23:2, 1152–1189.

65. With the words *logikē latreia* Paul appears to be 'taking up, in quotation marks as it were, a religious slogan common in certain circles at the time. In so doing he completely transforms the saying, while opposing it to those conceptions of spiritual worship so much in vogue at the time. Certainly no more the bloody animal sacrifices of the past, but not either the pure interiority of the Mystic. The Christian's spiritual worship involves an extreme of realism–the bodily offering of himself' (R. Corriveau, *The Liturgy of Life, A Study of the Ethical thought of St. Paul in his letters to the Early Christian Communities* [Studia 25; Bruxelles-Paris/Montréal: Desclée de Brouwer/Les Éditions Bellarmin, 1970] 179)

66. Cranfield, *Romans* 2.605. It is particularly clear from Rom. 1:5; 16:26 that the goal of Paul's ministry, expressed in non-cultic terms, was to bring about and encourage 'the obedience of faith'. This I take to mean 'an obedience motivated by and dependent upon faith' (cf. G. N. Davies, *Faith and Obedience in Romans* (JSNTS 39; Sheffield: JSOT, 1990] 28–30).

67. The verb *latreuein* is used in a quite general way in Acts 24:14; 27:23 and 2 Tim 1:3 to describe Paul's service to the God of Israel, according to the way of Christ. The portrayal of Paul's apostolic ministry in a more specifically cultic way has been investigated by A-M. Denis, 'La fonction apostolique et la liturgie nouvelle en esprit', *RSPT* 42 (1958) 401–436, 617–656. Note the use of *latreuein* to describe *prayer* (probably in connection with the morning and evening sacrifices at the temple) as the lifestyle of a pious Israelite in Lk. 2:37 (cf. Acts 26:7).

68. Cf. Rom. 13:6, where the civic authorities are God's servants (*leitourgoi theou*), and note the discussion of *leitourgein* and related terminology at the beginning of this chapter.

69. Cf. D. W. B. Robinson, 'The Priesthood of Paul in the Gospel of Hope', in *Reconciliation and Hope* (ed. R. J. Banks; Exeter: Paternoster, 1974) 231–245 (especially pp. 231f.). C. E. B. Cranfield (*Romans* 2.755–7) engages in special pleading when he argues that *leitourgos* is used to indicate that Paul fulfils a levitical-type ministry, 'subordinate and auxiliary to that of Christ the Priest'.

70. E. Ferguson ('Spiritual Sacrifice', 1189) shows how early the perspective was lost in early church history: 'What began in Christianity as a metaphorical and spiritual conception was by the age of Constantine ready to be taken literally again. The extension of sacrificial language had come to encompass *the ministry as a special priesthood* (Cyprian), *the table as an altar and buildings as temples* (Eusebius). Sacrifice was increasingly materialized and traditional content was put into the words. Sacrifice became again not only praise and thanksgiving but also *propitiatory* (Origen

and Cyprian). A blending and transformation of conceptions–pagan, philosophical, Jewish and Christian–created a new complex of ideas. We not only use words, but words use us' (my emphasis).

71. Cf. n. 17 above.

72. Since both *thysia* ('sacrifice') and *leitourgia* ('service') stand under the same article in the Greek it is possible to render the expression to mean ('the sacrificial service of your faith').

73. In the Greek world, the verb *spendō* was used to denote the pouring out of 'a portion of drink on the ground or on a cultic site as an offering to the gods.' (O. Michel, *TDNT* 7.528). In the LXX, such terminology was applied to drink offerings or libations of oil that were poured out over or beside a burnt offering with its accompanying cereal offering (e.g., Num. 15:3–10; Lev. 23:13,18). So Paul is indicating that he has a sacrifice to offer in connection with the sacrificial service coming from the faith of the Philippians. Cf. A. M. Denis, 'La fonction apostolique', 631–4.

74. Cf. D. E. Garland, 'The Composition and Unity of Philippians', *NovT* 27 (1985) 169–170. In contrast with those who are designated 'mutilators of the flesh', Christians are the true 'circumcision', 'who glory in Christ Jesus, and who put no confidence in the flesh'. Phil. 3:1 suggests that the notion of inward or spiritual circumcision (cf. Jer. 4:4; Rom. 2:28–9; Col. 2:11, 'not made with hands') is the key to understanding the nature of the worship or service involved.

75. Cf. C. F. D. Moule, 'Sanctuary and Sacrifice in the Church of the New Testament', *JTS* 1 (1950) 29–41 (esp. 39–41).

76. B. F. Westcott, *The Epistle to the Hebrews* (3rd ed.; London: Macmillan, 1914) 110. Again, noting the particular application of *engizein* in the LXX to the ministry of the priests (e.g. Exod. 19:22; Lev. 10:33; Ezek. 42:13; 43:19), Westcott (p189) argues in connection with Heb. 7:19 that all believers are, in virtue of their Christian faith, priests: 'that which was before (in a figure) the privilege of a class has become (in reality) the privilege of all'.

77. The verb *engizein* is used of Abraham's drawing near to God in prayer (Gen. 18:23) and in Eccl. 4:17 (ET 5:1), Hos. 12:7 (ET 12:6), Zeph. 3:2, Hag. 2:15, Isa. 29:13, 58:2, all Israel draws near to God, either in cultic worship or in prayer. Indeed, the people of God are characterised in Ps. 148:14 as 'those who draw near to him' (cf. Jud. 8:27). Similarly, *proserchesthai* is used to describe the action of all Israelites, coming before the Lord in solemn assembly (e.g., Exod. 16:9; 34:32; Num. 10:3–4). In Sir. 1:28,30; 2:1 and Philo (e.g., *Op. Mund.* 144, *Deus Imm.* VIII.161, *Plant.* 64), *proserchesthai* is used in the more general sense of having a relationship with God.

78. D. G. Peterson, *Hebrews and Perfection* 149–153.

79. H. Preisker, *TDNT* 2.331.

80. W. C. van Unnik ('The Christian's Freedom of Speech in the New Testament', *BJRL* 44 [1961–2] 485) argues that this term points to 'the free right to approach God, given in the sacrifice of Christ.'

81. O. Michel, *Der Brief an die Hebräer* (Meyers Kommentar, 7th ed.; Göttingen: Vandenhoeck & Ruprecht, 1975) 346. Cf. 1 Pet. 2:4. Michel (460 n. 2) rightly argues in connection with 12:22ff., 'one draws near to the good things of salvation by first grasping the word of God.'

82. It was noted previously that in the LXX this verb regularly denotes the service or worship of the people in general and that *leitourgein* has special reference to the priestly ministry. In Hebrews this distinction is not strictly observed. Although *latreuein* is used in 9:9 and 10:2 in the normal LXX sense to describe the service of all who sought to draw near to God by means of the Old Testament cult, in 8:5 and 13:10 it apparently refers to the sacrificial ministry of Jewish priests (cf. 9:6, contrast 10:11).

83. The 'acts that lead to death' (*nekrōn ergōn*, literally, 'dead works'), from which the conscience needs cleansing, must include those offences from which a person had to break away in order to become a Christian (cf. 6:1, 'repentance from acts that lead

to death'). Against Westcott (*Hebrews* 146), the writer cannot mean by this 'all the works corresponding with the Levitical system', since these 'works' are not such as would give a person a guilty conscience.

84. F. F. Bruce (*The Epistle to the Hebrews* [London/Edinburgh: Marshall, Morgan & Scott, 1964] 383 n.199) suggests that the present participle in 12:28 *paralambanontes* ('receiving') indicates that 'the people of Christ have not entered into their royal heritage with (Christ), although it is already theirs by promise.' This is consistent with the perspective of 13:14.

85. The expression *echōmen charin* is a common idiom for gratitude and should not be rendered 'let us hold on to (God's) grace.' Cf. H. W. Attridge, *The Epistle to the Hebrews* (Philadelphia: Fortress, 1989) 382 (especially n.69).

86. F. F. Bruce, *Hebrews* 384. According to H. Strathmann (*TDNT* 4.64), the essence of this service or worship is 'a manner of life which is pleasing to God and which is sustained both by gratitude and by a serious sense of responsibility.' Michel (*Hebräer* 477) inclines to the view that thanksgiving itself is the worship acceptable to God but acknowledges the possibility of the alternative understanding. Cf. H. W. Attridge, *Hebrews* 13–14, 384–5, regarding the authenticity of Hebrews 13 and it relation to the rest of the work.

87. Hebrews 12:29 is apparently an allusion to Deut. 4:24 (cf. Deut.9:3; Isa. 33:14), where Moses warned Israel not to pursue idolatry but to remain faithful to the Lord and to serve him alone. This clearly coincides with the emphasis of Hebrews on faithfulness to Jesus and his covenant (e.g., 10:26–39; 12:12–29).

88. Cf. Matt. 10:32 par.; Jn. 9:22; 12:42. O. Michel (*TDNT* 5.207–217) shows the wide range of meanings that can be conveyed by the terms *homologoun* and *homologia* in the New Testament, but unnecessaily restricts Heb. 13:15 to prayer and praise (pp 209–10) and limits the 'confession' of Heb. 3:1; 4:14; 10:23 to 'a firmly outlined, liturgically set tradition by which the community must abide' (p. 215).

89. In 13:12–14 the point is made that the sacrifice of Jesus was offered *outside the city of Jerusalem*, and it is this sacrifice which sanctifies his people. Such an interpretation of the death of Jesus suggests that it 'marks the abolition of the necessity of holy places for sanctification' (H. Koester, ' "Outside the Camp": Hebrews 13.9 –14', *HTR* 55 [1967] 22–25).

90. There is no basis for finding an allusion to 'eucharistic sacrifice' in 13:15. 'Our author is simply not thinking of the eucharist at all . . . It is later associations, not the words of the text itself, which have led commentators to see in this passage a reference to the eucharist' (H. W. Montefiore, *A Commentary on the Epistle to the Hebrews* [BNTC; London: Black, 1964] 248). Cf. R. Williamson, 'The Eucharist and the Epistle to the Hebrews', *NTS* 21 (1974–5) 309–310.

91. 'The new covenant community has a cult that is quite outside the realm of the cultic' (Attridge, *Hebrews* 401).

92. E. Käsemann, 'Worship and Everyday Life. A note on Romans 12', *New Testament Questions of Today* (ET, London: SCM, 1969) 191. He notes the parallel with 1 Pet. 2:5 and argues that the universal priesthood of all believers now appears as 'the eschatological worship of God which puts an end to every other cultus.'

93. Contra J. Jeremias, *Eucharistic Words*, 118–122, followed by I. H. Marshall, *Luke: Historian and Theologian* (Exeter: Paternoster, 1970) 204–6. I have discussed the relevant material from Acts more fully in *Engaging with God*, chap 5.

94. While it is true that the *koinōn-* words in the NT normally mean 'to share with someone in something', and that the terminology is fundamentally used with reference to the joint participation of believers in Christ and the blessings of the new covenant (cf. F. Hauck, *TDNT* 3.804–9), clearly there is a *mutual fellowship of believers that arises from this*. The context of Acts 2:42 suggests that *koinōnia* in the absolute refers to the latter in terms of its practical outworking in generous giving and the sharing of their lives together.

95. J. Behm, *TDNT* 3.730. Taking bread, giving thanks, breaking and distributing

it, was the normal method of saying grace and beginning a meal in Jewish culture. Jesus highlighted the theological significance of eating together as the community of the Messiah by his words spoken in association with these actions at the Last Supper. In the enjoyment of table fellowship they were to remember the basis of their fellowship in his redemptive death and the certainty of their hope of feasting together in the kingdom of God. Cf. n.25 above.

96. When Paul finally broke bread (presumably on behalf of everyone present) it was clearly to initiate an ordinary meal (Acts 20:11). The same could be said for Paul's action in Acts 27:35: he could hardly have been celebrating the Lord's Supper in that context! The adoption of the ancient Palestinian term 'the breaking of bread' as a title for the Lord's Supper is not formally attested until the second century AD (cf. Didache 14:1; Ignatius, *Eph.* 20:2).

97. For detailed discussion of synagogue services and their possible influence on Christian liturgical development, cf. R. T. Beckwith, 'The Jewish Background of Christian Worship', in *The Study of Liturgy* (ed. C. Jones, G. Wainwright, and E. Yarnold; London: SPCK, 1978) 39–51; and R. T. Beckwith, *Daily and Weekly Worship: From Jewish to Christian* (Alcuin/GROW Liturgical Study 1, 2nd ed.; Bramcote: Grove, 1989).

98. The prophetic ministry given to certain members of the Corinthian church required assessment and evaluation, which implied the possibility of challenging and even rejecting such contributions (1 Cor. 14:29; cf. 1 Thes. 5:21–2). This suggests that their prophecy did not carry the weight of being actual 'words from the Lord' in the Old Testament prophetic sense, yet it was distinguishable from other human words in that it was *the result of a revelation* (apokalypsis, v. 30), a prompting of the Spirit of God. Cf. W. A. Grudem, *The Gift of Prophecy in 1 Corinthians* (Lanham/New York/London: University Press of America, 1982) 54–73.

99. Markus Barth (*Ephesians 4–6*, 439) notes that the noun *katartismos*, which occurs only here in the NT, describes 'the dynamic *act* by which persons and things are properly conditioned'. Pastor-teachers in particular have the task of preparing God's people for their work of service (cf. his Comment VI, 477–484).

100. P. Vielhauer, *Oikodome. Aufsätze zum Neuen Testament* (Munich: Kaiser Verlag, 1979) 72. Cf. H. Ridderbos, *Paul: An Outline of his Theology* (ET, Grand Rapids: Eerdmans, 1975) 429–438, where the point is similarly made that edification involves both the *increase* and the *consolidation* of the church.

101. R. Y. K. Fung, 'Some Pauline Pictures of the Church', *EQ* 53 [1981] 95–96.

102. P. T. O'Brien, 'The Church as a Heavenly and Eschatological Entity', in *The Church in the Bible and the World* (ed. D. A. Carson; Grand Rapids/ Baker/ Paternoster, 1987) 111.

103. Translation of C. K. Barrett (*A Commentary on the First Epistle to the Corinthians* [BNTC 2nd ed.; London: Black, 1971] 86), based on the observation that in Plato (*Statesman* 259E, 260A) an *architektōn* contributes knowledge, not manual labour, but also assigns their task to individual workmen.

104. As R. Y. K. Fung ('Pauline Pictures', 101) rightly concludes from the general context. Although Paul asserts in 1 Cor. 6:19 that each individual Christian's body is 'a temple of the Holy Spirit', in 3:16 it is the congregation as the *corporate place of God's dwelling* that is most likely meant (cf. 2 Cor. 6:16; Eph. 2:21–2). Cf. G. D. Fee, *First Corinthians* 147–150.

105. Cf. D. A. Carson, *Showing the Spirit: A Theological Exposition of 1 Corinthians 12–14* (Homebush West/Grand Rapids: Lancer/Baker, 1988) 100–01.

106. So W. Richardson, 'Liturgical Order and Glossalalia in 1 Corinthians 14:26c–33a', *NTS* 32 (1986) 147. Contra E. Schweizer ('The Service of Worship', Int 13 [1959] 404), who overstates his case by arguing that 'Paul never speaks of edifying oneself; he always means edifying the congregation.'

107. R. P. Martin, *The Spirit and the Congregation* (Grand Rapids: Eerdmans, 1984) 70. Martin incorrectly concludes that Paul's *concession* here opposes any

concentration on personal experiences. It is the chapter as a whole that leads to Martin's conclusion.

108. Cf. my article 'Prayer in the Writings of Paul', in *Teach us to Pray: Prayer in the Bible and in the Church* (ed. D. A. Carson; Grand Rapids/Exeter: Baker/Paternoster, 1990).

109. F. Hauck (*TDNT* 3.805) confuses the issue by equating participation in the body and blood of Christ with 'union (sharing) with the heavenly Christ'. At the Supper, 'the participants have fellowship with God as their host because it is his table and he provides the spiritual blessings (cf. 1 Cor. 10:4). But this communion with God is not the same thing as participation in the body and blood of Jesus, and it is not achieved through eating bread and drinking wine in the sense that we somehow partake of Christ or God in so doing' (I. H. Marshall, *Last Supper and Lord's Supper* 123).

110. Cf. H. W. Beyer, *TDNT* 2.760.

111. C. K. Barrett, *First Corinthians* 232. He suggests that *koinōnia* must be translated 'common participation' to bring out its true meaning.

112. G. D. Fee, *First Corinthians* 468.

113. C. K. Barrett, *First Corinthians* 233. It is possible that Paul intended a double reference to the crucified body of Christ and the body of his people, without confusing those entities. Cf. J. A. T. Robinson, *The Body: A Study in Pauline Theology* (London: SCM, 1952) 47f.

114. Cf. B. W. Winter, 'The Lord's Supper at Corinth: An Alternative Reconstruction', *RTR* 37 (1978) 73–82, for the argument that the division was not so much between rich and poor as between 'the secure' (those guaranteed security, and thus food, by reason of membership of a household) and 'the insecure' (those who had no protection from a patron) in the social structure of Roman Corinth. For further discussion of various sociological factors that have been suggested cf. G. D. Fee, *First Corinthians* 533–4, 540–1 (and references).

115. Cf. G. D. Fee, *First Corinthians* 539–540. The holding of a *deipnon* in honour of a god was common in the Greco-Roman world (cf. J. Behm, *TDNT* 2 34–5).

116. J. Jeremias (*Eucharistic Words* 49–50) points out that, at the Passover, the blessing and distribution of the bread came during the meal (cf. Mk. 14:18–22; Lk. 22:17–19). Against the common assumption that there was an ordinary meal at Corinth and then the formal 'Lord's Supper', cf. G. Theissen, *The Social Setting of Pauline Christianity: Essays on Corinth* (ET, Philadelphia: Fortress, 1982) 152–3.

117. G. D. Fee, *First Corinthians* 557. Cf. his discussion of what Paul means by 'not recognizing the body' (pp. 562–4).

118. The verb *ekdechomai* in 11:33 carries its primary meaning of 'receive' here, which it often does in the context of hospitality (hence, 'welcome' or 'entertain'). NIV 'wait for each other' would normally be conveyed by *apekdechomai*. Cf. G. D. Fee, *First Corinthians* 567–8 and B. W. Winter, 'The Lord's Supper', 79–80.

119. H. Ridderbos, *Paul* 481.

120. R. J. Banks (*Paul's Idea of Community: The Early House Churches in their Historical Setting* [Sydney: ANZEA, 1979] 92) overstates the case when he says that it cannot be worship as such but edification that 'marks off their coming together from everything else that they are doing.' This ignores the fact that edification also takes place outside the assembly and that, from one point of view, the purpose of the assembly is also worship.

121. I. H. Marshall ('How far did the early Christians *worship* God?', 226–9) does not take adequate account of this, restricting the notion of worship to *response*, in order to avoid any suggestion that we can benefit God by what we do in church.

122. C. E. B. Cranfield, *Romans* 2.602. But he insists on talking about 'a Christian cultic worship', without justifying the use of such terminology.

123. Note that the writer describes his own work as a 'word of exhortation' (13:22, *logos tēs paraklēseōs*), suggesting that his method of teaching is a model for his readers to copy in their ministry to one another. I have developed this argument in 'The

Ministry of Encouragement', in *God who is Rich in Mercy* (ed. P. T. O'Brien and D. G. Peterson; Sydney/Grand Rapids: Lancer/Baker, 1986) 235–253.

124. P. E. Hughes, *A Commentary on the Epistle to the Hebrews* (Grand Rapids: Eerdmans, 1977) 148.

125. Something of the synagogue pattern may be reflected in the injunction to Timothy to attend to the public reading of scripture, to preaching (*tę paraklēsei*) and to teaching (*tę didaskalią*, 1 Tim. 4:13) and in the guidelines for public prayer in 1 Tim. 2:1–8.

126. R. J. Bauckham ('The Worship of Jesus in Apocalyptic Christianity', *NTS* 27 [1981] 329) notes that the contrast between the two groups of worshippers reaches its climax in the two visions that conclude the work. The vision of the fall of *Babylon* (17:1–19:10) represents the judgment coming upon human society in rebellion against God–the 'prostitute' seducing people away from the worship of the Creator by her corrupt practices. The vision of *Jerusalem* (21:9–22:9) portrays the future of the faithful in terms of a city where God himself dwells (21:22) and where his servants unceasingly do him priestly service (22:3).

127. P. J. J. Botha, 'God, emperor worship and society: Contemporary experiences and the book of Revelation', *Neot* 22 (1988) 97. Cf. K. Hopkins, 'Divine Emperors or the Symbolic Unity of the Roman Empire', in *Conquerors and Slaves* (Cambridge: University Press, 1978) 199 n.3. On the forms of the imperial cult see E. Ferguson, *Backgrounds of Early Christianity* (Grand Rapids: Eerdmans, 1987 164–5.

128. R. H. Mounce, *The Book of Revelation* (NICNT; Grand Rapids: Eerdmans, 1977) 259. The beast out of the earth is a deceiver (cf. v. 14). Elsewhere he is uniformly called the false prophet (16:13; 19:20; 20:10). Mounce suggests that 'in John's day the reference would be either to the local priests of the imperial cult or to the provincial council responsible for enforcing emperor worship throughout Asia.'

129. R. H. Mounce (*Revelation* 33) rightly asserts that 'while the picture of universal enforcement of the imperial cult given in Revelation 13 is a forecast rather than a descriptive account of the conditions under Domitian (AD 81–96), all the elements were present in the final decade of the first century from which a reasonable projection could be made.'

130. R. J. Bauckham, 'The Worship of Jesus', 329.

131. 'This chapter is the most powerful statement of the divinity of Christ in the New Testament, and it receives its power from the praise of God the Creator which precedes it' (J. Sweet, *Revelation* (Pelican Commentaries; London: SCM, 1979, 127).

132. E.g., J. J. O'Rourke, 'The Hymns of the Apocalypse', *CBQ* 30 (1968) 399–409.

133. E.g. L. Mowry, 'Revelation 4–5 and Early Christian Liturgical Usage', *JBL* 71 (1952) 75–84. D. E. Aune ('The Influence of Roman Imperial Court Ceremonial on the Apocalypse of John' *BR* 28 [1983] 5–26) argues persuasively for the influence of the practices of the Roman imperial cult on the visions of the Apocalypse and opposes the view that they reflect Christian liturgical practice.

134. G. Delling, *Worship in the New Testament* (ET, London: Darton, Longman & Todd, 1962) 47. L. Thompson ('Cult and Eschatology in the Apocalypse of John' *JR* 49 [1969] 330–350 [348–9] argues that, since John was writing a book of prophecy, 'he structured the hymnic material so that it would serve a prophetic function, as he knew it in the life of the community.'

135. G. Goldsworthy (*The Gospel in Revelation* [Exeter/ Flemington Markets: Paternoster/Lancer, 1984] 100–112) rightly argues that the hymns are part of 'a framework of explicitly gospel-oriented material which prevents [the Book of the Revelation] from being a piece of purely Judaistic apocalyptic as far as its perception of the end is concerned' (102).

136. G. Delling, *Worship in the New Testament* 45.

137. H. Ridderbos, *Paul* 481. In *Engaging with God* (pp 289–293) I have illustrated what it might be like to put into practice the theological principles illustrated in this chapter.

NOTES TO CHAPTER FOUR

1. The idea is also present in Dr. Hattori's essay, when he sees worship within the context of the covenant (pp. 28–29). Texts that point to the broader conception include Exod. 19:6; Ps. 15; Ps. 24; Micah 6:8

2. Cf. also T. Brienen, *De liturgie bij Johannes Calvijn* (Kampen: De Groot Goudriaan, 1987) 175ff.

3. Cf. Howard G. Hageman, *Pulpit and Table* (London: SCM, 1962) 130.

4. *Calvinism* (Amsterdam-Pretoria: Höveker en Wormser, n.d.) 31. (The lectures were originally given at Princeton, NJ, on 10 October 1898 and following.) Cf. also p. 62: 'A religion confined to the closet, the cell, or the church . . . Calvin abhors.' And p. 62: 'To be sure there is a concentration of religious light and life in the Church, but then in the walls of this church, there are wide open windows, and through these spacious windows the light of the Eternal has to radiate over the whole world.' Cf. also pp. 60–61.

5. *The Confession of 1967* (9.48), in Edward A. Dowey, Jr., *A Commentary on the Confession of 1967 and An Introduction to The Book of Confessions* (Philadelphia; Westminster, 1968) 23.

6. This saying from Psalm 124:8 was originally part of the medieval mass. It was privately said by the priest, who 'whispered it along with his private confession of sin as he entered the sanctuary to celebrate mass. Thus, it was not the beginning of the people's worship.' The words were taken over by Calvin to begin the morning worship of the whole congregation, but we no longer know why he did this. Cf. *Acts* (Grand Rapids: Christian Reformed Publishing House, 1968) 159.

7. In most Presbyterian churches of the same period the liturgy was hardly any different. Most of them followed the instructions given in the *Directory for Public Worship of God*, as issued by the famous Westminster Assembly (1645). This Directory shows the same austerity. It mentions only the following elements as necessary for a worship service: Scripture reading, prayer before the sermon, the sermon itself, prayer after the sermon and congregational singing. As late as 1929 the Act of Union declared that the Westminster Directory remains a normative standard for worship for the Church of Scotland: see John M. Barkley, *The Worship of the Reformed Church* (London: Lutterworth, 1966) 37. Cf. also J. H. Nichols, *Corporate Worship in the Reformed Tradition* (Philadelphia: Westminster, 1968). Before 1645 the Scottish service was equally austere: see W. McMillan, *The Worship of the Scottish Reformed Church, 16550–1638* (London: James Clarke, n.d. [but probably published in 1931 or 1932]) 127ff.

8. Cf. Biesterveld and H. H. Kuyper, *Kerkelijk Handboekje* (Kampen: J. H Bos, 1905) 13ff.

9. Cf. A. C. Barnard, *Die eredienst* (Pretoria: NG Boekhandel, 1981) 366f, and E. van der Schoot, *Hervormde Eredienst*'s (Gravenhage: Boekencentrum, 1950) 92ff.

10. Cf. Barnard, *De eredienst* 367.

11. Barnard, *De eredienst* 368.

12. Cf. Nichols, *Corporate Worship in the Reformed Tradition* 82.

13. Cf. Barnard, *De eredienst* 370.

14. Hageman, *Pulpit and Table* 37.

15. Cf. A. F. N. Lekkerkerker, 'Gereformeerde Liturgiek in de zestiende eeuw', *NTT* 6 (1951–52) 73.

16. *Acts*, 150.

17. This was the only service in the vernacular in the Middle Ages and naturally would strongly appeal to Zwingli.

18. Cf. E. Weismann, 'Der Predigtgottesdienst und die verwandte Formen', in *Leitourgia* (Kassel: Johannes Stauda Verlag) 3.22ff.; Nichols, *Corporate Worship* 71ff.

19. Hageman, *Pulpit and Table* 20.

20. Bard Thompson, *Liturgies of the Western Church* (Cleveland and New York: World Publishing Company, 1961) 143.

21. Cf. Barnard, *De eredienst* 293f.

22. Cf. Barnard, *De eredienst* 394ff.

23. Cf. Hageman, *Pulpit and Table* 23f.

24. Cf. the reissue (in ET) of the first edition of the *Institutes*, ed. Ford Lewis Battles (Atlanta: John Knox, 1975) 154, 166.

25. Cf. Brienen, *De liturgie bij Johannes Calvijn* 18ff.; Barnard, *De eredienst* 324ff.

26. J. H. Van der Laan ('De zondagmorgendienst van de Gereformeerde Kerken in Nederland', GTT [1983] 236f.) is doubtful whether the ancient church always had a worship service with both preaching and the Lord's Supper. For evidence he appeals to the famous letter of Pliny to the Emperor Trajan which speaks of a meeting with hymn singing before dawn and a meeting with a meal in the evening. It is questionable, however, whether this letter can bear the weight of this appeal. Pliny gives only a summary description of what happens in the Christian assemblies, which, moreover, is based not on his own experience but on what he has from hearsay.

27. W. D. Maxwell, *An Outline of Christian Worship* (London: Oxford University Press, 1963) 112. Cf. also *Acts*, 151f., where Bucer's and Calvin's Strasbourg liturgies are set side by side.

28. Cf. Barkley, *The Worship of the Reformed Church* 17.

29. Cf. Calvin's own statement, as given in Geddes MacGregor, *Corpus Christi* (London: MacMillan, 1959) 53f., and the description of a meeting of the French congregation in Strasbourg by a contemporary French student in Hageman, *Pulpit and Table* 27f.

30. Cf. Nichols, *Corporate Worship* 38ff.

31. Hageman, *Pulpit and Table* 16.

32. Hageman, *Pulpit and Table* 35.

33. Cf. Van der Schoot, *Hervormde Eredienst* 77ff.; Barnard, *De eredienst* 327ff.; Brienen, *op. cit.*, 132ff.

34. Cf. Nichols, *Corporate Worship* 75ff.

35. Van der Schoot, *Hervormde Eredienst* 84. Cf. W. F. Dankbaar, *Marten Micron. De Christelicke Ordinancien der Nederlandtse Ghemeinten te* (London, 1956). It was not a literal translation; he introduced some of his own ideas as well.

36. Cf. *Acts*, 152; Barnard, *De eredienst* 361.

37. Brienen, *De liturgie* 258.

38. *Ibid* 257ff.

39. Cf. *Acts*, 153. Cf. Nichols, *Corporate Worship* 78f.

40. Cf. the decision of the Synod of Middelburg, 1581, that such absolution was unnecessary, since the sermon is the proclamation of the forgiveness and retention of sin.

41. Hageman, *Pulpit and Table* 33. Cf. also Barnard,. *De eredienst* 364f.

42. Cf. McMillan, *The Worship of the Scottish Reformed Church, 1550–1638* 129, 136ff.

43. Cf. also the article on 'Liturgie' by F. de Jong, *Christelijke Encyclopedie* (Kampen: Kok, 1929) 4.468; Hageman, *Pulpit and Table* 33; Van der Schoot, *Hervormde Eeredienst* 111.

44. Cf. *Acts*, 170.

45. Cf. Van der Schoot, *Hervormde Eeredienst* 117ff., 123ff.; Hageman, *Pulpit and Table* 102ff. Kuyper wrote a volume of over 550 pages, called *Onze Eeredienst* (Kampen: Kok, 1911) containing 80 articles he had written in his paper *De Heraut*. When he became prime minister he had to stop work on the subject. After his premiership he wrote another 50 chapters. Together they were published in *Onze Eeredienst*.

46. For the full text, see Hageman, *Pulpit and Table* 104ff.

47. Cf. for this survey, Van der Laan, 'De zondagmorgendienst', 217–238.

48. Cf. I. John Hesselink, *On Being Reformed* (Ann Arbor: Servant, 1983) 23.

49. Cf. *Acts*, 64f. (the synodical decision), and 157ff. (an exposition of the liturgy itself by the committee).

50. Cf. *Acts*, 150.

51. Cf. Thompson, 197ff.

52. Quoted from F. Wendel, *Calvin* (London: Collins, 1963). Cf. *Institutes*, ed. by John T. McNeill (London: SCM, 1961) 2.1208 n. 50. Here the French edition of 1950 is quoted.

53. From the context it is clear that Calvin has the main Sunday service in mind here, a service in which people should both hear the sermon and partake of the Lord's Supper.

54. Calvin suggests that it may be due to a decree by Zephyrenus, who was Pope from 198–217, but he also believes that this Pope meant something quite different from what later on was decided by the Fourth Lateran Council, which made it into a law to have communion once a year. See also McNeil, *Institutes* 2.1422 n. 41.

55. Even a monthly celebration, which Calvin and Farel advocated in the *Ordonnances*, did not meet with the approval of the city council.

56. *Acts*, 152.

57. Barkley, *The Worship of the Reformed Church* 13.

58. This is not to deny that from Carolingian times a general confession was already known. After the year 1000 this confession entered the mass, being included after the sermon as an expanded *confiteor* said in the vernacular and thus wholly directed at the mass. Cf. J. G. Davies, *A Select Liturgical Lexicon* (London: Lutter-worth, 1965) 57, s.v, Confession.

59. Calvin adopted his words from Bucer, and his prayer of confession was afterwards used in most of the Reformed churches on the continent. We even find them, in paraphrased form, in Cranmer's *Book of Common Prayer*.

60. Cf. Nichols, *Corporate Worship* 41.

61. Hageman, *Pulpit and Table* 120. For this reason he also pleads for congregational responses to almost every part of the service. A Service Book should not be seen as a manual and guidebook for the minister only, but it should be present in all the pews, so that the members of the congregation can read or sing the responses, whenever required (p. 121).

62. Cf. Nichols, *Corporate Worship* 34.

63. *Ibid.* 35. Cf. also Brienen, *De liturgie* 194–211.

64. In the very first French psalter, published during his years in Strasbourg, we also find some 'canticles', i.e. metrical versions of the Decalogue and of the Song of Simeon. In a later edition we also find the hymn: 'I greet Thee, my sure Redeemer', attributed by some to Calvin himself (cf. Brienen, *De liturgie* 200).

65. Nichols, *Corporate Worship* 36f.

66. Cf. Nichols, *Ibid* 37.

67. Hesselink, *On Being Reformed* 27.

68. Cf. Brienen, *De liturgie* 164.

69. For the text see the *Acta* of Middelburg 1965, but also G. N. Lammens, 'De vooronderstellingen van de eredienst', in *'Houdt dan de lofzang gaande . . .'*, Opstellen aangeboden aan prof. dr. G. N. Lammens (Kampen: Kok, 1983) 15ff. (Lammens was the reporter of the committee).

70. Cf. *Acts*, 155ff.

71. Lammens, 'De vooronderstellingen van de eredienst', 22f.

72. *Acts*, 156.

73. Herman Ridderbos, *Paul: An Outline of His Theology* (Grand Rapids: Eerdmans, 1975) 481.

NOTES TO CHAPTER FIVE

1. The Willow Creek Community church in the suburbs of Chicago, Illinois, produces a Sunday morning programme designed to attract, entertain, and instruct people who have no background in (or tolerance for) Christian worship. Drama plays an important part in the programme. Churches following this model often arrange meetings for worship at another time: perhaps Sunday afternoon, or a week-night evening.

2. As J. Gresham Machen clearly demonstrated in the 'Fundamentalist-Modernist' controversy of the twenties. See his *Christianity and Liberalism* (NY: Macmillan, 1923).

3. J.-D. Benoit, *Liturgical Renewal: Studies in Catholic and Protestant Developments on the Continent* (Studies in Ministry and Worship; ed. G W. H Lampe; London, SCM, 1958) 71.

4. *Constitution on the Liturgy* n.37, cited in George Fitzgerald, *Handbook of the Mass* (NY: Paulist, 1982) 33–34

5. *Westminster Confession of Faith* I:6.

6. Robert G. Rayburn, *O Come. Let Us Worship: Corporate Worship in the Evangelical Church* (Grand Rapids: Baker, 1980).

7. Klaas Runia's description (chap.4 of this volume) of the similarity of the order of worship in the Dutch Reformed churches in Holland, the United States and South Africa at a time when no particular order was required illustrates the force of custom in following a pattern of worship. The Presbyterian churches followed a pattern that was similar.

8. David Peterson might seem to suggest this when he says, 'If Christians are meant to worship God in every sphere of life, it cannot be worship as such that brings them to church' [p. 82]. In a footnote, however, he recognizes that the same argument could be used against meeting for edification, and acknowledges that 'from one point of view' the purpose of the assembly is not only edification, but also worship [n. 120]. More emphatically, he points out that prayer, praise, and participation in the Lord's Supper are no less important than evangelism, benevolence, and service in life p.83. If his statements about the place of public worship seem to come as concessions, it is evidently because he wants to show the emphasis of the New Testament to correct common misunderstandings.

9. See my chapter, 'The Biblical Theology of the Church', in D. A. Carson, ed., *The Church in the Bible and the World* (Exeter: Paternoster, 1987) 13–24.

10. David Peterson points out the scope of these verses, as connected with Heb. 13:15,16. Certainly the author of Hebrews has in view worship that includes deeds as well as words. Yet festival assemblies were a central part of Israel's worship: to be told that we approach to the festival assembly of heaven, and enter the very presence of God (12:23), surely implies offering the fruit of our lips in corporate praise (cf. Heb. 10:19–25).

11. The *Directory* of the Westminster Assembly uses this language in its directions for the prayer before the sermon:

> And because we have been unprofitable hearers in times past, and now cannot of ourselves receive, as we should, the deep things of God, the mysteries of Jesus Christ, which require a spiritual discerning; to pray, that the Lord, who teacheth to profit, would graciously please to pour out the Spirit of grace, together with the outward means thereof, causing us to attain such a measure of the excellency of the knowledge of Christ Jesus our Lord, and, in him, of the things which belong to our peace, that we may account all things but as dross in comparison of him; and that we, tasting the first-fruits of the glory that is to be revealed, may long for a more full and perfect communion with him, that where he is, we may be also, and enjoy the fulness of those joys and pleasures which are at his right hand for evermore.

12. Hughes Oliphant Old, *Worship* (Guides to the Reformed Tradition; Atlanta: John Knox, 1985) 68f.

13. Old, *Worship* 75.

14. *WCF* I:6

15. See the discussion in E. P. Clowney, 'Distinctive Emphases in Presbyterian Church Polity', in *Pressing Toward the Mark: Essays Commemorating Fifty Years of the Orthodox Presbyterian Church* ed. C. G. Dennison and R. C. Gamble (Philadelphia: Orthodox Presbyterian Church, 1986) 100–105.

16. WCF XX:2. Note the semicolon after 'Word' and the reading '*if* matters of faith, or worship'. From the S. W. Carruthers edition of the original manuscript of the Confession written by Cornelius Burges in 1646.

17. WCF XXI:1

18. Calvin makes an important qualification here. Even though such proper laws have to be observed, they do not in themselves bind the conscience. 'For all obligation to observe laws looks to the general purpose, but does not consist in the things enjoined' (*Inst.* IV,x,5. A speed limit is not in itself a matter of conscience, but the purpose to protect human life.

19. J. I. Packer, 'The Puritan Approach to Worship', in *Diversity in Unity* (Papers read at the Puritan and Reformed Studies Conference, December, 1963), 4,5.

20. John Calvin, *Tracts and Treatises on the Doctrine and Worship of the Church*, vol. 2 (Edinburgh: Calvin Translation Society, 1849; reprint, Grand Rapids: Erdmans, 1958) 118: cf. p. 122. See also Article 32 of the *Belgic Confession*.

21. *Inst.* IV, x, 8 (McNeill, Battles v.2, p. 1187)

22. *Inst.* IV, x, 7.

23. *Inst.* IV, x, 8

24. *Inst.* IV, x, 27.

25. *Inst.* IV, x, 28.

26. *Inst.* IV, x, 29.

27. *Inst.* IV, x, 30.

28. For a different assessment see Ralph J. Gore, Jr., *The Pursuit of Plainness: Rethinking the Puritan Regulative Principle of Worship* (Ann Arbor, MI: University Microfilms International, 1990).

29. John Knox, *True and False Worship* (Dallas; Presbyterian Heritage Publications, 1988)2. (reprinted from *A Vindication of the Doctrine that the Sacrifice of the Mass Is Idolatry* [550] as published in David Laing, ed., *The Works of John Knox* [Edinburgh: James Thin, 1895] 29–70).

30. *Ibid.* 4.

31. Among the passages referred to by Knox: Jn. 10:5; 18:37; Eph. 2:20; Rev. 2:24,25; 1 Tim. 4:1–3; 1 Cor. 11:23.

32. Note the comments of K. L. Schmidt, although he does not indicate the Old Testament background of Paul's statement (*TDNT* 3. 159). For a differing interpretation see Peter T. O'Brien, *Colossians, Philemon* (WBC; Waco: Word Books, 1982) 142f.

33. The Westminster Divines cited Colossians 2:23. Their interpretation is supported by the NIV translation: 'Such regulations indeed have an appearance of wisdom, with their self-imposed worship, their false humility and their harsh treatment of the body, but they lack any value in restraining sensual indulgence.'

34. *Inst.* IV, x, 30.

35. Although in a service of dedication for a new organ, the instrument may be elevated to an element of worship – or almost a participant!

36. James Hastings Nichols, *Corporate Worship in the Reformed Tradition* 57.

37. As in an historical novel by a descendant of one such galley slave, Pierre Chamson, *La Superbe*.

38. Nichols, *Corporate Worship* 59.

39. Note the assurance of 1 Peter 1:3–9. God's elect, begotten by God's power in

the resurrection of Christ, have the inheritance kept for them, and they are kept for the inheritance. It is by faith that they are kept, and that they may be kept believing, God purifies their faith by trials, as gold in a furnace.

40. 'the kingdom of heaven belongs to such as these' (Matt. 19:14; Mk. 10:14; Lk. 18:16).

41. Nichols, *Corporate Worship* 103.

42. *Ibid.*

43. See John M. Barkley, *Worship of the Reformed Church* (Ecumenical Studies in Worship, No. 15; Atlanta: John Knox, 1967) 16.

44. Old, *Worship* 152–155.

45. See the works cited by Old and Nichols, and especially Barkley.

46. Reprinted with the title, *The Presbyterian Liturgies: Historical Sketches* (Grand Rapids: Baker, 1957).

47. David Peterson argues forcefully for this principle in chap. 3 of this volume.

NOTES TO CHAPTER SIX

1. Southey seems to have coined this phrase in the preface to his *Lives of the British Admirals* (1833–40). One of the earliest continental admirers of the Prayer Book was Isaac Casaubon (1559–1614); one of the latest is Samuel Leuenberger (see his *Archbishop Cranmer's Immortal Bequest* [ET: Grand Rapids: Eerdmans, 1990]). The influence of the Prayer Book in the Free Churches has been studied by A. E. Peaston, *The Prayer Book Tradition in the Free Churches* (London: James Clarke, 1964).

2. It has sometimes been held that Cranmer's sacramental doctrine was Zwinglian rather than Calvinistic. For the evidence against this view, see Peter Brooks, *Thomas Cranmer's Doctrine of the Eucharist* (London: Macmillan, 1965).

3. Anglican Evangelicals, such as John Wesley and Charles Simeon, are among those who have paid glowing tribute to the spiritual value of the Prayer Book liturgy in particular. With the English Bible, it has had a profound influence on the English language and English literature, so its appeal has undoubtedly been very widespread among Anglican worshippers.

4. From C. Jones, G. Wainwright, and E. Yarnold, ed., *The Study of Liturgy* (London: SPCK, 1978) 73–74, slightly amended.

5. See H. I. Bailey, *The Liturgy Compared with the Bible* (London: SPCK, 1845).

6. That Cranmer intended it as such (contrary to what has often been claimed), and always planned a further stage, see *The Study of Liturgy* 71–72.

7. See his much-quoted book *The Shape of the Liturgy* (London: Dacre Press, 1945).

8. See *An Australian Prayer Book, for use together with the Book of Common Prayer, 1662* (Sydney: Standing Committee of General Synod, 1978).

NOTES TO CHAPTER SEVEN

1. R. D. Preus, *NDT* 404–406.

2. J. Atkinson, *NDT* 401–404.

3. See Yoshiaki Hattori, chap.2 of this book, p.48.

4. See David Peterson, chap.3 of this book, p.52.

5. Graham Kendrick, ed., *Ten Worshipping Churches* (Bromley: MARC Europe, 1986) 8.

6. *LW* 41.233–235.

7. Cf. Einar Molland, *Konfesjonskunnskap* (Oslo, 1961) 181–221. *ET Christendom:*

The Christian Churches, Their Doctrines, Constitutional Forms and Ways of Worship (London, 1959). [Subsequent page numbers are to the Norwegian original.] Cf. Carl Fredrik Wisløff, *Kristne Kirkesamfunn, Reformasjonskirkene* (Oslo, 1988) 51–98; idem, *Martin Luthers Teologi* (Oslo, 1983) 11–40. Wisløff is one of the outstanding scholars of Lutheran Reformation theology. Cf. my article on Wisløff in *NDT* 726. On Lutheran Reformation theology, cf. further C. Bergendoff, *The Church of the Lutheran Reformation* (St Louis: Concordia, 1967); E. E. Cairns, *Christianity Through the Centuries* (Grand Rapids: Eerdmans, 1974) 311–326; Paul Althaus, *The Theology of Martin Luther* (Philadelphia: Fortress, 1966) 3–14.

8. In general, see the volume commemorating the 400th anniversary of the Augsburg Confession, *Die Bekenntnisschriften der evangelisch-lutherische Kirche, herausgegeben im Gedenkenjahr der Augsburgischen Konfession 1930* (5th ed'n; Gottingen: Vandenhoeck und Ruprecht, 1963). The text is both in Latin and German. An important document on Scripture is the *Formula of Concord* (1577); cf. also the *Book of Concord* (1580). The best critical edition of Luther's works is *Luthers Werke: Kritische Gesamtausgabe* (Weimar, 1883), often referred to as the *Weimar Ausgabe* (=*WA*). Cf. also Wisløff, *Martin Luthers Teologi* 54–78. To grasp the nature, continuities and discontinuities of Roman Catholic theology, it is helpful to compare the reports of the Council of Trent (1545–1563) with *The Documents of Vatican II* (1962–65), especially for our purposes all discussion of Scripture, tradition and revelation. Both sets of documents clearly insist that there is more than one source of authority springing from God's revelation (for Vatican II, see 'Revelation of God', 9). These positions should be compared with the stance taken by the Faith and Order Commission of the World Council of Churches, especially their treatment of Scripture and tradition (Faith and Order, 1963). I have discussed this at length in my book, *Quest for Authority: An Investigation of the Quest for Authority within the Ecumenical Movement from 1910 to 1974 and the Evangelical Response* (Nairobi, 1987) 165–214. See further J. A. Möhler, *Symbolik, oder Darstellung der dogmatischen Gegensatze der Katholiken und Protestanten nach ihren offentlichen Bekenntnisschriften* (6th ed'n; Mainz, 1843); Robert D. Preus, *The Theology of Post-Reformation Lutheranism: A Study of Theological Prolegomena*, vol.1 (St Louis: Concordia, 1970) *passim*, esp. pp.254–377 on the doctrine of Scripture; H. Fagerberg, *A New Look at the Lutheran Confessions 1529–1537* (tr. G. J. Lund; St Louis: Concordia, 1972) 15–62.

9. For examples of Lutherans who deny the possibility of adhering to *sola scriptura* today, see, for example, the many publications of Rudolf Bultmann, Werner G. Kümmel, and Ernst Käsemann: e.g. Werner G. Kümmel, *The Theology of the New Testament* (London: SCM, 1974) 14. Ernst Käsemann was deeply engaged in the Faith and Order studies of the WCC during the sixties, and was a key person in urging that the New Testament embraces mutually contradictory historical and theological traditions, making genuine theological unity based on the New Testament impossible: see my *Quest for Authority* 183–210. Cf. Gerhard Maier, *The End of the Historical-Critical Method* (tr. Edwin W. Leverenz and Rudolph F. Norden; St Louis: Concordia, 1977) 11: 'The general acceptance of Semler's basic concept that the Bible must be treated like any other book has plunged theology into an endless chain of perplexities and inner contradictions. This concept, which attempted with increasing satisfaction to show contradictions in the Bible, accomplished its utmost just in this. In its development, what began as a *charactisticum protestanticum* (Protestant character-istic) culminated in a universal Christian sickness.' Maier calls for an historical-biblical method: 'After the empirical end of the higher-critical method, we are faced with an immense task. This task is to develop an exegetical method which is in accord with revelation in the form of the Holy Scriptures. This includes surmounting the philosophically based cleavage between Scripture and the Word of God introduced by Semler and his colleagues. This implies nothing less than vanquishing English deism, French scepticism, and the German Enlightenment in the domain of theology' (p. 50).

10. *The Documents of Vatican II*, 'The Church'. Cf. the comprehensive study by

Carl Fredrik Wisløff, *Nattverd og Messe* (Oslo, 1957), ET *The Gift of Communion: Luther's Controversy with Rome on Eucharistic Sacrifice* (Minneapolis: Augsburg, 1964). [Subsequent references are to the Norwegian original.] Wisløff explores the various documents on both sides of the debate (Catholic and Lutheran) and points out the differences.

11. *LW* 12.187; cf. *WA* 17.1.32; 40.111.154.

12. In support of this view, see *inter alios* the following commentaries: O. Moe, *Apostelen Paulus brev til Romerne* (1948) 147ff.; Anders Nygren, *Commentary on Romans* (ET 1949) 157–158; R. C. H. Lenski, *The Interpretation of St Paul's Epistle to the Romans* (1936) 245. *Contra*, cf. Ernst Käsemann, *An die Romer* (4th ed'n 1980; ET 1980) 97–98 [page numbers from ET]; John Murray, *The Epistle to the Romans* (1960, 1965) 117.

13. See Althaus, *Theology 128–131*; cf. the quotations from 40.37.7 & 5.

14. Cf. Edmund Schlink, *Theologie der lutherischen Bekenntnisschriften* (München, 1948) 105–198; ET *Theology of the Lutheran Confessions* (Philadelphia: Fortress, 1975). See also J. O. Mæland, ed., *Konkordieboken [Book of Concord]: Den evangelisklutherske Kirkes bekjennelsesskrifter* (Oslo, 1985), especially the following sections: 'Den augsburgske bekjennelse', 29–31; 'Apologien', 71–128; 'De smalkaldiske artikler', 238–242, 246–254; 'Luthers lille katekisme', 281–285; 'Luthers Store Katekisme', 303–350; 'Konkordieformelen', 396–401. Cf. also Wisløff, *Martin Luthers Teologi*, chaps.4,6,12; *idem, Nattverd og Messe*; Althaus, *Theology*, chaps. 18–22.

15. *WA* 10.1.1,342. Cf. Wisløff, *Martin Luthers Teologi* 156.

16. Cf. Otto Clemen, *Luthers Werke in Auswahl*, 8 vols. (Leipzig, 1950) 4.428; cf. Wisløff, *Martin Luthers Teologi* 157.

17. *WA* 7.721; cf. also Althaus, *Theology* 289.

18. Schlink, *Theologie* 199–216; Mæland, ed., *Konkordieboken* 32,136,254,287, 365–372; Wisløff, *Martin Luthers Teologi* 123–135.

19. Schlink, *Theologie* 216–263; Mæland, ed., *Konkordieboken* 32,137,254,290, 273–281,481–500; Wisløff, *Martin Luthers Teologi*, chap.10, esp. pp.136–154 on the Lord's Supper; Althaus, *Theology*, chap.27, pp.375–403; Birgir Gulbrandsen, 'Nattverden i Norsk Kirkeliv' (doctoral dissertation, University of Oslo, 1948) 348. In this last work, the principles of 'free nattverd' – the practice of the Lord's Supper among Norwegian laypeople – are discussed.

20. Luther's *Great Catechism*; cf. Wisløff, *Martin Luthers Teologi* 155.

21. *Augsburg Confession*, articles 7–8, with further explanations in *Apologia* (same articles). See *Die Bekenntnisschriften, in loc.*

22. *WA* 7.721; cf. Althaus, *Theology* 281.

23. On the councils and the church, cf. *WA* 50.645.

24. Cf. Schlink, *Theologie*, chap.6 on the church, pp.264–305; Wisløff, *Martin Luthers Teologi*, chap.11; *WA* 30.111.340; Clemen, ed., *Luthers Werke in Auswahl* 4.127. In Mæland, ed., *Konkordieboken*, see articles 7,8,14,15,28, and compare explanations in *Apologia* (same articles).

25. See *The Documents of Vatican II* on 'The Church' Cf. 'Wisløff, *Nattverd og Messe; idem, Martin Luthers Teologi* 171–191.

26. *WA* 12.178. See also Ingen Lønning and Tarald Rasmussen, *Luthers Verker i utvalg*, 6 vols. (Oslo, 1979) 2.13; Clemen, ed., *Luthers Werke in Auswahl* 1.336.

27. *WA* 41.182, 186; 8.497. Cf. also Hans Kirsten, *Luther und die Frauenordination* (Lutherischer Rundblick, Heft III; 1973).

28. See Martin Luther, *Dass eine Christliche Versammelung oder Gemeinde Recht und Macht habe, alle Lehre zu urteilen und Lehrer ein- und abzusetzen, Grund und Ursache aus der Schrift* (Wittenberg, 1523) *passim*. See Luther's 'To the Christian Adel', *WA* 12.178; Lønning and Rasmussen, *Luthers Verker* 3.205–212; Schlink, *Theologie*, chap.6 (on the church); Mæland, ed., *Konkordieboken*, chap. 10; Wisløff, *Martin Luthers Teologi*, chap.12, pp.171–190.

29. For this paragraph, see Molland, *Konfesjonskunnskap* 208ff; Werner Elert, *The

Structure of Lutheranism (tr. Walter A. Hansen; St Louis: Concordia, 1962). The rest of the text is based on general studies of the Lutheran church and mission agencies, including my own experiences.

NOTES TO CHAPTER EIGHT

1. See Horton Davies, *The English Free Churches* (Oxford: Oxford University Press, 1952), which succinctly covers the entire history of the Free Churches up to the mid-twentieth century, and in more detail the same author's 5-volume work *Worship and Theology in England (1534–1965)* (Princeton, NJ: Princeton University Press London: Oxford University Press, 1960–1975). For the history of the early period see Michael R. Watts, *The Dissenters* (Oxford; Clarendon Press, 1978), which covers the period from the reformation to the French Revolution (1791).

2. See the standard histories of Methodism, Wesley's *Journal*, etc. For contemporary applications see Howard A. Snyder, *The Radical Wesley* (Downers Grove: Inter Varsity Press, 1980); *The Radical Wesley Reconsidered* (Papers by various authors; Bangor: Bangor Christian Trust, 1984).

3. See John F. New, *Anglican and Puritan* (London: A and C Black, 1964); Horton Davies, *The Worship of the English Puritans* (Westminster: Dacre Press, 1948); Peter Lewis, *The Genius of Puritanism* (Haywards Heath: Carey Press, 1975); and two collections of papers on worship given to the Westminster Conference for Historical Studies at Westminster Congregational Chapel, Buckingham Gate, London: *Anglican and Puritan Thinking* (1977) and *Spiritual Worship* (1985). For the Sabbatarianism of English Puritanism see the detailed studies by R. J. Bauckham in *From Sabbath to Lord's Day*, ed. D. A. Carson (Grand Rapids: Zondervan, 1982), chaps. 8, 9, 10, and esp. chap. 11, 'Sabbath and Sunday in the Protestant Tradition'.

3a. Michael Watts, *The Dissenters: From the Reformation to the French Revolution* (Oxford: University Press, 1986) 306, 307.

4. For the Victorian scene in general Owen Chadwick, *The Victorian Church*, 2 vols. (London: Adam and Charles Black, 1966, 1970).

4a. See F. R. Coad, *History of the Brethren Movement* (Exeter: Paternoster, 1976).

5. A notable protest to this trend came from the Congregational theologian and preacher P. T. Forsyth, in his *Positive Preaching and the Modern Mind* (London: Independent Press, 1949 [1907]).

6. Horton Davies, the Congregationalist historian, in vol. 5 of his massive historical study *Worship and Theology in England* (*op. cit.*), itemised what he perceived to be the major gains which by 1965 had changed the face of worship in the Free Churches. However, ten years later the Methodist, Donald English, in his book *God in the Gallery* (London: Epworth, 1975) 14, warned of the danger of people becoming 'connoisseurs of liturgical form' and 'waiting for the next form of service'. English's stress was that *the total church* has responsibility for its own worship and must never be on the sidelines. Moreover, he argues, liturgies must grow out of basic belief and not simply be collected from other traditions as one might collect ingredients for a recipe book. He concludes with his own 5 basic requirements (p. 165):

(a) Worship must be regular and expectant.

(b) Worship should be clearly relevant to the great revealed realities of the gospel enabling us to enter into the truth of God, man, salvation, the Church, the world and life.

(c) Worship must never be disassociated from life as a whole but must bring into itself the pressures and enjoyment of all things: 'Can I bring into worship the successes and the failures of my personal life, the pressures and comforts of the family, the grinding boredom or the absorbing interest of work, the exciting achievements and the degrading scandals of the world at large?' (p. 106).

(d) Worship cannot safely be separated from theology.

(e) The need for instruction in faith and life if our worship is to be in Spirit and in truth.

7. See W. J. Hollenweger, *The Pentecostals* (London: SCM, 1972) for a major historical study. David Barrett in 1989 gave the world population of Pentecostals for 1988 as 176 million.

8. See Peter Hocken, *Streams of Renewal* (Exeter: Paternoster, 1986) on the origins and early development of the movement; and Andrew Walker, *Restoring the Kingdom* (London: Hodder and Stoughton, 1985) for an appraisal of the various 'Restoration' streams. David Barrett in 1989 gave the world population of charismatic Christians (as distinct from Pentecostals) for 1988 as 123 million.

9. For a wide-ranging study of denominational responses, Catholic and Protestant, to the charismatic movement, see Killian McDonall, ed., *Power, Presence, Praise: Documents on the Charismatic Renewal*, 3 vols. (Collegeville, MN: Liturgical, 1980). For contrasting studies and positions outside the 'mainline' denominations see the strongly-worded critique of Victor Budgeon, *The Charismatics and the Word of God* (Welwyn: Evangelical Press, 1985). But note also the firm but irenic and sympathetic treatments by Donald Bridge, *Signs and Wonders Today* (Leicester: IVP, 1985) and Herbert Carson, *Spiritual Gifts for Today?* (Eastbourne: Kingsway, 1988).

10. Summarised, these are:
1. The Lord is more glorified.
2. There is more of the Lord's presence.
3. Here are the clearest manifestations of God.
4. There are more spiritual advantages.
5. It is more edifying.
6. It is a better security against apostasy.
7. Here the Lord works his greatest works.
8. Here is 'the nearest resemblance to heaven'.
9. It was especially valued by 'the most renowned servants of God' in Scripture.
10. It is more effective in prayer.
11. It emphasizes the federal headship of Christ.
12. There are more promises in Scripture given to it. It is interesting how frequently Clarkson crosses over from the Old dispensation to the New in his various Scripture 'proofs', recognizing a continuity in the matter of worship that must not be lost in the discontinuity.

11. *Preaching and Preachers* (London: Hodder and Stoughton, 1976) 97.

12. *Stewards of God's Grace* (Exeter: Paternoster, 1981) 64, 66.

13. See two challenging and perceptive studies by Howard A. Snyder: *New Wineskins: Changing the Man-made Structures of the Church* (London: Marshall, Morgan and Scott, 1977 Downes Grove: IVP, 1975); *The Community of the King* (Downes Grove: IVP, 1977).

14. See Gordon D. Fee, *The First Epistle to the Corinthians* (NICNT: Grand Rapids: Eerdmans, 1987) 19.

15. See D. A. Carson's detailed exegetical study of 1 Corinthians 12–14 in *Showing the Spirit: Theological Exposition of 1 Corinthians 12–14* (Grand Rapids: Baker, 1987), who remarks on 1 Corinthians 12:4–11 (p. 32): 'Paul's concern now is not so much with unity as with diversity. The triune God loves diversity – so much so, as someone has remarked, that when he sends a snowstorm he makes each flake different. We manufacture ice cubes. Doubtless the church is in some sense like a mighty army, but that does not mean we should think of ourselves as undifferentiated khaki. We should be more like an orchestra; each part making its own unique contribution to the symphonic harmony' (p. 32).

16. John Calvin, *Institutes of the Christian Religion*, 2 vols. (ed. John T. McNeill; Philadelphia, Westminster, 1977) IV. i. 5 (see also n. 11, *supra*, and related text). See also Peter Lewis, 'Preaching from Calvin to Bunyan', in *Spiritual Worship* (as in n.3, *supra*).

17. P. T. Forsyth, *Positive Preaching and the Modern Mind* 1, 56, 64, 75.

NOTES TO CHAPTER NINE

1. Os Guinness, in *Proclaim Christ Until He Comes* (Minneapolis: Worldwide Publications, 1990) 288.

2. What Americans would call 'announcements'.

NOTES TO CHAPTER TEN

1. These types belong both to reality and to fiction. Sor Juana Inés de la Cruz (1648–1695) was a Mexican poetess whose spiritual writings have inspired many because of her devotion to Christ and her mystic orientation. The story of Don Juan is an old tradition in Spanish Literature. The classic deceiver of women finally became a transcendental personality through the writings of Tirso de Molina. Lastly, the literature of chivalry is epitomized in the person of Don Quixote, the central figure in the great classic novel by Miguel de Cervantes.

2. Colombian writer Germán Arciniegas says: 'Because of a long series of experiences, the inhabitants of Hispano-America express themselves in Spanish, and along with their language they have retained the Catholic religion, Roman law and a tendency to quixotic flights of fancy' (*Latin America: A Cultural History* [London, Barrie and Rockliff: Cresset, 1969]) xxvi.

3. When Jesuit priests and other Catholic missionaries arrived in the Orient and Africa, there was a variety of responses to Catholic Christian presence. China and the Philippines were relatively open. Japan systematically closed its ranks against Christianity, and the period of success seen in the nineteenth century ended at the turn of the twentieth century for the Roman-French missions and the Russian church (today known as the Orthodox Church). After World War I Japan reopened to Christianity, but this time through the efforts of Protestantism. This context of opposition makes it hard to evaluate the role of Catholicism in the Orient. In Africa, Catholic Christianity experienced more or less the same fate as it had in the Orient. See Kenneth Scott Latourette, *The Great Century: North Africa and Asia 1800 A.D. – 1914 A.D.* (Grand Rapids: Zondervan, 1980) 6.6–20, 34–64, 253–295, 370–381.

4. Yoshiaki Hattori quotes R. Martin Archard regarding the term '*ābad* as an appropriate word for expressing worship: 'It extends to every domain of life. God must be served on all planes of human existence, as biblical legislation testifies. It is significant that Hebrew has one word to denote *work*, *service*, and *worship*: in biblical thought there is no watertight division between daily work and the adoration of God; in the very first page of Scripture manual activity and service of the Creator are inseparably linked' (p.212). For Leonard J. Coppes (*TWOT* 2.218), *hālal* 'was specially, though by no means uniquely (Ps. 146:1), congregational'. Helmer Ringgren (*TDOT* 3.406) also sees a cultic usage for the word. Nevertheless the exegetical work done in chaps. 2 and 3 of this book seems to broaden worship to include in it all issues of life. David Peterson says: 'It will be argued below that worship in the New Testament is essentially an engagement with God through faith in Jesus Christ and what he has done for us. Such faith will express itself in daily obedience or service to God in every aspect of life. What we do "in Church" must be considered as part of that engagement with God, but it is misleading to restrict the notion of worship to the congregational gathering' (p.52).

5. See Peter Wagner, ¡*Cuidado ahí vienen los Pentecostales*! (Miami: Editorial Vida, 1973) 113–134; Richard Quebedeaux, *The New Charismatics II* (New York: Harper & Row, 1974) 48–52.

6. G. W. Méndez, 'El Hombre Latinoamericano Hoy', paper presented at the Central American Theological Seminary, May 29, 1990.

7. Most of the materials in Spanish are translations from English works. In other

cases, worship is tangential and not the primary focus. See Rolando Gutiérrez-Cortés, *¿Holocausto o Adoración?* (México, D.F.: Editado por la Iglesia Bautista Horeb, n.d.).

8. Cf. Pablo Pérez, *Misión y Liberación* (México, D.F.: Publicaciones El Faro, 1976) 1–30; E. A. Núñez, *Liberation Theology* (Chicago: Moody, 1985) 8–20.

9. Núñez says: 'It can be said of the Christianization of Latin America that in general there was an imposition of medieval, Spanish, and Roman Christianity, but not an evangelization that would convert people to New Testament Christianity. The missionary effort resulted mainly in what we know as popular Catholic religiosity, and in a syncretism of European Christianity with the religion of the indigenous peoples. Today there are still those who worship their ancient gods as they bow before the images of Roman Catholic saints' (*Liberation Theology* 19).

10. Arciniegas (*Latin America* xxvi) says: '. . . the inhabitants of Hispano-America express themselves in Spanish, and along with their language they have retained the Catholic religion, Roman law . . .' Escobar observes: 'Concerning attitudes towards life, what Aranguren calls "disposition", catholicism has powerfully marked our continent. Along with the feudal view of life, this has been the common element between Spanish and Portuguese speaking people. In the realm of the intellect, the Iberian dominates the colonial, which results in a frozen scholasticism with few and occasional flashes of light. The opening would come with French thought' (Samuel Escobar, 'El contenido bíblico y el ropaje anglosajón en la Teología Latinoamericana', in *El Debate Contemporáneo sobre la Biblia*, ed. Pedro Savage [Barcelona: Ediciones Evangélicas Europeas, 1972] 25) [author's translation].

11. 'The popular sentiment, which was only imperfectly christianized, never had completely lost antipathy for the person who did not have to fight and did have to live chastely. The pride of chivalry, which had its roots in courage and love, distanced itself from the ecclesiastical ideal, just as did the unpolished popular sentiment. The degeneration of the clergy themselves did the rest, and thus now for centuries both the upper and lower classes have delighted in the sterotypes of the dishonest monk and of the fat and gluttonous priest'. (Johan Huizinga, *El Otoño de la Edad Medieval: Estudios sobre la forma de la vida y del espíritu durante los siglos XIV y XV en Francia y en los Países Bajos* [Madrid: Alianza Editorial, 1985] 250). There were, of course, Medieval Roman Catholics who were thoroughly comprehensive in their world view, such as Francis of Assisi and Thomas à Kempis. But we are dealing here with the dominant form of Medieval Catholicism that reached and formed much of Latin America.

12. Samuel Escobar, *La Fe Evangélica y las Teologías de la Liberación* (El Paso: Casa Bautista de Publicaciones, 1987) 18–21.

13. Guillermo W. Méndez, 'Las Buenas Nuevas que predicamos', *Kairós* 6, pp. 51–52.

14. Guillermo W. Méndez, 'El Reto Teológico para la Iglesia Evangélica en América Latina', paper presented at the Central American Theological Seminary (August, 1989). See also Guillermo W. Méndez, 'A todo el mundo, con todo el Evangelio, desde América Latina', *Boletín Teológico* (forthcoming). Both papers stress the wide gap between popular religiosity and social ethics: the first as an historical fact, in the aftermath of Roman Catholicism; the latter as a never-ending threat present in our Christian communication of the gospel.

15. In this regard we need to deepen our understanding of Liberation Theology's claim that ideology (in the Marxist sense) and idolatry go hand in hand. This is important because it is a sub-point of Marxism's classic criticism of religion. Here, we are told, it is not religion as such, but the gods of capitalism, against whom the poor must struggle, since they regularly oppress and overpower the poor. This interpretation understands the fight against idolatry in the Old Testament to be always in the context of political liberation from oppression. See Pablo Richard, 'Nuestra lucha en contra los ídolos', *La Lucha de los Dioses* (San José: Departamento Ecuménico de

Investigaciones, 1980), 9–32. Of course, this interpretation must explain why the people of God in the Old Testament were oppressed in the first place, what characterized the liberated people, from what they were liberated and for what or to what they were set free. It seems that the hasty identification of all these issues with the contemporary structure of oppressors and oppressed is to read into the text a heavy dose of Marxism not present in it. Expressed in another way, Liberationists tend to read the Bible with Marxist categories.

16. It is interesting how even the Eucharist is interpreted in a political way. This cultic element, linked to the Passover and therefore to the Exodus event, we are told, is thus rooted in the historical experience of the people of God. Today the Eucharist, Liberation Theology assumes, should have the same intention, but the content should be the political experience of the Latin American people. A criticism that could be levelled against this is that it moves the centre from the cross of Christ to the political arena, making the humanization of the poor through political means the goal of liturgy. See Rafael Avila, *Worship and Politics* (New York: Orbis, 1981) 5–72. For the political implications see pp. 73–106.

17. This is the attempt of Gustavo Gutiérrez in his important book, *We Drink from Our Own Wells* (New York: Orbis, 1983) 33–89. He proposes that spirituality is built upon the unique and renewing encounter with the living Christ in the struggle for freedom. See his interaction with the biblical text on pp. 33–89. In my view, Gutiérrez's lack of a defined metaphysical grid results in a faulty grasp of sin, and that in turn leads to a truncated spirituality. Regarding Liberation theology Costas has observed: 'God is so historicized, that he loses his otherness' (Orlando E. Costas, *The Church and Its Mission: A Shattering Critique from The Third World* [Wheaton: Tyndale House Publishers, 1974] 256).

18. Robert E Webber (*Common Roots: A Call to Evangelical Maturity* [Grand Rapido: Zondervan, 1978] 77) says: 'Among Evangelicals there is a growing demand to change the form of worship, to incorporate more variety in service and to realize a more creative and meaningful expression of worship.' Webber goes on to say that this is needed in North America because of the prevalence of man-centred worship: dry intellectualism focused on preaching, and then an over-emphasis on the emotional side of worship. Besides the biblical reasons invoked, this practical aspect of the discussion is what we see in Latin America as evolving from the contact between the independent tradition and the charismatic type of worship.

19. Among some old line pastors and missionaries there is still a firm belief that allowing bodily expressions of worship provides openings in one's theology through which pentecostal theology will creep in. Strictly on theological terms a Pentecostal is one who holds that (1) baptism in the Holy Spirit is a supernatural post-salvation existential event; (2) that one asks for this experience by prayer; and (3) and it manifests itself through speaking in tongues and the possible bestowal of other miraculous gifts. Charles Lalive d'Espinay says that by 1960 '80 percent of Latin American *evangélicos* were pentecostalists' ('Toward a Typology of Latin American Protestantism', *RRR* 10 [1968] 8). That high number is still claimed by charismatic leaders.

20. In this sense, it is worth remembering that the gospel will always challenge every culture. For a proper understanding of the interplay between culture and theology see the essay by D. A. Carson, 'Church and Mission: Reflections on Contextualization and the Third Horizon', in *The Church in the Bible and the World: An International Study* (ed. D. A. Carson; Exeter: Paternoster, 1987) 213–257.

21. Lalive d'Espinay ('Typology', 7) adds, 'The introduction of protestantism in this continent was to be the exclusive work of foreigners supported by foreign organizations.'

22. Of course, the freedom to do missionary work was one of the forces behind the efforts of dozens of missionary organizations and efforts to reach Latin America. This resulted in all sorts of tiny denominations and independent groups within Latin

America, each body cherishing its own emphases and styles. In spite of this, it is still possible to say that the vast majority of these groups and churches hold to the basic Reformation principles of *sola Scriptura, sola fide, sola gratia,* and *solo Christo.* Cf. Alianza Evangélica de Guatemala, Press Release, June 4, 1990.

23. It must be observed that out of the old traditional non-charismatic denominations have emerged younger national bodies with a charismatic theology. These indigenous churches tend to grow dramatically and are characterized by a tradition of lay leadership, urban culturation and attraction of the urban poor-features that are seldom seen in other large denominationations. Lalive d'Espinay ('Typology', 9) says, 'By contrast, a very significant number of pentecostalist churches have never passed through the stage of "mission churches" but *came* directly into existence either as "indigenous churches" or as "indigenized churches". If any could be regarded as starting as "mission churches", they evolved very quickly in the direction of autonomous national churches, given the nature of Pentecostalist encouragement to native (or national) leadership and local financial autonomy'.

24. In this regard, the extremes observed in the 'mother church' in the United States usually take place in the 'daughter church' in Latin America. An effervescent woman wandered into a liturgical service. As a pastor preached, she echoed his words with 'Praise the Lord!' Another woman leaned over to say, 'Excuse me, but we don't praise the Lord in the Lutheran Church.' A man down the pew corrected her: 'Yes we do; it is on page 19.' (I am indebted here to Paul Anderson, 'The Feud Between Form and Freedom', *CT* 30 [May 16, 1986] 66.) Costas says, 'The cultic structure follows more or less the format of the mother church. The worship service's rhythm lacks the spontaneity which characterizes the "Latin soul" ' (Orlando Costas, 'La Realidad de la Iglesia Evangélica Latinoamericana', in *Fe Cristiana y Latinoamérica Hoy* [ed., René Padilla, Buenos Aires: Ediciones Certeza, 1974] 46–47) [author's translation].

25. Webber (*Common Roots* 78) warns us: 'While the concern for content in Bible-oriented churches is certainly commendable, the focus is distorted when the content centers almost exclusively on the sermon, which, no matter how deep, can never represent all the content which a full service of worship ought to contain.'

26. In a dense argument on history, determinism and progress, Erazim Kohak, the personalist philosopher, says that 'in Christian thought, the motif of a return to the purity of the primitive church is far more common than any call for striving onward toward an ever better one' (*The Embers and the Stars* [Chicago: University Press, 1984] 163).

27. Note the pattern presented by Webber (*Common Roots* 101)/. But here, too, there is a fair bit of speculation in the order and structure of the pattern. It would be a great help if we admitted what we cannot know, or at least that of which we cannot be certain.

28. In this area there is room for freedom in details. For instance, O. Cullmann speaks of participation and freedom through 'perfectly free and unrestricted spiritual utterances' which, he argues, were also part of the greater 'fixed liturgical forms' (Oscar Cullmann, *Early Christian Worship* [Philadelphia: Westminster, 1953] 21). Although this seems also to imply the existence of a fixed pattern, as argued by Webber (*Common Roots* 99–104) I doubt that there was such a fixed pattern.

29. A pastor writes: 'For many congregations, worship has degenerated into mere convocations for the teaching of the Bible. A hymn or two, some announcements, and then the *pièce de résistance* – 20 minutes (or 40) of Bible teaching. The only liturgical furniture required is an overhead projector. Do not misunderstand. Bible teaching is integral to Christian worship. It is in the hearing of the Word of God that we are summoned to worship God in the first place. Without the proclamation of the Word, worship would be all effect with no cause. But without significant time in a Sunday service devoted to praise and thanksgiving, the service becomes all cause with no effect' (Ben Patterson, 'Worship is Forever', *CT* 29 [Feb. 1, 1985] 15).

30. Again another minister comes to our aid when he states where worship ought

to start: 'It starts with our daily personal contact with God. No one can worship once a week and become strong in the faith. The New Testament teaches that corporate worship is a must – Christ went to the synagogue as a 'custom' (LK. 4:16). But public worship alone can become ritual. Worship as part of the Christian lifestyle, however, provides vitality for the gathering of God's people' (Rob L. Hewell, 'The Vital Connection in Worship', *CT* 29 [April 5, 1989] 58).

31. The late Orlando Costas says that in this type of worship, 'there is no awareness of the needs of the individual as a member of a society where alienating situations take place which make him suffer along other members of the said society' (*The Church and Its Mission* 57). See also Peter Wagner, ¡*Cuidado ahi vienen los Pentecostales!* 155–168. Of course, Costas is speaking of insufficient contextualization.

32. 'Pentecostal worship makes the church appear as a *substitutive community* that comes to fill the vacuum left by the violent break of the recent convert with those who "shared with him in the pleasures of this world" ' (Wagner, *ibid.* 60).

33. David Peterson, 'Proposals for a Conference on the Subject of Worship', unpublished paper presented to the members of the Faith and Church Study Unit of the WEF Theological Commission, p. 1.

34. Commenting on the passage in Jn. 4, H. Greeven observes:

In John 4:20ss *proskynein* seems to have a wholly figurative sense. Yet the act of worship stands in the background. What Jesus says is that there is no one place to worship. The concrete act is lifted up into the sphere of Spirit and truth which now controls it. This does not mean total spiritualizing of worship but the possibility of true worship at all times and all places (*TDNT* 6. 949).

35. Pablo Deiros gives us an interesting account of pre-Columbian religion in his *Historia del Cristianismo en America Latina* (Viña del Mar: Facultad Latinoamericana de Estudios Teológicos, 1986) 10–29. See also Pablo Perez, *Misión y Liberación* 1–17.

36. In an interview article, 'Adeyemo: Islam Greatest Threat for Africa', *Action* (March-April, 1990) 25.

NOTES TO CHAPTER ELEVEN

1. The phrase based on Matt. 9:17 and parallels.

2. David Peterson, 'Worship in the New Testament', chap. 3 of this book, p. 90.

3. There are also negative examples that no-one would want to repeat, e.g., the abuses of the Lord's Supper described in 1 Cor. 11:17ff.

4. Some charismatics limit their definition of worship to the time of praise, and can be legitimately criticized for doing so. Peterson in fact argues that one part of a meeting cannot be 'the worship time' and another 'the edification time', since both occur together (Peterson, p. 83).

5. Peterson, 'Worship in the New Testament', 90.

6. Yoshiaki Hattori, 'Theology of Worship in the Old Testament', chap. 2 of this book, p. 23.

7. Is. 1:13 recognizes the possibility of offerings God does not find meaningful. See also Peterson, 'Worship', 67–68 *supra*, where he describes the concluding chapters of Romans under the 'umbrella' of acceptable worship.

8. Not unlike God's rejection of Israel's empty sacrifices,

9. The jibe to others is that they would not notice any difference in their services if the Holy Spirit did not come one week. The same routine would be followed anyway.

10. Peterson, 'Worship', 67.

11. Discordant notes on the guitar or piano, used to encourage singing in tongues, are particularly infuriating.

12. The idea of a volatile presence of the Spirit is not unbiblical. Cf. Luke 5:17,

'One day as he was teaching, . . . the power of the Lord was present for him to heal the sick.'

13. However, banners are popular, many portraying or expressing gospel truths in a way not dissimilar to stained glass art.

14. This parallels, at least in part, the emergency aid of the Spirit in prayer as described by Paul in Rom. 8:26-27.

15. The listeners heard them declaring the wonders of God (v. 11), but in such an uninhibited manner that some thought them drunk (v. 13).

16. Dancing as an expression of celebration and praise appears to have been common, e.g., Ex. 15:20; Judg. 11:34; 1 Sam. 21:11.

17. Hattori, 'Worship', 37, citing 2 Sam. 6:4-5; 1 Chron. 16:4-36, 41-42.

18. OHPs are also used to stop people burying their faces in song books, and to keep their hands free!

19. Peterson, 'Worship', 79–80. However, he also asks later why mutual ministry (including the spontaneous variety) is restricted in church life today to home groups or informal times. He goes on: 'Why is it not also encouraged in the formal gathering of the whole church? Many Christian traditions rightly emphasize the need for regular and systematic exposition of Scripture and the teaching of "sound doctrine" by those gifted and appointed for this task . . . However, if the balance of New Testament teaching is to be preserved, should there not be some space for the informal contributions of members?' (p. 00).

20. Adrian Plass, *The Sacred Diary of Adrian Plass* (Basingstoke: Marshall Pickering, 1987) 5-6

21. He notes it in respect of Rom.12-15, Eph. 4:12-16, and several passages in Hebrews (Peterson, 'Worship', 69–70, 74–75, 78).

22. Peterson, 'Worship', 78.

23. Hence a common ban on personal ministry to the opposite sex.

24. 'Worship', 77.

25. Peterson, 'Worship', 75.

26. A high premium has not usually been placed on homiletical skills, as charismatics often prefer to allow the Holy Spirit to apply the Word however presented. This can deteriorate into an emotionally charged end of sermon invitation to receive ministry, that invitation becoming almost another sermon in itself.

27. Both are common signs of the Spirit's presence, according to charismatics.

28. 'Worship', 71.

29. 'Worship', 82.

30. Glance at any neglected garden for proof.

31. This is a long-term development. Initially there is usually considerable abandon, but it often does not last. Where it does last, the reason may be either no strong leadership, or a leader who finds he can control more easily where there is little order.

NOTES TO CHAPTER TWELVE

1. Jonathan Lamb: *Draw Near to God: Worship in the Christian Union* (Leicester: UCCF, 1986) 5.

2. FOCUS-Zimbabwe: *Leaders' Training Manual* (1984) 15.

3. David Peterson, 'Worship in the New Testament', chap 3 *supra*, p. 67–70.

4. Gottfried Osei-Mensah, Personal testimony in IFES *Celebration '40* material.

5. Peterson, 'Worship', 81.

6. Pete Lowman, *The Day of His Power* (Leicester: IVP, 1983) 49.

7. Peterson, 'Worship', 65.

8. Pete Lowman, *The Day of His Power* 345.

9. The author surveyed a sample of twenty IFES-affiliated student movements around the world in order to gather data for this chapter. For a fuller analysis of her findings see 'Praise in every part' in *IFES REVIEW* No. 29 (October, 1990) 27–32.

10. Femi Adeleye, in *National Link* (Nigeria Fellowship of Evangelical Students, Benin, Nigeria; December, 1990) 1.

11. Jonathan Lamb, *Draw Near to God* 15.

12. Laurie Klein in *Mission Praise* (Basingstoke: Marshall, Morgan and Scott, 1983) 130.

13. Henry Williams Baker, 'O Praise ye the Lord', quoted from *Christian Praise* (Leicester: IVP, 1973 [Words edition]) 12.

14. Erik Routley, from the Preface to *Hymns Today and Tomorrow* (Nashville: Abingdon, 1964).

15. Christopher Idle; in *Church of England Newspaper* (1 September 1989).

16. Femi Adeleye in *National Link* (Nigeria Fellowship of Evangelical Students, Benin, Nigeria; September, 1989).

17. Spring Harvest is a large Christian convention that has taken place annually at Easter time in several different sites around the UK for the past decade. Drawing speakers and participants from many different churches, it offers teaching and celebration for all the family in a Christian holiday atmosphere. Speakers are broadly in sympathy with the doctrinal basis of the British Evangelical Alliance. In 1991 Spring Harvest offered eight such weeks in four different locations and expected to draw 80,000 participants. In the Spring of 1993, one week was devoted to meetings that focused more attention on exposition and teaching, and that was less characterized by 'charismatic' forms of worship. That week was dubbed 'Word Alive'.

18. Urbana is the triennial student missions convention sponsored by the Inter-Varsity Christian Fellowships of the USA and Canada. The 16th, with over 18,000 delegates from 95 nations, took place December 27–31, 1990 at the University of Illinois. God has used Urbana down the years to call many students into short- and long-term missionary service.

19. The Katoomba Youth Convention was started in the early '80s by two evangelical ministers to give young people in and around Sydney, Australia, exposure to good evangelical teaching.

20. InterVarsity Missions News Release, June 1990.

21. Allan Bloom, *The Closing of the American Mind* (New York: Simon and Shuster, 1987) 68–82.

22. R. Bibby and D. Posterski, *The Emerging Generation* (Toronto: Irwin, 1985).

23. Erik Routley, *Christian Hymns Observed* (London: Mowbray, 1982) 3.

24. Peterson, 'Worship', 69.

25. Lesslie Newbigin, *Foolishness to the Greeks* (London: SPCK, 1986).

26. Bloom, *The Closing of the American Mind* 25–26.

27. Bobby Sng, 'Student Work and the Church', *IFES REVIEW* (1982/2) 33.

28. Ian Darke, 'Living as a Militant', *IN TOUCH* (1989/3) 3. 'AGEUP' is an acronym for the name of the Peruvian student movement: Asociación de Grupos Evangélicos Universitarios de Peru.

29. John Stott, *Your Mind Matters* (Leicester: IVP, 1972) 27.

30. See, for example, O.R. Barclay, *Developing a Christian Mind* (Leicester: IVP 1984).

31. John Stott in *Our Link* [Union of Evangelical Students of India, Madras, India] (March-June, 1990) 16.

32. Goh Keat-Peng, 'Personal Growth: Letters to a Staff Friend', *IFES REVIEW* 28 (April, 1990) 8.

33. Jacques Ellul, *The Humiliation of the Word* (Grand Rapids: Eerdmans, 1985).

34. Ellul, *The Humiliation of the Word* 210.

35. Ellul, *The Humiliation of the Word* 210–211.

36. John W. Bachman: *Media: Between Wasteland and Wonderland* (Minneapolis: Augsburg, 1984) 25.

NOTES TO CHAPTER THIRTEEN

1. See Aristotle, *Nicomachean Ethics*, 1177b.

2. On the relation between action and contemplation see H. U. von Balthasar, 'Aktion und Kontemplation', in *Verbum Caro. Skizzen zur Theologie I* (Einsiedeln: Johannes Verlag, 1960) 245–259.

3. Aquinas, *Summa Theologica*, II–II, Q. 179, A. 2 and Q. 182, A. 3, 4.

4. See M. Weber, *The Protestant Ethic and the Spirit of Capitalism* (trans. T. Parsons; New York: Charles Scribner's Sons, 1958) 80.

5. For a critique of Luther's vocational understanding of work see M. Volf, *Work in the Spirit. Toward a Theology of Work* (New York: Oxford University Press, 1991) 105ff.

6. J. D. G. Dunn, *Romans 9–16* (Word Biblical Commentary 38B; Dallas: Word, 1988) 710.

7. See E. Käsemann, 'Worship in Everyday Life: A Note on Romans 12', in *New Testament Questions of Today* (ET; London: SCM, 1969), 188–195.

8. See D. Peterson, 'Worship in the New Testament', pp. 51ff.

9. See Y. Hattori, 'Worship in the Context of the Canonical Old Testament', p. 21 and, n. 1, p. 212.

10. According to the Atra-Hasis epic – and in this respect virtually all Mesopotamean myths of human creation agree – human beings were created in order to liberate the gods from strenuous labour. Creation of human beings was meant to solve the problem of lower gods refusing to do their work (see W. Zimmerli, 'Mensch und Arbeit im Alten Testament', in *Recht auf Arbeit – Sinn der Arbeit* [ed. J. Moltmann; München: Kaiser, 1979] 40–58, 52). In the Atra-Hasis epic, work is immediately related to the service of gods. In the Old Testament work is divorced from its immediate connection with cult and placed into service of culture. But as such, work is at the same time service to God.

11. See H. Arendt, *Vita Activa oder Vom tätigen Leben* (München: Pieper, 1981) 281ff.

12. O. Guinness, 'Mission in the Face of Modernity. Nine Checkpoints on Mission Without Worldliness in the Modern World' (a paper for the Plenary Session on the Impact of Modernization, presented at Lausanne II in Manila, July 11–20, 1989), 5.

13. Guinness, 7.

14. J. P. Miranda, *Marx and the Bible. A Critique of the Philosophy of Oppression* (trans. J. Eagleson; New York: Orbis Books, 1974) 35–76.

15. J. P. Miranda, 'Is Marxism Essentially Atheistic?' in *JES* 22 (1985) 509–515, 515 – italics mine.

16. Ibid.

17. In a somewhat less radical way, Käsemann proclaims that worship and ethics fall into one and that ethics is the only 'cult' that remains for Christians (Käsemann, 'Worship', 191f.).

18. See Hattori, 'Worship', pp. 44.

19. Peterson, 'Worship', p. 89.

20. In Eastern orthodox theology the summit of mystical life is sometimes perceived to consist 'in the personal encounter with Christ who speaks in our hearts by the Holy Spirit' (P. Evdokimov, *L'Orthodoxie* [Paris: Desclée de Brouwer, 1979] 113).

21. 'The Oxford Declaration on Christian Faith and Economics', in *Transformation* 7/2 (1990) 1–8, n. 30. For the background reflection on this formulation see Volf, *Work*, 136ff.

22. On the presence of God in creation in relation to worship see A. Schmemann, *Sacraments and Orthodoxy* (New York: Herder and Herder, 1965) 10ff.

23. See Peterson, 'Worship', pp. 76.

24. See P. Tillich, *Systematic Theology III: Life and the Spirit, History and the Kingdom of God* (Chicago: University of Chicago Press, 1963) 379f.

25. See Hattori, 'Worship', p. 36; and Peterson, 'Worship', p. 80.

26. V. Lossky, *The Mystical Theology of the Eastern Church* (Crestwood: St. Vladimir's Seminary Press, 1976) 9. For the same emphasis in the Catholic tradition see J. Cardinal Ratzinger, *Schauen auf den Durchbohrten. Versuche zu einer spirituellen Christologie* (Einsiedeln: Johannes Verlag, 1984) 18.

27. See on that Volf, *Work*, 98ff; M. Hengel, 'Die Arbeit im frühen Christentum', in *Th Beit* 17 (1986) 174–212, 180.

28. Though one should interpret the phrase as 'God's we are, being fellow workers' rather than 'we are labourers together *with* God' (so G. Fee, *The First Epistle to the Corinthians* [Grand Rapids: Eerdmans, 1987] 134), the agricultural imagery in the context suggests cooperation not only between Paul and Apollos but also of both of them with God: 'I planted the seed, Apollos watered it, but God made it grow' (1 Cor 3:6). The main point of the verse is, of course, that the work of both Paul and Apollos is useless unless God gives growth. But it implies also clearly that God cannot give growth to what Paul and Apollos (or some other human beings) have not planted and watered. The idea of apostles being co-workers with God is 'consistent with Paul's thought in general' (see C. K. Barrett, *A Commentary on the First Epistle to the Corinthians* [London: Black, 1968] 86).

29. On the contemplation as an activity see von Balthasar, 'Aktion', 245, 250.

30. Luther wrote: 'ne *vita activa* cum suis operibus et *vita contemplativa* cum suis speculationibus nos seducant' (WA 5, 85, 2f). On Luther's perspectives on *vita passiva* as distinct from *vita activa* and *vita contemplativa* in the context of a discussion about relation of theology to theory and practice see O. Bayer, 'Theologie und Philosophie in produktivem Konflikt' in *Neue Zeitschrift für Systematische Theologie und Religionsphilosophie* 32 (1990) 226–236, 234.

Index of Biblical Passages Discussed

Index of Names